MW00583620

THE MIGRANT'S JAIL

POLITICS AND SOCIETY IN MODERN AMERICA

Gary Gerstle, Elizabeth Hinton, Margaret O'Mara, and Julian E. Zelizer, Series Editors

For a full list of titles in the series, go to http://press.princeton.edu/series /politics-and-society-in-modern-america.

The Migrant's Jail

AN AMERICAN HISTORY
OF MASS INCARCERATION

BRIANNA NOFIL

PRINCETON UNIVERSITY PRESS

PRINCETON & OXFORD

Copyright © 2024 by Brianna Nofil

Princeton University Press is committed to the protection of copyright and the intellectual property our authors entrust to us. Copyright promotes the progress and integrity of knowledge. Thank you for supporting free speech and the global exchange of ideas by purchasing an authorized edition of this book. If you wish to reproduce or distribute any part of it in any form, please obtain permission.

Requests for permission to reproduce material from this work should be sent to permissions@press.princeton.edu

Published by Princeton University Press
41 William Street, Princeton, New Jersey 08540
99 Banbury Road, Oxford OX2 6JX

press.princeton.edu

All Rights Reserved

Library of Congress Cataloging-in-Publication Data

Names: Nofil, Brianna, 1989– author.
Title: The migrant's jail : an American history of mass incarceration / Brianna Nofil.
Description: Princeton, New Jersey : Princeton University Press, 2024. |
    Series: Politics and society in modern America | Includes bibliographical
    references and index.
Identifiers: LCCN 2024001085 (print) | LCCN 2024001086 (ebook) |
    ISBN 9780691237015 (hardback) | ISBN 9780691237039 (ebook)
Subjects: LCSH: United States—Emigration and immigration—Government
    policy. | Detention of persons—United States—History—20th century. |
    Noncitizen detention centers—United States—History—20th century. |
    Noncitizens—United States—Law and legislation—History—20th century. |
    Immigrants—United States—Law and legislation—History—20th century. |
    Prisons—United States—History—20th century. | Jails—United States—
    States—Finance—History—20th century.
Classification: LCC JV6483 .N64 2024 (print) | LCC JV6483 (ebook) |
    DDC 365/.470973—dc23/eng/20240412
LC record available at https://lccn.loc.gov/2024001085
LC ebook record available at https://lccn.loc.gov/2024001086

British Library Cataloging-in-Publication Data is available

Editorial: Priya Nelson and Emma Wagh
Production Editorial: Ali Parrington
Jacket/Cover Design: Katie Osborne
Production: Danielle Amatucci
Publicity: Kate Hensley, Maria Whelan, and Carmen Jimenez
Copyeditor: Elisabeth A. Graves

Jacket image: FPG / Staff / Getty Images

This book has been composed in Arno

Printed in the United States of America

10 9 8 7 6 5 4 3 2 1

CONTENTS

ILLUSTRATIONS

Figures

Tables

ACKNOWLEDGMENTS

THIS BOOK BEGAN AS a way to understand where I grew up: the swamps and sprawl of South Florida, a place that fosters an acute awareness of the risks immigrants, refugees, exiles, seasonal workers, and others take to build lives in the United States. Though the project's geography evolved, it remains, to me, an exploration of home and the people who made it. What a pleasure it is to thank the many people who helped make other places home, as well.

I owe the world to Mae Ngai, who stuck by me through (many) meandering paths and always treated me as more than my work, something I hope to emulate with my students. She is a model of how to think about the past and how to speak frankly about power in all its forms. Rebecca Kobrin has been a beacon for me in academia—a shining example of how to be a scholar and still be a person. I am glad to be among the multitudes of writers who have benefited from Elizabeth Blackmar's exceptional editing and razor-sharp thinking. At Columbia, I owe additional thanks to Nara Milanich, Ira Katznelson, Samuel K. Roberts, James Colgrove, and Stephanie McCurry for comments that helped me understand what I was doing and why I was doing it—and to Kate Daloz, who gave me the best job and made writing fun.

I met Gunther Peck during my junior year of college, when I was first beginning to think about detention; over many years of conversations about this project, his influence on my thinking has become indelible. As an undergraduate, I was fortunate to meet Karin Shapiro, Elizabeth Fenn, and Janet Ewald—women who made being a historian seem urgent and possible. Duke University's robust financial aid, as well as the Federal Pell Grant Program, enabled me to have a life and opportunities I never could have imagined.

I remain completely thrilled that Priya Nelson brought this book to Princeton University Press—truly a dream. I worked with infinitely patient and talented editorial assistants in Emma Wagh and Morgan Spehar. I thank, as well, Dimitri Karetnikov and the illustrations team for helping me get this many pictures into a book, Ali Parrington for piloting the book through production, and

Elisabeth Graves for copyediting. Kristina Shull and the second anonymous reviewer gave me rich, thoughtful comments that made this project better in every way. I am also grateful to the photojournalists who documented detention's rise and allowed me to republish their work here: Michelle Bogre, Michael Carlebach, and Tim Chapman.

This project would not have been possible without the skill and generosity of archivists across many institutions. I thank the National Archives D.C. staff for remaining calm when I pulled a (historic!) knife out of a manuscript box inside a federal building and for helping me navigate the Immigration and Naturalization Service records. (The knife has since been removed from the collection.) Chris Gushman, at the National Archives and Records Administration, New York, assisted me in accessing files amid pandemic closures. I spent an idyllic month at the University of Miami's Cuban Heritage Collection, the rare archive that offers daily *cafecito*, where I benefited from the expertise of Amanda Moreno and the support of a Goizueta Foundation Fellowship. At Duke's Rubenstein Rare Book and Manuscript Library, I thank Patrick Stawski for helping me gain access to closed portions of the Americans for Immigrant Justice Records. I am also indebted to the New Orleans Center for the Gulf South, the Gerald R. Ford Presidential Foundation, the American Historical Association, the New England Regional Fellowship Consortium, the Schlesinger Library, the University of Minnesota Social Welfare History Archive, the University of Chicago Special Collections, the Sallie Bingham Center for Women's History and Culture, and the Historical Society of Pennsylvania for financial support at various junctures of my research process.

An ACLS–Mellon Dissertation Completion Fellowship in 2019–20 gave me the essential time and resources to finish graduate school, and an ACLS Fellowship in 2022–23 gave me the space to write a book I'm proud of. At a time when humanities funding is increasingly scarce, I know how lucky I was to have this support. I am also grateful to the Jefferson Scholars Foundation at the University of Virginia, including Brian Balogh for his guidance and Lisa McGirr for her feedback on early chapters.

I cannot envision a nicer place to work, or nicer people to work with, than the William & Mary History Department. I am grateful to Chairs Frederick Corney and Tuska Benes for helping me survive starting a job during a pandemic, to Adrienne Petty for her consistently good advice, and to Julia Gaffield for so much eleventh hour help. Daneene Kelley and Annika Parks have saved me from many administrative catastrophes. And thanks especially to Nick Popper, who read all of this, answered too many questions, and generally made things better. Working with students at W&M has lived up to all the hype. I thank Claire Wyszynski, whose feedback on the manuscript made me think about this topic in new ways. And thanks to Benjamin Toyryla for excellent research assistance. I have called in far more favors than reasonable with the outstanding W&M library staff: My undying gratitude to Tyler Goldberger and Rick Mikulski, among others. W&M Faculty Summer Research Grants, as well as generous support from Keith and Sandy Dauer and the Tyler Endowment, made critical archive trips possible.

This project has been shaped through many workshops; perhaps the most transformative was the Hurst Institute for Legal History at the University of Wisconsin–Madison, expertly facilitated by Mitra Sharafi. I also benefited from workshops at the German Historical Institute's Bucerius Young Scholars Forum, the Heyman Center for the Humanities, the *Journal for Southern History* Manuscript Development Workshop, and the Columbia–Cambridge University Creating Borders Workshop. Feedback from audiences at the Duke University Forum for Scholars and Publics, the University of Toronto (In) Security Working Group, the William & Mary Law School Symposium on Mass Incarceration, and the University of Edinburgh American History Seminar helped me refine the interdisciplinary stakes of this research.

Over a decade of chapter edits, road trips, and overambitious party planning, not a day has gone by that I have not relied on Jake Purcell—an astounding thinker and dear friend. Jake and Zachary Levine made New York a joy. This book is one of a long list of things their support and unwavering commitment to the bit got me through. I am also grateful for the advice and friendship of Sam Rutherford, who inspires me as a person and a historian every day. Josh Schwartz read this entire manuscript; he improved every sentence of every chapter, bringing an eye for detail and narrative I have tried to live up to. It was a continuation of the remarkable generosity he and Jeannette Sharpless have always shown me. The influence of our long-enduring writing group with Scot McFarlane runs through each page of this book. I also benefited from a writing group organized by Alma Igra, a source of community and feedback in the years since graduating. My thanks, as well, to Nina Woodsum, Ivón Padilla-Rodriguez, Mookie Kideckel, Devon Golaszewski, Paul Katz, Nancy Ng Tam, Caroline Marris, Mallory Ditchey, Amy Zanoni, and Farren Yero, each of whom made the work more fun and more fulfilling. Lindsey Rupp, Catherine Miller, Katherine Canales, Elizabeth Zipprer, and Louis DeLillo taught me about urban planning, historic train renovation, password management, and a million other life-enriching things. And thank you to Nicole Iwata, the greatest friend imaginable, for making the book's graphs and for fifteen years of being there through it all.

The best part of going to grad school in New York was spending time with my Great-Aunt Lydia Nofil Gordon. Lydia was born in Manhattan's Little Syria neighborhood in 1928—as an immigration historian, it has been a gift to learn more about my own family's migration story and to connect with the Lebanese and Arab American communities in the city through her. My sister, Hillary, is everything I most admire in a person: funny, fearless, and willing to do some last-minute fact-checking. This book is a testament to my parents, Lori and Joseph, whose love, enthusiasm, and moral clarity are the foundation of everything.

It would be virtually impossible to tell the story of immigration detention without the work of local newspapers and journalists. This research is indebted to reporters, many of them in small towns and rural places, who asked questions about their communities' detention sites decades before immigrant incarceration became a locus of national attention. I am also grateful to the lawyers, legal aid groups, and community activists who have challenged migrant detention in the past and present (and who preserved their papers), including the Florida Immigrant Advocacy Center, now Americans for Immigrant Justice, who have been doing critical work in my home community for many decades. The history of immigration detention is long and infuriating, but it is also filled with stories of the people who have spent decades waging the ongoing fight for abolition, justice, and freedom.

A version of chapter 1 of this book first appeared in Brianna Nofil, "Policing, Profits, and the Rise of Immigration Detention in New York's 'Chinese Jails,'" *Law and History Review* 39, no. 4 (2021): 649–77.

Introduction

"Open arms for honorable immigrants; open jail doors for smuggled aliens"—that shall be the motto of the immigration department.

—U.S. IMMIGRATION COMMISSIONER HENRY CURRAN,
IN "JAIL FOR ALIENS," *LAKE SHORE NEWS*
(WOLCOTT, N.Y.), AUGUST 28, 1924

We want an answer to this question and we want it very FAST: when did we lose our goddamn rights to equal protection?

—LETTER FROM MIGRANTS INCARCERATED
AT MANATEE COUNTY JAIL, FLORIDA, 1998

IN NEW YORK'S NORTHERNMOST REACHES, a remote region of the state often called "the North Country," the county jails had many critics and few admirers. Throughout the 1920s, each new report from the Prison Association of New York lodged the same complaints about local jails' "glaring deficiencies and abuses": Jails were dangerously overcrowded (a surprising predicament for the decidedly uncrowded expanses just beneath the Canadian border), they were crumbling structural relics, and they were marred by episodes of bribery and corruption.[1] North Country jails held—at least in theory—local people accused of low-level infractions who did not generate a great deal of public sympathy. Even the Empire State's most avid reformers mustered little energy for campaigns of improvement, with one criminologist derisively describing the typical jail population as "bums, booze-fighters, [and] suspicious characters."[2]

Yet, when the prison commissioners entered Northern New York jails for annual inspections, they heard varying accents and foreign languages ringing

1

across the halls. Alongside the usual local suspects, inspectors encountered migrants awaiting hearings and deportations—the result of deals inked between counties and the federal immigration service over the previous twenty years.[3] Some of the people detained were Chinese laborers, ineligible for entry under the 1882 Chinese Exclusion Act. Following long voyages across the Pacific, Chinese migrants had used Canada as an entry point to the United States, often filing habeas corpus appeals demanding their freedom from New York lockups. Other cells held Canadians, for whom crossing the border for work and pleasure was a regular part of life. Now they found themselves "rotting in American jails," an alarmed British newspaper opined.[4] Canadians and Chinese shared the space with Italians and Jews attempting to evade new quota laws that had made legal migration an imposing, if not impossible, task. When Congress passed the 1929 Undesirable Aliens Act, criminalizing unauthorized entry into the United States, it trapped even more migrants in the jam-packed jails stationed along the southern and northern borders.[5]

These jails were sites of coercion and neglect—dozens of detained migrants died in Northern New York's dangerously overcrowded facilities while waiting for backlogged immigration hearings—but they were also sites where migrants lodged legal claims, plotted escapes, organized with aid groups, and fought for the right to stay in the United States. Migrants' presence created a predicament for Northern New York officials: On the one hand, jails filled with protesting people from around the globe were a liability. They brought bad press and bureaucratic headaches. On the other hand, migrants brought money. Each detained migrant represented a paycheck from the federal government to the local government, compensation for each night the immigration service "boarded" a person in the county jail. These paychecks had padded county budgets since the turn of the twentieth century and had made these small, peripheral towns integral to the federal work of deportation. While federal stations such as Ellis Island became the quintessential image of immigrant processing in the early twentieth century, it was at county jails that the U.S. government stretched its discretionary authority, held migrants for the longest durations, and forged enduring relationships between federal bureaucracy and local communities.

———

Nearly a century later, in the spring of 2019, towns in Louisiana would weigh many of the same concerns when considering how imprisoned migrants might keep county budgets in the black.⁶ Parishes throughout Louisiana had undertaken costly jail expansion projects in the prison-building booms of the 1980s and 1990s. Jackson Parish, for example, had room to hold 1,250 people in its jail, roughly one in thirteen of the parish's residents.⁷ In 2017, bipartisan criminal justice reform efforts in the Louisiana State Legislature successfully reduced sentences and lowered the number of people jailed in the state.⁸ With jail populations declining, local officials worried about how they would pay back construction bonds and retain corrections jobs. Many communities found an answer and an enthusiastic partner in Immigration and Customs Enforcement (ICE), signing contracts to incarcerate thousands of migrants in parish jails in exchange for about $70 per detained person, per night.

Parish jails housed migrants from Cuba, Haiti, Venezuela, India, Togo, and beyond. Many were asylum seekers, fleeing political violence and persecution, who had crossed the southern border before being sent to remote corners of Louisiana to await adjudication. They included men such as Walter Corrales, who was detained in a room with sixty other migrants in a Concordia Parish jail. Corrales had feared for his survival under the authoritarian Honduras government. Still, he called his time in Louisiana jails the worst days of his life.⁹ Sheriff Cranford Jordan of Winn Parish declared migrants like Corrales a "blessing." Their incarceration was keeping his jail open and his parish financially afloat.¹⁰

Despite decades of precedent for detaining migrants in local carceral facilities, even careful observers were caught off guard by what was occurring in Louisiana's jails. One attorney from the Southern Poverty Law Center said that while advocates knew criminal justice reform might lead rural jails to close and turn into immigration detention centers, they did not anticipate that jails would incarcerate both administratively detained migrants and those accused of criminal offenses in a shared space. Immigration detention in county jails, confessed a Louisiana law professor, "simply wasn't on anyone's radar." Both a century ago and today, county jails were and are foundational to the project of federal immigration law enforcement, but in both cases, they have operated with a staggering absence of oversight or public awareness.

This book demonstrates how a century of political, economic, and ideological exchange between the U.S. immigration bureaucracy and the criminal justice system gave rise to the world's largest system of migrant incarceration. Though court cases at the end of the nineteenth century made immigration regulation the sole prerogative of the federal government, it was the cooperation and resources of American counties and towns that made mass detention and deportation possible.[11] The enduring reliance on local jails shows that federal authorities have never had the capacity to implement restrictive immigration policies. The practice of migrant detention in jails reveals a web of political and financial incentives for local governments to collaborate with the immigration service, even as the Tenth Amendment of the Constitution granted localities leeway to refuse. Since the turn of the twentieth century, immigration agents have negotiated with sheriffs and city councils to determine how many migrants a local jail could detain and what price the federal government would pay. They transferred migrants between counties as they searched for cheaper rates and lower visibility. And they assigned detained persons a market value based on race, gender, and perceived criminality. In turn, federal and local authorities capitalized on the ill-defined rights of noncitizens to experiment with practices that saved money and streamlined the legal process of deportation. What began as temporary housing arrangements gradually gave way to a more expansive role for law enforcement in identifying and apprehending foreign-born people whom they suspected might be deportable. Across a century of intergovernmental collaboration, migrant incarceration remade the political economy of American jails and rewrote the constitutional rights of noncitizens.

A Century of Migrant Jailing

By adopting a broad chronological scope, *The Migrant's Jail* illustrates that immigration enforcement did not merely borrow the infrastructure, legal precedents, and practices of late twentieth-century criminal punishment.[12] Instead, in countless small towns, suburbs, and cities, migrant incarceration actively expanded the power and capacity of local, state, and federal governments to imprison. Migrant incarceration became a remarkably malleable tool for policymakers who sought to harden borders and engineer the nation's population: The physical spaces of detention were continually in flux, but its targets also frequently shifted as Congress prioritized different categories of people for expulsion.

The first four chapters of this book cover roughly the first half of the twentieth century. At the start of the twentieth century, the county jail was one of many components of an emerging migrant detention network—one that drew upon the United States' existing infrastructure for policing the vagrancy and mobility of subjects on society's fringes. Asylums, almshouses, workhouses, and charitable institutions all served as sites of confinement for noncitizens the United

States sought to eliminate.[13] Jails, however, had a particular utility because they existed in the vast majority of American communities, from the largest cities to the smallest outposts.[14] In the wake of the 1882 Chinese Exclusion Act, the immigration service began actively negotiating with county sheriffs to "board out" Chinese migrants in county jails. The Supreme Court declared in 1896 that migrant detention was "not imprisonment in a legal sense," yet this administrative incarceration moved thousands of Chinese men, as well as a smaller number of women and children, through a shared carceral infrastructure.[15]

For migrants apprehended near a major port of entry, such as New York, San Francisco, Seattle, or Philadelphia, the immigration service maintained federal detention space, where migrants would await hearings, recover from illness, or prepare for a return trip.[16] Away from U.S. urban centers—for example, in Upstate New York along a relatively unpatrolled border—the process of deportation was far more fragmented. As Chinese migrants turned to the courts to assert due process rights, immigration officials reimagined jailing as a practice that could streamline removals and discourage lengthy legal battles. When the late nineteenth-century courts gave the immigration service the green light to detain as part of the sovereign power to exclude, the bureaucracy saw potential. Although it was federal agents who typically took migrants into custody, sheriffs and local officials would amplify the messaging and augment the manpower of the immigration service.

The decentralized nature of early migrant detention created both opportunities and challenges for the state. Partnering with localities demanded flexibility and extensive bureaucratic labor from a fledgling federal agency with an expanding mandate: By the 1920s, the immigration service was enforcing quota laws, literacy tests, and anti-trafficking provisions, alongside legislation barring migration from Asia. With each additional immigration restriction, new groups within the nation and at the nation's gates became vulnerable to detention and deportation. Immigration officials contended with inquiries from sheriffs complaining that neighboring counties received better monetary rates and from embassies wondering why their nationals were behind bars, highlighting the interlocking local, national, and international scales of deportation. However, jails also *granted* the federal government tremendous flexibility. They offered the immigration service a dispersed network of spaces to use, expanding the agency's reach far beyond ports and borderlands. When crises arose—uprisings, escapes, lawsuits—there was always another jail the immigration service could turn to. Jails could likewise serve as a means of institutional self-preservation, a way to minimize visibility when the agency's practices came under scrutiny. From its earliest days, detention was not simply a closed space or a stagnant waiting zone. It was a process by which the state strategically contained and circulated migrants across a growing carceral network, rewarding those who could keep migrants alive and out of sight at the lowest cost.[17]

Why did localities choose to work with the immigration service?[18] The most obvious incentive for cooperation was money. As the federal government made detention an arena of economic exchange, it became something localities argued they could not afford to refuse. The case for contracting jail space often cited local unemployment numbers, new services the locality could fund, and the potential for lower tax rates.[19] Sheriffs and other elected officials found ways to personally profit, by pocketing federal money, gifting new jail contracts to associates, and leveraging their federal relationships in campaigns for reelection. Once communities came to rely on the income from detention, and in many cases, expanded their jails to accommodate the federal government, they needed the United States' demand for jail space to persist. This book shows that migrant incarceration (whether public or private) has always been a moneymaking enterprise: Local entities competed for federal revenue long before private prison companies moved into the business of detaining migrants in the 1980s.

However, the long history of migrant incarceration also shows that financial incentives were not the only means of inducing local cooperation. The immigration service could not always afford the rates sheriffs demanded, and aiding in detention was far from a lucrative undertaking for every community. To ensure local cooperation the immigration service constructed unauthorized migration as an existential, racialized threat that demanded the assistance and resources of localities. In the 1920s, when concerned citizens and embassies criticized the policy of detaining migrant families in jails, federal bureaucrats proposed a "campaign of education" aimed at skeptical mayors and police chiefs.[20] They stressed the alleged domestic consequences of unauthorized migrants, often in terms of employment, dependency, and crime, reframing immigration law enforcement as a subject of local jurisdiction and relevancy— an issue that should be equally of concern to sheriffs and city councils as it was to Congress.[21] These efforts further infused myths of immigration's harm into local, as well as national, discourses. Rationales for cooperation linked the courts' visions of immigration law as a matter of foreign policy and national identity with localities' arguments for immigration law as a means of regulating health, welfare, and safety.[22] It was a vision that invited, and perhaps demanded, an intergovernmental approach.[23]

Postwar migrant detention solidified federal dependence on local jails and spurred the development of other carceral spaces: from internment camps to skyscraper detention sites to privately run migrant detention centers. The immigration service spent much of the 1940s collaborating with fellow government agencies to facilitate the wartime incarceration of "enemy aliens," a project that borrowed the labor, infrastructure, and legal precedents of the U.S. deportation regime. After the war ended, efforts shifted to investigating and imprisoning noncitizens with communist affiliations, many of whom faced months and years of detention as they pursued extensive legal battles against their deportation orders. In the aftermath of World War II, accusations that the United States was operating migrant gulags or concentration camps proliferated in American towns hosting detention sites, as well as in the international press—a damning association as the Unites States proclaimed itself a beacon of democracy and human rights in the postwar world. Concerns about geopolitical optics, alongside ongoing discontent about the expense of incarceration, brought a first round of liberal reform to migrant jailing.

When changes came to the detention system, they affected migrants unevenly.[24] In the 1950s, the immigration service piloted a policy of "supervisory parole" rather than outright imprisonment, a shift that predominantly freed European migrants from jails and detention centers. At the same time that the nation lauded its own progressiveness in reducing the incarceration of noncitizens, the federal government was building new detention sites and forging new contracts for the capture of Mexican migrants and "war brides" arriving from Asia. This infrastructure laid the foundation for an even more expansive detention system in the 1970s and 1980s, when refugees began arriving in large numbers from the Caribbean and Central America—groups that challenged the United States' vision of its asylum system as a pathway to citizenship for European, anti-communist dissidents.[25] Buoyed by racist conceptions of the "criminal alien," policymakers lobbied for more detention laws and more detention beds as part of a national war on crime. These initiatives conveyed to the American public that nonwhite migrants, including refugees, were a threat requiring the same strategies of surveillance and control the state deployed against citizens of color.

By the latter decades of the twentieth century, a diverse set of American communities began taking migration control into their own hands, marking what some scholars have described as a new era of immigration federalism.[26] A resurgent nativist movement followed the 1965 passage of the Hart-Celler Act, a landmark law that opened pathways for legal migration from Asia, Latin

America, and Africa while closing doors for migrants from Mexico. With public outrage on their side, states and localities made greater demands of the
federal immigration service—rather than courting localities, the immigration
service now had to rein in its overenthusiastic local partners.[27] When noncitizens were convicted of crimes, towns such as Miami Beach flooded the immigration service with bills for increased incarceration costs, arguing that all
crime committed by unauthorized migrants was a failure of federal immigration policy.[28] When towns such as Moline, Illinois, observed growing Mexican
communities, they deployed local police into bars and workplaces to enforce
immigration law themselves.[29] And as the number of migrants susceptible to
Reagan-era "mandatory detention" policies grew, communities invested
unprecedented municipal money into becoming featured players in the jail
bed economy.

Towns and cities throughout the United States recognized detained migrants as a racialized source of financial capital; working with the immigration
service became a way to bankroll carceral expansion without requiring the approval (or even the tax dollars) of voters. Municipalities built and enlarged jails
on speculation, confident that the immigration service would fill them. They
then reinvested proceeds from migrant incarceration into local law enforcement, expanding police forces and corrections departments as jails grew. This
intertwined system of carceral growth had stark consequences for both citizens
and noncitizens facing incarceration, a group disproportionately composed of
poor people of color. Using incarceration as a tool of border control provided
a facade of tough, punitive state response to unauthorized migration—one that
belied the uneven, slipshod reality of how the federal government policed
borders.

Finding the Forgotten Jail

At the center of migrant incarceration's rise and endurance is the county jail.
A flourishing field of scholarship on immigration detention has concentrated
on moments when migrant incarceration became more centralized and the
federal government took on a greater role: In particular, scholars have offered
rich examinations of the buildup of federal detention facilities since the 1980s,
illustrating how Cold War tensions, a globalized war on drugs, and a late
twentieth-century bipartisan embrace of mass imprisonment drove migrant
incarceration.[30] This book shifts our periodization and our focus via a national
account of how migrants and officials negotiated detention from the turn of

the twentieth century to the present. This approach exposes the roots of the heterogeneous landscape of private, federal, and local detention sites that migrants navigate today. It explains how local officials' decisions and discretion shaped and constrained the much-noted and oft-criticized discretionary power of immigration bureaucrats.[31] And it shows the remarkable persistence of county jails and intergovernmental agreements as the cornerstone of migration control. As federal sites such as El Centro in Southern California and the Krome Service Processing Center in Miami became the most visible, contentious examples of detention in the second half of the twentieth century, the immigration service continued to quietly contract with hundreds of jails around the country. Migrants in these jails experienced different forms of violence and faced different obstacles in demanding accountability. Their stories, too, are central to the history of mass incarceration.

Jails differ from other carceral institutions in the U.S. criminal justice system—namely, prisons—in two key ways. First, they are locally operated. Jails are typically administered by a sheriff or department of corrections, and municipal politics heavily influence jails' funding, conditions, and population. Second, jails hold various categories of detained persons. They detain people awaiting trial, who may or may not be released from jail with payment of bail, alongside people convicted of crimes (usually misdemeanors, with sentences of a year or less); people awaiting transfers to prison; and, as this book emphasizes, people accused of violating federal law, whom localities detain at the behest of the federal government.[32] Jails, historically and presently, have very high turnover rates compared with prisons. In 2021, people were admitted to U.S. jails almost seven million times—some for hours, others for months—compared with about 421,000 admissions to state and federal prisons.[33] Because of the disparities in local budgets and priorities, the conditions of jails vary tremendously. A jail could be a retrofitted barn in a rural community designed to hold a dozen people, or it could be an urban multibuilding complex employing hundreds and incarcerating even more.[34] The immigration service contracted with both.

From Progressive-era calls for their abolition to lawsuits in the 1970s and 1980s that publicized unconstitutional conditions, jails were continually under fire in the twentieth-century United States. Their inadequacy was a rare point of consensus among policymakers, penologists, and activists. The immigration service regularly pointed to the deficiencies of jails as a rationale for building more migrant detention facilities of its own. As historian Melanie Newport's work on Chicago's Cook County Jail has shown, pushes for reform counterintuitively produced carceral expansion—the drive to build a "better" jail meant more funding for jailing.[35] This pattern was similarly visible in immigration detention. The failures of jail reform and the success of jailed people in securing legal interventions created demand for alternative spaces of migrant incarceration, often under the guise of humanitarian concern or paternalism. When localities' enthusiasm for cooperation waned, policymakers advocated for creative new avenues of carceral expansion, pioneering some of the nation's first federal jails, private detention facilities, and federal migrant detention centers, as well as repurposing warehouses, military bases, office buildings, and motels into sites of incarceration. We, too, want to remove migrants from violent, dangerous jails, federal officials said. Give us more money and resources to do so.

These local spaces, where the fates of migrants were still unsettled, became the center of legal and political battles about the nation's ability to exclude and deport, as well as the nation's ethical obligation to outsiders. Migrants' captivity and migrants' activism provoked local debates and critiques about what it meant to incarcerate people who, in many cases, had not been accused of a crime.[36] Long before detention dominated national headlines, questions about its morality proliferated in host communities: Was migrant detention a form of punishment? Was it Christian? Was it the right kind of business for local leaders to pursue?

The question of which outsiders the United States had an obligation to was inseparable from ideas of who was too poor, too radical, too sick, and above all, too racially different to be a citizen. Detention was most politically popular when it involved eliminating people deemed racially unassimilable or unfit for citizenship—people whom many Americans imagined might *belong* in jail. Migrant incarceration built on long lineages of how the United States policed the mobility of poor and nonwhite people, relying on both administrative police power and local vigilantism: from the recapture of fugitive slaves, to the removal and containment of Indigenous people, to the jailing of marginalized groups under local and federal vagrancy laws.[37] All of these, too, had been intergovernmental projects that familiarized Americans with the immobilization of people denied full political and constitutional rights.[38] The jail became a space that amplified and refracted Americans' existing ideas about guilt, criminality, and race. Some detainees—notably Chinese, Mexican, and Afro-Caribbean migrants—became guilty by their association with jails, which confirmed Americans' suspicions about these groups' illegality and lawlessness. At other times, as when European migrants were detained, the jail could represent the excesses of extreme immigration law enforcement,

prompting political soul-searching and efforts for relief. Through its many in-
carnations, the expansion of migrant incarceration relied on its power as a tool
of coercion; federal officials hoped that the threat of an indefinite jail stay
would pressure migrants to abandon legal appeals and would deter unwanted
migrants from coming to the United States in the first place.

By paying close attention to legal decisions affecting American jails, this
book emphasizes the interconnected experiences of citizens and noncitizens
in carceral institutions. Though they are often conceptualized as two parallel
systems of incarceration, the developments and politics of American penal
policy had major reverberations for migrants in civil detention. Lawsuits that
brought jails under court orders, legislation that established new types of carceral institutions, and highly publicized prison uprisings all affected how the
state approached migrant incarceration, in part because migrants were *already*
in shared local institutions. Still, migrants and their advocates often relied on
rhetoric that positioned administrative detainees as more deserving of constitutional protections and less deserving of jail time than people who had been
accused or convicted of criminal charges—a group disproportionately made
up of Black Americans. Jailing migrants was egregious, advocates claimed
throughout the twentieth century, because it treated a migrant like a "common
criminal." This reasoning positioned individuals imprisoned for criminal
charges as the "real" threat, more deserving of the horrific conditions of human
warehousing. Though observers often attempted to draw lines of merit and
culpability between those targeted for administrative and criminal offenses,
people of all citizenship statuses would suffer under a system that prioritized
control and suppressed dissent.

Resistance, Federalism, and the Law

Despite the best efforts of law enforcement and policymakers to create a system of incarceration that would serve their own interests, few groups influenced the trajectory of detention more than migrants themselves. Through
individual and collective resistance, migrants challenged the state's power to
detain, as well as the relationship between the federal government and localities. An archive that centers on institutional power still offers ways to witness
how migrants pushed back against the capriciousness of jailing and removal.[39]
The material evidence of migrants' lived experience is scattered among the
records of bureaucrats and lawyers. It takes many forms: a butter knife carved
into a key by an Italian attempting to break out of a detention cell, letters from
Chinese migrants offering to expose their smugglers' secrets in exchange for

freedom from jail, political speeches drawing parallels between Jim Crow and migrant incarceration, funeral programs for an asylum seeker who died in a Florida jail and another for a migrant child who drowned in a Coast Guard apprehension at sea. Archives contain thousands of affidavits from detained people, testimonies that attempt to make experiences of persecution legible to the legal apparatus of the United States.[40]

These sources are complemented by migrants' letters and petitions, writing that excoriated the contradictions between professed American ideals and the system of incarceration without trial they encountered. "Do you Americans like when people suffer? Does God give Americans power to do evil things?" wrote a Haitian migrant interdicted at sea.[41] A Cuban in Louisiana described his incarceration as a form of state-sponsored disappearance: "[Since] Oct. 2, 1995, I have been kidnapped by the [immigration] service in parish jails."[42] Another letter by a group of asylum seekers held in Florida framed the United States' actions as the latest in a long list of hypocrisies: "The U.S. is going to China, Cuba, and several other countries telling them about civil rights violations; the Indians was run off their land by the U.S. Put on the reservation. Now [the immigration service] have [migrants] hiding here in the Manatee County Jail."[43] Migrants' protests and critiques of state power led officials to think of the jail as a tool to thwart resistance: Transferring migrants between jails was an effort to separate them from the solidarity they found in one another. The practice also produced a disparate and scattered archive, one easy to overlook in federal immigration records alone.

One of the ways that migrants attempted to secure their freedom and undercut the legitimacy of detention was through the courts. This book examines both routine, individual petitions, requesting habeas corpus or reprieve through bail, and more complex legal challenges to jail conditions and the immigration agency's power to incarcerate. Incarcerated or detained noncitizens "sit at the intersection of two powerful lines of deference," writes legal scholar Emma Kaufman.[44] In cases involving the immigration status of foreign nationals, courts have historically deferred to the political branches, which have near-complete sovereign authority in dictating entry and exclusion. And in cases involving prisons and jails, courts have routinely deferred to policies curbing the constitutional rights of incarcerated people. Despite a series of more liberal rulings for prisoners' rights in the 1970s, the 1980s saw a judicial retreat from rights recognition in favor of arguments that stressed the peculiarity of carceral institutions and recognized the broad power of prison officials to restrict rights in the name of "legitimate penological interests."[45] Together, these two lines of deference have vested extraordinary power in sheriffs and other jail workers tasked with policing the day-to-day lives of people with few rights and only the narrowest paths to judicial recourse.

The plenary power doctrine, crystallized by the courts at the turn of the twentieth century, dictates that the executive and legislative branches are responsible for immigration policy decisions and that courts should only rarely, if ever, entertain challenges to decisions about who is admitted or expelled. *Plenary power,* a term similarly invoked in Indian affairs and in cases involving the political status of U.S. territories, indicates complete and *absolute* authority. The power over immigration was affirmed in the 1889 case of *Chae Chan Ping v. United States,* in which the Supreme Court ruled that the government could exclude a noncitizen on whatever grounds it deemed necessary.[46] "Jurisdiction over its own territory . . . is an incident of every independent nation. It is a part of its independence," the Court declared, describing migration control as a by-product of foreign affairs and immigration as an act of "foreign aggression and encroachment." Individual constitutional rights became secondary; Congress held the power to discriminate against arriving migrants on the basis of race, gender, political affiliation, or any other category it deemed relevant.[47] To say that the nation could not deny foreigners was to compromise nationhood itself.

Plenary power also bore a corollary notion: that federal authority over immigration was indivisible and that states and counties had no independent role in immigration law's development and administration.[48] This doctrine upended the nineteenth-century U.S. immigration regime, which was characterized by the creation and energetic enforcement of immigration laws by state and local officials.[49] Though the courts dictated that localities could not produce or execute immigration policy, there was much more ambiguity about how the federal government might delegate power to localities. The history of migrant incarceration shows how federalism could be used to both serve and undercut the interests of migrants: Reliance on localities enabled unprecedented, large-scale deportations in some moments and incapacitated the immigration service in others.[50] These intergovernmental relationships were perpetually in flux. It was not uncommon for communities to embrace a role in the deportation state one year and denounce it the next. And unwillingness to cooperate was not always progressive: Localities pushed back against the immigration service's requests for reasons that had little to do with concern for migrants' rights.[51] Local refusals to detain could be strategies to negotiate more money, reactions to poor media coverage, or efforts to refocus jail space on "local" crime.

Local actors did not control the core aspects of immigration—decisions about the admission and removal of noncitizens—yet they held significant power in shaping the enforcement of immigration law. *The Migrant's Jail* shows how the vast, virtually unchecked plenary power of Congress and the president to create immigration policy devolved to empower a broad range of bureaucrats, contractors, and local officials. The distinctive standing of immigration law gave rise to a bureaucracy that operated with stunning autonomy: It was insulated from judicial intervention; it resisted oversight and administrative norms at every juncture; and it used subcontracting, transfers, and intergovernmental agreements to further distance itself from accountability.[52] Against imposing odds, migrants returned to court again and again, often securing victories on procedural grounds. Even when they did not win, their legal cases were critical in bringing detention into public consciousness and creating a paper trail of abuses of power.

———

The Migrant's Jail tells a national story about local institutions. The United States currently has 2,850 county jails, most of which have existed in some form for more than a century—to make any generalizations about these disparate spaces is treacherous business.[53] In writing this book, I have strived for regional coverage, to show that detention was a process taking place across the nation. I place particular emphasis on localities where migrant jailing moved from a local issue to a point of national reckoning. Often this occurred in unexpected places such as Malone, New York, and Galveston, Texas, in the beginning of the twentieth century and Immokalee, Florida; York, Pennsylvania; and Avoyelles Parish, Louisiana, at the end. These communities differ in virtually every way, from demographics to geography, politics to population—yet each of them chose to work closely with the immigration service to expel the people the nation had deemed dangerous, undesirable, or otherwise "illegal."

In 2023, ICE detained an average of 28,289 migrants per night, down from a pre-COVID peak of 49,403 migrants per night in 2019. (Figure 1.) Even this reduced number is roughly twelve times as many people as the agency detained fifty years ago. Detention is the backbone of the U.S. border enforcement regime, relying not just on private prison companies and federal detention centers but on the hundreds of city and county jails that contract with the immigration service.[54] The cruelties and injustices are manifold. But they are not new.

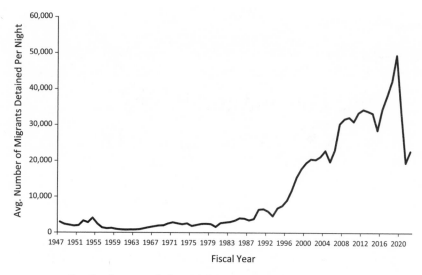

FIGURE 1. Graph of average daily population in immigration custody, 1947–2022. *Source:* Compiled from U.S. Department of Justice appropriations hearings, U.S. Department of Homeland Security appropriations hearings, and Immigration and Naturalization Service annual reports.

"Here, almost daily, Federal officers call for aliens," a local writer observed in Upstate New York in 1927. "They are handcuffed. They are led through the main streets of this village to be photographed. Yet [the] spotlight that plays around Ellis Island is not trained upon small county jails."[55] It has been nearly one hundred years since this journalist encountered migrants from Asia, Europe, and Latin America detained, out of sight and out of mind, in the rural jails along the Canadian border. Today, debates over federalism have come to the forefront in fights about sanctuary cities, migrant busing, and how local law enforcement works (or refuses to work) with ICE. The questions raised by these fights are the same ones that migrants and their advocates confronted, shivering in a converted barn against the New York winter. Who is responsible for detaining migrants? What is the relationship between a seemingly unaccountable federal immigration enforcement bureaucracy and a local municipality? Does a locality have to cooperate when the federal immigration service requests, or in some cases, *demands*, its assistance? And most importantly: How can a self-proclaimed nation of immigrants also be a place that imprisons tens of thousands of immigrants, exiles, and refugees?

1

Policing and Profits in
New York's Chinese Jails

IN 1903, a journalist named Poultney Bigelow traveled to Malone, New York, a mill town in a region of the Empire State so remote that the state's own senator declared it "the Siberia of New York."[1] Bigelow was something of an accidental muckraker. The son of a powerful U.S. statesman, he had quickly lost interest in his law degree and instead carved out a career in international reporting. He preferred the topic of corruption, writing exposés of foreign governments as well as the questionable dealings of his own family members.[2] Malone was the county seat of Franklin County, fourteen miles south of the border and home to ten thousand residents, many of them dairy farmers. It was not a location that frequently saw well-connected writers pass through town.[3]

Bigelow came to Malone to explore what he called "the back door to the state of New York." The halls of Ellis Island were the front door, where Jews, Romanians, Croats, and Italians entered to become citizens. But the northern reaches of New York were something else entirely, Bigelow warned in his dispatch. It was a land of unregulated entry and local corruption, far from the consciousness of most Americans.

The journalist's report focused not on the physical borderlands or the local immigration station or even the courthouse. Instead, it centered on the Franklin County Jail, a three-story, brick structure with six steel cells that had been "properly condemned" by the state commissioner of prisons for its dangerous conditions.[4] In the jail sat dozens of Chinese migrants, most of whom had been apprehended after crossing the Canadian border and nearly all of whom claimed to be U.S. citizens. The town was in the process of building a new jail or "detention house" exclusively to detain the rising number of people arriving in violation of the 1882 Chinese Exclusion Act, a law that banned Chinese laborers from admission to the United States. The law had been fueled by grass-roots activism that claimed Chinese migrants were, in the words of the San Francisco mayor, "a threat to everything that goes to make up American civilization."[5] Lawmakers, unions, and everyday Americans latched onto a shared understanding that Chinese were a separate race, with customs, habits, and bodies that made them fundamentally unassimilable and dangerous. When Congress codified the exclusion law, it became the United States' first federal policy banning entry on the basis of race and nationality—a culmination of decades of political organizing and messaging about the so-called Chinese Problem, much of which centered on California and the Pacific Northwest.[6] Despite its West Coast roots, the law's reverberations echoed nationwide.

Bigelow anticipated a familiar story, as communities throughout the United States were expelling Chinese residents through local policies and, more commonly, through vigilante violence.[7] But after speaking with Franklin County Sheriff Ernest Douglass, the writer was surprised to find that the sheriff treated Chinese migrants "like pets," emphasizing that they were easier to take care of than jailed Americans. Sheriff Douglass, an imposing man who had been elected for his "fearless integrity" and long career in law enforcement, had good reason to be enthusiastic about Chinese migration.[8] He earned about a dollar a week from the federal government for each "federal prisoner" held at the Franklin County Jail.[9] In the previous three years, the sheriff had pocketed $20,000 from migrant incarceration.[10] "The Sheriff has therefore a direct pecuniary interest in detaining the Chinaman as long as possible," Bigelow concluded.

Even beyond the troubling financial implications of this arrangement, Bigelow suggested that there was something fundamentally odd about the situation in Northern New York. These "Chinese prisoners" claimed to have been born in the United States, making them U.S. citizens.[11] They were not accused of committing a crime. And yet, they were stuck in American jails for month upon month. Under common law, individuals suspected of crimes were innocent until proven guilty. In the case of Chinese migrants, Bigelow observed, "we put them in jail first and let them prove their innocence afterwards."[12] The county jail was a liminal space in a literal sense—a holding zone for individuals crossing national boundaries. But it was also a liminal space in a figurative sense—a space that blurred the lines between punishment and administrative process, local authority and federal control, the prisoner and the citizen.

This chapter explores the United States' earliest efforts to develop an immigration detention system in Northern New York. By the early twentieth century, the Supreme Court had sharply curtailed cities' and states' ability to *create* immigration law, demarcating immigration as the exclusive jurisdiction of the federal government, yet localities proved critical to *carrying out* immigration law.[13] A cornerstone of this cooperation came through towns and cities granting the federal government use of local jails. Immigration policing moved Chinese migrants from a more fluid category of "entrant" into the new category of "Chinese prisoner," creating a form of legibility from which communities could profit.[14] Rather than viewing Chinese prisoners as a threat to law and order, New York border towns instead viewed them as a low-risk, high-reward population that channeled federal money into rural communities. Migrants' incarceration transformed them into a potential commodity.[15]

Localities' focus on fees and revenue created tension with the efforts of the federal government. Chinese migrants may have been desirable to local officials, but their unauthorized presence in the United States, the expense of their incarceration, and their use of the courts to resist exclusion laws threatened a nascent federal Bureau of Immigration eager to assert its enforcement power. Chinese migrants in Northern New York, like Chinese migrants throughout the country, successfully utilized habeas corpus petitions to undercut the legal barriers posed by the Chinese Exclusion Act. The petitions claimed that the jailed Chinese men were U.S. citizens, unlawfully detained by the immigration service.

Detention was a miserable affair. The food was unappetizing and unfamiliar. The jails were petri dishes for outbreaks of illness, including smallpox. Most men slept on the floor, and minors were incarcerated alongside adults. But if Chinese migrants could survive the months of captivity, the federal government's lack of evidence to refute their claims of citizenship meant that most would eventually be freed. While Chinese migrants were detained, they were actively carving out exceptions and resisting regulation through the law.[16]

Much of the scholarship on detention in the early twentieth century has focused on the West Coast and on the development of the Angel Island Immigration Station in particular. Scholars have typically characterized the detention of Chinese migrants in this era as relatively brief, with detention beyond a couple of weeks a notable exception.[17] However, before the West Coast had Angel Island, it had another facility. Commonly known as the "detention shed," the notoriously ill-kept structure stood at the end of a wharf in San Francisco Bay, where the odor of sewage, seawater, and bile permeated every wooden corner. The Pacific Mail Steamship Company bore the cost of detention for migrants it brought to the United States, a policy that paralleled the one in place for steamship companies transporting European migrants to the East Coast.[18] By 1902, Frank Sargent, the commissioner-general of immigration, conceded that the shed was a liability and called for its abolition—a move that would not occur for another eight years.[19]

Nonetheless, Sargent also emphasized that the San Francisco detention shed was vastly preferable to its alternative. "But for [the shed] our officers here would have had no place other than the jails of the city in which to keep the men and I hardly think the jails are a proper place to detain immigrants," he opined.[20] Sargent made no mention that this improper place had already become the de facto solution for the immigration service along the U.S. land borders. Detentions in Northern New York were significantly longer than detentions in San Francisco, which observers attributed to financial incentives for sheriffs and a lack of resources for immigration officials operating at the nation's peripheries. Data I compiled from jail ledger books in Northern New York's Essex County show that the average length of detention for a Chinese migrant awaiting investigation or appeal in 1901 and 1902 was a staggering 114 days—migrants spent nearly four months in a remote county jail, a space designed for only the shortest-term stays. (Figure 2.) By comparison, scholars have estimated that the average detention at Angel Island ranged from ten days to a month.[21]

Though the U.S. West received far more attention for its Chinese communities and its rampant anti-Chinese violence, more than three-quarters of Chinese apprehended between 1901 and 1903 crossed the border east of Ohio.[22] In 1903, Commissioner-General Sargent wrote that the agency had been misappropriating its limited resources, enacting "an idle ceremony" of cursory examinations as foreign passengers departed ships. The real enforcement issues, he insisted, were at America's land borders.[23] As Northern New York became a preferred route of entry for Chinese migrants, congestion at local jails created demand for new, racialized spaces of incarceration. The New York State Prison Commission called these sites "Chinese jails" and their denizens "the Chinese prisoners." Despite the Supreme Court's insistence in the 1893 case of Fong Yue Ting v. United States that deportation was a purely civil process, the state of New York acknowledged these sites for what they were: the first wave of immigration prisons in the United States.[24]

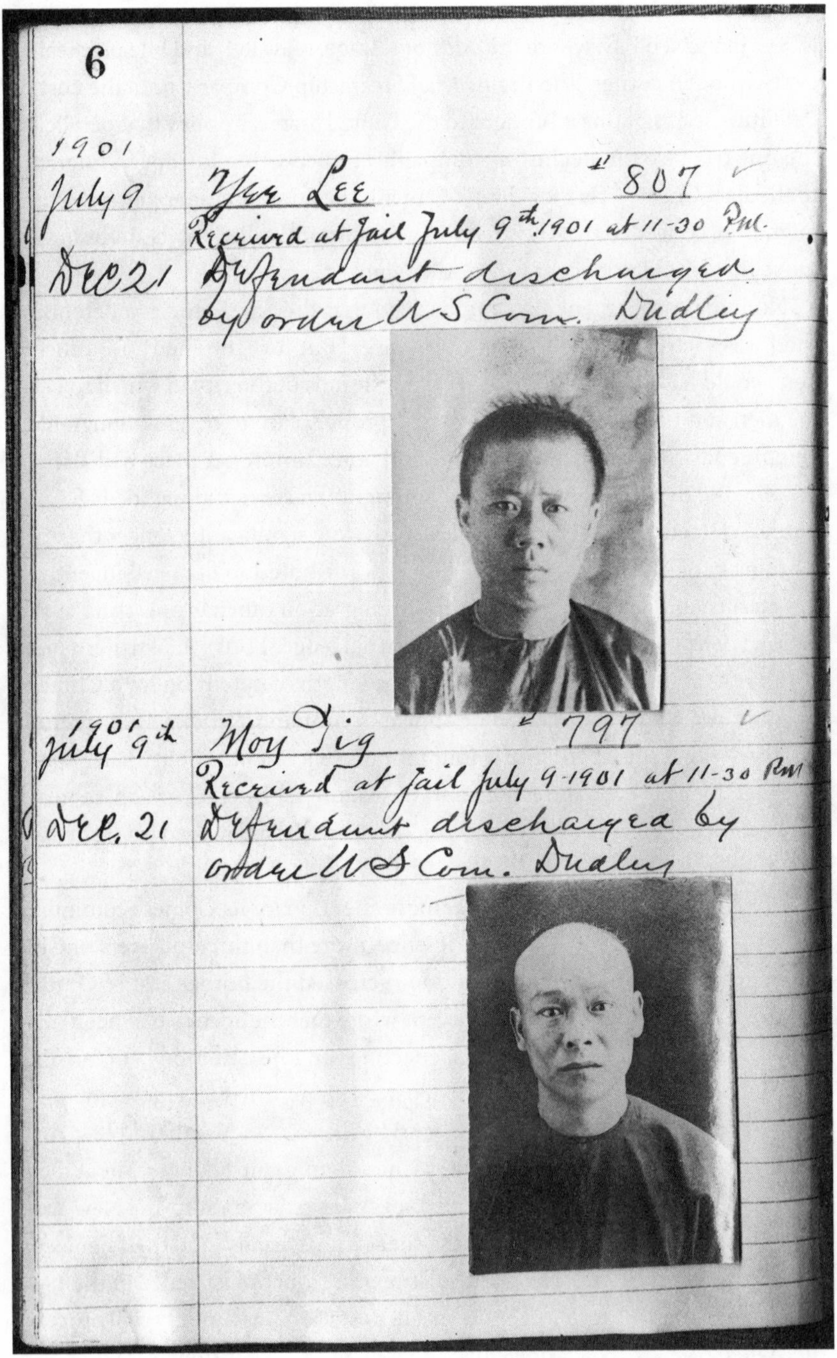
6
1901
July 9 Yee Lee #807
Received at jail July 9th 1901 at 11-30 P.M.
Dec 21 Defendant discharged by order U S Com. Dudley
1901 July 9th Moy Jig #797
Received at jail July 9-1901 at 11-30 PM
Dec. 21 Defendant discharged by order U S Com. Dudley

FIGURE 2. Port Henry Jail Ledger, Vol. 2 of 2, 1901, 6–7 (*above* and *overleaf*). County jail ledgers note the dates migrants entered and exited the jail, as well as the outcome of their cases. Courtesy of Town of Moriah Historical Society, Museum of Chinese in America Collection.

1901

July 9   Yee Nom   ✓ #808
          Recived at Jail July 9-1901 at 11.30 P.M.

1902

Feb 26   Defendant released by discharge
7 P.M.   by order Com. Dudley

1901
July 9th   Wong Gong Yu
          Recived at Jail July 9th 1901 at 11-30 P.M.
Oct 19   Defendant discharged by order of
12 M-Oct 19 U.S Commissioner F.W. Dudley

FIGURE 2. (continued)

Chinese Migrants at Malone

Chinese laborers had traversed the U.S.-Canada border since the passage of the 1882 Chinese Exclusion Act: They rafted in overcrowded rowboats across the Niagara River, they hid in the cargo of trains that crisscrossed the two nations, and they journeyed across what the immigration service deemed the "wild districts" of rural Montana, Idaho, and Washington.[25] The four thousand-mile northern border was an immense expanse of land, presenting endless opportunities for smugglers to move across its mountain ranges, rivers, and two flanking oceans.[26] Those who passed into Northern New York entered the ancestral lands of Iroquoian and Algonquian peoples.[27] The four counties that built Chinese jails were primarily Mohawk territory, bisected by the U.S.-Canada border.[28] (Figure 3.)

Most Chinese who crossed into the North Country traveled by trains departing from Montreal, disembarking just north of the boundary line and walking across the border on foot.[29] Sometimes their crossings were facilitated by networks of Chinese in Montreal, who prepped migrants for interrogations and provided witnesses who could testify to their identities.[30] Other times entry was brokered by enterprising New Yorkers, as federal officials griped about a lack of law enforcement intervention.[31] While the United States excluded groups of Chinese based on occupation and labor status, the Canadian government attempted to deter migration with a $50 head tax on all Chinese laborers in 1885, which increased to $500 by 1903. In the years following the passage of the Chinese Exclusion Act, American policymakers suggested that Canada's more lenient policies had "practically nullified" U.S. border enforcement efforts.[32]

In communities such as Malone, Chinese migrants entered with the expectation of arrest. Then, at a hearing before a U.S. immigration commissioner, migrants would claim that they had been born in the United States. The Bureau of Immigration had little recourse in proving these testimonies false; agents attempted to discredit the witnesses by highlighting inconsistencies in their testimonies and hoped that the courts would err on their side. In nearly all cases in which the courts sided with the government, a Chinese migrant would appeal the decision of the immigration officer and, if the resources were available, secure legal representation.[33] In Northern New York, virtually all cases were taken by Robert M. Moore, described by one observer as an attorney who "knows all the ins and outs of the Chinese business better than the government officials themselves."[34] Moore was in his mid-thirties—a self-trained,

Canada

Montréal

Malone Clinton

Canton

Franklin Plattsburgh

St. Lawrence

Essex Port Henry

Vermont

• Cities with Chinese Jails
▆ NY Counties with Chinese Jails
▢ NY Counties

FIGURE 3. Map of four Northern New York counties that detained significant numbers of Chinese migrants. Map by Jordan Landrum.

Canadian-born former schoolteacher who had never attended university.[35] That the U.S. government was regularly being bested by a country lawyer did not improve immigration officials' faith in the judicial system.

Through its liberal appeal process, the Bureau of Immigration contended that the courts were in effect "doing that thing which is expressly forbidden by law and treaty, to wit, naturalizing Chinamen."[36] Between 1895 and 1905, at least 5,714 Chinese were admitted as citizens after entering through the northern boundary.[37] And even when the United States did manage to successfully reject migrants, removal from the East Coast was a tremendously expensive project; by 1904, deportations from New York and New England represented the bureau's largest per capita expense.[38]

The root of the bureau's problem was that when Chinese claimed U.S. citizenship, the district court virtually always granted habeas corpus, moving their case from an administrative tribunal to a full legal hearing.[39] In September 1903, the bureau sent Special Assistant Attorney John L. Lott to Malone to observe the processing of sixty Chinese men picked up by immigration officials near the border. Several Chinese travelers were bound for Cuba, using Malone as a stopover before continuing south. Several were returning laborers who held appropriate documentation. The remaining forty-five "were seeking to enter upon the pretended claim that they had been born in the United States," Lott reported.[40] After the district court granted habeas corpus for those declaring citizenship, the detained men met with lawyers and interpreters—in Lott's words, "[furnishing] the opportunity to perfect the fraud" by crafting stories about family relations, birthplaces, and migration histories that could be confirmed by outside witnesses.[41] The bureau claimed that, because the immigration officer at Malone did not possess the singular authority to deny admission, the entire system of border law enforcement could be easily undermined. Lott concluded his report with a recommendation: The only way to end such "gross frauds" was to close the port of Malone and transfer all Chinese cases to a neighboring Vermont district where the courts had opted not to review writs of habeas corpus.[42] The bureau saw its relationship to the federal courts as a critical determinant of its success in the region—critical enough to contemplate the costly project of shutting down an entire immigration station in order to drive migrants into a district where the courts had been more favorable to the agency.

Aside from the immigration service, the presence of Chinese migrants in Northern New York was also of interest to a more reform-minded group: the New York State Commission of Prisons, an investigatory body tasked with maintaining a basic level of decency in New York's carceral institutions.[43] The commission had a thankless job, particularly when it came to jails. Cornelius V. Collins, the New York superintendent of prisons, called county jails "the fatally weak point" of the Empire State's carceral system, while the Prison Association of New York editorialized that "the work of manufacturing criminals could hardly be done more effectually than it is by our jail system."[44] When Chinese migrants arrived in Malone, officials brought them to the second floor of the Franklin County Jail, where they encountered cells of about thirty-five square feet apiece. The jail's second floor was designed to hold twelve people. At the time of the Prison Commission's 1900 visit, investigators counted forty Chinese men detained in the facility, some in "hammock bunks," others sleeping on the floor. The commission discovered another forty-four Chinese men huddled in the jail attic, a space never intended to house people. Perhaps the most visceral element of the jail was the smell. In a space without proper ventilation, new arrivals were immersed in an odor that inspectors described as overpowering and sickening.[45]

The overcrowded conditions at Franklin County Jail produced jurisdictional friction between the federal government and the State Commission of Prisons. The commission noted that the county jail was encouraged to accommodate federal prisoners but that the sheriff "[was] not compelled to receive prisoners at the jail" when it was already filled to capacity.[46] The jail clearly violated state laws requiring the separation and classification of prisoners—men from women, violent offenders from nonviolent offenders—but the commission offered few remedies, short of closing the nation's borders.[47] The inability of the nation to effectively enforce its immigration laws had generated a local predicament that local government had little ability to address.[48] The federal government owned and operated large immigration detention spaces at Ellis Island and in San Francisco Bay; in Baltimore, Philadelphia, and Boston it had access to detention stations operated by steamship companies.[49] Since 1880, the government used a federal prison at McNeil Island, off the coast of Washington, to detain Chinese migrants with criminal charges (including a common allegation of "unlawful presence") whom it struggled to deport.[50] However, the United States had no short-term federal jails and no real plan for how removal would look in rural extremities. County jails, alongside an assemblage of other coercive institutions including mental hospitals, almshouses, and private detention homes, became the solution.[51]

While the commission bemoaned the dangerous jail conditions, a new phenomenon was concurrently rising in Malone: the birth of the town's so-called Chinese business. A growing number of locals and visitors were receiving federal money for watching, arresting, keeping, and examining Chinese migrants. Four deputy marshals who patrolled the border each received a $7,300 annual salary, the U.S. commissioner earned fees for each defendant, and the U.S. Marshals earned fees for each arrest.[52] Witnesses arriving from New York City and Boston to testify in the Chinese citizenship cases each cost the federal government an average of $40.80 for travel and lodging. Most critically, the sheriff could reap a substantial sum of money from Chinese migration. The Franklin County sheriff earned fifty cents a day for the board of each prisoner. For detained Chinese, these stays lasted anywhere from a week to eighteen months.[53] By September 1900, Sheriff Douglass held ninety-one Chinese prisoners in the Franklin County Jail, collecting $45.50 per day. "The Chinese business has flourished like a green-bay tree in Malone," observed a reporter from the nearby town of Plattsburgh.[54] The townspeople's potential profit off "Malone's monopoly" complicated the enforcement of Chinese exclusion laws.[55] If the sheriff could now make a year's salary in a single month of holding one hundred Chinese migrants, what incentive did the system have to move efficiently?[56]

Despite denials and acquittals, Malone's association with corruption was hard to shake. Even if the federal government could not prove a region-wide conspiracy, it remained alarmed by the court's deferrals to habeas corpus claims and Malone's low rate of expulsion. In the autumn of 1900, U.S. District Attorney George B. Curtis ordered Chinese inspectors to move the forty-eight Chinese migrants detained at the Franklin County Jail fifty miles east to Platts-burgh for examination and detention, disregarding a law mandating that migrants be tried by the commissioner nearest to their point of entry.[57] The district attorney reported that "the atmosphere in Malone is favorable to the Chinese" and implied that officials at Malone actively thwarted the depor-tation of Chinese migrants. Sheriff Douglass responded that he would not "surrender the Chinese prisoners" unless U.S. Commissioner F. G. Paddock ordered him to do so.[58] Losing Chinese migrants was a blow to the local econ-omy. Malone would forfeit the federal money for boarding at its jail, as well as money circulated into local businesses for jail groceries, hotel rooms for wit-nesses, and railroad tickets.[59] One newspaper's estimate put Malone's financial losses at $50,000 per year if the "Chinese business" moved east.[60]

Several months later, a Treasury Department investigation into Malone reiterated the district attorney's request that Chinese migrants be transferred, turning Plattsburgh into the main hub of immigrant adjudication. Much of the impetus for the move came from anxieties around how Commissioner Pad-dock ruled in Chinese cases. "It is not alleged that Mr. Paddock has been guilty of any wrongdoing," a Malone paper wrote, "but his construction of the Chi-nese exclusion act has been so radically different from that of treasury officials that it has been decided that no more Chinese cases shall be taken before him."[61] Paddock published a forcible rebuke to accusations that he had mis-handled Chinese cases, instead blaming the federal government's feeble evi-dence against migrants. "It was practically impossible for the government to produce testimony to contradict the testimony of the defendants," Paddock said, gesturing to the difficulty of confirming the prior locations and contacts of transient Chinese laborers. In the previous nine months, Paddock had heard 162 Chinese cases and had deported only twenty-seven people. However, in many of those cases the district attorney failed to submit any evidence to sup-port the government's case.[62]

With Commissioner Paddock's resignation several months after the move, Franklin County leaders were hopeful that the "Chinese business" would return to town.[63] Weeks later, the federal government unceremoniously reintroduced Chinese migrants to the Franklin County Jail, even though trials in Malone had not officially resumed. This was a result of the rising number of Chinese arrests and the limited space at Plattsburgh facilities; the *Brooklyn Eagle* reported in the spring of 1901 that the Franklin County Jail held 229 Chinese men—likely an all-time high.[64]

The Rise of the Chinese Jail

As controversy and allegations of corruption swirled, the decision to move Chinese migrants from Malone to Plattsburgh signaled a larger shift in the detention economy. By 1901, the rising number of Chinese migrants moving through Northern New York led the immigration service to recruit more upstate counties as collaborators in migrant incarceration. The 1901 State Commission of Prisons report indicated that federal officials had committed Chinese migrants to county jails in St. Lawrence, Clinton, and Essex counties, in addition to Franklin. Nearly all of the jails were holding well over their maximum capacity, with inspectors tallying 460 detained Chinese migrants across the four county jails.[65] Overcrowding led local officials to envision a new approach to migrant incarceration: Rather than trying to squeeze federal prisoners into overextended jails, they could create separate facilities specifically to incarcerate Chinese migrants and attract federal business. (Figure 4.)

In 1901, Plattsburgh became the first town in New York to build a facility exclusively for holding Chinese laborers, a decision fueled by the number of migrants it received in the wake of Malone's corruption scandal. Sheriff James P. Cunningham announced the completion of the "new Chinese jail" in May and transferred eighty Chinese men from the county jail to the new site. The jail resembled an Adirondack lumber camp, with bunk beds, a long dining table, and a cookstove.[66] Over the next several years, all four New York counties holding substantial numbers of Chinese men created separate sites for their detention, distinct from the county jails. The formation of these sites served multiple ends: They kept the State Prison Commission at bay, they ensured that counties would continue to receive cohorts to detain, and they cemented an association between Chinese people and illegality, moving the phrase "Chinese jail" firmly into the local vernacular. Once Clinton County built a Chinese jail, it compelled neighboring counties to build similar facilities to compete in the informal economy for Chinese prisoners.

JAIL, MALONE, FRANKLIN COUNTY, N. Y.

FIGURE 4. County Jail (*above*) and the Chinese Jail (*overleaf*)—also called "detention building for Chinese" or "Chinese detention house"—in Franklin County, New York, 1902. *Source:* Prison Association of New York, *Annual Report of the Prison Association of New York for the Year 1902* (Albany: Argus Co. Printers, 1903).

MALONE, N. Y., DETENTION BUILDING FOR CHINESE.

FIGURE 4. (*continued*)

With the detention economy expanding, all four Northern New York counties arrived at similar conclusions about the value of jailed Chinese people:
They were a potential commodity that the community should fight for. When
a train of Chinese migrants arrived in Plattsburgh in 1901, the town emphasized that the men were, in many ways, ideal prisoners—a description that

drew from racist characterizations of Chinese and conveyed to locals that cooperation with federal immigration law enforcement was a desirable arrangement.[67] Mainstream racist thought at the time of the exclusion acts characterized Chinese men as docile, subservient, and effeminate—as a semi-slave or "coolie" race.[68] Nativists and labor groups decried these traits as a threat to American democracy and manhood, fundamentally incompatible with American citizenship. But this characterization was highly compatible with the traits that made a model prisoner.

New York towns did not desire Chinese residents, but the *Chinese prisoner* filled a distinct social and economic role: His potential social threat had been neutralized by his lack of freedom, and his economic benefit outweighed his potential danger. The agreements had novelty for the citizens of Northern New York. At St. Lawrence and Clinton counties, hundreds of residents gathered outside the jails to watch and photograph Chinese migrants in scenes reminiscent of spectators at a zoo.[69] Though the jail was undeniably congested, a St. Lawrence journalist reported that Chinese prisoners "appeared to be as much at home and as happy as if they were safely quartered in New York's Chinatown."[70] At the detention station in nearby Richford, Vermont, also along the U.S.-Canada border, the *Boston Globe* praised the serenity and "cheerfulness" of Chinese prisoners. "Time is nothing to the Chinaman. His patience is greater than that of any other man on Earth."[71] In one particularly outrageous declaration, a St. Lawrence newspaper suggested that Chinese migrants enjoyed New York jails so much that they took "pleasure trips" to the United States at Americans' expense.[72]

These claims had an insidious effect, turning the jail into a space that produced and confirmed racial difference. Local governments insisted that they could keep Chinese migrants in abhorrent conditions with no real impact on their well-being, thus validating cost-cutting measures and reiterating the "otherness" of Chinese detainees compared with the American prisoner. One sheriff made the claim quite explicitly, arguing that "four Chinamen can make themselves comfortable where one white man would think himself crowded."[73] Overcrowding, he suggested, was only a concern to white prisoners. Local and federal officials ignored the dangerous conditions Chinese migrants faced in jails, but they also obscured the intentional way Chinese migrants were navigating the U.S. legal system, a system in which a stay in jail was a route to recourse in American courts.

Beyond the insistences that jails were practically resorts, some observers reckoned quite explicitly with the ethical stakes of holding thousands of migrants in county and Chinese jails. One upstate resident expressed distress at the inefficiency of the U.S. legal system in discerning between American-born Chinese and those making false claims to citizenship. He suggested that the U.S. government needed to either pass a *more* restrictive law, disallowing even Chinese American citizens from leaving the country, or repeal the Exclusion Act altogether. The severe but ultimately unenforceable laws, the writer suggested, had led the United States to traffic in cruelty: "It is painful to think that in a country professedly Christian, men are being arrested and hauled to jail for no other reason than that they were not born with white skin."[74] A reverend, one of the era's many Protestant missionaries who advocated that Chinese souls could be saved through Christian conversion, articulated a similar point about race in the *Western Christian Advocate*.[75] The minister argued that American cities had jails filled with European immigrants "against whom actual crimes have been proven" and yet faced no exclusion mandates, while Chinese at Malone were incarcerated merely for crossing a border.[76] Others feared what the "Chinese business" said about the "character" of Upstate New York towns, drawing racialized comparisons to border towns along the U.S.-Mexico line.[77] Commentary from Malone conveyed concern about an unjust, un-Christian system of incarceration without due process. It also expressed an underlying anxiety about criminality and corruption that residents associated with the presence of racialized groups.[78]

The State Commission of Prisons remained a critical voice throughout the peak years of Chinese migration, even as Chinese jails mitigated the overcrowding at county facilities.[79] What the federal government deemed "acceptable conditions" for holding migrants was never especially clear, reflecting a nationwide absence of standards for county jails. With competition for prisoners mounting, New York counties made more aggressive claims for why their county most deserved Chinese detainees, often based on the quality and capacity of their jails. When news of a Clinton County facility exclusively for Chinese migrants circulated in 1902, St. Lawrence County contended that Chinese migrants should be sent to its jail instead, boasting of the facility's sanitation, ventilation, and undercrowding.[80] Despite annual inspection reports filled with blistering criticism, the New York State Prison Commission had limited political power to improve conditions in jails. Since stays were thought to be brief and since jails had little rehabilitative mission, New York's most ambitious reformers and criminologists poured their energy into the state's prisons rather than its small-town jails.[81] However, as Chinese migrants pushed Northern New York jails exponentially over capacity, the federal government intervened in select situations, removing migrants from certain jails and distributing them among other facilities.[82]

Competition among counties for federal deals provoked rising criticism about where federal cash was going. In 1901, the federal government paid New York county jails $4.00 per week for boarding each Chinese person. Bigelow, the reporter from *Collier's*, wrote: "The sheriff grows fat on this sort of boarding house and is eager to get all the Chinese boarders he can find. . . . [N]ine-tenths of the $4 per week he gets in clear profit."[83] Sheriffs profiting from the local jail was not unique to counties with federal boarders. A relic of the English model of jailing, sheriffs throughout the country received set fees for tasks such as serving a summons and fulfilling a warrant of arrest, along with a nightly fee for each person held in jail.[84] Reformers and criminologists suggested that the fee system led to longer jail stays and incentivized sheriffs to starve prisoners to maximize the fees received for their sustenance.[85] By the early twentieth century, Americans were interrogating the role of fees in government not just for sheriffs but for lawyers, judges, immigration bureaucrats, and other public workers.[86]

While sheriffs profiting from incarceration was a long-standing practice, the boarding of federal prisoners created unprecedented opportunities. Unlike jailing locals, jailing outsiders and noncitizens had little obvious political cost: These people were mobile and unlikely to become local voters—and sheriff, after all, was an elected position.[87] A stay for drunkenness or petit larceny might be just a few hours before release on bond, whereas Chinese detentions regularly stretched on for six months and longer, resulting in a bigger payday. Still, critics of the fee system found success in the region. Northern New York counties ended the practice long before the state of New York formally eliminated fees for sheriffs in 1917.[88]

Abolishment of the fee system became yet another point for communities to leverage when seeking federal prisoners. In 1901, St. Lawrence County reasoned that the federal government should prioritize sending it prisoners because the county paid its sheriff a set salary. By early 1902, Franklin County had also made sheriff a salaried position, explicitly stating that the sheriff could receive no additional funds for the care of Chinese migrants.[89] Yet, even as sheriffs' payments became more regulated, the construction of new jails opened new pathways for locals to profit. When St. Lawrence County decided to build a Chinese detention facility in 1904, for example, U.S. Commissioner Fred William Dudley gifted the lease contract to his law partner.[90]

The federal government cemented Franklin County's role as the hub of Chinese incarceration in Northern New York in 1903 when it brokered an agreement with the Canadian Pacific Railway Company. The new policy required the railway to examine all Chinese travelers coming from steamships before delivering Chinese passengers directly to U.S. inspection stations at four designated points along the Canadian border, including Malone.[91] Officials were hopeful that consolidating migrants at a few locations would reduce the labor of negotiating with individual counties. Jails gave the immigration service flexible space, but they also required extensive relationship management between federal and local governments. The new system hardly stopped unauthorized border crossing—Chinese migration strategies adapted and evolved with each bureaucratic roadblock.

The Trial of Sing Tuck

Alongside confidence that the Canadian Pacific Railway agreement would provide a "serious check" on Chinese entry via the northern border, there were a number of other reasons for the immigration bureaucracy to feel optimistic in 1903.[92] Under Commissioner-General Sargent, the Bureau of Immigration made major strides toward centralization and professionalization, with employees expressing a new enthusiasm that the scientific and organizational tools of the agency could block Chinese migration.[93] The Bureau of Immigration was reorganized under the Department of Commerce and Labor and embraced an aggressive stance on stopping immigration fraud. In Northern New York, detentions shortened; Essex County jail ledger books show that the average stay for detained Chinese reached sixty-five days, over a month briefer than the average incarceration in 1902. Still, the immigration service did not find much more success in disproving claims of citizenship. While it managed to deport fifty-two Chinese migrants from Essex County in 1903, compared with just a dozen in 1902, an uptick in overall arrivals meant that the rate of deportation was only about 6.5 percent in 1903, compared with about 15 percent in 1902.[94]

The disjuncture between the immigration service's and the courts' interpretation of the burden of proof remained a source of tension. If Chinese migrants could continue to walk across the border, file habeas petitions in the United States, and be released with a discharge certificate, the federal government claimed that it would be incapacitated by the sheer volume of cases and the expense of detention.[95] The immigration service needed a way to curtail the use of habeas corpus and firmly shut New York's "back door." When a group of thirty-two Chinese men crossed the Canadian border in October 1903, Sargent's immigration service saw an opportunity.

FIGURE 5. Photograph of Sing Tuck, 1903, a defendant in the 1904 Supreme
Court case challenging whether Chinese migrants must exhaust administrative
remedies before accessing the courts. *Source:* File 14/3733, Chinese Exclusion
Case Files, National Archives and Records Administration, New York City.

Complaints that Chinese migrants had immobilized the legal apparatus of
Northern New York were central to the case of *Sing Tuck*, the landmark Supreme Court case born out of Malone.[96] As was routine, the thirty-two men
appeared before an immigration inspector and received what *The Nation* derided as "a mockery of a hearing."[97] (Figure 5.) Sing Tuck and his cohort then
secured representation by Robert M. Moore, who was now dividing his time
between Chinese cases in Northern New York and defending clients in high-
profile New York City murder trials.[98] Moore petitioned for a writ of habeas

corpus, alleging that his clients had been deprived of their liberty without cause. The case took nearly a year to decide, during which time immigrant processing in Northern New York came to a near standstill, trapping hundreds of Chinese migrants in the jails of the North Country.

Sing Tuck centered on the question of how the immigration service should proceed in exclusion cases involving a claim of nativity. The case's legal journey began in the district court in December 1903, which ruled that immigration officials had the right to adjudicate admission and exclusion even when citizenship claims were at stake and remanded the Chinese migrants into the custody of immigration officials at Malone. Several months later, the Court of Appeals ruled in Sing Tuck's favor, dictating that individuals claiming citizenship were entitled to a judicial review of their status. Immigration authorities were exasperated. In the previous six months, writs of habeas corpus had been granted to 326 "alleged Chinese citizens" in Malone, compared with just 115 in all of San Francisco. For all of the public scrutiny of unauthorized immigration in the U.S. West, Malone officials suggested, critics had only scratched the surface of the issue at America's lesser-known points of entry.[99] Authorities saw *Sing Tuck* as a last-ditch effort to maintain control over the northern border. They appealed the case to the Supreme Court.[100]

As the case wound its way through the courts, locals described conditions at the Malone detention house as "exceedingly bad, with a tendency to grow worse," and "a matter of grave concern."[101] Meanwhile, Chinese migrants kept arriving. By the spring of 1904, the numbers had crept so high that authorities were once again relying on Franklin County Jail to hold forty Chinese migrants, with an additional 168 migrants in the Chinese detention house. When 149 Chinese migrants crossed the border into Malone in November 1903, local authorities converted a vacant tannery into an additional makeshift detention facility.[102]

With the number of Chinese warehoused in the county jail, the federal station, and the tannery rising, the stakes of *Sing Tuck* grew higher. The banishment or admission of hundreds of Chinese migrants stalled in Northern New York could become a powerful image of the immigration service's strength or lack thereof. The legality of the exclusion process was on the line in the case, but the federal government also cited the "overflowing" detention house in its justification of why the Supreme Court should move *Sing Tuck* to the top of its docket. For immigration officials, the jail was the physical embodiment of the Chinese threat and the danger of the Court of Appeals decision: an American institution, overrun and incapacitated by the movement of foreigners, leaving the entire community vulnerable.[103]

In April 1904, *Sing Tuck* became the first Supreme Court decision requiring exhaustion of federal administrative remedies, typically hearings before immigration officials, before an immigration case could move to judicial proceedings.[104] Moore had argued that Chinese defendants who claimed to be citizens had distinct rights in the United States. Foremost among them was a right to habeas corpus and a trial in front of a judge rather than an administrative officer. The process in place at Malone, where a Chinese person was asked a series of questions by an immigration inspector who then had final say over his case, was not due process of law but, rather, "a pretended trial and adjudication," carried out by an employee who was "in no sense a judicial officer."[105] Moore alleged that a claim of citizenship was a legal question whose jurisdiction belonged to the courts, not an administrative question whose decision could be tasked to executive officers.

The case cut to the heart of the issue in Northern New York. In instances in which a migrant was excluded from the United States, the decision of the immigration officials was final and not reviewable by the courts—the crux of the plenary power doctrine. However, as Justice David Brewer noted in the dissent, this act only applied when the parties involved were "aliens," and virtually all Chinese migrants entering through the Canadian border claimed that they were U.S. citizens. To argue that Chinese who claimed to be citizens could not access the courts suggested that any American citizen seeking to reenter the United States "would be compelled to bring with him two witnesses to prove the place of birth or else be denied his right to return," wrote Brewer. "No such rule is enforced against an American citizen of Anglo-Saxon descent, and if this be, as claimed, a government of laws and not of men, I do not think it should be enforced against American citizens of Chinese descent."[106]

The majority of the Court disagreed, with seven of the nine justices ruling in favor of the immigration service. "A mere allegation of citizenship by a person of Chinese descent is not sufficient to oust the inspector of jurisdiction under the alien immigrant law and allow a resort to the courts," the decision dictated.[107] The only way that a migrant could receive a writ of habeas corpus after being denied entry was to appeal to the secretary of commerce and labor. Justice Oliver Wendell Holmes Jr. argued that detention was not unlawful, given that the Chinese migrants had done little to establish their citizenship. He further argued that such detention would not be unlawful *even if* the parties were citizens of the United States, as detention was not punishment but an administrative process that enabled investigations.[108] Though the decision effectively distanced Chinese migrants from due process, there were some notes of hope for migrants and their attorneys: Justice Holmes refused to endorse more restrictive rules or regulations of administrative procedures, such as allowing immigration officials to choose witnesses or to deny counsel the ability to participate in administrative hearings.[109] Though the decisions stripped Chinese migrants of one reliable path to the courts, it did not fully remove procedural protections in immigration service hearings.[110]

With the *Sing Tuck* ruling in June 1904, immigration authorities in Northern New York loudly declared victory over border crossers and fraudulent citizens. The 187 Chinese men remaining at Malone, most of whom had been jailed in Northern New York for more than six months, boarded Canadian Pacific Railway cars to Vancouver and then a ship for the nearly three-week journey back to China.[111] In its annual report, the Bureau of Immigration remarked that it was more successfully deporting Chinese migrants from Northern New York counties, as they could now be excluded with a single administrative hearing. The immigration service noted success in communities where comparatively few Chinese lived, which it credited to the *Sing Tuck* decision.[112] Historian Lucy Salyer has described the case as a high point of judicial deference to the Bureau of Immigration.[113]

Though federal officials were elated, locals noted that the end of the informal economy of Chinese smuggling meant financial consequences for their community. At the Malone detention house, the staff downsized from eighteen employees to seven following the ruling. "While closing one of the detention houses and the removing of many of the guards, some of whom had their families here, will mean a money loss to the town, very few of our citizens will regret the change," the *Ogdensburg Journal* reported.[114] Though residents frequently spoke of the economic benefits that Chinese smuggling had brought to their region, few were willing to advocate against the U.S. immigration service in a key legal battle. By the end of 1905, St. Lawrence County declared Chinese prisoners "a thing of the past," noting that the cost of incarceration throughout the region had increased without federal subsidies.[115] Many of the Chinese jails continued to function in some form.[116] In 1907, St. Lawrence County and Essex County wrote open letters to their congressman, urging him to make "every honest endeavor" to bring Chinese prisoners *back* to their counties. Malone's neighbors protested that the Franklin County Jail received virtually all Chinese people captured in Northern New York, which they declared "discrimination" against their counties.[117]

Others with a financial stake in migrant jailing made similar pleas: The Port Henry landlord offered to reduce the rent on the Chinese jail for several months while the Canadian legislature debated new head taxes, eager to keep the government from backing out of its real estate arrangement any sooner than necessary.[118] As border crossings waned, the immigration service planned to close the smaller immigration stations along the Canadian border, including Malone.[119] Immigration through Northern New York spiked again from 1910 to 1911 amid rumors that the Canadian head tax for Chinese entrants would soon double, as well as a favorable Court of Appeals decision that challenged the ability of officials in Malone to arrest Chinese under general immigration law.[120] Still, the number of Chinese in Northern New York never matched the peak of the pre–*Sing Tuck* era. But beyond New York, the Chinese business boomed for years to come.

On the peripheries of immigration law enforcement and on the peripheries of the nation, Northern New York was a crucible where critical themes of legality, migration, and race played out in the early twentieth century. The bureaucratic negotiations on the northern border raised questions about the paradox of "administrative incarceration" that the United States would continue to wrestle with for decades to come and that would soon spread to other communities reckoning with requests from the federal government to jail migrants for deportation. The immigration service's experiences in the North Country taught it two key lessons: that incarceration could serve as a tool of border control and that some localities were eager to be in the incarceration business.

2

Negotiating Freedom in
an Era of Exclusion

THE GEOGRAPHY OF jailing and migration was perpetually in flux in the early years of the twentieth century. While Northern New York was a hub for a relatively short time, jails throughout the United States held Chinese migrants awaiting hearings and deportations. Much like the New York records, the archive of Chinese detention in local jails in the rest of the United States is dominated by authorities' accounts of days detained, fees received, and legal battles waged. In spite of the decentralized landscape of jails and the limited source base, we can still catch glimpses of how migrants experienced prolonged incarceration.

There were fleeting moments of celebration. In a county jail in St. Paul, Minnesota, for example, jailers allowed detained Chinese men to gather in one cell for Chinese New Year.[1] There were many more moments of grief. When Ng Wing died in the county jail of Brownsville, Texas, officials permitted other detained Chinese migrants to attend his burial services. They placed candles at the foot of Ng Wing's grave.[2] There were moments of fear. In Rochester, New York, the jail caught on fire in the middle of the night, terrifying migrants, who watched the flames from a handcuffed line in the yard.[3]

Some Chinese laborers escaped from jail despite imposing obstacles. In Luna County Jail, a frequent site of migrant detention in New Mexico, escape required scaling an adobe wall topped with cacti.[4] Officials in Montgomery, Alabama, apprehended and jailed two migrants fleeing from a deportation train that traveled cross-country from Norfolk to San Francisco.[5] Migrants were particularly likely to attempt escape as the date of deportation approached, with some managing to abscond from China-bound ships in the harbor.[6]

Other migrants stayed put and wrote letters to friends and family in the United States complaining about jail rations and seeking money for stamps and snacks. Many migrants felt hopeless, particularly as cases such as *Sing Tuck* narrowed their chance of reaching the courts. "My mind is all mixed now, I don't know what to do while I am here. My tears always run, my eyes haven't been dry for a long time. . . . I expect deportation but don't know when. No use to fight the case and spend the money," wrote Jung Ai, from a county jail in Buffalo, New York. His fellow countryman, Yee Gue Bon Yick, wrote to a loved one, "We are suffering here and confined in this jail like a fish in the net. . . . [W]e are suffering terribly no words can express it."[7]

Immigration bureaucrats and their local collaborators were negotiating captivity on a daily basis. They set the monetary rates that made migrant incarceration a desirable local investment, and they expanded detention infrastructure to secure federal deals. However, they were also negotiating freedom. Authorities had significant discretion in detention and deportation and faced difficult questions about which migrants should be granted greater liberties. Should sick migrants be held in the jail? Should Chinese migrants who were especially cooperative or especially Christian be subjected to the same conditions as others? Which cases should the Bureau of Immigration prioritize with its limited resources for deportation? In turn, migrants faced related questions: Was it worth it to challenge this system in ways that went beyond habeas corpus claims? And if they wanted to fight, how?

With the passage of the 1892 Geary Act, questions of the immigration service's prosecutorial discretion came to the forefront. The Geary Act extended the Chinese Exclusion Act for an additional ten years and introduced a host of other requirements for Chinese residents in the United States: The law required that they register for a certificate of residence and establish, with the support of at least one white witness, that they had proof to land or reside in the United States. Failure to carry a certificate meant jail time and removal, making unprecedented numbers of Chinese migrants vulnerable to incarceration. From the law's earliest days, policymakers complained that the immigration service's limited budget made the Geary Act "a dead letter upon the statute book"—a law they could only afford to enforce in highly select circumstances, giving rise to a regime of unpredictable discretionary power.[8] This chapter shows that officials' choices involved not only whether Chinese migrants would be deported but also whether they would be jailed, whether they could access bail, and what sorts of spaces would be used for detention. The decisions bureaucrats made reflected the financial limitations of the agency, yet they also showed an agency attuned to the political liabilities of incarceration. The immigration service sought to demonstrate that it was effectively enforcing anti-Chinese legislation, particularly against migrants deemed deviant or criminal, but it also lessened or ceased the use of detention in cases that incurred critical media and political attention.

Just as authorities, both bureaucrats and the courts, had tremendous discretion in exclusion and removal proceedings, they also had tremendous authority in granting and revoking privileges to migrants caught in the web of incarceration. These decisions gave rise to new ideas about what made a migrant "deserving" of freedom: Factors included race, gender, religion, time in the United States, behavior in jail, and any other criteria immigration officials and judges deemed salient. In some cases, the decentralized system worked to migrants' advantage, allowing them to leverage relationships with local officials for greater freedom. Other times, the lack of formal rules made it easier for judges to deny detained migrants access to bail, leaving them in jail for the duration of their proceedings. This chapter expands our view of Chinese migrant incarceration beyond Northern New York and asks what freedom meant to migrants jailed for violating immigration laws. It shows the many forms resistance took during the early decades of the twentieth century: from daring escapes, to mobilizing media and political attention, to courtroom fights for reprieve through bail. The state attempted to make Chinese migrants nameless, faceless line items on a county budget, who patiently tolerated jailing and accepted exile. Instead, at every possible juncture, Chinese migrants pushed back against the cruelty and arbitrariness of administrative incarceration.

Surviving *Sing Tuck*

In January 1904, Chinese men detained at the Franklin County Jail wrote a letter pleading for help. "There are many deaths [occurring] in this wooden detention house," they told a Chinese American identified as Mr. Fong, who had previously inquired about the conditions at Malone. Detention in Franklin County had always been unpleasant, but now something was different. While the court deliberated about the *Sing Tuck* case, the site's population had swelled. The cramped conditions bred disease, including pneumonia, typhoid, and mumps. The illnesses confirmed Americans' suspicions that Chinese migrants brought dangerous and contagious contaminants to their communities, with one local writer declaring them "a constant menace to the health of the place."[9]

Death haunted the detention site. Chinese migrants watched healthy young men—some of whom had shared the long voyage from China to Montreal to the United States, some of whom were strangers—waste away in a foreign jail. To die far from home posed the threat of an eternity in a liminal space; historian Beth Lew-Williams notes that most of the migrants hailed from China's Guangdong Province, where tradition held that burial in one's home community, with the proper rites and rituals, was necessary to transform into an ancestor.[10] "We, who are here, are much frightened," the men wrote. "We earnest beg you to devise plans and consult with lawyers to do something to get us out of this dark hold."[11]

Sing Tuck's legal decision had immense implications for the future of Chinese migration, effectively cutting off the most significant route for Chinese migrants to access the courts. But the long legal process also had dire, immediate consequences for Chinese still trapped in Malone. Seventeen Chinese men and adolescents died in the county's facilities before the conclusion of the case.[12] (Figure 6.) Countless others became seriously ill. The commissioner-general of immigration described these deaths as natural and inevitable, pathologizing migrants' "peculiar habits" and physical inactivity.[13] Even when a migrant contracted a case of typhoid fever, a disease marked by weakness and abdominal cramping, officials complained that the man would not exercise.[14] Their deaths became yet another marker of racial difference and physical inferiority—more evidence that the Chinese detainee was unlike the American prisoner.

Local accounts present a clearer picture of how incarceration produced illness. In the second week of January 1904, three Chinese men died in a detention house that was holding nearly 130 people. The immigration service sent a doctor to investigate. Dr. Robert John Wilding, a Malone physician, found "dangerously sick" men huddled for warmth in a corner of the jail.[15] It was the dead of winter, and the temperature in Malone barely hovered above zero degrees Fahrenheit. The doctor observed high rates of heart disease, respiratory illness, and "congestion of the kidney and liver." He concluded, "[While] the men are confined to such close quarters, I am afraid that there will be many more such cases."[16] Heeding the doctor's warning, Malone officials opened a second and then a third detention site.

Several more men died in the days following Dr. Wilding's visit, sparking alarm from locals who had once praised the community's deportation work. The *Malone Farmer's* report on the doctor's visit concluded with a call to arms about jailing in Malone. "The present Chinese exclusion law

FIGURE 6. Interiors of the Chinese Jail at Malone, New York, showing the sleeping quarters, the dining room, and the kitchen. The jail employed a Chinese cook (*upper left*). *Source: Collier's Weekly* 31, no. 24 (Sept. 12, 1903).

and its administration is a shame upon civilized government," the writer implored.

> Some new system ought to be adopted other than the one now in operation of conflating the Celestials for months in jails or detention houses for no other cause than seeking to enter this prosperous country. . . . [T]here ought to be some other way of handling them other than placing them behind locked doors and barred windows.[17]

As conditions deteriorated in Malone, some detainees launched desperate appeals to find a way out. One migrant, Wong Chune, known to his jailers as "Billy," made a remarkable attempt at freedom. (Figure 7.) Even in a packed

FIGURE 7. Photograph of Wong Chune, also known as Billy, 1904, photographed by the Bureau of Immigration. *Source:* File 14/3653, Chinese Exclusion Case Files, National Archives and Records Administration, New York City.

detention house, Billy stood out. He was much older than his counterparts, with thinning hair and a lined face. Most notably, he was missing his left eye.[18]

While his disability made him particularly unlikely to gain admission to the United States, Billy had endeared himself to immigration officials during his long five months at the Malone jail. He spoke excellent English, a desirable skill in a region perpetually short of translators. In January 1904, he penned a dramatic, English-language appeal to the immigration service.[19] While it is impossible to say whether Billy's sentiments were sincere, strategic, or some combination of the two, one thing was clear: He told immigration authorities exactly what they wanted to hear. The Malone attorney whom U.S. authorities loathed? Billy had grown tired of him, too. If Robert Moore was such a good lawyer, why were all these migrants still incarcerated? The jailers and immigration officials had always treated him kindly, Billy wrote. And so, in exchange, he was ready to tell them exactly how so many Chinese migrants were making it to Malone.

Authorities had already expended significant money and resources to understand the smuggling routes across the northern border. Much of what Billy told them about coaching, the path through Montreal, and hired witnesses purporting to be family members, the agency had already surmised. However, Billy did offer what the bureau described as "very valuable" specifics. Moore— the attorney who typically represented Chinese clients—was working with Chinese brokers in the United States, including a man named Chin Park. Immigration officials had long been mistrustful of Park, the rare Chinese resident of Northern New York.[20] Park operated a boarding house and a Chinese restaurant, which he relocated between Malone and Plattsburgh as the locus of the detention business shifted.[21] Billy claimed that Moore received at least $100 from Park and his fellow brokers for each migrant for whom he successfully secured admission into the country. This confirmed immigration officials' suspicions of a grand conspiracy of Chinese migration and was evidence that the fight they were waging in *Sing Tuck* was worthwhile—keeping Chinese migrants out of the courts and ending the successful use of habeas corpus was the highest priority.

Billy hoped that revealing this information would garner him something in return.[22] His gamble paid off. After receiving his letter, Malone officials decided to grant Billy "some liberties." He was permitted to leave the detention house to provide medical assistance at the boarding house where the immigration service had moved the sickest migrants. The position meant risking his own health, but it also granted Billy mobility between the town's multiple detention sites. Authorities trusted him.[23] Billy was a steadfast nurse, caring for the ill and translating between the doctor and patients. Dr. Wilding credited Billy with saving at least two lives.

Then, at the end of January, Billy bolted. He was expected back at the jail, but he never showed. He purchased a new set of American clothes, plus a pair of tinted glasses to conceal his missing eye, and boarded a train to New York City. After more than 150 days of incarceration, and weeks of witnessing the death and despair of his countrymen, Billy was a free man.

His escape was an enormous embarrassment to the immigration service. Bureaucrats at the district level strained to explain to their bosses how this had happened and why they had let a Chinese migrant freely leave the jail. Marshals captured Billy three and a half months later in New Jersey, following an extensive pursuit that mobilized networks and contacts throughout the Northeast. The immigration official in charge of Malone promised the commissioner-general that no liberties of the type extended to Billy would ever be granted again.[24] The saga further undermined officials' claims that Chinese migrants passively accepted incarceration. As the well-worn legal channels appeared in jeopardy with the Supreme Court, incarcerated people like Billy went to extraordinary lengths to plot their freedom. They negotiated systems of power at every turn and could be savvy operators in exploiting tensions between federal officials and local interlopers.

We know very little about the seventeen migrants who died at Malone during *Sing Tuck*'s adjudication, some of whom Billy had aided. (Figure 8.) The youngest of them, Ark Toy, was just seventeen years old.[25] Most deaths were described as sudden and swift, though it is clear from their limited preserved writing that people in the jail felt terror as they watched conditions worsen. Their immigration files are characteristically short on details. Migrants refused to answer any of the inquiries about their families, their hometowns, or their journeys to the United States, as they had been carefully coached to do. Certainly, some of the men had heard stories about what jail in New York would be like—that detentions were long but that eventually the habeas petitions came through. We do not know whether they understood what was different in this moment and why they were stalled as the Supreme Court deliberated.

Even in death, there was bureaucracy. When a migrant succumbed to illness in detention, the immigration service began the process of searching for family, a task complicated by migrants' false names and family histories. Relatives received a telegram that plainly informed them of the death and said "expenses must be paid before body forwarded." Some migrants' family and friends were unable to afford the full cost and sent smaller sums of money. In other cases, Chinese brokers intervened and paid the bill—some migrants had joined mutual aid organizations that promised to repatriate their bones in the event of a death abroad, enabling them to have a proper Chinese burial and ensuring that they could protect their descendants from the afterlife.[26] Internally, the immigration service suggested that the chore of locating associates of the deceased could be worthwhile if it helped to expose smuggling rings.[27] Unclaimed bodies were buried in an unmarked potter's field in Malone. Officials wrote the checks: $20 for a coffin, $10 for embalming, $2 to dig a hole.[28]

FIGURE 8. Photographs of fifteen Chinese migrants who died in detention at Malone, New York, between 1902 and 1904. From left to right, descending, their names were recorded as Lee Quon (File 14/3790), Yuen Lee (14/3792), Ming Sun (14/3905), Lim Mow (14/3764), Hong Sang (14/3752), Ng Sing (14/3662), Mee Lee (14/3893), Chong Wing (14/3802), Hong Quai Yong (34/210), Lee Yuen (14/3792), Yah Tai (14/3818), Bing Get (14/3983), Fong Hoo (14/3854), Ark Toy (14/3945), and Lee Qin (14/3918). *Source:* Chinese Exclusion Case Files, National Archives and Records Administration, New York City.

For agents of the immigration service, the burial expenses were just another bill, an expense of faithfully enforcing the Chinese Exclusion Act. They were following the orders of Congress, they reassured themselves. When the local immigration commissioner was told of the death of seventeen-year-old Ark Toy, he said that he regretted to hear the news. He then quickly added the caveat, "[Y]et of course I know it was unavoidable."[29]

The Shifting Geography of Chinese Jails

The conclusion of *Sing Tuck*, and the attention it brought to smuggling in Northern New York, altered the geography of Chinese migration. The same year the case concluded, the Bureau of Immigration dispatched its first immigration inspectors to New Mexico and Arizona, tasked with monitoring and prohibiting the entry of unwanted migrants.[30] "Having been practically defeated at every turn along the Canadian frontier," an immigration inspector wrote in 1906, Chinese migrants turned their attention southward.[31] From 1907 to 1909, U.S. officials arrested 2,492 Chinese migrants for illegal entry along the Mexican border.[32] As migrants moved through Mexico and into the Southwest, immigration authorities adopted an even more aggressive strategy of surveillance and policing than they had used on the northern border, relying on immigration officials, train conductors, consular workers, and informants on both sides of the dividing line.[33] It was a dramatic rupture. For most of the nineteenth century, officials in the southern borderlands had focused on collecting customs duties, paying little attention to unauthorized entry across the barely marked boundary.[34]

While the bureau's enforcement strategies and geographies evolved, the reliance on local jails remained consistent. In 1908, the *El Paso Herald* reported that a record ninety Chinese migrants had been captured in one day of apprehensions along the border: The United States held fifty-six at the El Paso jail and distributed the others throughout smaller jails in New Mexico and Texas.[35] Detentions were rarely as long as in Northern New York, though the average length of detention for a Chinese migrant at El Paso still stretched to twenty-eight days in 1908. Local officials complained that this had brought considerable expense and liability to the El Paso immigration office, which threatened to defer strict enforcement of the law until it found more detention space.[36] Even as new immigration laws made migrants of other nationalities more vulnerable to deportation, Chinese migrants continued to be disproportionately targeted for jailing and removal. In Los Angeles, the Chinese-American League of Justice asserted that authorities more commonly detained Chinese migrants in local jails, whereas Mexican and Japanese migrants were sent to private detention houses or placed under surveillance in hotels.[37]

Throughout the United States, immigration officials jailed Chinese migrants of all social classes and immigration statuses. Some had been accused of smuggling their countrymen, some had just crossed the border, some had lived in the United States for years. Immigration officials, as well as vigilante citizens, pursued not only the "illegal alien" at the nation's borders but also the "illegal resident," who could be apprehended at work, at home, and on the road.[38] The Geary Act had produced a state of constant vigilance and vulnerability for residents of Chinese ancestry.[39] Interior enforcement was spearheaded by special agents known as "Chinese catchers," who carried out raids in cities far from the border, often with the assistance of local law enforcement.[40] In Helena, Montana, five Chinese men were lodged in the local jail after Chinese catchers entered a boarding house and demanded that all Chinese patrons produce residence papers. Men leapt over fences, hid in alleyways, and threatened agents with a pitchfork in desperate attempts to avoid apprehension.[41]

In urban centers such as San Francisco and Los Angeles, jails became crossroads where migrants detained for immigration offenses encountered fellow countrymen incarcerated for a growing list of zoning laws and public health ordinances targeting Chinatowns. (Figure 9.) The jail was the physical intersection of criminal and administrative laws policing Chinese communities.[42] Still, officials and the media drew a line between migrants held on criminal versus administrative charges. In describing the population at the local jail in 1907, the *Los Angeles Times* wrote that there were sixteen Chinese but "only one who is 'bad,' the others being held for deportation."[43] In theory, civil detainees were required to be segregated from criminal detainees within a jail; it is unlikely this happened often. While newspapers would have been reluctant to describe violators of the Chinese Exclusion Act as *good*, per se, they still portrayed the deportees as more defensible than Chinese migrants held for nonimmigration offenses. It foreshadowed a dichotomy of good and bad migrants that would be further enshrined into law in coming years, as a criminal conviction became the foremost indicator of moral inadequacy and the metric by which officials would prioritize deportation and removal.

As the Bureau of Immigration dispatched inspectors and undercover agents to pursue smugglers working between Mexico and the United States, they also detained growing numbers of Chinese migrants to testify as witnesses in the state's cases against alleged traffickers. In some cases, Chinese witnesses

"OUT OF THE FRYING PAN INTO THE FIRE".

FIGURE 9. "Out of the Frying Pan into the Fire," *The Wasp*, 1877. This cover illustration depicts San Francisco authorities enforcing the Cubic Air Ordinance, a law used to surveil and police Chinese workplaces and homes. Though this is a typically dehumanizing depiction of Chinese migrants, the caption references the hypocrisy of authorities in decrying public health conditions in Chinatown while moving Chinese residents to county jails where health and sanitation were even worse. *Source: The Wasp* 2, no. 83 (Aug. 1877–July 1878), Bancroft Library, University of California, Berkeley.

received fees from the federal government. One Los Angeles report described witnesses as the "aristocrats" of the jail's Chinese population: Other federal detainees produced fees for their local jailers; migrant witnesses stood to profit from the U.S. immigration system themselves.[44] Though it is difficult to say for certain how Chinese migrants held for various charges related to one another, the local media often assumed a social hierarchy of detainees within the

jail, while also imposing a moral hierarchy when describing the jail's population to American readers.

Outside of New York, most reports of jails overcrowded with migrants
came from California and the southern border states. However, the Bureau of
Immigration records also show a more irregular use of county jails farther
from land borders. In these cases, migrants faced long incarcerations until officials could secure them passage to a seaport on one of the deportation trains
crisscrossing the nation, picking up migrants at various jails, asylums, and
hospitals along the way.[45] On February 28, 1909, a U.S. marshal for the Southern District of Ohio wrote to the commissioner general of immigration about
the case of Long Chong, a Chinese man who had been in Cincinnati's Hamilton County Jail for two months. Long Chong's health was failing, and the
marshal had "no doubt" the conditions of the jail were to blame.[46] In regions
farther away from major migration routes, migrants like Long Chong struggled
to secure legal representation and faced the experience of being the only Chinese migrant at a county jail. Due to isolation by language, and often by the
built environment of the jail itself, the experience resembled solitary confinement.[47] Several years prior and 1,800 miles away, authorities detained Hum
Chim for more than three months in Butte, Montana's Silver Bow County Jail.
Local officials had little knowledge of whether immigration clerks in Washington or San Francisco were making progress on his case and worried that he
could be held many more months as the bureau focused on regions of higher
priority.[48] "If he were a white man no doubt someone would have come to his
aid and secured his release on habeas corpus proceedings months ago," wrote
the *Butte Miner*—something that also likely would have occurred had Hum
Chim been apprehended at a place like Malone, where attorneys capitalized
on the high volume of Chinese clients.[49]

Occasionally, Chinese migrants found advocates who went beyond attorneys
alone, typically because of the severity of their cases or because of their personal
connections. In the summer of 1906, immigration officials encountered Pang
Sho Yin crossing the Detroit River by rowboat in the dead of night, accompanied by a Canadian he had paid to aid his border crossing.[50] (Figure 10.) Pang
Sho Yin was a thirty-four-year-old father of two, who claimed to have been
born in San Francisco before spending thirty years as a farmer in China.[51] His
case received national media coverage, in part because it illustrated the debilitating psychological effects of migrant detention. After a commissioner ordered Pang Sho Yin deported, a wealthy American uncle intervened and hired
a lawyer who brought the case to the U.S. Court of Appeals. As his detention

FIGURE 10. Pang Sho Yin, a Chinese migrant detained for eleven months, primarily in Detroit's Wayne County Jail, 1906. Pang Sho Yin purchased this suit in Windsor, Canada, before paying a Canadian smuggler to transport him across the Detroit River. *Source:* File 261A, Chinese Exclusion Case Files, National Archives and Records Administration, Chicago.

dragged on, first in a jail in Lansing, Michigan, and then in Detroit's Wayne County Jail, Pang Sho Yin's behavior grew desperate and erratic. He wept when jailers approached his cell. He paced barefoot, mumbling to himself. He stopped eating. The local media evocatively described him as "grieving himself to death," in near-total isolation.[52]

Pang Sho Yin's case provoked alarm from many circles. Detroit's congressman Edwin Denby, who had spent some of his childhood in China, declared the Wayne County Jail episode "the most striking example of the inhumanity of our system toward the Chinaman that I have ever heard of."[53] Denby was the son of a minister and brought a missionary's energy to his advocacy, speaking of both the "stupidity" of Pang Sho Yin and the Christian obligation to aid the hapless and downtrodden. Much of the rhetoric around the Michigan jail paralleled the moral discourse and American exceptionalism encountered in Northern New York. Pang Sho Yin's story, a Connecticut newspaper wrote, might be acceptable in Russia or China, but it was shocking to witness it in a "Christian and civilized country."[54] Whereas immigration officials and local jailers continually passed the buck for incarceration, suggesting that it was simply incidental or unavoidable, the op-ed minced few words: American policies and choices "made a lunatic of Pang." Under political pressure, the appeals court released Pang Sho Yin on a technicality after eleven months in jail.[55]

Reflecting on Pang Sho Yin's detention in 1909, the *Detroit Free Press* editorialized that the infamous case had revealed "the almost despotic power of the immigration office."[56] Increasingly, the Detroit media noted, some of the same precedents and procedures of Chinese exclusion were being weaponized against Europeans and Canadians crossing the northern border. These migrants, too, were jailed based on questionable statements taken by administrative officials, with appeals heard by a secretive Board of Special Inquiry composed of yet more immigration bureaucrats.[57] The United States had used Chinese immigration to establish the key tenets of the plenary power doctrine, cementing the sovereign right of the federal government to determine entry and exclusion, the limited power of the courts to overturn administrative decisions, the scant due process rights owed to noncitizens, and the use of detention as a tool of border control. The courts had crafted a system that championed the administrative powers of immigration bureaucrats, who in turn delegated much of the labor of removal to sheriffs, private business interests, and local officials. Yet, as the *Detroit Free Press* foresaw, Chinese migrants would not be the only ones to suffer under plenary power's reign.

Getting out of Jail

One of the most vexing issues facing both jailers and migrants around the United States was whether Chinese migrants had the right to *leave* the local jail when being held for deportation. The Supreme Court hesitated to establish a standardized policy on bail throughout the exclusion era, leaving significant discretion in the hands of local authorities and district courts. In the late nineteenth century, local and federal officials expressed discomfort with Chinese bail bondsmen in California, who provided bonds both to free migrants from detention and to vouch that they would not become public charges.[58] Predictably, authorities suspected bondsmen of conspiring to defraud the immigration service, with one judge claiming that a quarter of a million bonds had been forfeited in Chinese habeas corpus cases.[59] Among the Geary Act's many tools for distancing Chinese from due process, such as requiring white witnesses and

allowing arrest without a warrant, it also denied bail to Chinese migrants pending habeas corpus. Still, there was considerable disagreement on whether this
statute absolutely precluded admission to bail in cases pending appeal or pending deportation, particularly for Chinese who resided in the United States.[60]

The lack of standardization created an inconsistent practice of release from
detention for jailed Chinese migrants. Bail decisions differed by geographic
location and by the presence of agencies willing to underwrite bonds but could
also differ within the same districts depending on how sympathetic local officials deemed a person's case. Controversy continued to follow bondsmen: In
Northern New York multiple New Yorkers were indicted for furnishing "straw"
(worthless) bail for Chinese migrants, as officials fretted that bail had become
one more avenue through which savvy operators could profit from unauthorized Chinese migration.[61] Discussions about bail illustrated how courts and
communities spoke about which migrants *deserved* to be in jail—a conversa-
tion that would become even more contentious as the demographics of migrants diversified in the coming years. At the same time, the proliferation of
bail cases confirmed that migrants were not content to wait out their removals
and hearings behind bars; instead, they actively agitated for freedom from jail.

A case that arrived in the Southern District of Georgia exemplifies the ways
that the courts thought about administrative power and the morality of migrants at the beginning of the twentieth century. Georgia was hardly an epicenter of Chinese migration, though Geary Act registrations showed sizable
Chinese communities in the cities of Atlanta, Macon, and Augusta.[62] In 1904,
immigration authorities in Augusta apprehended two Chinese men, Fah
Chung and Foong King. Both had been born in the British colony of Hong
Kong. They claimed that their birthplace made them British subjects, not subject to the Chinese Exclusion Act. The court denied their claim, granting final
orders of deportation in June 1904.[63] While they appealed the decision of the
district court, their lawyers filed a separate lawsuit, arguing that Fah Chung
and Foong King were eligible for release on bail while the Circuit Court of
Appeals reviewed their case.[64]

Two months after the initial order of deportation, with both men detained
in Augusta's Richmond County Jail, their bail claim came before a district
court judge, Emory Speer. In his decision, Judge Speer weighed the costs and
benefits of offering bail to deportable migrants but also considered the broader
constitutional stakes of creating a subclass of "unbailable" individuals in the
American legal system. "To refuse bail to any person whose liberty on American soil is at stake, even though he be an undesirable immigrant, seems upon

first impression to be in ill accordance with the humane and benignant principles of our constitutional law," Speer began. The Eighth Amendment of the
Constitution prohibited excessive bail—the standard that would be upheld if
the legal rights of an American citizen or even a noncitizen were at stake.[65] But
an individual who had been ordered deported was in a different category altogether, the judge declared:

> [The] order of deportation of a Chinese person who has plainly violated
> the exclusion act . . . does not deal with "legal rights," as that expression is
> generally understood. It merely involved the pretended claim to remain in
> this country of an individual, who, against settled American policy, and
> against the positive command of our statutes, as surreptitiously and fraudu-
> lently obtruded his unacceptable presence among our people.[66]

The judge acknowledged that the rule of bail had been "marked by some vari-
ance" and that the Supreme Court had made no final declaration on the subject. There was no statute that expressly authorized the court to grant bail to
Chinese migrants but also no ruling that explicitly *prohibited* it.[67] Thus, he said,
it was necessarily a matter of discretion.

Even as the judge made a strong pronouncement against granting bail, he
still carved out exceptions. The judge cited two recent Georgia cases in which
a denial of bail "would be abhorrent to that general sense of justice." The first
was the case of a Chinese girl who had accompanied a missionary couple
to receive a Christian education in the United States but lacked the proper
documents. Such a girl, the judge insisted, had no business being detained
"amid the vile associations of the common jail." In the second case, the court
granted bail to Kol Lee, a Chinese laundry owner and nineteen-year resident
of Georgia, after his arrest for not carrying a residence certificate.[68] Lee was a
widely known proprietor with deep community ties, a judge observed. He had
eagerly produced paperwork when asked by immigration authorities, and thus
they decided that his violation of the law was unintentional; he was given the
benefit of the doubt by the district court.[69] Implicit in these decisions was an
understanding that detention in jail was a punishment in practice, if not in the
letter of the law. Jailing meant suffering, and officials used discretion to protect
Chinese migrants they considered undeserving of such treatment.

In 1911, the Supreme Court case of *Chin Ying Don v. Billings* tested the idea
that sympathetic or "worthy" Chinese migrants might be eligible for a reprieve
from the county jail. Newspapers described Jem Yuen as "a Chinese boy locked
up in Boston," whose legal case raised "the ticklish question of personal rights

that may work havoc with immigration regulations in the United States."[70] Jem Yuen's father, Chin Ying Don, was a Chinese merchant living in Boston, one of the few categories of Chinese nationals eligible for admission under the Chinese Exclusion Act. Immigration authorities questioned Jem Yuen's paternity but were most skeptical about his claim to be a minor. On the grounds that Jem Yuen had been denied a fair hearing, his attorneys appealed the decision to the Supreme Court.

Jem Yuen's predicament forced the Supreme Court to reckon not only with questions of liberty and bail but also with the mundane business of court backlogs. At the time Jem Yuen's case reached the docket, the Supreme Court estimated that it would be *three years* before his case could be heard. In the meantime, Jem Yuen's health deteriorated. "Because of confinement and unaccustomed food, it is stated that he is now suffering 'great impairment of health,'" a newspaper reported, noting that Jem Yuen experienced anxiety attacks and fainting spells and had recently required stitches after a fall.[71] His family feared that he would not survive the long legal process. Bail may not have been a legal imperative, but Jem Yuen's advocates argued that it would be a humane act of discretion.[72]

The *Jem Yuen* case bore many trademarks of Chinese Exclusion legal battles: District courts claimed that under the plenary power doctrine they had no jurisdiction to review decisions made by immigration authorities, the plaintiffs' lawyers stressed that Jem Yuen bore fewer rights than an accused criminal, and immigration authorities reiterated that the detainee must make an affirmative case of his right to stay in the United States.[73] But the case also became a stage for examining the stakes of migrant incarceration. Jem Yuen's lawyer, Warren Ozro Kyle, launched a scathing critique of the federal government's detention practices: He asked what it meant for the United States to be a place where an adolescent, the son of a legal resident, suffering from debilitating health problems, had to remain in jail for three years to receive a fair immigration hearing. Immigration authorities countered that Jem Yuen's incarceration was, in a sense, voluntary. The young man could give up his claim at any time and return to China. Kyle dismissed this argument as absurd.

> The government has no right to starve him out, compel abandonment of case, prevent the inquiry demanded by law and justice, and deprive the resident father of his rights. It is not just to say: "Go back to China if you don't like it." ... Must we insist on the martyrdom of years of imprisonment to obtain justice?[74]

Supreme Court Justice Oliver Wendell Holmes Jr. wrote in an August 1910 letter to Kyle that he did not believe he had the power to "intermeddle" with Jem Yuen's case and that he was obligated to defer to the authority of immigration officials. "This imprisonment is unlike the imprisonment of an indicted man," Justice Holmes insisted, repeating that Chinese migrants had no presumption of innocence.[75] He denied the appeal for bail. The secretary of labor wrote that he regretted Jem Yuen would remain in jail for so long; however, he blamed this on the migrant's failure to weigh the costs that immigration and a prolonged legal battle might have.[76] Jem Yuen eventually abandoned his appeal and returned to China before the Supreme Court heard his case, cornered into what his opponents declared a "voluntary" departure. Cases like Jem Yuen's underscored the ways that plenary power and the discretionary authority of immigration bureaucrats empowered the nexus between immigration and incarceration and the ways that jails could be used to coerce migrants into the outcomes that the state desired.

Other legal cases similarly highlighted the ways that jails and lack of access to bail could hinder migrants' ability to secure aid. In Oregon, local debate arose when immigration authorities claimed that they could hold a Chinese migrant named Chin Wah completely incommunicado in the county jail, refusing to allow him visitors or mail from the outside. Chin Wah received gifts of flowers, fruit, and Chinese delicacies, which authorities feared could contain messages of instruction to assist him in his hearing. Officials argued that denial of bail was the only way to weaken Portland's "Underground Railroad," in which Chinese would be released and trained to answer immigration screening questions.[77] A distinct advantage of the jail was that it cut migrants off from Chinatowns and from the social worlds and collective knowledge that could aid them in the immigration process. By releasing a migrant from jail, even for a short time, state power was undermined—a point further reinforced to the immigration service through cases like Billy's in Malone.[78] Internally, the immigration service expressed that it had been "somewhat embarrassed" because its records failed to indicate why Chin Wah was arrested in the first place.[79] Nonetheless, the court erred on the immigration service's side. The bureau distributed copies of the *Chin Wah* case to every district in the country, to "stop the frequent practice of admitting Chinese to bail in insignificant amounts."[80] Once again, local jails served as a place to negotiate and refine what would become nationwide enforcement practices.

Bail remained a discretionary power, not solely for the cases of "sympathetic" migrants but for the sake of county jails struggling to accommodate growing numbers of federal prisoners. In the 1903 case of a Chinese man named Ah Tai, the district court refused to make a broad ruling about admissibility of bail but suggested that bail could be a critical tool in managing the local justice apparatus. Judge Lowell wrote, "[Were] bail never taken [in Chinese Exclusion cases] the jails might be overcrowded, and the recent arrests in this city show that this danger is not imaginary."[81] Together, the corpus of bail cases exemplifies how Chinese migrants throughout the country were assessed around a range of qualities not formally written in law. Gender, age, religion, character, duration of time spent in the United States, and conditions of local jails were not established legal criteria for more liberal rulings in bail decisions. But in practice, these factors often made the difference between freedom and captivity for Chinese migrants in deportation proceedings.

————

For the early immigration service, the jail became a means of reining in the mobility of unauthorized migrants and stretching the power of a limited federal agency. Unauthorized migrants were a threat because they moved where they were not permitted to move and crossed borders they were not authorized to cross. The jail's power came in immobilizing racialized migrant groups and perpetuating an illusion of control over American borders.

Yet, at the same time, jails embodied Americans' larger fears about the inefficiency of the immigration service. The presence of large numbers of Chinese migrants in local jails confirmed the porousness of national borders, even as the budget for expulsion grew. And in a moment when Americans were especially concerned with government waste and corruption, both the smuggling of migrants and their subsequent incarceration created boundless opportunities for profit. Immigration authorities came to see immobilization as a key to winning the battle against unwanted Chinese migrants: Freedom at any phase of the proceedings meant that migrants could connect with Chinese American communities and prepare their legal cases with greater ease or could skip bail and disappear into the nation. Federal officials envisaged incarceration as a central component of the deportation machine and a critical way to perform sovereign power. Authorities took the local space most associated with deviancy and lawbreaking and argued that this was where Chinese migrants belonged: They were not just surplus labor or unassimilable foreigners; they were prisoners who had violated federal laws. Detention was a tool of punishment and coercion, which authorities hoped would lead migrants to abandon their fights to stay in the United States.

Extended incarceration could be a way to break migrants' bodies, as they contracted illnesses and wasted away from the lack of proper food. It was also a way to break them psychologically. When Detroit officials finally told Pang Sho Yin that his case had been discharged, he stared at them blankly. "So completely has his mind been shattered by his bewildering ordeal in jail," wrote the local paper, that he could not process the news.[82] In the first years of the twentieth century, Chinese migrants envisioned incarceration as a means to an end, as their habeas corpus claims signaled a flickering light at the end of a long tunnel. But with legal channels narrowing, more migrants spent their time in cells anticipating when a ship or deportation train would arrive.

As immigration law evolved and quota laws made new groups vulnerable to exclusion and deportation during the 1910s and 1920s, Northern New York's detention business changed. Immigration officials now asked counties to detain a growing population of white migrants. Some were women who had been trafficked for "immoral" purposes. Some were Europeans trying to evade the low quotas of their native countries. Some were Canadians who were accustomed to crossing back and forth across the border but were now deterred by literacy tests and head taxes. These changing demographics challenged the ways that courts, politicians, and observers thought about migrant detention, making the practice increasingly contentious and undesirable. Throughout the 1910s, immigration officials reported that sheriffs in New York—including their once-reliable allies in Franklin County—had grown reluctant to grant federal authorities access to their jails, complicating the agency's enforcement efforts.[83] If incarceration was now central to the practice of exclusion and removal, what would happen if local governments no longer wanted to play ball?

3

A Kaleidoscopic Affair

RETHINKING THE PROGRESSIVE-ERA MIGRANT JAIL

IN THE AUTUMN OF 1924, New York Governor Al Smith called for a premature end to hunting season in the Adirondacks. Forest fires had ravaged the region, and the move was necessary to conserve the white-tailed deer population, the governor announced to the disappointed hunters of New York.[1] On November 10, 1924, the state troopers deployed to surveil the singed forests stumbled upon something else entirely: a lone makeshift shack in the woods, about thirty-four miles outside of Malone.[2]

Authorities assumed that the shack belonged to rogue hunters. But when they entered, they found ten Irish men, abandoned and starving. The young men had paid a man named Edward Cronk $50 to $70 each to bring them across the Canadian border and into the United States. They had met Cronk, a former New York state police officer, in Montreal, and he assured them that he could pull certain strings to assist their legal passage. Instead, he took their money, smuggled them across the border, and deserted them in the dense woods, insisting that he would return when they could safely travel to New York City. The ten Irishmen were lodged in the Franklin County Jail to await deportation decisions—the same site that, two decades prior, held hundreds of Chinese migrants for removal.

Edward Cronk, prolific trafficker of both liquor and people, was a thorn in the side of Northern New York law enforcement.[3] Troopers apprehended Cronk shortly after discovering the migrants. He swiftly escaped the Franklin County Jail, as authorities pursued him with bloodhounds through downtown Malone.[4] Aside from generating considerable local drama, Cronk's exploits illustrated a broader shift: New laws had transformed the landscape of illegal immigration, both in Northern New York and throughout the nation. The previous decade had brought a flurry of immigration laws, from anti–"white slavery" measures to literacy tests to the infamous quota laws, which for the first time capped how many immigrants could legally immigrate from European countries. Each of these laws created new incentives for illegal entry and a new enthusiasm for removal, with immigration officials looking not just to expel migrants at the borders but to locate, surveil, and banish migrants from within the nation.[5]

When the United States passed the 1910 Mann Act—a law making it a felony to transport any woman or girl "for the purpose of prostitution or debauchery"—border authorities apprehended more noncitizen women traversing borders.[6] When the United States instituted literacy tests in 1917, border authorities encountered illiterate Quebecois immigrants, many of whom had crossed the border for decades, sneaking across rivers to dodge immigration authorities.[7] And when the United States implemented national quotas with the 1924 Johnson-Reed Act, thousands of would-be immigrants from Europe hid in trains and cars to be trafficked alongside contraband liquor into the United States, solidifying an association between immigrants and vice.[8] "The deportation mill is a kaleidoscopic affair," a reporter for the *Detroit Free Press* observed in 1929. "Caucasians, Celestials, Negroes, Indians, and Mexicans passing through it. And there is at least as much variety in circumstances of the many cases."[9]

The jailing of migrants did not end with the Chinese jails. Instead, the jail became integral to enforcing a growing list of immigration laws in the first three decades of the twentieth century; in turn, the incarceration of migrants and other federal prisoners provoked a national reckoning with the role of the county jail. At the turn of the twentieth century, even avid reformers declared jails a lost cause, with the American Prison Association maintaining virtually no statistics on local sites. In the 1920s, criminologists began collecting data about the immigration service's use of local jails, suggesting that enforcement of immigration law would be impossible without expanded carceral infrastructure to match. Questions about the future of migrant incarceration arose locally, as towns wrestled with the ethics of holding the undocumented entrant together with the "common criminal," and internationally, as foreign nations inquired about why their citizens were incarcerated in squalid American institutions. Pressures from borderland counties whose jails were stretched thin by restrictive immigration laws, along with newly collected data about jail conditions, were key factors in the 1930 creation of the Bureau of Prisons

(BOP) and the nation's first federal jails, firmly intertwining immigration law and the buildup of carceral infrastructure.[10]

The discourse around county jails and federal prisoners shifted dramatically between the peak of Chinese migration into New York and the late 1920s, even across some of the same counties. Communities had transformed detained Chinese migrants into lucrative commodities—something for counties to fight *for*, rather than fight against. But in the 1920s and into the 1930s, many sheriffs and locals perceived the new amalgamation of migrant prisoners as a burden on the system, a wrench in the gears of an already struggling carceral apparatus.

Several factors explain this shift. First, the 1919 ratification of the Eighteenth Amendment, prohibiting the manufacture, sale, or transportation of alcohol, produced a soaring number of federal offenses and offenders; the number of federal prisoners was four times higher in 1930 than it was in 1915.[11] Prohibition-related arrests were most concentrated in border counties that now contended with both bootleggers and migrant smugglers, alongside rising arrests for narcotics and organized crime—notably, criminal charges that also disproportionately targeted foreign-born people.[12] By the start of the 1930s, nearly all New York county jails housed federal offenders, which left many communities less than enthused.[13] Perhaps most critically, the mounting federal arrests also meant that the federal government placed significant pressure on New York City's jails, triggering a showdown between the city and the federal government that a small border town like Malone lacked the leverage to pursue. Second, the migrants who filled county jails after the peak of Chinese migration through New York were less easily classified.[14] Northern New York counties saw the "Chinese prisoner" as a worthwhile investment because he could be cared for at little expense and created few problems for the sheriff. Local officials spoke of "the Chinese" as a racialized collective: All Chinese prisoners ate the same food, had the same customs, generated the same sum of federal money. Holding a variety of migrants from different countries, accused of violating different laws, alongside a rising number of other federal prisoners, posed a very different challenge than a simple dichotomy between "Chinese prisoners" and the general population.

Progressive-era reformers viewed both immigration and criminal justice as realms where standardization and expertise could improve the efficacy and fairness of the state.[15] Jails inched closer to the mainstream of criminology in the 1920s and 1930s, in part because reform-minded criminologists cast jail inhabitants as sympathetic and redeemable. Tales of migrants, and in

particular white migrant women, trapped in "a human dumping ground" became a tool for political mobilization.[16] Locals, politicians, and the courts
envisioned the jail as a place where *some* racialized groups belonged, a place
that might even be a desirable alternative to their lives abroad—an understanding reinforced by the growing ubiquity of eugenics in both scholarship
and society.[17] These same officials expressed serious discomfort when women,
children, and European migrants were subject to the same conditions. This
chapter begins with a return to Northern New York, to examine how the communities that had once praised Chinese detainees developed a more complicated relationship with the "immigrant prisoner." It then turns to migrants
elsewhere in the country, looking to Michigan, Florida, and Texas. While the
regional relationship between immigration law enforcement and municipalities varied, towns throughout the United States confronted shared questions:
Were local jails the best solution for federal prisoners, and exactly how much
cooperation did localities owe the immigration service?

The Changing Face of Northern New York Jails

Through the first decade of the twentieth century, the United States maintained what historian Torrie Hester describes as "two parallel deportation
policies": one for Chinese migrants and one for everyone else.[18] Non-Chinese
migrants had little access to the federal courts. They received a decision from
an immigration agent and could be deported for a broad range of offenses,
from coming to the United States as a contract laborer to belonging to an
expanding list of excludable categories, including paupers, polygamists, convicts, the disabled and ill, and those likely to become a public charge. Appeals
went through administrative Boards of Special Inquiry. Unlike Chinese migrants, few Europeans in deportation proceedings saw a judge unless the
courts determined that they were asking a new legal question or lodging a
procedural challenge.[19]

Northern New York became an arena for testing this two-prong process
in 1909, when officials apprehended Wong You and three other Chinese men
near Malone and processed them under the general immigration deportation
law that typically only applied to Europeans. Wong You's attorney countered
that since his client was Chinese, he could *only* be deported under the proto-
cols of Chinese exclusion.[20] The Supreme Court disagreed, ruling that immigration authorities did not need to go through the "more cumbersome
proceedings" of the Chinese Exclusion Act.[21] This made it considerably more

difficult for Chinese migrants to win appeals and access the courts. The ruling dramatically streamlined deportations for Chinese migrants: In 1913, the New York district reported that it had held more than 1,100 deportation hearings for Chinese migrants under general immigration law and had secured deportation in about 90 percent of all cases.[22] When the Immigration Act of 1917 wrote the precedent into law, due process rights for migrants in removal proceedings were permanently reduced—all deportations firmly resided in a separate realm of administrative law, with fewer routes to access judicial review than ever before. But even as Chinese removal cases bore less and less resemblance to the judicial proceedings of a criminal trial, one element remained consistent: Deportable migrants still moved through America's jails.

Even before the introduction of quotas, immigration authorities had noticed the demographics of jailed migrants change. In Northern New York, officials paid increased attention to the supposed exploitation of young white women who crossed American borders as sex workers.[23] In 1909, as part of a nationwide Bureau of Immigration dragnet against sex trafficking, U.S. Immigration Inspector David Lehrhaupt arrived in Watertown, New York, a mill town about twenty-five miles from the Canadian border.[24] River Street, a road along the banks of the Black River, had a paper factory, a pulp mill, and according to some sources, as many as eleven houses of prostitution.[25] At 56 River Street, Lehrhaupt arrested a Canadian migrant named Alda Rol and carted her to the county jail to await deportation—the first of a string of raids and deportations that would come to River Street as women cycled across the northern border, through the small town, to the county jail, and eventually back to Canada.[26]

Women faced extended incarcerations not just for their own deportations but also as witnesses in the state's cases against traffickers. The 1910 Mann Act used the Commerce Clause to make the foreign or interstate transportation of women a felony, officially putting the federal government in the business of fighting so-called white slavery. In a 1912 St. Lawrence County case, two Canadian women, Elizabeth Belle Julian and Agnes Bertrand, were jailed for more than four months pending the trial of a local man accused of transporting them for immoral purposes.[27] When the U.S. Grand Jury finally heard the testimonies of Julian and Bertrand, the trafficker was sentenced to just four days in jail, a marginal outcome relative to the women's four-month imprisonment.[28]

The jailing of migrant women who had been trafficked or who engaged in sex work intersected with Progressive-era battles over how to best address the "fallen woman."[29] Some women's organizations hesitated to cooperate with deportation efforts because they objected to sending women back to countries where they would face hardship and diminished chances of reform.[30] To secure the support of women's organizations, the immigration service sought to position immigration policing—and even incarceration—as a humane intervention in the lives of wayward women. In 1915, the commissioner-general of immigration recommended that officials should avoid "to the fullest extent possible" the incarceration of women and girls in local jails, boarding them instead with reform-minded philanthropic groups.[31] His declaration, known as Rule 22, marked the first time the immigration service formally disavowed holding a category of deportable persons in jails.[32]

Rule 22 encountered pushback from districts that agreed that white women should not be jailed but questioned whether they needed to follow the same protocol for women of color. In 1917, immigration authorities in Jacksonville complained that they had to detain "colored alien prostitutes ... of an extremely low character" in private houses at a rate of $2.50 a day, when they could hold the women in jail for just forty cents.[33] In a highly segregated Jim Crow southern city, separating Black and white migrants served a social role, as well as an economic one.[34] Women's detention was similarly contentious on the southern border, where Mexican women were the largest nationality excluded and deported on prostitution charges.[35] Following an investigation into white slavery in the Southwest, the commissioner-general lodged an impassioned defense of holding Mexican women in county jails, citing the cost savings and the relative "freedom" granted to jail detainees.[36] Even as officials presented jailing as in women's best interest, budgetary concerns were never far from mind.

World War I created a new condition of statelessness for both migrants and immigration officials to navigate, adding another major hurdle to the bureau's removal efforts in the 1910s and 1920s.[37] Deportation was not a one-way street. It required the cooperation of other sovereign nations that did not always share U.S. priorities. Individuals born in Macedonia before the war, for example, had Turkish citizenship. But as Macedonia became part of the Greek Republic, the Greek government refused to issue passports for Macedonian deportees. More and more migrants were deported from the United States to countries where they had never lived, exposing the hollowness of "national origin" as a meaningful category of identity.[38] In other cases, foreign governments dragged their feet on issuing documentation for racialized citizens they were not eager to see return: For example, James Sullivan, a Black British citizen, spent more than six months in a Northern New York jail as the British government stalled on sending a passport.[39] Authorities announced that another British subject in Northern New York had become "violently insane" while awaiting his passport to the West Indies; he was transferred to a mental institution, one of a growing class of deportees detained in asylums and hospitals.[40]

Delays became so dire that in 1927 the secretary of labor called on Congress to pass retaliatory legislation lowering immigration quotas from countries that declined to take back deportees.[41] As they confronted the cases of "undeportables," authorities questioned how long was *too* long to hold someone in a county jail. Though the courts had dictated that a deportee must be removed within a "reasonable time," there was considerable legal uncertainty about what that meant, particularly amid the new world of passport controls and citizenship loss.[42] In some cases, judges decided that four months was beyond "reasonable"; in other cases judges decreed that any detention longer than thirty days exceeded reasonable limits. Judge E. H. Lacombe concluded in a 1915 case that prolonged detentions were "unfortunate, but certainly not illegal."[43]

While immigration restrictions around sex, welfare, and disability all expanded routes to removal, no decree upended U.S. immigration law more than the passage of national origins quotas. The quota laws were the culmination of years of nativist organizing, buttressed by the racism and pseudoscience of the eugenics movement. They solidified into law what had become a commonly accepted maxim in the United States: There existed a hierarchy of races with a hierarchy of intellectual and democratic potentials. For eugenicists like the Immigration Restriction League, the nation's survival depended on curbing the entry and membership of the least desirable groups.[44] In 1919, Congress imposed a head tax of $8.00 on Canadians and Mexicans, and two years later the United States passed an Emergency Quota Act, restricting immigration to 350,000 people per year. Both policies triggered prolific smuggling and border running by Europeans who sought to avoid the taxes, failed to secure a place under the quota, or simply wanted to circumvent the increasingly complicated process of legal immigration. In 1924, Congress further reduced the quotas and made them permanent. Under the new system, immigrants from Southern and Eastern Europe competed for a fraction of the quota spots allocated to nations of "high-quality," "old-stock" origins, such as Britain, Germany, and Norway. Notions of racial purity were at the center of U.S. immigration law. While some Europeans faced higher barriers to entry, Asian immigrants became virtually ineligible for admission altogether, cementing the boundary between white and nonwhite foreigners.[45]

With the quota laws in effect, local media reported that Northern New York's jails were again in crisis, facing strain unseen since the peak of Chinese migration twenty years prior. In Franklin County, men slept in the jail hallways, while the sheriff housed migrant women in his own quarters.[46] Officials wrestled a knife away from a Finnish man who attempted to cut his throat when his long incarceration became too much to bear.[47] The overcrowding in New York's jails was due in part to Prohibition, but the sheriff declared the immigration service the county's "greatest offender" because of how long it detained people in the facility.[48] The emerging gatekeeping regime presented related, but distinct, challenges for members of tribal nations. With the passage of the Indian Citizenship Act of 1924, Indigenous people in the United States became citizens, while those outside the United States became classified as aliens. In 1925, Paul Diabo, a Mohawk ironworker from Kahnawake, a First Nations reserve located on Quebec's side of the St. Lawrence River, attempted to cross the border into New York for work, as he had done for more than a decade. He found himself detained and deported for violations of immigration law, now marked an alien under the new citizenship regime. Though the Supreme Court would later affirm that Indigenous people had the right to pass through the border as Indigenous nationals, tribal members had to contend with much of the same surveillance and bureaucracy that shaped the experiences of migrants.[49]

Once again, local observers raised ethical questions about using incarceration as a tool of border control. In a 1925 article from a Plattsburgh newspaper, one observer wrote that "some accused of murder and some who have tried to sneak across an imaginary line, drawn on the same soil and on which the same sun shines, boys and girls, men and women, sick and well, are all thrown into the same hopper and sifted as chance dictates." The newspaper's description laid bare the fiction of borders, belittling them as an "imaginary line" and highlighting the ways that people in the U.S.-Canada borderlands understood the interconnectedness of their local communities. The author drew on the tried-and-true dichotomy of the innocent immigrant girl versus the hardened criminal. In Clinton County Jail, a woman accused of narcotics trafficking, who was in the final stages of tuberculosis, shared a bed "with a healthy alien girl capable of a bright future whose only crime was that of trying to enter this land of the free in the face of an immigration law she could not understand or appreciate."[50] The image evoked women's aid groups' fears that the enforcement mechanisms of immigration law served to further corrupt young white women. As county jails stretched to house the evolving amalgam of federal offenders, a new idea gained momentum: federal jails.

The Fight to End Boarding Out

The push for federal jails was spearheaded by the criminologist Hastings H. Hart, a mustachioed pastor turned social worker and the chairman of the American Prison Association's committee on jails.[51] (Figure 11.) One contemporary described Hart as "an invincible crusader for jail conditions," responsible for forcing the subject of jails onto the agenda of the American Prison Association.[52] "The most amazing thing is the indifference of the entire United States on this subject [of jails]. Nobody seems to care anything about it," Hart told Congress.[53] Under Hart's leadership, the American Prison Association established its first permanent committee on jails in 1923. "[I] expect to hold the chairmanship for the rest of my life, because nobody else wants the job," Hart quipped.[54]

Along with the lack of attention came a lack of data. In 1923, under the auspices of the newly formed American Prison Association jail committee, Hart wrote to 130 judges to describe the government's predicament: Because the United States maintained no jails for violators of federal laws, it outsourced thousands of prisoners to city, county, and state jails. The federal government had virtually no statistics on these people, their locations, or their offenses.[55] In an effort to paint a more complete portrait of the relationship between the local carceral state and the federal government, Hart spent years collecting data about federal boarders from more than nine hundred jails and workhouses.[56] In 1926, he published the first comprehensive survey of federal prisoners in county jails, revealing that the United States held 65,000 federal prisoners in local jails annually, with an average of about 6,300 incarcerated on federal charges on any given night.[57] Each agreement for jail space was individually negotiated between the U.S. Marshals and local authorities. Some locales were more successful than others, with nightly rates ranging from twenty cents a day for jails in Puerto Rico to $3.00 a day for jails in Alaska.[58]

For Hart, a longtime critic of the local jail's "destructive influence," the scale of boarding out was stomach churning. He proposed that the federal government create a modern, humane jail system of its own, focused on the U.S.-Canada and the U.S.-Mexico borders.[59] The jails would be owned and operated by the federal government and would hold migrants, pretrial defendants, and people sentenced to brief incarcerations for federal infractions. Federal jails were not an easy solution. They required new allotments from the national budget, the transformation of a centuries-old boarding-out system, and, potentially, the development an entirely new federal agency. But attempts

FIGURE 11. Photograph of Hastings Hornell Hart, 1915: social worker, penologist, and president of the American Prison Association, 1921–22. Courtesy of the Minnesota Historical Society.

to improve county jails had proved difficult, if not impossible. The Department of Justice had only two inspectors overseeing the roughly 1,100 jails used by the federal government.[60] The United States could end its contract with a county jail, but it could not appropriate federal money to improve county facilities, even when the stress of federal prisoners contributed to jails' deterioration.[61] The impetus was on the locality to keep the jail in acceptable condition, and in most cases, investing in the local lockup was not a priority—especially not at the federal government's going rates.

Money was a major source of tension in intergovernmental collaboration. Local communities argued that they were not being fairly compensated for jail space. The federal government argued that it could barely afford the rates it was paying. The Bureau of Immigration had long operated on a shoestring budget, and by the late 1920s it had resorted to multiple cost-saving measures, from docking employees' pay two and a half days per month to promoting the merits of "voluntary departure" to detained migrants.[62] Across the United States, growing populations of migrants were held in flux because the agency did not have the money to deport them. In 1926, Buffalo had seven hundred unserved warrants for deportation and several hundred deportation hearings pending.[63] Detention bills reached as high as $14 per day, causing the entire district office to operate at a loss. With debts accumulating, the district director threatened to release all migrants from jail and stop making new arrests if they did not receive more funding. "Nothing short of absolute chaos would be the result," the official ominously predicted.[64] Authorities argued that the financial costs of unauthorized migration were made worse by the number of deportable "alien criminals" in New York state prisons, some of whom would never be deported. At the same time Hart was completing his research, the state of New York began compiling new data on its prison population, claiming that 23 percent of the state's convicts were noncitizens.[65]

In 1926, New York took one of the first steps in challenging the practice of boarding out. Effective March 1, 1927, a new state law empowered sheriffs to refuse federal prisoners if the jail was full or if their presence would violate rules mandating the separation of violent and nonviolent offenders.[66] The law had limited impact: Localities still felt pressure from the federal government to accept prisoners and feared retaliation if they refused.[67] The occasional sheriff did draw a line in the sand. In 1929, Sheriff A. L. Senecal of Plattsburgh, New York, refused to accept any more people detained by the federal government until the thirteen held at his jail had been removed. Some migrants had been awaiting deportation for five months, the sheriff reported, while others did not have sufficient clothing to survive the brutal New York winter.[68] The U.S. deputy marshal desperately tried to convince local authorities to budge; he had twelve migrants waiting to be arraigned and no jails to hold them.

Compared with small towns and rural places, cities had greater leverage in negotiating with the federal government over jail space. In New York City, the relationship between municipal penal institutions and the federal government reached a stalemate. Sheriff David H. Knott, who oversaw the Ludlow Street Jail on Manhattan's Lower East Side, reported in 1921 that the federal government had not paid the city for use of jail space in two years.[69] "The City of New York does not seek to make any money on Uncle Sam, but neither can I be a party to Father Knickerbocker being nicked," the sheriff lamented.[70] Unlike the obsequious "Chinese prisoners" of twenty years prior, the sheriff found federal prisoners to be entitled and demanding, in one case requesting a cell with southern exposure.[71] In 1926, the New York City commissioner of correction informed federal authorities that the city would not renew its contract after an investigation revealed that the arrangement had cost taxpayers $126,821.55 over the previous five years.[72] In 1925, a Boston judge suspended sentencing on liquor cases, as every county jail in Massachusetts was over capacity.[73] The city of Baltimore followed New York City's lead and refused federal prisoners unless the government raised its rates.[74] In New York City, Boston, and Baltimore, most people incarcerated on federal charges were bootleggers. Because these cities had immigration stations with space for detention, they did not rely heavily on county jails to hold migrants. Still, as major cities hurled ultimatums, federal jails seemed like a more urgent, necessary solution.

In their pursuit of federal intervention, Hastings Hart and his allies also argued that the construction of federal jails would play a moral role. Though rhetoric of moral reform had infused discussions of prison reform throughout U.S. history, advocates argued that the jail had particular importance because its inhabitants were *more* reformable. People in jail were the "small fish" of the criminal justice system: rumrunners, witnesses in criminal trials, those who could not afford bond, and of course, border crossers. Joseph C. Hutcheson Jr., a federal judge from Texas and one of Hart's collaborators, wrote that "a county jail ought to be the most reformatory prison in the state. . . . [No] missionary work in the world is of a higher order."[75] He called on his fellow federal judges to avail themselves of every means to keep people *out* of the nation's crumbling jails until a more humane system could be devised. If federal jails were approved, "judges and prisoners alike may well feel, that at last, on this dull earth, Justice and Mercy are reconciled and the judge and the brother are one," Hutcheson beseeched an audience in 1925.[76] To true believers like Hutcheson, federal jails were not a dull bureaucratic solution—they were a revelation.

Or were they? Policymakers and penologists had good reason to believe that federal jails would not be a silver bullet. Federal prisons had been around since 1891 and had hardly solved the issues plaguing modern penitentiaries.[77] For federal prisoners with sentences over a year, the United States had three prisons, at Leavenworth, Kansas; Atlanta, Georgia; and McNeil Island in Puget Sound in Washington. The federal government had recently completed work on the Industrial Institute for Women at Alderson, West Virginia, and also oversaw an assemblage of work camps and training schools. Federal prisons had significant problems. Leavenworth had double the number of inmates it was built to hold, McNeil Island struggled to reliably provide clean water, and Atlanta had men sleeping in dark basements and corridors because they had run out of cells.[78] Would federal jails be any better? Policymakers contemplated and equivocated until finally, in 1929, a new immigration law pushed borderland jails over the edge.

Criminalizing Unlawful Entry

In 1923, R. B. Sims, the superintendent of the Arizona State Prison, wrote to the governor of Arizona to complain about the prison's relationship with the immigration service. Again and again, Sims and the county sheriff released Mexican migrants for deportation, only to see them return to the United States days later. The immigration service's present method of "dumping" Mexicans just across the border was "an absolute farce," the superintendent declared. If the federal government could not find a better way to keep Mexicans from crossing the border, deportation "might just as well be abolished."[79] Secretary of Labor James J. Davis suggested that remedying the problem identified by Sims and others required a more punitive approach to immigration law, something that went beyond simple removal. "No prohibitive law can successfully be enforced without a deterrent penalty," Secretary Davis implored Congress.[80]

On March 4, 1929, the day of Herbert Hoover's inauguration, Congress passed S. 5094, making unlawful entry into the United States a misdemeanor punishable by one year of imprisonment, a $1,000 fine, or both.[81] If a person entered without authorization for a second time, that person faced felony charges and two years imprisonment, a $2,000 fine, or both. Congress had contemplated making illegal immigration a crime during early drafts of the 1882 Chinese Exclusion Act but had settled on a watered-down version that cut the provision in hopes of maintaining stronger diplomatic relations with China.[82] In 1929, Congress's most extreme nativist factions would finally get their way. The new law, known colloquially as the Undesirable Aliens Act, dramatically raised the stakes of deportation, making it tantamount to permanent banishment under threat of felony prosecution.[83] The secretary of labor wrote that the 1929 law "in some particulars, . . . is the most drastic general immigration law ever enacted," delivering "stern punishment" to those who violated immigration law.[84] After decades of the immigration service insisting that deportation proceedings were a solely administrative procedure, the 1929 law reclassified illegal entry as a *criminal* offense with criminal consequences. In the words of one Northern New York newspaper, the new policy "put teeth in immigration law."[85]

Though illegal entry along the northern frontier remained a concern for the immigration service, the U.S.-Mexico border eclipsed the U.S.-Canada border as an agency priority. Removals along the southern border were skyrocketing, accelerated by the 1924 creation of the U.S. Border Patrol. In 1925, there were just 1,751 expulsions from the southern border; by 1929 the number surpassed fifteen thousand.[86] In the early 1920s, restrictionists' efforts to include Mexicans in the quota laws failed due to the Harding administration's reluctance to antagonize Mexico, as well as pressure from southwestern congressmen whose constituents profited from inexpensive workers.[87] After the quotas' passage, anxieties about Mexican labor suppressing wages continued to fester, matched with concerns about the violence allegedly fostered by migrant smuggling and so-called Mexican criminality.[88] Coleman Blease, a South Carolina Democrat and avowed white supremacist, introduced S. 5094 to the Senate in December 1928, where it received little pushback.[89] Lawmakers saw the bill as a concession to those who had fought for a Mexican quota and assured growers that the law would not impact their access to labor. They also saw it as critical to maintaining the racial composition of the nation. Like the quota laws before it, the new law confirmed that a white American race, descended from Europe, was the linchpin of national identity and would be jealously defended against groups deemed unassimilable or otherwise inferior.[90]

Historians have argued that a limited budget and workforce meant that the immigration service enforced the Undesirable Aliens Act erratically and selectively.[91] Between 1930 and 1936, the service brought more than forty thousand criminal cases against unlawful entrants and won convictions in 90 percent of those cases—still representing only a fraction of the total number of migrants entering the country without authorization. Nativist legislators grumbled that, as was the case with the Geary Act, Congress made the law unenforceable by failing to provide adequate appropriations—a problem soon made worse by depression-era budget cuts. The vast majority of removals were carried out via voluntary departures, in which migrants paid for their own return, rather than via the formal deportation system.[92] The legal system was similarly unprepared: Courts in some border districts met only once a year, further prolonging the pretrial detention of migrants charged under S. 5094.[93] In the law's first year, migrants in county jails averaged nearly a month of detention prior to criminal trial.[94]

TABLE 1. Immigration Prisoners (Sentenced) Received at
County Jails, FY 1929–1930

	Men	Women
Number of Prisoners	4,619	195
Total Time Served (days)	210,076	8,452
Average Sentence (days)	51	48
Average Age (years)	24.6	25.2

Source: Data from File 55639/731, Record Group 85, National Archives and
Records Administration, Washington, D.C.

Yet, even if the law was not enforced to its fullest extent, its repercussions
were strongly felt in border communities. County jails now held migrants
awaiting deportation, as well as migrants serving *criminal sentences*—in the
first year after the law's passage county jails held nearly five thousand migrants
sentenced to jail time for illegal entry (Table 1).[95] Particularly in counties near
U.S. borders, jails were incarcerating dual populations of migrants: one administrative and one criminal, both in the local lockup. Just six months after the
law's passage, the assistant U.S. attorney advised immigration districts to
charge migrants under Section 2 of the 1929 law, a misdemeanor charge that
brought a maximum imprisonment of a year, rather than Section 1, a felony
charge that brought up to two years imprisonment.[96] Lax enforcement of the
law was partially a result of immigration service funding and manpower, but
it was also a result of jail overcrowding.

Though Congress crafted the 1929 law with Mexican migrants in mind, it
created immediate changes for upstate immigration law enforcement. With the
law's passage, sixty-five new immigration inspectors were sent to Northern New
York, and the immigration station in Clinton County was upgraded to a "port
of entry," with inspectors on duty twenty-four hours a day.[97] By the summer of
1930, detainees at Northern New York's county jails were again double-booked
in cells, with outdoor time cut in half.[98] When the New York State Prison Commission investigators visited the Clinton County Jail, they found that immigration prisoners knew little about the status of their cases, how long they would
be held, or what the next steps in their cases might be. At the Franklin County
Jail, inspectors discovered a migrant woman with three young children who had
been held in the facility for more than a month on a charge of illegal entry.[99]
Authorities in Malone said that they "regretted" the illegal detentions of
children.[100] "It is hoped that a federal institution will soon be provided in this

part of the country which will be equipped to take care of all United States prisoners," the report stated, again agitating for federal intervention and carceral expansion as the singular solution to humanitarian injustices.[101]

The effects of the 1929 law also stirred international alarm, catapulting the most local of American institutions onto a global stage. In December 1929, a London newspaper printed a story about Canadian border crossers sharing cells with "common criminals."[102] In 1931, the British consul launched an investigation into the experiences of English and Canadian deportees in Arizona county jails; he suggested that the United States establish more "detention camps . . . similar to those already in use at San Francisco and Ellis Island," in order to segregate the migrant prisoner from the rest of the incarcerated population.[103] Concerns about white women continued to be central to these critiques. When authorities detained Marie Scriver, an eighteen-year-old Canadian, in a Detroit jail for three weeks on a charge of illegal border crossing, the Canadian press was horrified. An editorial proclaimed Scriver a "pretty Canadian miss," who had "attempted innocent passage between the two countries." The media stressed that she was unlike the jail's "real" criminals, but as a young, white woman she was also unlike other immigrant prisoners.[104] Historian Mae Ngai has argued that the laws of the 1920s gave rise to a discourse of "deserving and undeserving illegal immigrants" and "just and unjust deportations," a framing that extended to the county jail.[105] Mexicans made up the vast majority of apprehensions and prosecutions under the 1929 law, yet European and Canadian migrants commanded disproportionate attention.[106]

The surge of arrests under the Undesirable Aliens Act accelerated organizing for federal intervention. The growing deportation system, which fostered coordination between the federal government, district immigration offices, and thousands of localities, had expanded the state's administrative capacity. In turn, it expanded Americans' ideas about what the state was capable of and what responsibilities it bore. At a 1929 congressional hearing, Walter W. Nicholson, a member of the New York State Commission of Correction, said that arrests and sentencing for Prohibition, narcotics, and border crossing had "utterly destroyed" the sheriff's ability to enforce local laws.[107] An appropriations appeal from the secretary of labor articulated what had been clear on the ground in Upstate New York—the "already deplorable situation" in jails had been made "immeasurably worse" by the 1929 law.[108] The New York State Commission of Correction reported that federal prisoners were warehoused in fifty of the sixty-six county jails in New York.[109] To even the Prison Commission's surprise, the largest share of federal prisoners in New York jails were *not* bootleggers but, by a narrow margin, people held for violation of immigration law.[110]

Making Intergovernmental Cooperation Work

While Northern New York jails had become a flash point of concern about incarceration, cities and towns throughout the nation were reckoning with their evolving role in the deportation state. In 1923, the Bureau of Immigration sent a memo to each of its districts requesting information about the "nature and extent of cooperation between our service and the state, municipal, and other public authorities in your district."[111] The immigration service wanted to know how much "alien reliefers" cost the government and also sought to understand the relationship between immigration agents and local law enforcement.[112] The bureau received responses from across the country, documenting a range of experiences with local governments. Together, these dispatches offered a snapshot of an increasingly, though unevenly, interconnected carceral state—one that facilitated cooperation between scales of government as well as across carceral and welfare institutions.[113]

In some cases, police and localities were eager to help the immigration service. In Texas, police joined Border Patrol officers to scout migrants crossing the Rio Grande. In Portland, Maine, the State Board of Charities prepared monthly reports on all potentially deportable migrants held in state almshouses. In New York Harbor, the Jersey City Police patrolled the water around Ellis Island to look for escapees. In California and Washington, the states employed a "state deportation agent," who tracked migrants held in state institutions and brought their cases to the immigration service.[114] San Francisco immigration officials incentivized police with small cash rewards for identifying smuggled Chinese migrants, while Portland, Maine, immigration officials offered their most cooperative police officers trips accompanying transcontinental deportation parties.[115]

Yet, in other communities, collaboration between immigration and local law enforcement was, in the words of the Pittsburgh immigration office, "practically nil." Pittsburgh officials reported that the local police rarely aided in immigration cases because they believed that the work was of "too little importance." An inspector from Cincinnati indicated that his office more frequently learned about deportable migrants from newspapers than from law enforcement. In Georgia, the immigration service griped that local arrest records did not indicate whether an apprehended person was foreign-born. The

Atlanta immigration service admitted that it made little effort to contact sheriffs and wardens because local law enforcement did not have the resources to pursue deportations.[116] The Los Angeles office noted that ever since the money from immigration prisoners began flowing to the county budget, rather than directly to the sheriff and his deputies, there had been considerably less enthusiasm for working with the immigration service.[117]

One pressing issue for the Bureau of Immigration was whether local law enforcement agencies notified the service when they had migrants in their custody. People with criminal convictions were a particular priority for removal, as the 1917 Immigration Act enabled deportation for any criminal conviction within five years of entry.[118] In the immigration service's ideal vision of this relationship, prisons and jails would hold deportable migrants until the Bureau of Immigration could relieve them, an informal prototype for today's system of immigration detainers, through which Immigration and Customs Enforcement can request that a local jail hold people until ICE takes them into custody. Because of the service's finite resources and limited detention space, this could mean weeks and months of additional incarceration. Migrants were justifiably furious when they were detained beyond the end of their criminal sentences. In 1924, twenty-six Greek and Turkish men detained in New York's Washington County Jail for violation of the Passport Act of 1920 petitioned the secretary of labor.[119] (Figure 12.) They were still incarcerated a week after their sentence had ended, with little indication of when they might be freed.[120] Some local authorities stopped alerting the immigration service to the cases of deportable persons after the immigration service failed to pursue the cases. An inspector in Winnipeg defined the problem plainly: "[T]he solution of the smuggling and illegal entry problem is more money."[121]

Other communities were unwilling to oblige the immigration service's request that they hold migrants in custody longer than the courts dictated, citing a range of legal, logistical, and ethical concerns. The New York superintendent of prisons wrote that "we have no authority, morally or legally, to hold [the alien prisoner] beyond the expiration of his term," emphasizing that federal authorities had ample time to acquire a warrant for deportation while a person was serving a sentence.[122] In Atlanta, a judge wrote to the Department of Labor that migrants were being removed from the United States Penitentiary, Atlanta, upon completion of their prison sentence and moved to Georgia jails to await deportation for as long as three or four months. "This jail is very uncomfortable and unwholesome, and it does not seem right to keep a man who is not charged with any crime there for that length of time," the judge wrote.[123] The assistant

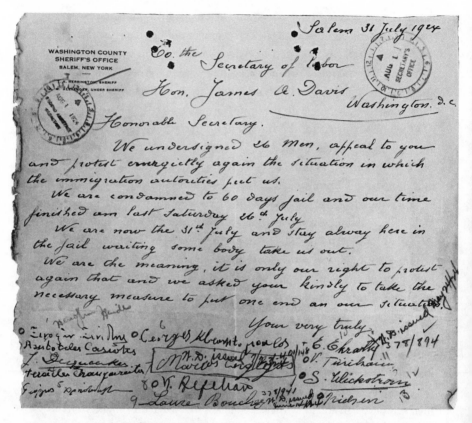

FIGURE 12. Petition from twenty-six migrants detained in New York's Washington County Jail, 1924, protesting that immigration officials had held them in jail after the expiration of their sentence. *Source:* File 54933-351-D, Record Group 85, National Archives and Records Administration, Washington, D.C.

secretary of labor suggested that the Georgia judge could use discretion in offering relief to detained migrants, writing that New York City had observed "a sort of gentlemen's agreement rule" where migrants held for more than four months without bail or deportation were discharged on habeas corpus.[124]

Perhaps the most prescient analysis of federal-local collaborations came from an immigration official in El Paso in 1923. In order to get local institutions on board with the project of immigration law enforcement, he wrote, the federal government needed to create incentives to cooperation:

Our officers have been impressed with the necessity of carrying on our propaganda; they become missionaries and never let up in endeavoring to sell the Service to the public generally. It can readily be appreciated that what will appeal to one man will not appeal to another. Railroad men must understand that the immigration laws are enforced to their advantage. Police officers must be given to understand that by helping us, they help themselves; they rid themselves of troublesome problems, and in return secure much valuable aid from immigration officers. Institutions generally are glad to be rid of maintenance expenses. In other words, if we cannot appeal to a man's patriotism, loyalty, etc. we appeal to his self-interest.[125]

The letter suggested that the Bureau of Immigration should see itself as having something to sell—community safety, rule of law, sovereign borders—and should view the public as customers. This signaled a reversal from how the immigration service had tended to see itself in prior decades—as a customer, in search of the infrastructure and manpower that localities provided. It was an appeal that the immigration officials should see themselves as the ones with the *power*, even if they did not necessarily have the resources to match. In the first decade of the twentieth century, financial incentives were often sufficient to secure local cooperation in jailing migrants in the counties the immigration service relied on. However, by the 1920s, the expanding scale of deportation, the reduced potential for sheriffs to personally profit, and the changing demographics of people jailed for immigration offenses meant that the immigration service needed to sell migrant detention as a political project, not just an economic one.

One way federal cooperation was marketed to communities was as a means of crime control, a potent argument as emerging academic fields such as sociology and criminology drew statistical connections between immigration, race, and criminality.[126] Along the northern border, the immigration service identified seventy-five major smuggling gangs operating in the greater Detroit area, bringing roughly twenty thousand Europeans into the United States each month.[127] Detroit's Wayne County Jail routinely held between 100 and 150 migrants for deportation.[128] A 1929 article in the *Detroit Free Press* documented the diversity of cases in the jail; it held a Scottish family who had been in jail seven months, an interracial couple made up of a previously deported Canadian woman and an African American man, and a number of Chinese laborers.[129] While some of these migrants were apprehended crossing the border, growing numbers were picked up post-entry, as the immigration service raided immigrant coffeehouses, pool halls, and workplaces under the auspices of targeting organized crime.[130] The immigration service worked alongside

Detroit police to spearhead what the Bureau of Immigration director declared a "deportation war" and basked in glowing media coverage claiming that the removal of undesirable migrants was ameliorating urban crime rates.[131] Detroit's war grew more aggressive in the early 1930s, as Secretary of Labor William Doak proclaimed mass deportations as a solution for alleviating American unemployment. Doak's critics in Detroit accused his agents of illegal search and seizure, inhumane punishments, and abuse of power.[132] Doak countered that his critics had an "America last" attitude, prioritizing the rights of the foreigner above the interests of the nation.[133]

Controversy over Detroit's deportation tactics meant more unwanted attention for the overcrowded Wayne County Jail. In 1932, an Indian man named Mohammed Box attempted to hang himself after being detained in the jail for more than six months. Box told the sheriff that he would rather die than be imprisoned one more day. Wayne County officials were shaken by the incident; the sheriff demanded that the federal government cut the "red tape" that put migrants' lives at risk.[134] "Why even a murderer would get speedier action than these men," the sheriff declared.[135] Instances of red tape abounded: Seventeen-year-old Edward Argot was "lost" in the Detroit jail for eight months, while officials searched for his birth records. After finding him sobbing in a cell, officials released Argot on probation, and he was later adopted by the jail's barber.[136] Argot shared the jail with Nellie Elash, who was incarcerated for six weeks while the United States attempted to deport her to Poland. Elash was Canadian by birth and had never so much as stepped foot in Poland—she had attained the citizenship via marriage to her Polish ex-husband.[137]

One consistency through all the detainees' stories was the agonizing uncertainty that detention wrought. While days stretched into weeks into months, migrants received little information about the progress of their cases: Would their documents ever be found? Would an attorney make the bureaucracy budge? Exactly how long would they be in this jail? Once illegal entry was turned into a federal crime, effectively all immigration law enforcement could be a crime control project, regardless of whether noncitizens had committed an offense aside from entering the nation.

In other locations, detention was seen less as retribution for a criminal act and more as a proactive measure to prevent lawbreaking. In South Florida, the Bureau of Immigration relied on county jails to detain migrants from the Bahamas and Cuba, as well as migrants from China and Europe who used Caribbean stopovers before entering the United States. Immigration authorities in Florida became particularly concerned about the number of seamen deserting foreign ships. In 1925, a German named Arthur Rudolph Bucholtz was found cooking in a Miami restaurant after absconding from a freighter a month prior.[138] To avoid paying penalty fees for defectors like Bucholtz, shipping companies asked to detain crews at the Dade County Jail while boats were docked. Immigration authorities obliged, so long as the company paid for their board. Maritime workers, now incarcerated merely as a precaution, were aghast: They wrote letters from jail calling their imprisonment "against all international law" and a violation of their human rights.[139]

Officials in Miami had heard tales from their colleagues of the bureaucratic fallout created by absconding seamen. North of Miami, in the Florida cities of Jacksonville and Tampa, immigration officials spent considerable time and energy searching for missing seamen in the towns' Chinese laundries.[140] When seamen were located, their apprehension and incarceration could be a performance and a warning to other workers: Years later, in Mobile, Alabama, local officials paraded handcuffed seamen through the streets, before delivering them to the jail. The detained men wrote in a letter that they had been "degraded and humiliated," before being tossed into a roach-infested jail.[141] Officials accused them of exaggerating the horrors of the Alabama lockup.[142] Yet, in internal communications, officials expressed fear that such letters from detainees could constitute petitions for habeas corpus if they reached judges and that the courts might be more likely to grant freedom because of jail conditions. "A jail within a jail within a jail describe this hell hole. No air, no sunlight, just a cage built between four walls," declared the detained maritime laborers of Mobile.[143]

On the U.S.-Mexico border, the South Texas island of Galveston was among the nation's busiest ports of immigration and most controversial sites of detention. Following the demise of their immigration station in a 1915 hurricane, local officials began channeling European migrants into Galveston County Jail, while sending migrants from elsewhere to the Nueces County Jail in Corpus Christi.[144] Galveston's migrants were held on a dark, windowless floor of the jail, where they contended with perpetual louse problems and a single bathtub for dozens of inmates.[145]

Conditions facing women at the jail were especially dire. In 1928, an immigration inspector filed a report on a Mexican woman named Gertrudis

Hernandez de Rodriguez, after a jailer was found "loving her up" at the Galveston facility. At least two other jailers had previously assaulted Rodriguez at Galveston. Though the report referred to "improper relations between this woman, the jailors, and probably other inmates," the power differential between a Mexican woman awaiting deportation and the white jail workers was undeniable.[146] The immigration service explored alternative arrangements for women and children throughout the 1920s, but European women received priority for transfers out of the jail. The *Galveston Daily News* noted that jail was a particular hardship for women "from the better class families," abandoning women like Hernandez to endure an environment that left them vulnerable to both the whims of bureaucracy and the predations of their jailers.[147] It reinforced the idea that racialized migrants were disorderly, and perhaps criminal, while others were merely unlucky or unfortunate.

In many cities where the immigration service operated, it encountered an occasional angry op-ed about immigration detention or about the agency's behavior—federal-local collaboration had its critics, but they were routinely dismissed. Galveston was different. The immigration service in Galveston was met with a sustained local crusade to move migrants out of the local jail, a campaign that reflected Galveston's reputation as a site of incarceration for Europeans. In August 1925, members of the Galveston chapter of the League of Women Voters wrote to their senator to express concern about the "dreadful conditions which exist in regard to the detention of deportees in this part of the world." They elaborated that "these deportees, while they have broken some law of the country (many unwittingly) are not in the true sense of the word criminals."[148] The letter concluded with an appeal to civic pride, arguing that the city's reputation was on the line and that a place like New York City would never tolerate such treatment. The Galveston Chamber of Commerce similarly agitated for the "establishment of a concentration camp or station" that would specifically serve migrants.[149]

Critics in Galveston were not arguing against incarceration broadly; they specifically argued against incarceration in the *jail*, reiterating criminologists' comments about the uniquely dire conditions of America's local carceral institutions. Jailing migrants in Galveston, critics asserted, was a moral atrocity and a civic embarrassment, which exposed the interconnected local and global scales of deportation. Migrants not destined for Mexico typically faced longer detentions, as immigration officials navigated travel documents and shifting borders, but in places like Galveston they benefited from the interventions of local groups concerned about their treatment. White migrants raised alarm and mobilized political organizing, as Mexican migrants suffered in relative obscurity—a disparity that would become even starker in coming decades.

———

On August 5, 1930, Northern New York's *Plattsburgh Sentinel* published an editorial celebrating the Hoover administration's newly interventionist stance on "criminal affairs." Hoover transformed crime control into a national priority: The state invested in prisons, streamlined federal criminal recordkeeping, and collected new crime statistics through projects such as the National Commission on Law Observance and Enforcement.[150] Nonetheless, the editorial said, the dangerous, overcrowded county jails of the North Country and of the nation continued to get the short end of the stick; the situation demanded "radical change" in the form of a federal jail.[151] The change the *Plattsburgh Sentinel* sought was on the horizon. Conversations about congestion and unrest culminated in the Act of May 14, 1930, which created the Federal Bureau of Prisons and officially sanctioned the construction of federal jails. The advent of the BOP marked a new era for the federal government, confirming that American crime control would be a shared national and local project. It was a shift driven not just by concern about liquor law and gangsters but also by concern about illegal entry and the nation's capacity to deport.

Even as the creation of the BOP expanded the federal government's carceral investments, it still permitted the practice of boarding out federal prisoners in local facilities. The federal government was under no illusions that it could replace its reliance on county jails overnight. One vocal critic of this caveat was the National Association for the Advancement of Colored People (NAACP), an organization that had spent much of the 1920s fighting to abolish convict leasing and expand the due process protections of Black criminal defendants.[152] The NAACP argued that continuing to permit boarding out would do "irreparable injustice to Negro prisoners," who in years prior had been relegated to the worst local institutions when federal prisons became overcrowded.[153] In 1929, the Department of Justice leased two hundred Black men from the United States Penitentiary, Atlanta, to a Chatham County convict camp for road construction work, despite the state and federal governments' insistence that convict leasing had ended.[154] The NAACP spent five months attempting to add language to the BOP legislation that would specifically address racial disparities in boarding-out practices but ultimately settled for the BOP's assurances that the agency would make "every effort" to avoid discrimination.[155] Racist discrimination permeated the practice for both noncitizens and citizens alike. Over the coming years, Mexican migrants would be among the most vulnerable to the forced labor and discriminatory boarding-out practices the NAACP feared.

With the federal green light, the BOP built quickly. By 1933, the United States had established federal jails in New York City; La Tuna, Texas; New Orleans, Louisiana; and Milan, Michigan, all municipalities proximate to a land border or port of entry. The opening of La Tuna swiftly reshaped the local detention economy in El Paso.[156] (Figure 13.) In 1932, the county downsized the sheriff's office in anticipation of losing $82,000 of annual payment for holding federal prisoners.[157] But El Paso overestimated how dramatically the federal jail would curtail business. Within months of opening, La Tuna was over capacity, and by the spring of 1933 the federal government was again transferring people to the El Paso jail, buoyed by an uptick of immigration raids and Mexican repatriation efforts.[158] Migrants also continued to pass through Galveston; in 1938, Secretary of Labor Frances Perkins received a letter from Rabbi Henry Cohen condemning the warehousing of migrants in the Galveston jail. "The well-being, morally and physically, of the immigrants has been sacrificed to Economy. Thrift might be applied elsewhere that human life may be bettered!" the rabbi implored.[159]

Since the federal government did not have adequate detention space in its new federal facilities, officials focused on weeding out county jails with the most egregious conditions and designating them ineligible for future federal contracts. In 1935, 477 county and city jails housed federal prisoners, just a third of the number of local jails the agency used at its peak.[160] But by 1939, the BOP reported that the number of local jails used for boarding out had crept back up to 691.[161] In the decade following the BOP's creation, observers reported only marginal improvements in the condition of local jails, even as the agency offered financial incentives to the best-kept facilities. "Few things have been discussed so much, damned so long and loudly, and had so little done about them as the jails and the weather," sighed a lawmaker at a 1940 meeting of the National Jail Association.[162] Other criminologists demanded the complete abolition of the county jail, suggesting that the BOP's failures proved that jail was an institution incapable of reform.[163]

The early trials of federal jails exemplified what would become a pattern for the immigration service over the remainder of the twentieth century. Frustrations with local jails—the conditions, the costs, the challenge of negotiating

FIGURE 13. La Tuna, one of the nation's first federal jails, opened in El Paso County, Texas, 1932. Courtesy of the El Paso Public Library, Border Heritage Center, Otis A. Aultman Collection, A5903.

with hundreds of individual municipalities—would regularly lead the immigration service to explore alternatives. Crises of legitimacy for the immigration service's detention practices led to carceral expansion, often in the name of reform. However, the immigration service never fully broke its bond with local jails. As policymakers embraced immigration law as the foremost tool of ensuring the "good stock" of the American citizenry, mechanisms for disposing of unwanted men, women, and children became all the more essential. Jails were the safety valve of a rapidly expanding detention apparatus. They were rarely the first choice, but their vast geographic coverage gave the immigration service a potential detention site in nearly every county in the United States.

For the migrants who found themselves trapped inside, jails were unbearable. Some detained people threatened their own lives in desperate appeals for freedom. Some mobilized attorneys and embassies, begging someone to care about an all-but-invisible population. Others suffered quietly as they endured violence from jailers and other inmates. All experienced the blistering monotony of day after day staring at blank cell walls in a foreign land. Whether it was incarceration in a brand-new federal facility or incarceration under the eye of a county sheriff, the result was the same: state-sponsored punishment for violating an imaginary line.

4

"A Concentration Camp of Their Own"

DETENTION IN AND AFTER WAR

WORLD WAR II UPENDED patterns of immigration to the United States. The danger of moving through war zones, alongside an intentionally byzantine wartime visa bureaucracy, left U.S. immigration quotas largely unfilled in the years leading up to and during the conflict.[1] The Immigration and Naturalization Service, however, would not have a quiet war.

In the months preceding the United States' official entry into the conflict, the Department of Justice (DOJ) drew up blueprints for an enemy alien program targeting German, Italian, and Japanese nationals residing in the United States. The DOJ designated the INS, created by a 1933 merger between the Bureau of Immigration and the Bureau of Naturalization, as its "custodial agency," tasked with detaining people suspected of being enemy aliens in immigration stations, hotels, hospitals, and local jails. For immigration officials who had spent much of the prior decades refining their capacity to incarcerate, the onset of war created opportunities to reimagine carceral space and revisit relationships with local law enforcement, all in the name of protecting the nation from totalitarianism. Two days after Japan's attack on Pearl Harbor, the INS detained nearly one thousand people deemed suspicious foreign nationals. In less than a week, it had detained more than 2,200.[2]

This chapter shows how the immigration service transformed ideology and political affiliation into a central justification for detaining noncitizens in the 1940s and 1950s and how global conflict transformed migrant incarceration into a national security imperative. When the war ended in 1945, the INS shifted its resources to tackle the postwar problem of "subversives," noncitizens the

United States feared brought dangerous ideas to American shores. These people fit many descriptions: Korean émigrés who had protested Japanese imperialism, Greek dockworkers stranded in the United States during wartime, Guatemalan civil rights leaders, Italian composers, German war brides.[3] What they had in common was a connection to communism or other "un-American" ideologies. As global war gave way to a new conflict of the "free world" of the United States and Western Europe versus the communist Soviet Union, American leaders expressed fears about migrants' transnational ties and potential communist infiltration via underprotected borders.[4] Just as exceptional curtailments of civil liberties were green-lit during wartime, the Cold War state of emergency allowed officials more discretion in detaining noncitizens they labeled dangerous; any affiliation with the Communist Party effectively became a violation of immigration law. Laws enabling ideological exclusion and deportation had been on the books since the eighteenth century, and the immigration service had targeted European anarchists and Bolsheviks as well as anticolonial Asian activists in the 1910s and 1920s, but campaigns against migrants with supposedly dangerous ideas took on a renewed intensity in the postwar world.[5]

Over the course of the 1950s, the DOJ fervently defended the state's detention power for "radical aliens" as a power insulated from constitutional and administrative norms. In cases brought by noncitizens detained at Ellis Island on the East Coast and Terminal Island on the West Coast, the immigration bureaucracy argued that it did not need to follow the Administrative Procedure Act, that it could hold migrants without bail, and that it could detain a migrant indefinitely if deportation was not possible. However, the global rise of fascism, as well as the atrocities of the Holocaust, armed activists with examples of oppressive state power, which they invoked in often-damning comparisons to the expanding reach of the DOJ and INS. Groups such as the American Committee for Protection of Foreign Born (ACPFB) and the American Civil Liberties Union (ACLU) mobilized mass publicity campaigns on behalf of detainees. Members of Congress introduced private bills for the relief of certain migrants. And incarcerated persons undertook highly visible acts of resistance, from lawsuits to protests to hunger strikes. Much of the media attention in the postwar period focused on the high-profile cases of Europeans facing years of jail time pending deportation hearings, due in part to extensive litigation undertaken on their behalf. In 1952, these critics secured a major victory when the INS proclaimed that it would *abandon* migrant incarceration in all but exceptional circumstances.

Yet, as this chapter shows, the U.S. migrant incarceration landscape extended far beyond the European causes célèbres who became the face of detention's postwar abuses. The postwar period was defined by a contradiction: INS detention infrastructure rapidly expanded in an age of government-proclaimed abolition. When World War II began, the United States had re-purposed tools of border control to meet its new detention mandate. By war's end, the United States took the technology and spaces developed in wartime and turned them toward policing Mexican migrants: men, women, and children whom the United States deemed surplus labor in the postwar world. As Americans increasingly saw some detained noncitizens as individuals, with personal narratives and campaigns devoted to their freedom, they viewed Mexican migrants as a racialized collective, a faceless "wave" of cheap labor, that could be removed via informal proceedings rather than legal deportation. Camps that once held enemy Germans became hubs for incarcerating Mexican farmworkers. Aircrafts that deployed paratroopers became planes to airlift deportees. Factories that had produced military vehicles were converted to urban detention centers. Critics also retained the language of wartime incarceration, lodging accusations of "concentration camps" both when Chinese war brides were detained in West Coast skyscrapers and when Mexicans were held in overcrowded jail centers along the southern border.

Still, protests about a diffused detention system targeting Mexicans or a West Coast immigration office warehousing the Chinese wives of American servicemen failed to mobilize the same national outcry or achieve the same success in courts as cases involving Europeans.[6] The events of the 1940s and 1950s reaffirmed that the DOJ's ability to detain migrants without political interference or scandal depended heavily on who it was detaining. Race, nationality, and gender continued to be significant factors in whose jailings Americans envisioned as just.

Policing the Enemy Alien

The history of wartime incarceration fits somewhat uneasily in the history of migrant incarceration—despite INS involvement, much of the incarceration was carried out via executive orders rather than under immigration laws, and the system targeted large numbers of citizens as well as permanent residents and noncitizens. In 2019, *Pacific Standard* published an article titled "The Legacy of Japanese Internment Lives on in Migrant Detention."[7] Yet the inverse was perhaps equally true. The legacy of migrant incarceration in the first decades of the twentieth century—its technologies, infrastructure, legal precedents, and workforce—had laid critical groundwork for Japanese incarceration and wartime internment.

In California's South Pedro Bay, just yards from mainland Los Angeles, sat Terminal Island, a site where Japanese fishermen had reeled in nets of sardines and albacore tuna since the early twentieth century. The island was a distinctly transnational place: Residents spoke a mixed dialect of Japanese and English, community centers showed Japanese films and dramas, and children attended elementary schools that celebrated both American and Japanese holidays. Terminal Island was also a key West Coast port; the federal government was uneasy about the presence of foreign-born Japanese residing nearby and surveilled the community for months before the United States entered the war. Hours after the December 1941 attack on Pearl Harbor, the FBI, the INS, and Los Angeles police began banging on doors, ransacking homes, and making arrests. First they apprehended community leaders, then teachers and priests, and finally, all Japan-born fishermen.[8] Though the FBI took the lead, the INS also made arrests, apprehending eighty-seven Japanese fishermen on the basis of "unspecified irregularities in their Immigration Status."[9] INS agents drew on their experiences raiding Chinatowns at the turn of the twentieth century and searching immigrant homes and businesses in the urban "deportations delirium" of the 1920s and 1930s.[10] As in many prior cases, they did not have warrants.[11] In February 1942, the federal government ordered a full evacuation of Terminal Island. "It was one of the saddest moments in my life," a Japanese pastor said of crossing the drawbridge to leave home for the final time.[12]

A month after the raids, the island that had once been home to more than five thousand Japanese residents resembled a deserted mining town, with piles of junk, smoldering fires, and broken furniture from the lives uprooted. The land had been "'cleaned' of the alien menace," the Los Angeles Times praised.[13]

The fishermen arrested by the INS were sent to internment camps throughout the country, including Fort Lincoln, a frigid North Dakota outpost just south of Bismarck. As the men disembarked trains, they were greeted by Border Patrol agents armed with submachine guns—yet another mobilization of the federal government's police power over migrants.

The INS-run enemy alien program ran parallel to the confinement of ethnic Japanese by the War Relocation Authority, a wartime federal agency that operated the massive incarceration camps for Nisei, U.S. citizens of Japanese descent, as well as Issei, first-generation immigrants from Japan. These camps, with their rows of identical, tar paper–covered barracks slicing through desert landscapes, became the most enduring image of U.S. wartime incarceration.[14] However, these were only one element in a vast, interagency carceral network built to accommodate the U.S. wartime detention demands—a system historian Tetsuden Kashima calls "rife with internal competition, lack of coordination, and *ad hoc* decisionmaking." Between 1941 and 1943, the INS operated at least sixty-five facilities for the internment of enemy nationals.[15] Federal officials believed that they had greater skill in adjudicating loyalty among the "Caucasian race" than among Japanese nationals. A 1942 survey among California district attorneys, sheriffs, and police chiefs similarly found that local law enforcement identified Japanese as the group most likely to commit espionage.[16] While most apprehended Italians and Germans were released by the DOJ, most apprehended Japanese were sent to INS-run camps.[17]

The scale and circumstances of wartime incarceration were unprecedented, but as prior chapters have illustrated, this was not the first time the INS had managed a fluid, nationwide network of carceral sites. Compared with the other agencies involved—some of which, like the War Relocation Authority, had not existed until the war began—the INS boasted significant incarceration experience. The roundup of "enemy aliens" relied on existing INS barracks and beds at Ellis Island, Angel Island, Seattle, and four other large immigration stations.[18] When the INS moved noncitizens to internment camps, it placed them on the same deportation trains, supervised by the same deportation officer who had expelled thousands of migrants from the United States in the prior two decades.[19] And beyond the agency's own immigration stations, the INS also looked to familiar partners for jail space. When the federal government secured the Los Angeles County Jail as a staging ground for interning people of Japanese descent (as well as smaller numbers of Germans and Italians), it built upon decades of borrowing that same jail space as a staging ground for repatriation and deportation campaigns involving Mexican migrants.[20] (Figure 14.) Jails and other sites of migrant incarceration provided flexible space that could be reimagined for whichever project of racial control and removal the state deemed most pressing.

Some of the people the INS detained during the war were longtime residents of the United States; others were forced to cross U.S. borders for the sole purpose of being incarcerated in INS facilities. In January 1942, ministers of foreign affairs from the United States and various Latin American countries agreed to an "inter-American removal process," in which Axis nationals would be transported to the United States for internment. American officials exerted considerable pressure on their Latin American neighbors to consent to the project, envisioning Japanese Latin Americans as a pool of people who could

FIGURE 14. Japanese nationals detained at Los Angeles County Jail in the days following the attack on Pearl Harbor, 1941. *Source: Los Angeles Times* Photographic Archive, Library Special Collections, Charles E. Young Research Library, University of California, Los Angeles.

be exchanged for U.S. citizens trapped in Axis nations. Some nations, such as Brazil, refused, assuring the United States that they could surveil the Japanese community themselves.[21] Other nations, most notably Peru, were enthusiastic partners. Through this initiative, the INS detained people like the Shibayama family, a mother and father along with their six children, who in March 1944 were apprehended by local law enforcement in Peru and passed into U.S. custody.[22] Even though the federal government had all but demanded the arrival of Japanese Latin Americans, they were classified as "illegal aliens" upon arrival. This was, in part, a recognition of the power to detain under immigration law. Officials feared that Latin American detainees in U.S. territory would attempt to file habeas corpus claims in federal courts and hoped that classifying them as immigration law violators would curtail their legal options.[23] The Shibayamas became eight of the more than two thousand Japanese Peruvians interned in prison camps run by the immigration service.

The journey from Peru to the United States took three weeks by boat. Officials seized the Shibayamas' Peruvian identity documents, separated them from one another aboard the *U.S.S. Cuba,* and granted them only sparing moments above deck. When the family disembarked their ship in New Orleans, officials immediately asked them to disrobe. They were sprayed with the carcinogenic pesticide DDT—the same humiliating and dangerous process that the INS developed for Mexican migrants crossing the border.[24] Beginning in the 1910s, the U.S. Public Health Service had constructed disinfection plants at major points of entry along the U.S.-Mexico line, arguing that an "iron-clad quarantine" was the only way to prevent the spread of disease across borders. All people traversing the border from Mexico, said a Public Health Service surgeon in 1918, were "considered as likely to be vermin infested."[25] Decades later, and despite considerable protest from affected migrants, these invasive practices persisted, now attaching the stigma of biological threat to Japanese arriving from Latin America.

The categorization of "illegal entrant" would continue to shape the lives of forced migrants long after they left internment camps. Isamu Shibayama had been just thirteen when he and his siblings were arrested. By the time he was sixteen, the war was over, and Peru refused to take his family back. Isamu became a very young man without a country. While he was serving in the U.S. military during the Korean War, a supervisor attempted to help Isamu naturalize so that he could obtain a higher security clearance—the INS denied his application because he had not been legally admitted to the United States and the agency reopened deportation proceedings against his entire family. Though the Shibayamas were eventually granted temporary relief and gained legal status, Isamu would spend the rest of his life fighting for redress for the ways his family had suffered: first in the U.S. courts, after Japanese Peruvians were denied the $20,000 restitution checks granted to incarcerated Japanese Americans, and later in international human rights tribunals.

The Battle over Ellis Island

As the war ended, the Soviet Union began a dogged, often bloody march of installing communist regimes throughout the nations of Eastern European. The Soviet-U.S. relationship quickly soured, as the United States saw the spread of communism as a threat to its political influence in Europe and its economic interests worldwide.[26] In the immediate aftermath of World War II, the INS expanded its apprehension efforts for "foreign-born radicals," some of whom were seized at the border and some of whom were arrested after years of living in the United States.[27] The prior decades had confirmed that deportations were subject to few constitutional safeguards and thus "offered a convenient way to attack individual Communists while the other mechanisms of repression were being developed," writes historian Ellen Schrecker.[28] Prior to World War II, most of policymakers' rationales for detention suggested that if the United States released deportable migrants, they could escape the reach of immigration authorities. Postwar, the DOJ explicitly acknowledged that it was wielding immigration detention as a national security tool, a way to eliminate dangerous radicals who were "walking the streets" of the United States.[29] Migrants could not be released, and in many cases, could not even know the evidence being used against them, because it would compromise the safety of the American public.

Throughout the 1940s, Congressman Sam Hobbs, an Alabama Democrat, repeatedly introduced legislation to expand the detention power of the DOJ and the agency he called "the immigration and deportation service."[30] Though none of his proposed bills ever passed both houses of Congress, a bill Hobbs introduced in 1949, H.R. 10, would become a road map for the legislative expansion of the government's detention power. H.R. 10 authorized the *lifetime detention* of noncitizens suspected of subversive activity or affiliation. It did so through two key provisions: The first offered the government the power to detain migrants until their deportation was possible—a day that for many deportees would never come, particularly as nations such as the Soviet Union closed their borders. The second exempted the INS from the Administrative Procedure Act of 1946, a law governing how federal agencies developed rules and regulations. Though few individuals had more at stake in agency power than migrants in deportation proceedings, the courts had been inconclusive as to whether they were eligible for the Administrative Procedure Act's protections.[31]

Hobbs's persistent efforts to expand the DOJ's detention authority triggered alarm from civil liberties activists. In an age where nearly every attorney or organization representing the rights of noncitizens was deemed a potential communist, defending people with radical affiliations was a delicate balancing act.[32] At mid-century, the American Committee for Protection of Foreign Born was pivotal in focusing public attention on the issue of detention and shifting the way the practice was perceived. Its main rhetorical tactic involved comparing proposed legislation with totalitarianism.[33] Through bulletins and flyers decrying Hobbs's plan to create "Concentration Camps in America," activists reframed detention not just in carceral terms but in distinctly fascist ones. The group accused the INS of "Gestapo tactics" and distributed photographs of

American families with mothers, often labor leaders, whom the United States was in the process of deporting or denaturalizing. Its message emphasized that violations of civil liberties would impact noncitizens first, before reaching into the lives of citizens as well.

Despite the ACPFB's best efforts, the spike in anticommunist sentiment accompanying the onset of the Korean War birthed an even more expansive version of the Hobbs framework: the Internal Security Act of 1950.[34] The new law, also known as the McCarran Act, required the registration of Communist Party members and authorized the exclusion and retroactive deportation of communists and members of other "subversive groups," including Fascist or Nazi Party members. The law deemed it "immaterial" how long ago or for what amount of time a noncitizen had been affiliated with such a political group.[35] In practice, this meant that entire steamships of displaced persons arriving from nations such as Italy, where inspectors would be hard-pressed to find anyone without a fleeting "affiliation" to that nation's totalitarian government, now faced extended detentions. The legislation also contained a subsection called the Emergency Detention Act, permitting the detention of any person, including citizens, who might commit "espionage or sabotage" if the president declared an "internal security emergency." The bill's sponsors cited the 1944 Supreme Court case of *Korematsu v. United States* and other legal rulings upholding Japanese wartime incarceration to argue that the Constitution sanctioned the detention of disloyal citizens—a provision that terrified the ACPFB as well as African American civil rights groups, who feared that the law would be weaponized against Black radicals and critics of the government.[36]

The Internal Security Act triggered immediate chaos for the U.S. detention system. Two weeks after it was signed, immigration officials in New York City detained nearly one thousand people, pushing detention infrastructure to its brink. Thirteen thousand seamen were held on ships in the harbor while the immigration service investigated their backgrounds and political beliefs. The State Department temporarily stopped issuing visas due to lack of investigatory capacity.[37] At the center of this administrative maelstrom, in the shadow of the Statue of Liberty, was Ellis Island.

———

In the first half of the twentieth century, jails were the most common site of immigration detention for most of the country; centralized federal stations such as Ellis Island and Angel Island were notable exceptions. Though Ellis

Island had detention facilities, at the peak of the site's use, only a small fraction of migrants would see them. Prior to the quota laws, about 2 percent of arrivals at Ellis Island were excluded, typically on the basis of illness, disability, or poverty.[38] The role of Ellis Island shifted with the passage of the 1924 Johnson-Reed Act, as migrants who arrived in excess of their nation's quota could be detained in Upper New York Bay until officials arranged for their deportation. Still, towns throughout the United States invoked Ellis Island as the gold standard of detention, a stark contrast to the ramshackle jail conditions in the rest of the country.[39]

By the postwar period, America's storied immigration hub had become a de facto detention center for a mix of immigrants, visitors, stowaways, unaccompanied children, displaced persons, and political dissidents from across the globe. About one-third of Ellis Island detainees sought entry to the United States with status not yet determined, while the other two-thirds awaited deportation.[40]

The question of whether Ellis Island had become a prison created tension for immigration administrators trying to explain the site's evolving role to the public. The INS suggested that the site was more a "self-contained city" than the concentration camp its critics described. The media fixated on stories of women attempting to make the dormitories livable by hanging up lace curtains or scrubbing the decades of grime from the walls.[41] (Figure 15.) This emphasis on domestic life underscored that these were not the temporary medical evaluations of the early twentieth century; immigrant families were living substantial periods of their lives within the walls of detention sites, as the government probed their potentially subversive pasts.

In an effort to garner more favorable press coverage of the island, officials invited journalists to tour the detention facilities on an annual basis. In 1948, a journalist reported that German migrants had surrounded the tour group, pleading their cases and declaring their love of democracy. The migrants yelled to the reporters that the detention conditions and food had been temporarily improved to impress the media. Other times the press tours seemed to veer into bribery—before a 1949 tour, all reporters were fed a filet mignon lunch at the island's cafeteria. When reporters inquired whether this was the kind of food served to detainees, the Ellis Island commissioner laughed and replied, "There are only so many filets to a steer."[42]

Dissatisfied with media portrayals, people detained at Ellis Island took action to reshape the narrative of their incarceration. In 1948, five men began a hunger strike to protest their detention without bail. Gerhart Eisler, a man the

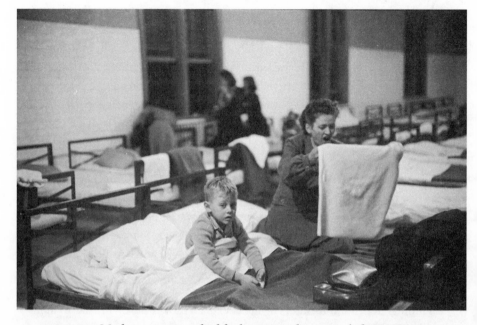

FIGURE 15. Mother preparing a bed for her son in the women's detention barracks at Ellis Island, 1950. *Life Magazine* described Ellis Island as "a gray and gloomy place suddenly full of bewildered people who have become victims of American politics," in text accompanying images by photographer Alfred Eisenstaedt. The article stressed the long delays caused by the McCarran Act, as officials interrogated migrants about their political affiliations. *Source:* Alfred Eisenstaedt / *LIFE* Picture Collection / Shutterstock.

DOJ declared "the brains" of the Communist Party in the United States, alongside four other labor organizers, wrote a letter to Attorney General Tom Clark on February 25, 1948:

> On your order we have been locked up in Ellis Island under what the Nazis called "protective arrest." . . . If you are permitted to imprison people like us and deny us our freedom on bail because we oppose your administration program of war, imperialist aggression, anti-labor legislation and destruction of civil rights—then no one in America is safe.[43]

The letter concluded that the detainees anticipated broad support from "all true Americans," particularly organized labor and African Americans, groups whom they saw as particularly vulnerable to the vagaries of DOJ power. The hunger strike lasted nearly six days, after which the court relented and released four of the five men on $3,500 bail each.[44] The night Eisler and his cohort posted bail, several hundred protesters gathered in Times Square, chanting "Deport Jim Crow" and demanding the dismissal of charges against the hunger strikers.[45]

The crowd's invocation of Jim Crow highlighted an evolving strategy of immigrants' rights activists: linking the prejudice faced by Black Americans to that encountered by noncitizens.[46] During the Hobbs bill fight, many activists had drawn similar connections, labeling Hobbs a racist Dixiecrat and noting that the majority of the bill's support came from "poll tax states."[47] Black migrants, including one of Eisler's fellow hunger strikers, also found themselves incarcerated in Ellis Island's "McCarran Wing."[48] Immigration officials detained Claudia Jones, a Trinidad-born communist activist and intellectual, for nearly a year before her 1955 deportation. In a letter from Ellis Island, Jones identified parallels between the racialized exclusion of Black Americans and that of Black noncitizens, writing of "the 15 million Negro Americans, whose sons serve in jimcrow units in Korea, they are no strangers to the second-class, jimcrow justice likewise meted out to West Indians of foreign birth."[49] C.L.R. James, a Trinidadian author, activist, and longtime target of U.S. surveillance, similarly used his four months on Ellis Island to launch a broad critique of American state power. He produced an essay on *Moby Dick*, which he mailed to every member of Congress. The central theme of the novel, James wrote, was "how the society of free individualism would give birth to totalitarianism and be unable to defend itself against it."[50] The "sailors, renegades, and castaways" aboard the *Pequod* were not terribly different from the diverse migrants he found himself detained alongside at postwar Ellis Island. Both Jones and James stressed the "insoluble contradictions" posed by a detention center filled with ideological dissidents from around the globe—most of whom received nary a hint of due process—as the United States celebrated its own liberalism and exceptionality in the postwar world.[51]

Stories of "Ellis Island's Prisoners" became a powerful organizing tool for groups like the ACPFB. Some campaigns focused on detained persons who were notable because of their fame or the fame of their interlocutors: When the immigration service detained the Nobel Prize–winning scientist Irene Joliot-Curie in 1948, Albert Einstein personally wired the DOJ requesting her release.[52] Others were notable for the novelty of their cases. In 1953, the United States detained a teenage stowaway named Karl-Heinz Pfeiffer, who had walked from Poland to West Germany before sneaking onto a Pan American Airways flight bound for New York.[53] The media pointed to Pfeiffer's yearlong detention as evidence of the severe enforcement of the new immigration law.[54] Perhaps the most widely reported and cited of the "Ellis Island Prisoner" tales was the case of Ellen Knauff. The DOJ excluded Knauff based on secret evidence and deemed her ineligible for judicial review, two administrative powers granted by the McCarran Act. Her case created a precedent that legal scholar Charles D. Weisselberg calls "the Supreme Court's fullest statements of the plenary power doctrine," confirming the sweeping power of Congress to confine and exclude noncitizens without due process and without judicial intervention.[55]

Ellen Knauff's immigration journey had been a complex one. She was born in Germany in 1915 and fled to Czechoslovakia after Adolf Hitler rose to power.[56] In 1939, she traveled to England as a refugee, where she served in the Royal Air Force and married an American serviceman. On August 14, 1948, Knauff attempted to enter the United States under the War Brides Act of 1945; instead, she was apprehended and placed in detention at Ellis Island. Two months later, the assistant commissioner of immigration recommended her permanent exclusion without a hearing on the grounds that her admission would be prejudicial to the interests of the United States.[57] The DOJ refused to disclose the evidence against Knauff, claiming that it would put the nation at risk.[58] Knauff remained in Ellis Island detention until the Supreme Court agreed to hear her case in December 1949—more than a year after her initial arrival. In a four-to-three decision, the Court ruled that the president had the power to impose additional restrictions and prohibitions on entry into the United States during a "national emergency," including detaining and removing a noncitizen without a hearing.[59] The power over entry and exclusion was carried out on the ground not by the president but by immigration officials. As ACLU attorney Arthur Garfield Hays observed, immigration agents served as "the arresting officers, stenographers, judges, and executioners," vested with a virtually unreviewable power.[60] The Supreme Court cited *Fong Yue Ting v. United States* and *Nishimura Ekiu v. United States* in declaring that the admission of aliens to the country represented a sovereign right of the United States under any standard of entry the executive branch determined.[61] In a particularly blunt invocation of plenary power, the Court asserted, "Whatever the procedure authorized by Congress is, it is due process as far as an alien denied entry is concerned."[62]

The Supreme Court's ruling evoked a massive outpouring of support for Knauff, due in part to the sensitive media coverage the case received. Knauff was an ideal victim to illustrate the excesses of detention power: young,

European, the wife of an American serviceman.[63] Throughout the trial, the ACLU methodically delivered information to the *St. Louis Post-Dispatch*, which ran a series of fifteen sympathetic editorials on her case. Multiple congressmen introduced bills to free Knauff, citing the dangers of "holding a girl prisoner, on unreleased evidence."[64] In March 1951, the attorney general relented and granted Knauff a full exclusion hearing before a Board of Special Inquiry. Knauff was freed through administrative discretion after nearly three years of detention and legal limbo.[65] When the DOJ was forced to show evidence to justify its decision—both to the judiciary and to the public—its case against Knauff crumbled.[66]

Detention on the West Coast

Though Ellis Island captured most of the public attention in the postwar period, the detention landscape of the West Coast was rapidly changing as well. In 1938, the Bureau of Prisons opened a new facility at Terminal Island, Los Angeles, one of several federal jails promised to disgruntled sheriffs and municipalities. The jail sat just yards from the harbor where Japanese migrants had built a thriving fishing community. Terminal Island was the BOP's crown jewel: a $2 million project with rows of identical steel cells, three lookout towers, and a machine gun for every guard. (Figure 16.) If the county jails used at the beginning of the century were often little more than repurposed barns, Los Angeles's new federal jail was something very different.[67]

Twelve years after the Terminal Island jail opened its doors, it became the site of one of the most high-profile postwar immigration detention legal battles, testing the limits of noncitizen incarceration justified on security grounds. The case of the "Terminal Island Four" was a campaign for four noncitizens— Miriam Stevenson, a British dance instructor; David Hyun, a Korean architect; Frank Carlson, a former Communist Party educator from Poland; and Harry Carlisle, a writer from England—all detained for their alleged affiliation with the Communist Party.[68] When the DOJ originally arrested the four defendants in 1949 and 1950 they were granted bail and released. But after the passage of the Internal Security Act, the DOJ issued new warrants for their arrest. The 1950 law gave the attorney general the power to detain migrants considered "dangerous" without bail, while stipulating that communists and anarchists were *presumptively* dangerous.

The case of *Carlson v. Landon* landed in the Supreme Court in November 1951. One of its major legal questions centered on who bore the burden of

FIGURE 16. Interior view of cells at the Terminal Island federal jail in the Los Angeles Harbor, 1938. Courtesy of University of Southern California Libraries and California Historical Society.

proof in immigration detention cases: Was it the DOJ's obligation to show evidence that a detained person represented a flight risk or a danger to the community, or was it the detained people's burden to prove they were not? Justice Felix Frankfurter wrote in a personal letter to Justice Robert H. Jackson that he did not "give a damn about these aliens" but, rather, feared that the Terminal Island Four ruling could effectively make *all* ideological deportees ineligible for bail.[69] Jackson countered that incarceration without bond had been the exception rather than the rule even under the new security legislation and insisted that Frankfurter's anxiety about mass detention without bail was unfounded. Though Jackson conceded some discomfort about denying bail, he could not find a strong enough legal logic to deny the attorney general the right to exercise administrative discretion.[70]

In March 1952, the Supreme Court approved the detention of noncitizens pending deportation hearings, for any amount of time, if the state considered them a danger to the public interest. "Detention is necessarily a part of this deportation procedure," read the Court's decision. "Otherwise aliens arrested

222

for deportation would have opportunities to hurt the United States during the pendency of deportation proceedings."[71] The attorney general was not required to identify specific acts of sabotage or subversive activity; supporting the Communist Party's philosophy qualified as "adequate grounds" for detention without bail. The INS reveled in the Court's decision, swiftly apprehending and returning to jail people it had previously released on bail.[72]

With expanding legal powers to detain, the INS also continued to experiment with detention space that was further removed from the carceral infrastructure of prisons and jails.[73] In 1940, a fire destroyed Angel Island. The fire came just three years before the United States repealed fifteen separate Chinese exclusion statutes, deeming the laws politically untenable during a global conflict in which China was a U.S. ally.[74] Immigration officials refocused attention on policing Chinese women entering through the 1945 War Brides Act, the same law under which Ellen Knauff had arrived. Women from China faced intense scrutiny as officials clung to long-standing fears about Chinese migrants perpetrating a vast conspiracy against the United States.[75] With Angel Island in ashes, officials turned to a downtown San Francisco office building, 630 Sansome, as their new center of migrant incarceration. (Figure 17.)

Despite the protests of American GIs who found themselves unable to communicate with their detained spouses, authorities held 450 people in 630 Sansome each night while investigating their immigration cases. The majority of those detained were wives of servicemen, as well as an occasional Chinese student, diplomat, or scientist.[76] Migrants regularly waited several months for a Board of Special Inquiry hearing.[77] Civil liberties activists argued that the cause was not understaffing but, rather, a deliberate effort on the part of the INS to limit communication between families.

Leong Bick Ha, the wife of U.S. Army Sergeant Ng Bak Teung, was one of nearly four thousand Chinese migrants detained at 630 Sansome between 1946 and 1948.[78] INS officials detained women on one floor of the building and men on another, separating Leong Bick Ha and her fifteen-year-old son. As marriage and birth certificates were rarely issued in rural China, the limited INS workforce relied on its own investigatory tools and administrative discretion.[79] In the meantime, Leong Bick Ha waited. The building had no outdoor recreation area; she sat on her bed for hours on end. She ate unfamiliar foods and was allowed little contact with her son or the outside world. After three months of delays, Leong Bick Ha received her official interview—she was so anxious that immigration officials prescribed her sedatives.[80] The inspector asked her exhaustive questions about her husband's dietary habits, about their

FIGURE 17. U.S. Appraiser's Building at 630 Sansome Street, San Francisco, ca. 1940s. The building became a site of detention, primarily for Chinese women, in the 1940s; Immigration and Customs Enforcement continues to operate a field office out of it today. Courtesy of Alan J. Canterbury, San Francisco History Center, San Francisco Public Library.

matchmaker in China, and about who had been present at their wedding sixteen years prior.[81] The night after her immigration interview, feeling more uncertain than ever about her future, Leong Bick Ha hanged herself in a shower stall on the building's thirteenth floor.[82]

Leong Bick Ha's story was not an isolated tragedy. On June 2, 1948, Gin Hop, a veteran and Chinese herbalist in Aberdeen, Washington, received a phone call from his attorney. "Your wife is sitting on a wall hundreds of feet in the air and threatening to jump," the lawyer told him.[83] Gin Hop's wife, Heng Loy, had been detained for six months and faced imminent deportation after failing to convince authorities of her marriage's legitimacy. Many San Franciscans first became aware of the unmarked downtown detention center as Heng Loy's crisis unfolded. A crowd of five thousand people gathered below and witnessed a police officer jerk the woman away from the ledge.

The English-language San Francisco media praised the heroics of the police officers and immigration inspectors in preventing Heng Loy's death. They paid little attention to the plight of the migrants in the office building.[84] The Chinese-language media in San Francisco, however, painted their incarceration as both a humanitarian tragedy and a disaster for the United States' global reputation; the *Chinese Pacific Weekly* wrote: "If the Chinese Communists were seeking for material to make their anti-American attacks, the case of Leong Bick Ha and Heng Loy would furnish them with their best propaganda material."[85] Following Leong Bick Ha's death, one hundred Chinese women undertook a hunger strike, a remarkable gesture dismissed by immigration officials, who insisted that such strikes rarely lasted long.[86] Still, officials at the detention station feared that more deaths were imminent, with the station's director predicting an "epidemic of suicides, particularly if these long detentions continue."[87] Within a few years, suicide attempts in immigration custody had become so commonplace that they received an entire section in the INS Detention Officers Manual. The guidelines instructed officers in cold bureaucratic language not to remove a body but to take photographs and put all the details in writing.[88]

While the detention of the Terminal Island Four activated the now-familiar advocacy of the ACPFB, the plight of the detainees at 630 Sansome became visible only when detainees took the most extreme measures. Holding thousands of war brides in a county jail would have created devastating Cold War optics for the immigration service, even if Americans viewed Chinese women with suspicion—but who would have suspected that a regular financial district office building was a site of migrant incarceration?

Humane Administration and the Mexican Exception

Concurrent with the legal battles and agency experiments with new sites of detention was the passage of the first comprehensive immigration law since 1917: the 1952 Immigration and Nationality Act, also known as the McCarran-Walter Act. The law was, in the words of historian Mae Ngai, "less an overhaul than a hardening of existing policy."[89] Despite growing concern about the viability of an unequal system of quotas in the postwar world, the 1952 legislation maintained the quota system. Legislators attempted to downplay the quotas' racist underpinnings, instead reframing them as a sociologically based tool to maintain the nation's "cultural balance."[90]

Detention policy was one area of significant change under the McCarran-Walter Act. The 1952 legislation endorsed detention only in exceptional circumstances, calling instead for a range of parole alternatives. The legislation's passage is often interpreted by scholars as a triumph in the history of migrant incarceration: a rare moment in which the state imagined and implemented an alternative to jailing.[91] These accounts can overlook how oppressive the systems of parole became for migrants caught in new surveillance regimes. And for the thousands of migrants who were *not* granted parole in the years following 1952, the reports of detention's end were greatly exaggerated. The same year that Ellis Island finally closed its doors, the INS was laying plans to radically remake detention in the Southwest.

The federal government's denouncement of migrant incarceration was the culmination of years of progressive groups' activism. Policymakers questioned whether administrative detention, like other civil rights problems at home, was a reputational liability and contradiction to the United States' human rights rhetoric abroad.[92] At the 1952 hearings for the new immigration law, groups such as the ACLU, the Hebrew Sheltering and Immigrant Aid Society, and the International Longshoremen's and Warehousemen's Union wielded the language of fascist repression and civil rights violation that the ACPFB had pioneered. They benefited from the exhaustion the *Knauff* case and others like it had produced: Many lawmakers were weary of the extended drama of Ellis Island prisoners and felt uneasy about the precedent of unrestrained noncitizen detention. The turn away from detention was part of a growing deinstitutionalization movement at mid-century, as frustrations with institutional conditions gained traction and the Supreme Court set new constitutional limits on civil confinement.[93]

The future of detention was also a question of economics. In the bill's hearings one of the most forceful rebukes came from a surprising source. Welburn Mayock, the attorney for American President Lines, Ltd.—the largest American shipping company in the Pacific—evocatively condemned the "skyscraper concentration camp" at 630 Sansome.[94] Despite moralist language, Mayock's primary concern was money; his client had a significant financial interest in eliminating immigration detention. Since the late nineteenth century, the United States had required steamship companies to pay for the detention and return of migrants the nation rejected, as well as for crew members of their steamships who absconded.[95] Companies that did not promptly foot the bill faced stiff penalties and could be barred from American ports.[96]

Steamship companies insisted that it should not be their responsibility to adjudicate U.S. immigration law, yet, for much of the twentieth century, shipping and passenger traffic were big enough business that profits far outweighed penalties.[97] By the 1950s, airlines were footing the bill as well; in the case of the German teen stowaway Karl-Heinz Pfeiffer, Pan American Airways received a $300 fine, alongside a $1,500 bill for Pfeiffer's yearlong stay on Ellis Island.[98] American President Lines had paid an estimated $550,000 in detention expenses in the prior five years, including substantial fees for the women detained at 630 Sansome. Pressure from private industry became a major factor in the government's disavowal of migrant detention; President Truman called removing the "archaic requirement" that required companies to pay detention costs a strength of a law otherwise riddled with discrimination.[99]

In response to ideological and economic pressure, the 1952 law placed a six-month limit on migrant detention. If a migrant could not be deported within that time frame, the system of "supervisory parole" was activated. Parole was not a "humane," or even noncarceral, alternative to detention. It was an effort, in the words of one Louisiana senator, "to make conditions so distasteful [migrants] would not want to live in the United States."[100] Authorities required paroled migrants to appear in person before an immigration officer at scheduled intervals, to offer information about their whereabouts and activities, and, perhaps most disturbingly, to submit to medical and psychiatric examinations at the government's discretion.[101] The new policy further fused the criminal and immigration systems by inflicting punishments of fines and jail time on migrants who did not follow its long list of rules. An ACPFB representative explained, "[The] noncitizen becomes a walking jail, with the disadvantage that he has to supply his own food and lodging."[102]

Following the new policy's passage, the ACPFB collected letters from parolees that it used to highlight the social and economic costs of surveillance. "Reporting weekly to Ellis Island means losing half a day's work at least. For many, weekly reporting makes it impossible to hold a job and support our families," wrote one parolee.[103] Clara Gelman worked as a neonatal nurse; she had to explain to her patients and boss that she could be arrested if she did not take a particular day off work to report to immigration officials. "Many people get the idea that since I'm on probation, that I must have committed some sort of crime," she wrote. "Since the welfare and health of the new born baby and mother are entrusted in my hands, some people become suspicious of me." Gelman declared supervisory parole "a living death," a practice that produced both social alienation and material loss for the noncitizens under its watch.[104]

Supervisory parole also failed to bring migrant detention to a standstill. The INS commenced the new detention policy in November 1954; that year, the INS had reported the highest number of detentions in the service's history—more than half a million migrants were detained, and of that number, 83,000 migrants were held in three hundred contracted state, county, and city jails.[105] Under the revised policy, the DOJ announced plans to close six seaport detention facilities including Ellis Island. Migrants would be released "so long as they appear to be deserving of their personal liberty," decreed Attorney General Brownell.[106] The following year, Brownell proudly reported a 100 percent reduction in detentions. The Eisenhower administration had brought about "the abolition of indiscriminate detention," the attorney general said, emphasizing that most migrants had appeared for their hearings without the use of incarceration.[107]

Despite the attorney general's praise of the nondetention policy, when Ellis Island finally shuttered in 1954, the immigration service moved several dozen detainees to the Federal House of Detention in New York City and the Westchester County Jail. The ACLU insisted that holding migrants in local jails was "contradictory to the letter and spirit" of the 1952 law.[108] The law gave the attorney general authority to acquire land, build new detention facilities, and remodel or repair buildings, sheds, and office quarters for migrant detention. Yet there was nothing in the law specifying that jails or prisons could be used as a place of detention. A few weeks later, the sheriff of Westchester County demanded that the INS stop sending migrants to his facility, expressing discomfort with holding people in jail without a charge.[109] Though the INS eventually transferred the Ellis Island migrants to an Upper West Side hotel, the agency refused to concede that jails and prisons were off-limits for the immigration service. After all, it had fifty years of precedent on its side.[110]

The chief caveat to the "end of detention" narrative perpetuated in scholarship and by policymakers at the time was that detention was expanding, not retreating, at the U.S.-Mexico border. Officials rationalized this contradiction by arguing that detention along the southern border was fundamentally *different* from the detention practices that had become a locus of controversy. These detentions were shorter. There were rarely long legal battles. And they involved Mexican laborers rather than European radicals. Yet arguments *for* detention along the southern border also often made the same claims about detention as a national security imperative that undergirded internal security legislation of the 1940s and 1950s. During a 1953 visit to California, Attorney General Brownell observed that "the flow of illegal aliens into California from Mexico is critical and endangering national security," providing an "easy avenue" not just for Mexican laborers but for alleged subversives from all over the world.[111] His argument echoed what immigration officials had been insisting for decades: National security was impossible without aggressive border securitization.[112] Detention in the mid-century Southwest became an important trial run for incarceration efforts in the second half of the twentieth century: The INS actively courted sheriffs and local cooperation while also relentlessly pursuing federal money for immigration-specific detention sites that reduced dependence on localities. In the 1920s, officials had fought for federal jails that could hold a variety of federal offenders. With the advent of "Operation Wetback," federal officials requested millions of dollars for carceral sites specialized for facilitating mass deportations.[113]

Southern border detentions were frequently brief, averaging between two and three days until the next bus, train, or airplane returned to Mexico.[114] Most Mexican migrants did not engage in extended legal battles against their deportations, and in fact, very few Mexicans saw a courtroom at all. The immigration service pressured Mexicans to accept "voluntary departures," moving swiftly from a brief detention stint to a return trip.[115] A voluntary departure enabled migrants to avoid jail time in the present and in the future: As there was little legal or bureaucratic adjudication, there would be minimal detention while awaiting removal; and since migrants would not acquire a formal record of deportation, they were less likely to receive a criminal sentence for illegal entry should they return. Detention statistics compiled by the INS erratically included and excluded Mexicans from their calculations of how many detentions the agency had carried out.[116] Attorney General Brownell adopted a similarly evasive rhetorical approach, claiming in 1955 that only seventy-five migrants were detained, "not counting Mexican wetbacks."[117]

Unlike the ideological dissidents who dominated the immigration discourse in the rest of the country, migrants detained in the Southwest were primarily agricultural workers. Many were braceros, temporary workers from Mexico brought in to alleviate U.S wartime labor shortages, who had over-stayed their contracts.[118] Others were unauthorized migrants, some of whom had been unable to secure a highly competitive Bracero permit and some who chose to skip the bureaucracy and cross the border without authorization. Mexican migrants were concentrated in the Southwest, where the INS spent the vast majority of its enforcement budget, yet the INS also worked with jails adjacent to farming communities in the rest of the country—from Rock Island County Jail, on the border of Iowa and Illinois, where migrants had cultivated corn and soybeans, to Klamath County Jail, in Oregon's Klamath Basin, where migrants had grown potatoes and sugar beets.[119] Mexicans were not the only people caught in a system of incarceration that the attorney general insisted did not exist. Athel Esther Johnson, a thirty-seven-year-old Jamaican farm-worker, was detained alongside Mexican migrants in a Spokane, Washington, jail for overstaying a wartime labor permit. Media reports, as well as other detained persons, remarked upon Johnson's racial and cultural difference from what had now become the prototypical Mexican "immigration prisoner."[120]

In 1953, the Eisenhower administration initiated "Operation Wetback," a federal campaign and spectacle intended to drive migrant workers toward the Bracero Program and to curtail what INS Commissioner Joseph Swing declared "an actual invasion of the United States."[121] Between 1953 and 1955 the INS apprehended and removed 801,069 Mexican migrants from work camps, bars, and the streets of American communities, as fawning media coverage celebrated the heroics of the Border Patrol's war on Mexicans.[122] Historian Kelly Lytle Hernández has described Operation Wetback as a new form of crime control mechanism, as the Border Patrol "[recoded] migration control as a site of policing crime and punishing criminals," thus making its work compatible with American understandings of how emerging social problems ought to be managed.[123] As in other overpoliced communities, an interaction with law enforcement for Mexican migrants now culminated in incarceration. Detention sites became the staging ground for the convoys of transportation that would remove Mexican migrants en masse. In Operation Wetback's first full year, the INS detained 508,566 migrants across three hundred local jails, as well as in INS-operated facilities.[124]

On the ground, immigration officials leaned into fearmongering about the dangerous border crosser and detainee, recasting *every* Mexican migrant as a potential threat. Immigration authorities used the growing numbers of escapes from detention camps as evidence that Mexican migrants were not the passive laborers they had once envisioned, a fear heightened by ongoing efforts to organize Mexican farmworkers, miners, and factory workers.[125] Racialized accusations of criminality helped to justify Mexicans' "exceptional" detention. In 1954, the *New York Times* claimed that "crime follows the illegal immigrant," while the Hidalgo County sheriff alleged that 85 percent of the felonies in his county were committed by unauthorized Mexican migrants.[126] The popular perception of the Mexican migrant as criminal was further reinforced by media coverage of overcrowded county jails, as INS deportation efforts pushed border jails three and four times over capacity.[127] The media coverage paid little attention to whether Mexicans in jail had committed a non-entry-related crime; crossing the border was itself a criminal offense. Regardless of whether crime "followed" the unauthorized migrant, the unauthorized migrant was also, by definition, criminal.

In his 1955 State of the Union address, President Eisenhower celebrated the "end" of detention, proclaiming that "[through] humane administration, the Department of Justice is doing what it legally can to alleviate hardships. . . . [E]xcept for criminal offenders, the imprisonment of aliens awaiting admission or deportation has been stopped."[128] The irony was not lost on migrants and their advocates that in the first State of the Union since the president had instituted the mass deportations of Operation Wetback, he was extolling the immigration service's compassionate choices. Reports would soon show that concern for the humanity of migrants stopped somewhere north of the southern border.

Money and Labor in the New Southwest Detention Economy

For sheriffs along the southern border, working with the federal government was business as usual. Marshals maintained relationships throughout Texas, California, Arizona, and New Mexico, using local facilities to hold Chinese migrants at the turn of the twentieth century and Mexicans for the decades after.[129] Federal officials relied on small-town jails such as those in New Mexico's Silver City and Deming, two towns with fewer than seven thousand residents each in 1950.[130] They also looked to larger sites such as Pima County Jail in Tucson, Arizona, which reaped around $11,000 for detaining migrants in 1929. By 1955, the county earned just over $55,000 annually for incarcerating people in what Pima County Sheriff Waldon Burr referred to as the jail's "federal wetback tank."[131] Deportation work for marshals could become all-consuming; in 1953, an Arizona marshal, Ben McKinney, reported that he was handling 1,200 "wetback" cases a month, with more than five hundred migrants caged in Arizona county jails.[132]

While some sheriffs were eager to partner with the federal government, others found the work a source of frustration, especially when it came to negotiating their agreements. As the BOP undertook more routine inspections of contracted jails, localities griped that the federal government asked them for too much in exchange for too little. In 1936, the federal government received a deluge of angry letters from sheriffs after suggesting that localities were responsible for covering the costs of shoes and clothing for federal detainees. "I sometimes wonder why we bother with Federal Prisoners," wrote Sheriff "Boots" Fletcher of Colfax County, New Mexico, a rural community in the state's northeast corner. "I can't make a dime out of it. . . . I get a little annoyed at the constant nagging and constant complaining about matters that are purely whimsical."[133] The tensions remained twenty years later. A U.S. prison inspector's request that a jail in Corpus Christi, Texas, improve food, hire two additional guards, and provide better medical care, a delouser, and a disciplinary cellblock was met with outrage by local officials, who claimed that they were not breaking even on the $1.07 per night the federal government paid.[134]

Despite tensions, many counties pursued the expansion of their jails to rectify dangerous conditions and maintain positive relations with the federal government. Marshals were aware of the power they held in counties' financial futures. In a tongue-in-cheek letter to the El Paso sheriff, a U.S. marshal wrote that on many occasions the sheriff did not know how his office would pay its bills, when conveniently "you would receive a check for $7,000 or $8,000 from your old Uncle through the marshal's office. This would cause you to smile like a jackass eating cactus." The marshal concluded that "El Paso County would be in a Hell of a Fix without the marshal's office."[135] In the 1940s, Cameron County, Texas's southernmost district, doubled the size of its jail at the request of the U.S. Marshals and Border Patrol.[136] A decade later, the BOP honored the county for incarcerating more federal prisoners than any other county jail in the United States.[137] The threat of removing federally detained people was used by the federal government to coerce localities into carceral expansion, and in turn, communities reinvested federal proceeds into funding the enlargement of jails.[138] Sheriffs' investments in jails could be advantageous for their political careers. When Sheriff Odem Dolan of Nueces County, Texas, ran for reelection in 1956, he printed newspaper ads claiming to have saved Nueces County taxpayers more than $17,500 through his efforts to secure federal prisoners.[139] Though the federal government's shift to federal jails and labor camps made some progress in reducing "boarding out," its continuing footprint in southwestern jails indicated that it had hardly eliminated the use of local facilities.

———

As the BOP initiated construction on federal jails in the 1930s, it focused its efforts on the Southwest. The southern border received one of the nation's first federal jails, La Tuna, which opened in 1932. In its first year, more than 90 percent of the jail's population were Mexican migrants convicted of illegal entry.[140] La Tuna boasted proximity to the border and an expansive labor program. In the barren desert locale, BOP officials praised the "astonishing way" that Mexican migrants grew alfalfa and corn "right out of that sand."[141] La Tuna was followed by the creation of Tucson Prison Camp #10, a convict labor encampment located eight miles up an isolated section of the Catalina Mountains, opened in 1933 to alleviate overcrowding at La Tuna.[142] The camp became notorious for its high number of escapes, as migrants fled from brutal work constructing highways through a punishing landscape.[143]

By the postwar period, La Tuna, the Tucson Prison Camp, and the INS network of local jails were all overcrowded. Immigration officials urged the construction of centralized, federally operated migrant detention centers that would make it easier to criminally prosecute Mexican migrants for illegal entry and carry out mass "voluntary departures." The INS hoped that permanent facilities would send a message that the deportation boom was not an aberration and that the "intensity and vigor of the present enforcement drive" would be an enduring reality along the southern border.[144]

In the summer of 1952, the INS initiated construction on a new detention site in Brownsville, a town of just under forty thousand residents located in the southern tip of Texas. Though the DOJ promoted the new detention site as an economic engine and a national security imperative, Brownsville residents expressed serious doubts, embracing the terminology of "concentration camps" used to attack detention elsewhere in the United States.[145] While critics in Galveston thirty years prior had demanded a "concentration camp" as a desirable alternative to detention in the local jail, the term now suggested something not just carceral but potentially genocidal. Both Mexican and Texan newspapers used phrases such as "our new concentration camp" and "Korean type wire stockades" or even a passing comparison to Dachau when decrying the proposed Cameron County site.[146] The *Brownsville Herald* sponsored a contest for readers to submit names for the new detention site, with responses that nodded to the carceral and racialized space: "Mexicalcatraz," "Sultry Siberia," "Uncle Sam's Wetback Hotel."[147]

Texas Congressman Lloyd M. Bentsen adamantly fought the proposed detention site in his district, which INS officials attributed to fears that local governments would lose income from holding migrants in county jails.[148] Cameron County had built a larger jail to accommodate the immigration service's prisoners. How was the county supposed to anticipate, implored Representative Bentsen, that the immigration service would decide "to go into the prison business on a grandiose scale"?[149] One Texas newspaper conceded that Rio Grande Valley counties should have never expanded their jails: "Now apparently they are stuck with big jails and nobody to put in them but each other. The immigration service and the Border Patrol prefer a concentration camp of their own."[150] A new detention site was not just a moral stain, locals argued, it was an economic disaster.

Other observers suggested that Brownsville's skepticism toward the proposed detention site went beyond concerns about jail revenue—it was a way of undercutting immigration law enforcement to protect the interests of South Texas's wealthy grower class. A lack of Border Patrol activity in South Texas had been a "poorly guarded secret" in the 1950s, as locals claimed that the federal government was infringing on their rights and interfering with their way of life.[151] Landowners took dramatic measures to prevent this interference: One grower placed boards with nails sticking out of them on the road leading to his property, aiming to puncture the tires of any Border Patrol official who came along, while other growers drew firearms on Border Patrol agents who crossed their property lines.[152] What first appeared to be a fight about detention logistics was also a referendum about the access to inexpensive labor that sustained the entire region.

Due in part to local opposition, the INS selected a new location for its detention site sixty miles west of Brownsville in the border town of McAllen, Texas, transforming a temporary Border Patrol holding site into a more permanent detention facility.[153] (Figure 18.) Authorities located secondhand barracks a few hundred miles away in Crystal City, Texas, which had been used to detain Latin Americans of Japanese and German citizenship as an "enemy alien" wartime internment camp.[154] Crystal City had been the largest of the wartime sites administered by the INS; notably, it served as a "family internment center," as officials feared that separating Latin American families might

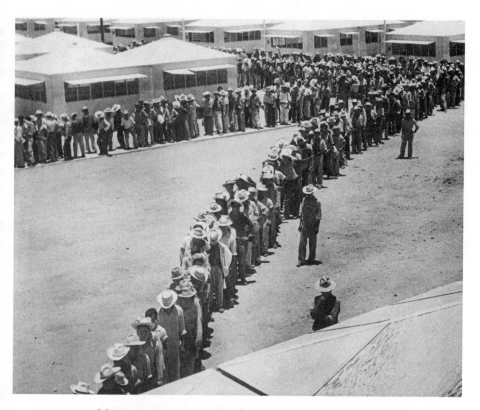

FIGURE 18. Mexican migrants awaiting deportation at McAllen Detention Center, McAllen, Texas, ca. early 1950s. *Source:* Texas American Federation of Labor–Congress of Industrial Organizations Mexican American Affairs Committee Records, Special Collections, University of Texas at Arlington Libraries.

fuel anti-American propaganda.[155] Federal officials transported the buildings to McAllen in 1952, in a rather unsubtle illustration of the DOJ's shifting priorities.[156] A few months after Operation Wetback commenced, the camp held as many as three thousand migrants per night.[157]

The INS envisioned McAllen as a centralized "transit detention center" for its multipronged deportation efforts. C-46 planes, used years prior to drop American paratroopers into the European theater, landed in McAllen carrying Mexican passengers from as far away as Illinois. During a Midwestern campaign of Operation Wetback, the INS converted a former Studebaker Corporation plant in Chicago into an enormous detention site, moving migrants between a repurposed war production factory and McAllen's repurposed

FIGURE 19. Immigration officials loading men and boys onto Valley Service deportation buses at McAllen Detention Center, McAllen, Texas, to be driven to Laredo, Texas, ca. 1953. *Source:* Texas American Federation of Labor–Congress of Industrial Organizations Mexican American Affairs Committee Records, Special Collections, University of Texas at Arlington Libraries.

enemy alien camp. After landing in McAllen, migrants might board a fleet of old school buses to Zapata, Texas, a destination selected for its isolation. From there migrants entered a part of Mexico so remote that many would walk fifteen to twenty miles to find the highway.[158] Other migrants waited at McAllen to be transported east to Port Isabel, where they would board ships belonging to private shipping companies that hauled bananas, cement, and other cargo from Mexico to the United States.[159] (Figure 19.) Years prior, Pacific shipping companies had campaigned for an end to detention; now shipping companies would capitalize on it. Still other migrants would ride another C-46 plane, taking them from McAllen deep into the interior of Mexico—a solution that sidestepped the seasickness and terrible conditions of the cargo ships but which cost considerably more for the immigration service.[160] Having a detention hub gave the United States the capacity to gather together large numbers of migrants to fill its various modes of transit; it was a system of removal made possible by decommissioned wartime technologies and spaces, as well as the collaboration of private companies.

While the INS offered endless assurances that this form of detention was different—that its short-term nature meant that it was nothing like the weeks and months of detention migrants experienced in the early twentieth century—these new sites were still fundamentally spaces of coercion. Even a space designed to hold 640 people a night was taxed by the apprehensions of Operation Wetback, triggering more protests and escapes and opening new channels for exploitation.[161] In 1954, local growers contacted *The Monitor* to accuse immigration officials of "robbing" Mexican migrants at the detention camp.[162] That July, the INS had moved as many as fifty busloads of migrants a day from McAllen to El Paso for deportation. Farmers reported that they had seen INS officials demanding that Mexican migrants turn over all of their money (save a single dollar) to cover the cost of the trip to El Paso. The INS responded that the Border Patrol had "statutory authority to request funds" from migrants to defray the cost of their transportation. "Request!" one farmer exclaimed. "Any request to a man in jail is an order."[163] Migrants pushed back against the carceral space, even in their relatively short time inhabiting it: Historian Jennifer Cullison found evidence that in the early months of the camp, men detained at McAllen broke the camp's cots in protest, while officials reported women defacing barrack walls with lipstick.[164]

Migrants were particularly vulnerable to exploitation in their working conditions as they moved from county jails to federal sites. Federal laws prohibited county jails from hiring out or contracting the labor of U.S. prisoners; local officials could face misdemeanor charges for violating the policy.[165] However, the postwar southwestern sites often incorporated labor into their mission, bringing them in line with federal prison labor programs.[166] In 1950, the DOJ secured Congress's permission to "put an alien to some useful work," at a rate of no more than $1.00 per day. Congress mandated that the labor be voluntary and related to the maintenance of the detention facility.

The hypocrisy of detention centers employing Mexican migrants was not lost on South Texans. In 1955, tensions flared following the publication of a brief news story documenting migrants performing renovations at the McAllen facility. In an editorial titled "Don't Pay Your Wetbacks; The Border Patrol Doesn't," the *Brownsville Herald* spoke to angry local employers: "Know what you've been doing wrong? Why, you've been paying your wetbacks. . . . [T]he poor devils can't work for a dollar because the Border Patrol makes a living picking them up, putting them in the concentration camps and shipping them to Mexico."[167] Even though Congress appropriated funds for paying migrants, officials often incentivized detained persons with cigarettes and extra outdoor time rather than monetary compensation.[168] Migrants also performed work that went far beyond camp maintenance—at the Federal Prison Camp at Florence, Arizona, they were tasked with fighting forest fires, aiding with flood relief, and making repairs to local homes and churches.[169] Though unacknowledged by federal officials, this was a genuine divergence from both the detention of European subversives and the detention of migrants in earlier decades. Mexicans, perceived as the consummate disposable laborer, were coerced into work even as the nation shoved them out the door.[170] The power dynamics at sites like McAllen did not become any less lopsided just because the deportations were quicker.

———

In some ways, the repeated insistences of immigration officials that southern border detention was fundamentally different from detention in the rest of the country were accurate. The southern border forecasted a new era in which a network of local and federal sites of migrant incarceration would work together, if not quite in lockstep. But observers of detention on the southern border would have also seen many recognizable patterns: the ways detention collided with both local agendas and international diplomacy, the tension with sheriffs who resented federal prisoners but also relied on them, and the ways that the immigration service needed to "sell" migrant detention to communities whose priorities did not always neatly align with the federal government's own. Perhaps most importantly, even as the United States apprehended, jailed, and forcibly removed hundreds of thousands of Mexican migrants, it did not encounter the same degree of nationwide protest as it had with Europeans. For an agency concerned with the ideological viability of migrant incarceration, its success in expanding migrant detention in the Southwest proved that incarceration could still be a powerful tool, even in an age of proclaimed abolition.

Historians have often conceived of detention in the postwar period as an aberration—a period of hysteria, characterized by extreme jurisprudence and an out-of-control DOJ. However, the logics of detention, legal precedents, and new models of detention space deployed at Ellis Island, on the West Coast, and along the southern border would shape the landscape of immigration detention and incarceration for decades to come. At Ellis Island, Ellen Knauff's story revealed the growing use of detention not just as a tool of security but as a tool of migrant deterrence. She wrote in her 1952 memoir that detention was a means of destroying the spirit of people seeking citizenship in a nation hostile to their presence: "Many people do die on Ellis Island. They don't die physically, but a sort of mental death. . . . [P]eople are shut away from the outside world long enough, most of them will stop caring about what happens in the world, as well as to themselves."[171] Knauff's words were prophetic. For a nation searching for a way to restrict immigration, breaking migrants' will to fight could be as effective as legal channels of refusal and removal.

On the West Coast, the legal precedents set by *Carlson v. Landon* defined detainees' rights, both in and outside of the realm of immigration. In the late 1960s, amid rising national concern about crime and President Nixon's agitation for "law and order," some criminologists and policymakers began advocating for "preventive detention" without bail for criminal offenders. "Preventive Detention: Latest Concentration Camp Move?" read the banner of the February 11, 1969, issue of the *Baltimore Afro-American*, echoing the rhetoric that ACPFB had relied on in its fight against detention several decades prior. The *Afro-American* identified the connection between the 1950s policies and the new legislation, noting that "historically, the main thrust of such blatantly unconstitutional legislation has been against political dissidents, not the burglary and rape criminals."[172] *Carlson* was later cited in upholding the 1984 Bail Reform Act, a law permitting pretrial detention without bail if a criminal defendant was deemed a threat to communities.[173] Attorneys arguing for pretrial incarceration sans bail found a powerful logic in *Carlson*—that detention without bail could be justified even outside of wartime, on the grounds of defendants' alleged danger.

Expansion in the Southwest signaled that the federal government was ready to make serious investments in a permanent system of migrant incarceration. In McAllen's final years its population diversified: It detained migrants from twenty-seven nations, including an alleged Russian spy, several dozen absconding Greek seamen, and Cubans fleeing Fidel Castro's revolution—evidence that the U.S. government's half-hearted commitment to ending detention had already begun to wane.[174] In the 1960s, the INS consolidated smaller detention sites such as McAllen in favor of larger sites. The INS moved most of the migrants held at McAllen to a new high-security facility at Port Isabel, Texas, in 1961; by the early 1970s, about one hundred thousand Mexicans were removed through Port Isabel annually.[175] The average length of detention began to tick up across the 1960s and reached 14.2 days in 1961, with the INS turning an eye toward detaining people who overstayed visas alongside Mexican migrant laborers.[176] This mix of local and federal infrastructure would endure, holding not just Mexican migrants but asylum seekers from the Caribbean, Central America, and beyond in the years to come.

5

Disorderly Expansion

RESISTING DETENTION IN THE 1970S

ON DECEMBER 12, 1972, a leaking fifty-six-foot sailboat called *Saint Sauveur* docked on the shore of Pompano Beach, Florida, carrying sixty-five Haitian asylum seekers—many malnourished, some pregnant, all fleeing the regime of Haitian dictator Jean-Claude Duvalier. The boat was first spotted by the residents of a beachside condominium. "How they got here is by the wind and tide and the grace of God," mused one condo resident who had brought food down to the migrants. "The boat looks like a garbage scow. You should have seen us out there at 6 o'clock in the morning trying to speak French." The initial media coverage of the migrants' arrival uniformly referred to the Haitians as refugees and described their oppression as political prisoners in Haitian jails. When a reporter asked one English-speaking migrant why he had left Haiti, he simply answered, "Because they wanted to kill me."[1]

Six months later, the asylum seekers from *Saint Sauveur* sat in Florida jails, detained on $1,000 bonds they had little chance of affording. They were joined by dozens more Haitian rafters who had arrived in the United States soon after.[2] Despite the decades-long project to reduce the immigration service's reliance on local facilities, by 1976, the INS had contracted with thirty-eight Florida county and city jails to imprison migrants, including refugees and asylum seekers. The United States would deny virtually all Haitians' claims for asylum following their stint in a Florida jail.

The actions of the U.S. government transformed Haitians into a new prototype of illegality: the illegitimate asylum seeker, seen as a disruptive, racialized threat who used the refugee system as a legal loophole. As immigration scholars have noted, a desire to deter migration from Haiti was central to President Ronald Reagan's 1981 decision to institute "mandatory detention" for people making asylum claims, a shift that fueled the massive expansion of immigration detention in the 1980s.[3] But detention was not suddenly reborn in a moment of perceived crisis. It was gradually expanded throughout the 1970s, as immigration officials capitalized on public anger toward both crime and illegal immigration. In the same decade that saw bipartisan support for Vietnamese refugee admissions and bipartisan pressure toward the Nixon administration to do more for Soviet Jewish refugees, the nation's first major group of Black asylum seekers was greeted not with special admissions programs or generous social services but with the architecture of criminal punishment.[4]

This detention of Haitian asylum seekers occurred within a wider context of the multiple, often overlapping ways in which the INS was rethinking carceral space. Haitians' incarceration built upon existing patterns of jailing Mexicans, who had become the focus of the detention system in the preceding decades. Haitian migrants shared jails with migrants from Mexico, moved through detention centers originally constructed to facilitate deportations to Mexico, and encountered an immigration service that had rebranded itself as a branch of law enforcement, largely fixated on policing migrant labor crossing the southern border. Unlike Mexican migrants, who found themselves in a revolving door of arrivals and deportations, Haitians bore specific legal rights as asylum seekers; it was not uncommon for their hearings and appeals to last months. Even as the INS explored new ways to stunt these rights and expedite removals, the backlogged asylum process typically meant more time in the United States. The INS decided that this would also mean more time in detention. This chapter focuses on two connected stories: how the INS embraced detention as a solution for an increasingly heterogeneous group of people crossing U.S. borders and the growing coalitions of people—unions, pastors, civil rights activists, migrants, politicians—pushing back against detention's ubiquity.

As the United States lacked a uniform refugee law, significant discretion rested with the president and Congress in determining how to respond to each group lodging claims for asylum. The nation's response depended most heavily on how the potential refugees advanced the U.S. foreign policy agenda, though it also reflected domestic concerns about race and dependency. In incarcerating Haitians, the INS capitalized on the national enthusiasm for warehousing racialized subjects and a persistent anxiety about Black criminality, fortified by urban uprisings, the Black Power movement, and a burgeoning war on drugs.[5] The agency's invocations of global instability and looming social burden were not always successful in securing the budget increases it desired, but it had a potent side effect: convincing states and municipalities that expelling migrants should be a local priority.

A century prior, the 1875 Supreme Court case of *Chy Lung v. Freeman* marked a watershed decision for the federalization of immigration power, striking down California's imposition of bonds on certain arriving migrants. However, this precedent still left the door slightly ajar for local control, arguing that in the absence of federal legislation, states might create laws to protect themselves from foreign paupers and criminals.[6] This was effectively the argument that states and localities lodged in the years following the 1965 Hart-Celler Act: They had been "abandoned" by the federal government; their communities were being overrun with poor, dangerous migrants; and the dearth of federal intervention meant that state and local governments could fill the void to protect the safety and health of their constituents. Though the federal government's ambitions for deportation and border control grew, there was, in the words of political scientist Donald Kettl, "no eagerness to grow the federal bureaucracy, nor even to define sharply what federal policy ought to be."[7] Enlisting localities as the foot soldiers of immigration law enforcement enabled a diffusion of political consequences and further obscured who held power over immigration. Immigration law enforcement continued a long-running pattern of being "administratively disorderly," with the federal government ignoring or encouraging local overreach in some moments and discouraging it in others.

When immigration officials returned to local jails, hoping to use them once again as detention space, they encountered a system under greater pressure than ever before. Rising numbers of arrests across the 1970s meant that jail space was at a premium. Overcrowding sparked a rash of lawsuits exposing abysmal institutional conditions. And incarcerated people were making loud claims for freedom from and dignity within carceral institutions.[8] The immigration service had a renewed interest in detention as a tool of deterrence and expulsion, but it was also facing unprecedented competition for jail space. The agency's decisions in this decade—in responding both to Haitians crossing the Atlantic and to Mexicans and other Latin Americans crossing the border—would be foundational for imagining the role of incarceration and local immigration policing in the second half of the twentieth century.

Detention and the Interior Border

The passage of the 1965 Hart-Celler Act marked, in some ways, a major civil rights victory—for the first time in decades, admission to the United States would not be based on an assumed hierarchy of desirable and inferior nationalities. With President Lyndon B. Johnson's signature, the law abolished the national origins quotas and explicitly prohibited visa discrimination on the basis of race, sex, nationality, country of birth, or place of residence.[9] At the bill's signing, with the Statue of Liberty poised in the background, President Johnson condemned the "un-American" quota laws that had been on the books since 1924 and announced that the nation had now patched "a very deep and painful flaw in the fabric of American justice."[10] As with the repeal of the Chinese Exclusion Act during World War II, lawmakers hoped that this change would improve the nation's international reputation, creating a more egalitarian system of admission better aligned with the United States' professed commitment to equality under the law. Still, many members of Congress hoped that it would not be *too* egalitarian—the bill's sponsors sought to make immigration more equitable for the nations of Europe, but they remained resistant to increasing immigration from Asia, Latin America, and Africa.

The great irony of the 1965 law was that it opened paths for the very people policymakers promised would not come: Migrants from Asia, Latin America, and Africa would be the primary beneficiaries of new visa preferences for family members and for people with certain in-demand occupations. The legislation that President Johnson claimed would be a mostly symbolic gesture did, in fact, transform the racial and ethnic demographics of the United States. Still, the law did not remove numerical limits; it merely made them "colorblind," placing an annual ceiling of 290,000 on total immigration to the United States. For the first time, this included a quota for the Western Hemisphere, capped at 120,000 people. Following the principle of formal equality, Congress later set a country quota of twenty thousand for each Western Hemisphere nation. This meant that Mexico, a country that averaged an annual fifty thousand people seeking permanent residence in the United States in the late 1950s, now had the same quota as small nations such as Suriname and Paraguay.[11] Mexicans who, a few years prior, might have legally entered the country as guest workers under the Bracero Program were now labeled illegal immigrants when they journeyed across the Rio Grande, in excess of their country's low quota. There remained significant demand for their labor and effectively no legal paths for them to enter the country. At the same time as the United States embraced a more liberal immigration policy, that same law reproduced and naturalized the problem of illegal immigration.[12]

Throughout the 1970s, public alarm stoked by both the media and the agency itself pressured the INS to stem what Commissioner Leonard F. Chapman declared a "silent invasion" of unauthorized migrants.[13] Chapman saw mass deportations as a silver bullet solution for the U.S. economy, suggesting that the expulsion of migrant workers could create a million new jobs for

Americans overnight, as well as producing billions of dollars in savings from migrants' "illegally acquired" welfare benefits.[14] However, the agency's aspirations were continually stymied by a familiar concern—a shortage of funding and space. In 1974, amid efforts to balance the federal budget, the Ford administration cut the appropriations for deportation activities by nearly 70 percent, necessitating substantial adjustments in the immigration service's local operations.[15] "Our nation's jails and holding areas are literally bursting at the seams, and often we cannot find any place that will accept aliens whom we believe must be detained," reported one INS official.[16]

Jails were bursting because of the aggressive anti-crime politics of the late 1960s and early 1970s. Legislation such as the Safe Streets Act of 1968 intensified the war on crime, allocating tens of millions of dollars to "modernize" police departments with AR-15s and armored tanks and to create a reserve of federal grants to support ill-defined municipal innovation in criminal justice. Communities of color faced heightened levels of surveillance and disruption as militarized police flooded their neighborhoods.[17] These laws and their aftereffects catalyzed a new push for jail construction, focused on replacing older, smaller jails with larger, more modern facilities that would lodge the rising number of people being arrested.[18] While crime control legislation had massive ramifications for the people caught in the web of criminal punishment, it also had implications for the nation's enforcement of immigration laws.

By the 1970s, many police departments saw enforcing immigration law—or at the very least, facilitating INS enforcement of these laws—as part of their mission. The collaboration reflected INS success in branding unauthorized immigration as a crime control and welfare problem during the "Operation Wetback" era, blurring lines of jurisdiction. From 1968 to 1978, the number of migrants turned over to the INS by police increased by a stunning one hundred thousand apprehensions annually. (Figure 20.) Local police and federal officials embraced the use of detainers, which transferred noncitizens from local to INS custody either after arrest for minor offenses or upon completion of a criminal sentence for more serious offenses.[19] Latina/o citizens and legal residents encountered discriminatory policing and racial profiling while moving within the nation, as a veil of suspected illegality closely followed anyone who "looked" Mexican.[20] The immigration service proudly told Congress that police departments throughout the United States were eager to participate in thwarting "illegal immigrants," whom they perceived as a threat to the security of the community, seizing on stereotypes associating Mexicans with gangs and the drug trade.[21]

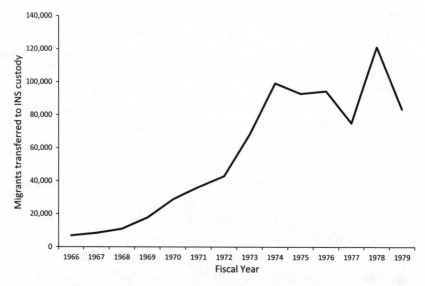

FIGURE 20. Graph of transfers into Immigration and Naturalization Service (INS) custody after apprehension by other law enforcement agencies, 1966–1979. *Source:* Immigration and Naturalization Service annual reports.

Budget limitations forced the INS to make decisions about where to prioritize enforcement, often to the chagrin of localities. In 1975 testimony to Congress, Commissioner Chapman described a delicate balance, in which the agency tried not to apprehend more people than it had the resources to deport. Sometimes this meant halting apprehensions altogether. In January 1975, the INS announced that it would discontinue deportations in the state of Nevada until the beginning of the next fiscal year. It cost the agency $20 to house a migrant overnight in Nevada county jails, plus an additional $30 to transport a migrant to the federal detention facility at El Centro—virtually impossible on the district office's monthly budget of $470 for deportation and detention expenses.[22] A month later, the INS reported that monthly arrests of unauthorized migrants working at Las Vegas gambling resorts had dropped from 208 to eighteen due to a lack of funding.[23] The governor of Nevada decried this move as a total abdication of responsibility by the federal government, stoking accompanying public outrage.[24] If undocumented migrants were as serious a threat as the INS insisted, how could it justify abandoning localities?

Frustrated with perceived federal inaction, municipalities sought ways to take immigration law enforcement into their own hands. Some major immigrant hubs such as Los Angeles and San Diego debated the power of police to arrest people they suspected of being unauthorized migrants, weighing paranoia about migrant criminality against concerns of alienating their cities' sizable Latina/o constituencies.[25] Questions of law enforcement's role in border control also reached communities rarely thought of as major migrant destinations, such as Moline, Illinois, a Midwestern town of around forty thousand residents, perched on the bluffs of the Mississippi River.[26] In September 1975, Mayor Earl L. Wendt called for the Moline Police Department to crack down on migrants, citing concerns about the town's unemployment rate.[27] The following month, the Moline Police Department raided three taverns frequented by Mexicans and Mexican Americans. Police locked the bar doors and demanded that every patron produce identification.[28] Officers forced several dozen patrons, including three legal residents, out of the taverns, shoving them against police wagons and searching them for weapons before taking them to the jail for alleged violations of U.S. immigration laws. Municipalities again contended that a dearth of INS enforcement meant that it fell to them to target and apprehend migrants in their communities. "Do you know how many immigration officers there are in the state of Illinois outside Chicago?" Mayor Wendt asked a reporter. "There is one, and he operates out of Springfield. I have never seen him."[29]

Catalyzed by episodes like the Moline raids and the protests of the Congressional Hispanic Caucus and the Mexican American Legal Defense and Educational Fund, Attorney General Griffin Bell issued a statement in 1978 clarifying that local police agencies were *not* authorized to enforce U.S. immigration law.[30] The attorney general instructed local authorities not to "stop and question, detain, arrest or place an immigration hold on any person, not suspected of crime, solely on the ground they are deportable aliens"—a directive that caused a temporary dip in total number of migrants turned over to the INS by police.[31] Still, these federal directives were crafted to keep INS-police collaborations on constitutionally solid ground, not to hamper collaboration between the agencies. The immigration service's commitment to keeping the police out of immigration enforcement proved tenuous at best. In 1980, the agency wrote a letter to the DOJ Civil Rights Commission stating that local police had *implicit* authority to enforce the criminal provisions of immigration law. Though the INS reiterated that police could not make arrests solely on the grounds that someone might be undocumented, it also encouraged police to notify the INS of any persons in local custody whom they *suspected* might be unauthorized migrants. Local police could still target people they suspected of being "illegal." They just needed to do so under the guise of pursuing some other criminal offense.[32]

The Search for Detention Space

Concurrent with fights about the imprecise boundaries of law enforcement jurisdiction was a reckoning about the role of incarceration in carrying out deportations and removals. In 1975, the INS opened a facility at Brooklyn Navy Yard, the agency's first detention center not located along the U.S.-Mexico border—unlike locales like Ellis Island that also served as sites of admission, the Brooklyn site was designed exclusively for detention. The federal government poured $530,000 into renovating a building that could hold up to 316 people and which the INS defensively described as "definitely not a jail."[33]

Prior to the Brooklyn facility's opening, the INS sent women in the New York City region to Rikers Island, the overcrowded nexus of the city's jail system.[34] The INS conceded that this arrangement was far from ideal and used the image of migrant women held at an embattled Rikers as a tool to push for new federal space.[35] Locating detention space in urban centers proved especially vexing for the agency. Detention in rural areas was relatively straightforward, with jails less overcrowded and local authorities more willing to cooperate with the INS. In some cases, local communities even allowed the INS to detain migrants for a few days at no charge at all. However, in cities such as Los Angeles, the INS paid $62 per night to detain men and a staggering $102 per night to detain women.[36] In Philadelphia, there was no space available at all, as Mayor Frank Rizzo's notoriously aggressive policing filled the jails.[37] The INS complained that in some urban areas, local police had become "openly hostile to the Federal agents," whom they viewed as competing for sparse bed space.[38]

The new facility in New York joined three other federal INS sites—one in Southern California, El Centro, and two in southern Texas, at El Paso and Port Isabel—each of which dated back to the 1950s and 1960s. In 1977 hearings before Congress, the INS displayed a series of flattering photographs of these facilities, trumpeting the success of its "voluntary" detention labor programs and stressing the humane conditions of federal immigration detention centers compared with county jails.[39] The INS insisted to Congress that unlike the nation's eternally broken, prohibitively expensive jails, federal migrant detention sites were *working*. The agency required more of them.

Where the INS wanted detention space most was the "major trouble area" of Miami.[40] In 1976, the immigration service apprehended about seven thousand migrants in the Miami district, whom they boarded at thirty-eight Florida county jails, juvenile detention facilities, and police lockups. A federal detention site in Florida would be a critical addition to the INS arsenal, officials argued to Congress. Some lawmakers questioned why they should pursue federal detention space when it cost less to detain people in a jail. The INS countered that bottom-line numbers did not fully encapsulate the challenges of relying on local sites: By warehousing migrants in jails, the immigration service strained the resources of police departments and spent countless hours negotiating with local authorities. Boarding out may have saved the agency some money, but the INS insisted that it created logistical and legal issues that superseded its financial benefits.

The challenges of boarding out were exemplified by events taking place in the jails of Lubbock, Texas. Though the government operated three service processing centers near the U.S.-Mexico border, jails remained critical for Border Patrol offices in towns such as Lubbock, located six hours from the closest federal detention site. Beginning in 1977, the city of Lubbock permitted the Border Patrol to house migrants alongside local people in the city jail.[41] Several months later, city commissioners merged the county and city jails, transferring all people detained on criminal charges to the county facility; they allowed the Border Patrol to continue using the now-abandoned city jail as a detention space.[42] Between 1977 and 1981, the Border Patrol detained more than seven thousand Mexican migrants in the Lubbock City Jail.[43]

Once police stopped using the city jail, facility conditions went from bad to worse. Migrants testified that they slept on cardboard boxes and sheet metal bunks, their cells were filled with trash, and they were offered neither towels nor soap.[44] A lawsuit about jail conditions revealed a breakdown of the relationship between the immigration service and the city. The Lubbock police chief assumed that the detained migrants were the responsibility of the Border Patrol, while the Border Patrol assumed that the city was providing bed, board, and oversight. Both sides had, in the words of the circuit court, "assumed away responsibility," leaving migrants to suffer in a largely unsupervised facility.[45]

In a 1986 ruling, the court decided that because migrants' imprisonment did not result from a conviction for a crime, the Eighth Amendment's prohibition of cruel and unusual punishment did not apply. This was a "sloppy system of cooperation between federal and local authorities," the judge said, not a case of willful abuse.[46] The case drove home the ways in which detention of Mexican migrants was different from what asylum seekers would encounter in Florida—because detentions in Lubbock rarely exceeded a few nights, the district court concluded that conditions were not serious enough to be constitutional violations. The judge denied the plaintiffs relief because they failed to show that either the INS or Lubbock County *intended* to punish migrants by subjecting them to such conditions. The argument that both groups believed the other was overseeing conditions at the jail was somehow enough to protect both groups from liability. Still, cases like *Ortega v. Rowe* foreshadowed many of the legal and logistical challenges the INS faced in the 1970s and 1980s: As the average length of detention became weeks, rather than days, what sort of facility would the INS require? And as the federal government began to explicitly describe detention as a *deterrent* to future migration, did this cross a line into punishment?[47]

Alongside local jails and federal migrant detention sites, the INS also relied on federal jails run by the BOP, which became central to the agency's pursuit of migrant smugglers working across the borders. Throughout the 1970s, INS officials observed an uptick in the use of coyotes, or migrant smugglers, who charged high fees to facilitate passage across mountains, rivers, and deserts.[48] As the Border Patrol budget increased, migrants became less likely to cross the border in highly policed urban areas and more likely to enlist assistance. In 1972, the INS arrested 4,500 alleged smugglers. Within four years, that number more than doubled to 9,600 apprehensions.[49]

In decades prior, the immigration service would have detained only a fraction of the smuggled migrants to testify in criminal cases against alleged traffickers. However, a 1971 appeals court decision required that the INS detain *every* migrant apprehended after being smuggled, transported, or harbored until questioned by the defendant's attorney, causing massive backlogs in smuggling cases. At San Diego's Metropolitan Correctional Center, a twelve-story federal jail completed in 1974, about 20 to 30 percent of all people detained were migrant witnesses in criminal cases against alleged coyotes, known in the legal system as "material witnesses."[50] Localities and the federal government cited the rising number of witnesses as justification for constructing more federal jails. In 1978, detention infrastructure in Los Angeles was so strained that the INS detained migrants in makeshift pens in the basement of a federal building, as well as in a chain-link enclosure in a dark government warehouse.[51] Material witnesses from the Los Angeles area were frequently transferred to the federal jail at San Diego, where it became "virtually impossible" for either the defense or the prosecution to prepare their cases. Both policymakers and the courts insisted that Los Angeles needed a new, multistory metropolitan correctional center modeled after the one in San Diego.[52]

Children held as witnesses in smuggling cases posed a distinct challenge to a carceral system designed primarily with adult men in mind. From August 1979 to August 1980, fifteen thousand migrants were jailed as material witnesses, including nine hundred juveniles. On August 4, 1980, the *New York Times* ran a front-page story on Sylvia Alvarado, a ten-year-old girl from El Salvador, whose grandmother was held as a material witness in the county jail after paying a smuggler to cross the U.S.-Mexico border.[53] The girl had been detained at the Cameron County juvenile detention center in Brownsville, Texas, for about a month and a half. Herman Baca, chairperson of the Committee on Chicano Rights, Inc., a San Diego–based civil rights group, lodged multiple complaints to the Carter administration about how the material witness system treated children: The INS imprisoned minors as young as two years old without their parents and, in Baca's words, "simply toss[ed]" children back into Mexico when they were no longer needed for trials.[54] Even when children were released into foster homes or private custody, they still went through the BOP intake process, leading to the spectacle of jail officials attempting to take mug shots and fingerprints (or more frequently, footprints) of squirming toddlers. Activists feared that BOP records would prevent children from legally crossing the border in the future, effectively giving some children a criminal record of border crossing before they reached elementary school.[55] For the INS, the mounting number of witnesses reinforced that it needed more detention beds—particularly for women and children, the costliest populations to detain.

As the INS appealed to Congress for more detention space, the elephant in the room was supervisory parole, the supposed humane revolution of mid-century immigration law enforcement. The immigration service was, in theory, not supposed to be detaining many migrants at all. The agency had quietly changed its tune: By the 1970s, the INS insisted that release on bond had become insufficient to guarantee that migrants would show up for hearings and deportations. In New York City, the service claimed that 92 percent of all migrants released on their own recognizance or on bond failed to appear for deportation, and about 40 percent of migrants failed to appear nationwide. In the previous several years, the INS had increased the standard immigration bond from $500 to $2,000; it claimed to have still breached $1.5 million of bonds in 1976.[56]

In 1978, the INS commissioned a study of bond-setting practices in immigration law as compared with criminal law. The final report offered a scathing critique of how the INS used bail. The investigator found few written standards for immigration bonds, no discernible patterns in how officials set bail levels, and little evidence to show that one amount of bond was more effective than another. The examination of bonds highlighted two elements of how immigration policy functioned in the 1970s: the enormous discretionary power of INS officers in dictating freedom or captivity and the way that allegedly administrative tools were being weaponized by the agency to deter and discipline migrants. High bail, the study said, had become a form of "indirect punishment" against people accused of immigration violations.[57] The INS failed to heed the warning of its own study. Within a decade, the immigration service would argue in internal documents that migrants who jumped bail should face *criminal* prosecution, rather than deportation alone.[58]

It was into this environment—one of contested battles over enforcement, prolific racial profiling, and budget shortfalls and surges—that Haitian asylum seekers arrived during the 1970s. Though the immigration service had spent most of the previous decades focused on how to restrain and control Mexican laborers, it now faced migrants from a different part of the world, fleeing violence at the hands of an allied political leader. What would it mean to incorporate asylum seekers into this evolving nexus of border control and federal-local police power?

From Haiti to Immokalee

Most Haitians who arrived in Florida throughout the 1970s came not as immigrants but as asylum seekers; they faced enormous political challenges in gaining refugee status under a system built to privilege the claims of individuals from communist countries. In U.S. law, refugees are people fleeing persecution or the threat of persecution in their home country. They are forced migrants, rather than voluntary ones, a dichotomy that is virtually never as clear-cut as legislators attempt to make it.[59] U.S. refugee law had been intimately connected to foreign affairs as well as domestic concerns. In the wake of World War II, the United States imagined refugees as European anti-communists, perhaps best exemplified by the tens of thousands of Hungarians fleeing a violent Soviet takeover, whom the United States welcomed in the 1950s.[60]

Though the United States extended admission to select groups of refugees, the Truman administration rejected the United Nations 1951 Convention Relating to the Status of Refugees. The agreement required signatories to avoid involuntary repatriation of anyone who faced likely persecution in Europe on the basis of race, religion, national origin, or political beliefs. The United States was wary of the costs of open-ended commitments to refugees, particularly as destabilizing events in nations outside of Europe suggested that the world's refugee dilemma would not be constrained to one continent.[61] By the 1970s, the United States' conception of refugees had edged toward a broader geo-graphic scope, as Americans' ideas about what made a citizen inched away from the ethnonational and racial and toward shared adherence to ideological values and commitments to individual rights—a landmark achievement of the era's overlapping civil rights movements.[62] From 1962 to 1979, the United States paroled more than six hundred thousand Cuban refugees and more than two hundred thousand Indochinese refugees, hailing from Vietnam, Laos, and Cambodia.[63] Yet, even as immigration law liberalized, refugee law remained stubbornly tied to its anti-communist roots. The Hart-Celler Act reified the existing definition of "refugee" and granted them just 6 percent (around ten thousand visas) of the annual U.S. admissions quota.[64]

Haitian asylum seekers discovered throughout the 1970s that the ways the United States assessed information about "persecution" had a decidedly political bent. Jean-Claude Duvalier ("Baby Doc") took over leadership of Haiti from his father, the self-proclaimed "President for Life" François Duvalier, in 1971. With the transfer of power, Haiti's paramilitary force, the Tonton Macoute, shifted patterns of interrogating, arresting, and torturing Haitian citizens away from urban centers and toward rural provinces where the government could claim less responsibility for the security forces' actions.[65] As a result, most Hai-tians arriving in South Florida in the 1970s were rural peasants who had encoun-tered a new degree of terror and repression under Baby Doc.[66] The younger Duvalier capitalized on Cold War tensions, expressing anti-communist senti-ments to U.S. Ambassador Clinton E. Knox and voicing concern that the Soviet fleet in Cuba might invade Haiti.[67] Despite well-documented allegations of state violence, the U.S. government appeared cautiously optimistic about the reign of Jean-Claude Duvalier, restoring aid to Haiti and offering American technical advisors to help the country restructure its customs and postal services.[68] The United States, almost without exception, classified Haitians as "economic mi-grants," ineligible for the protections of asylum.

By the end of the 1970s, Amnesty International concluded that the transi-tion in presidency from father to son had not altered the nature of the regime in any substantial way.[69] Critics of Duvalier highlighted the interconnected political and economic situations in Haiti—as Judge James L. King wrote in 1980, "[M]uch of Haiti's poverty is a result of Duvalier's efforts to maintain power. Indeed, it could be said that Duvalier had made his country weak so that he could be strong."[70] American policymakers, however, saw two risks in acknowledging Haitians as political refugees: Doing so would undermine the U.S.-Haiti strategic relationship and might encourage more Haitians to seek asylum. The pattern of rejections incurred massive pushback from people in varied South Florida circles, who argued that the denial of Haitians' asylum claims was a human rights atrocity and that Haitians' incarceration in U.S. jails was an alarming break from precedent.

In the first year of significant migration from Haiti, the INS claimed that holding Haitian refugees in Florida jails was standard practice due to the migrants' lack of documentation.[71] These claims rang hollow to observers, who pointed out that Cubans had been arriving on U.S. shores without authorization for decades and had not faced detention. Under the 1952 immigration law, the INS had the discretion to either parole or detain persons who were in the process of applying for admission to the United States; the agency used this discretion to move Haitians directly from Florida beaches into Florida jails. "At one point we were incarcerating all Haitian males," Richard Gullage, INS district director for Miami, later testified about the initial years of Haitian migration. "To my knowledge, that has never been done [before] with Haitians or any other immigrant group."[72]

The county jail in Immokalee, Florida, became the epicenter of Haitian detention controversies. (Figure 21.) Immokalee was a rural community in southwestern Florida, just north of the Everglades and about a two-hour drive from downtown Miami. Most of Immokalee's residents were agricultural laborers. The town had a wealthy planter class, as well as a large farmworker population, the majority of whom were Black.[73] Immokalee was home to the Collier County Stockade, a small facility that offered the INS good rates, an enthusiastic warden, and a location unlikely to ever become as overcrowded as jails in Miami.[74] The INS sent a first group of Haitians to Immokalee in 1973. By September 1975, more than three hundred Haitian migrants had been moved to the jail, which reportedly held four times more refugees than locals.[75]

The first years of Haitian migrants' time in Florida jails were rife with uncertainty for both the asylum seekers and the agency. The INS had the discretionary power to waive bond and release people from detention, but it did so unpredictably and erratically. In June 1973, the INS freed several dozen Haitian migrants from Dade County Jail, issuing them into the custody of the Haitian Information Center, a nonprofit organization based in Miami.[76] Reverend James E. Jenkins, a minister at Friendship Missionary Church in Miami's Liberty City neighborhood, used the moment to affirm solidarity among African Americans and Black migrants in Miami, as well as a shared understanding of the inequalities driving both the immigration and the

FIGURE 21. Haitian migrants detained at Collier County Stockade, Florida, 1978. Used by permission of Michelle Bogre, American Committee for Protection of Foreign Born Records, University of Michigan Library, Joseph A. Labadie Collection, Special Collections Research Center.

criminal justice systems. "Now you are aware of what thousands of black brothers and sisters are suffering behind bars—many not guilty of anything but trying to attain freedom while being U.S. citizens," he told an audience of newly freed asylum seekers.[77] While he envisioned himself as an intermediary between Miami's "militant" and "moderate" Black communities, Reverend Jenkins's fury at the INS was unmissable: He criticized the hypocrisy and racism of the agency's actions and said that physical violence was not off the table when it came to protecting Haitians from deportation.[78] A few months later, the INS rejected advocates' appeals to release another group of migrants into their custody, claiming frustration that some of the previous parolees had not shown up for hearings.[79] By January 1974, a judge had upheld the federal government's right to incarcerate and remove Haitian asylum seekers, sparking protests from Jenkins and others in Miami.[80]

With hope for release dwindling, Haitian asylum seekers inside Florida jails made their frustrations known. On October 2, 1975, Haitian migrants at

Immokalee initiated a hunger strike. Four days later, all but six of the Immokalee stockade's Haitian residents refused to eat. The hunger strikers complained of inadequate access to supervised medical leave and limited recreational time, a problem worsened by Immokalee employing only half the number of recommended guards.[81] "I am fasting now to be free," said Willeme August from an Immokalee cell. "I left my country because of persecution, but I find it here. Men have to be free. Here they treat me like I am an animal, so I will not eat until they set me free."[82]

In response to resistance, the INS experimented with dispersing migrants through its network of municipal jails to deter organizing, distance legal aid, and appease local communities. When Neil Sonnett, a young lawyer representing Haitian migrants at Immokalee, called the stockade on October 7, 1975, he was stunned to learn that his clients had been removed from Collier County in the dead of night and scattered across four central Florida jails, as well as the federal detention facility in Port Isabel, Texas. The move brought an unceremonious end to the hunger strike. The INS deputy director implicitly confirmed advocates' suspicions that the relocations were a retaliatory measure. "They were causing embarrassment to the Immokalee facility," the director said. "They were refusing to eat and complaining they didn't like the stockade, so we moved them."[83]

The day before the move, a local newspaper ran a story discussing Immokalee city commissioners' growing discontent with the negative publicity the hunger strike had generated.[84] The city cast its relationship with the federal government as one of cooperation and shared purpose, yet there was an economic incentive underlying Immokalee's involvement. It cost the warden just $1.50 per night to house and feed each detained person, while the INS paid the county $6.00, bringing in a 400 percent surplus.[85] This was all the more significant in a rural economy with high unemployment and a largely transient labor force.[86] "We would anticipate housing more [Haitians] there in the future," an INS district official said of Immokalee in 1975. "[We] intend to use [Immokalee] unless the county commission refuses us. I'm sure they liked the money."[87]

Making Haitians Illegal

Haitian migrants were not the only noncitizens behind bars at Immokalee. On a sign affixed to a stockade wall, jailers listed the names of Haitians in their custody. The last entry was not a name but a description reading simply:

"25 wetbacks." This was later crossed out and amended to "40 wetbacks"—still nameless, a number and a slur.[88] Haitians shared the Collier County Stockade with Mexican seasonal workers apprehended in the immigration service's surge of interior enforcement efforts. Mexican migrants moved to Collier County in greater numbers throughout the 1970s, as the African American agricultural workforce left for other industries.[89] By the late 1970s, the jail detained as many as two hundred Mexican migrants per day. The numbers were inconsistent, ebbing and flowing when immigration agents found the resources to raid the work camps of southwest Florida.[90] While the raids consistently turned up undocumented workers, primarily from Mexico, as well as a smaller number from Jamaica, they also generated enforcement penalties for employers. In a May 1976 raid, the agency issued fifty-seven citations to Immokalee growers for illegally using migrant child labor.[91] The two groups—Haitian refugees and Mexican migrant workers—that populated jails like Collier County's reflected dueling INS priorities. The agency pursued highly visible responses to Mexican workers and their employers, while simultaneously transforming Haitians into a new prototype of illegality: the illegitimate asylum seeker.

The question of detention was embedded in a larger battle over Haitians' access to fair asylum hearings under a system that had prematurely decided they were not real refugees. Lawyers working at Immokalee observed a shifting set of rules across the 1970s: Whereas the INS had once given attorneys the names of Haitians in detention, by 1976 the agency refused to release any information unless lawyers already had a migrant's name, accusing attorneys of "ambulance chasing."[92] Judge James L. King would later observe that "the actions of lawyers representing Haitians were seen (by the INS) *as part of the Haitian problem.*"[93] Internally, the INS Miami office pursued a bureaucratic scheme it referred to as the "Haitian Program," meant to alleviate the buildup of fifteen thousand Haitian asylum hearings. Over the duration of the Haitian Program, the agency adjudicated the claims of four thousand Haitian asylum seekers in sped-up trials that left immigration lawyers triple-booked at courtrooms across South Florida.[94] Not one of the migrants processed under the accelerated hearings of the Haitian Program received asylum. Agency officials described this arrangement as a valid use of their discretionary authority, necessary to contain what they described in department memos as the "Haitian threat."[95]

The earliest mentions of the Haitian Program began with Associate Attorney General Michael J. Egan, who had grown concerned with the mounting

backlog of Haitian asylum cases in Miami. In July 1978, Egan issued a vague
directive to the INS to process Haitian migrants' claims more quickly and
to suspend work permits for asylum seekers.[96] Egan's order then moved
down the line through the INS, allowing various bureaucrats to add instructions to the plan. On July 14, 1978, Acting INS Commissioner for Enforcement
Charles C. Sava wrote to INS Deputy Commissioner Mario T. Noto, "I believe
the best, most practical deterrent to this problem is expulsion from the United
States. This is a process that Enforcement properly has the lead role in. We will
get the cases moved to hearings swiftly and keep things rolling."[97] That same
month, INS Regional Commissioner Armand J. Salturelli traveled to Miami
to survey the "Haitian Situation" and initiated two changes in policy: ending
the practice of suspending deportation proceedings when a migrant made an
asylum claim and ending the practice of allowing noncitizens ten days to prepare applications to withhold deportation. Salturelli noted that both revised
policies would violate INS operating instructions and simply suggested that
the INS should suspend its procedures "insofar as the Haitians are concerned."[98] When it came to Haitian asylum seekers, even the agency's own
rules did not apply. It was another incarnation of what historian S. Deborah
Kang has observed about the INS along the U.S.-Mexico border in the first
half of the twentieth century—this was not just a law enforcement agency but
an agency actively making and remaking immigration law.[99]

Migration from the Caribbean disrupted how the United States envisioned
its asylum system working and who the nation envisioned the system
serving—namely, communist defectors from Europe who neatly fit into U.S.
Cold War narratives. The "Haitian threat" invoked tropes of Black disobedience and disorder and brought them to bear on border control: Haitians represented the possibility of uncontrollable, unconstrained mobility and of an
asylum system that officials perceived as open to exploitation.[100] The United
States had imagined itself as geographically insulated from the massive cross-
border movements that followed World War II in Europe and Asia.[101] Haitian
asylum seekers, undertaking a dangerous eight hundred-mile ocean journey
across the Greater Antilles, confirmed the naivety of this belief. Internally, the
INS suggested that the scale of this migration necessitated overhauls of the
asylum process: "All supervisory personnel are hereby ordered to take *whatever
action they deem necessary* to keep these [Haitian] cases moving throughout the
system," the deputy director in charge of the Haitian Program told his subordinates.[102] The comment mirrored the judiciary's description of plenary power
at mid-century—that "whatever the procedure authorized by Congress is, it

is due process as far as an alien denied entry is concerned."[103] However, now the rules were being made not by Congress but by immigration officials operating with scant congressional oversight.

The Haitian Program was even more alarming because it began just months after what many immigrants' rights advocates hoped would be a turning point for more progressive policies. On April 7, 1977, President Carter nominated Leonel J. Castillo as the first Latino to serve as INS commissioner. Castillo committed to improving federal border detention sites. His efforts included installing soccer fields and ping-pong tables, providing Spanish-language reading material, and playing films for detainees—all moves that infuriated critics.[104] With the encouragement of the Mexican government, Castillo changed the name of the "alien detention centers" to "service processing centers" and urged INS officials to adopt the term "undocumented alien" rather than "illegal alien."[105] Carter's nominee became a controversial figure among politicians of both parties, who accused Castillo of coddling migrants with "get soft" policies.[106]

Commissioner Castillo declared that under his administration, INS detention centers would be required to meet the minimum standards of the BOP, marking the agency's first attempt to create service-wide detention standards. The move was partially a product of Castillo's ideological leanings, but it was also a consequence of the litigious political climate of the 1970s. Across the country, incarcerated people were bringing successful class action litigation against prisons and jails, much of it asserting that institutional conditions constituted cruel and unusual punishment.[107] To the new commissioner, INS detention centers, operating under even less regulation than state prisons, looked like a major liability. If migrants were undertaking hunger strikes and the INS was receiving scathing letters from the Mexican government, it stood to reason that litigation would not be far behind.[108]

Though much of Castillo's focus was on the southern border, the growing number of asylum seekers in Florida made the state impossible to ignore. In November 1977, Castillo announced that the INS would end the policy of imprisoning Haitian migrants prior to hearings and would offer them work permits.[109] He called Haitians "our own hemisphere boat cases," drawing a line between the plight of Vietnamese refugees and the plight of Haitian asylum seekers. Castillo emphasized that seeking asylum was a protected act under international law.[110] However, when migration from Haiti spiked again in spring and summer of 1978, the INS had second thoughts about the more liberal policy.[111] In September 1978, the INS reneged on Castillo's promise, announcing that no new work permits would be issued or renewed. Detention was reinstituted as the de facto response. Within a month, all INS-contracted local jails were full. The INS positioned its lack of facilities as a looming crisis for the entire community, one that foretold crime, dependency, and disease.[112] By the end of 1979, the agency detained nine thousand Haitian asylum seekers under immigration proceedings.[113] "We're not in the business of jailing people, but we have no other place to put them," said Gullage.[114] With several thousand migrants in custody and the INS bankrolling counties throughout Florida, Gullage's claim fell flat.

A judge struck down the Haitian Program in a 1981 class action lawsuit brought by the Miami-based Haitian Refugee Center on behalf of four thousand jailed Haitian migrants. In *Haitian Refugee Center v. Civiletti*, the center argued that the Haitian Program was a violation of Haitian migrants' due process rights and that the INS program systematically discriminated against their claims for asylum. The plaintiffs relied heavily on internal INS memorandums detailing the arbitrary ways bureaucrats drove the program forward and the way expedited hearings exclusively impacted Haitian asylum seekers. Judge King declared the program "offensive to every notion of constitutional due process and equal protection."[115] Despite the judge's passionate denouncement of the Haitian Program, the court did not extend legal status to migrants, nor did it place any significant checks on INS power. Instead, the court ordered the INS to adhere to the principles of due process and equal protection when formulating a new plan for processing Haitian asylum seekers. The decision offered a strong condemnation of INS actions but offered little direction for how to reform the agency's behavior and the tremendous discretionary power that made the Haitian Program possible. While the courts proved willing to break the tradition of judicial noninterference to address egregious agency abuses of power, the plenary power doctrine still restrained how far they would intervene in regulating immigration.

Living and Dying in Immigration Purgatory

Migrants' experiences in Florida jails were rife with abuse, much of it echoing the violence and injustice that had caused them to flee their homeland in the first place. The irony of this treatment was compounded by an immigration service that continually insisted detention was a humane response to a complex problem. "I'm probably less interested in having these people incarcerated than the Haitian Refugee Center," an INS director said in February 1979, "but

I cannot let them loose on the streets without a job, a place to stay, or anything to eat."[116] The argument neatly obscured how the INS had produced much of this economic vulnerability by erratically granting and rescinding work authorization. Haitian migrants and their advocates charged that detention was not about sheltering a vulnerable community. It was about punishing Black asylum seekers, whom U.S. leaders viewed as fraudulent refugees and economic liabilities.

One way that Haitian advocates highlighted the cruelty of jailing migrants was by emphasizing the number of suicide attempts that occurred under INS supervision, a problem all too familiar for migrant incarceration sites. In 1977, a man named Georges Pierre, who had been in detention for nearly a year, attempted suicide in the El Paso federal detention facility. From the hospital, Pierre eviscerated the United States' superficial asylum process: His interview with immigration authorities had been just fifteen minutes long. He did not have sufficient opportunity to explain the full details of his case. He felt intimidated by immigration authorities, whom he feared could be collaborators of the Haitian government. "I keep thinking about what would happen if I had to go back home. I can't sleep at night for thinking," Pierre said. "I tried to kill myself in the Detention Center. I wanted to die because I have been in jail so long and I think I will be sent back to Haiti."[117]

While examples of migrants resorting to drastic measures abounded, the loss of Turenne Deville became a particular rallying point for the Haitian community in and outside of detention. Deville, a twenty-seven-year-old Haitian stonemason, had paid a trafficker $400 to facilitate his passage to Florida.[118] Alongside forty-eight other Haitian and Jamaican asylum seekers, he rode an overloaded sailboat to Boca Raton before police discovered him in the back of a U-Haul truck during a traffic stop.[119] From October 1973 until March 1974, Deville sat in Florida jails: first in Miami and then in Dade City, a rural community in central Florida, after Miami jails became overcrowded.[120] On the night of March 14, 1974, Deville used a bedsheet to hang himself in his Dade City jail cell, just hours after authorities informed him that he was being returned to Miami to board a boat to Haiti.

On March 23, 1974, Reverend Jenkins's Liberty City church held a funeral service for Deville, printing his affidavit for asylum in the service program.[121] Deville's testimony was rife with tragic parallels. He had spoken of his arbitrary jailing in Haiti after clashing with the Tonton Macoute and of the unbearable conditions in Haitian jails: the lack of food, the abysmal sanitation, the astronomical bail. "I must find a place for security for my life," Deville said. "In

Haiti, there is no justice. The poor must die prematurely, often asphyxiated in jail." The funeral program highlighted the intentional cruelty of American immigration policy, invoking a long tradition of making mourning political within the Black freedom struggle.[122] The bottom of the program read:

> We the Black people of the Model City and all concerned human beings of Dade County, do hereby declare that our Black Haitian Brother Turenne Deville is now and forever, as long as there are concerned citizens, in Dade County, he is a citizen of Dade County and our community.[123]

Grieving Deville underscored another important element of the resistance to Haitians' imprisonment: organizing among the Black community of South Florida. (Figure 22.) In the 1960s and early 1970s groups such as the NAACP had opposed some immigrants' rights projects, viewing undocumented labor as a threat to the economic prospects of poor Black workers.[124] However, the treatment of Haitians turned immigration into a national civil rights issue. Following Deville's death, Cain Bollard, head of the Laborer's Union of North America, a union predominately composed of Black members, rallied to raise bond money for the remaining Haitian asylum seekers in Dade County jails. "A lot of Cuban people come into this area and they're not put into jail. . . . Why do they do the Haitians like that? It must be because they're black," Bollard concluded.[125] In 1974, a network of Black churches raised $10,000 to cover bond expenses for the latest group of migrants.[126] Though the federal government presented Haitians' status as "economic migrants" as a settled fact, in American communities where people had deep ties to Haiti and the Caribbean, the government's actions were understood as a political whitewashing of a complex reality.

In December 1978, activists mobilized around another case that they believed epitomized the deliberate cruelty of detention: the incarceration of an eight-year-old Haitian girl in the West Palm Beach City Jail. Reverend Gérard Jean-Juste, a Catholic priest and relentless advocate for South Florida's Haitian community, discovered Rosalene Dorsainvil, crying and barefoot, in the corner of a cell. She had arrived on a boat from Haiti with her father two weeks earlier and had been in the jail ever since. The INS called the child's detention an "unfortunate and regrettable" mistake, which it attributed to a breakdown in communication between the INS and jail officials.[127] Haitian advocates called Dorsainvil "a pawn and a hostage" to an immigration bureaucracy eager to force her father's return to Haiti and deter other migrants.[128]

The Dorsainvil case illustrated how migrant detention could become a point of fracture within localities, as policymakers and law enforcement butted

FIGURE 22. Miami protest against the incarceration of Haitian asylum seekers, 1975. Courtesy of Tim Chapman, Tim Chapman Collection, HistoryMiami Museum, 2013-334-75-1.

heads over enforcement. Eva Williams Mack and Ruby Bullock, West Palm Beach's first African American commissioners, arrived at the West Palm Beach City Jail on January 17, 1979, and asked to see where the jail detained refugees. "We don't give tours of the jail," replied Police Chief William Barnes. The commissioners told Barnes that they had received complaints of a detained woman who was bleeding from hemorrhoids but had not received medical treatment. They observed that the migrants appeared to be wearing the same tattered clothes they had arrived in weeks prior. Chief Barnes would not budge.[129] The day after the city commissioners attempted to tour the jail, the West Palm Beach police chief announced that the asylum seekers would be moved to Immokalee. Lawyers who worked between the two counties described Immokalee as "ten times worse" than the West Palm Beach jail and declared the transfer "a typical coverup" intended to deflect political attention.[130] When West Palm Beach's contract with the DOJ expired in March 1979, the commissioners successfully advocated that access to medical care and interpreters be added to the contract—perhaps the first time that a city had negotiated better migrant care in a contract with the federal government.[131]

By the late 1970s, grievances among jailed Haitians focused not just on the substandard food and the lack of information but also on intimidation and abject abuse by local officials. Lucien Calixte had served in the Haitian Marines and had been a guard to the elder Duvalier before fleeing the country in 1978. The INS transferred him six times between three South Florida jails. Calixte refused to depart voluntarily, despite repeated INS threats that he would be "returned to Haiti in handcuffs" regardless of whether he pursued his asylum claim. At nearly every facility, Calixte and others engaged in some form of hunger strike and were greeted with increasingly militarized responses. In Immokalee, Calixte claimed that guards had picked up dining hall benches and had used them "as weapons to make us move," before handcuffing the protestors and putting them on buses to a jail seventy miles away in Belle Glade, Florida. At a jail in Fort Pierce, Florida, he described cells covered with trash and toilets that did not flush. "We made noise to call the guards, because we did not want to be in that cell which was filthy. The guards came and sprayed us with tear gas. Some men fell to the ground because they were so overcome by the gas," Calixte testified.[132]

The INS initially denied reports of abuse as "absolute lies" and accused the South Florida media of contriving a more dramatic story.[133] However, two Haitian American community members had captured photographs of jail employees violently forcing Calixte and his cohort onto buses from the jail in Belle Glade to the jail in Fort Pierce. "[The hunger strikers] were so weak and even then the police were beating and beating them," said Sister Pierre Marie Armand, a Catholic nun and one of the photographers. When a reporter confronted an INS official with the photographs, the official paused and shifted the agency's narrative: "Unfortunately, things like that happen every day. There is nothing we can do about it. The guards are uneducated and underpaid. Anytime anyone acts up they are quick to exert their authority."[134]

Immokalee's warden, described by the local paper as "a classic good old boy," did not deny that his guards used force in controlling hunger strikers.[135] "We had lots of fun there for a few minutes. There was some bloodshed and we cracked some heads," James Lester admitted.[136] The warden insisted that this was a proportionate response to the migrants' resistance, claiming that they had thrown food around the cafeteria, spilled coffee on the floor, and urinated in their cells. "If I were a guest in someone else's country, I would try to obey their laws and act with some dignity," said Lester.[137] The images from Immokalee resembled the scenes of law enforcement brutality against Black protestors that had become widespread in the urban uprisings of prior years. Both the INS and local officials implicitly asked why these poor Black migrants couldn't just be grateful for their incarceration, for their scraps of American support, for their shadow of due process. They were uninvited guests. Didn't they know how much worse it could be?

The disparity between the INS public relations narrative regarding use of force and the warden's explicit confession of violence exemplified the agency's contradictory public messaging. When abuse at the local level became impossible to deny, the INS immediately distanced itself from its contractees, arguing that the agency should not be held responsible for the actions of ignorant guards and that complete oversight of county jails was an impossibility. Wardens like Lester were painted as "bad apples" rather than reflections of systemic problems, a claim made all the more egregious as Black prisoners throughout the country exposed and challenged the conditions inside American prisons and jails.[138] Agreements with localities provided the federal agency with a level of insulation from the worst abuses, as it capitalized on stereotypes of racist, uneducated rural workers whose actions did not represent the directives of the federal government. Federal officials weaponized the ambiguity around federalism to suggest that it was local officials who had corrupted immigration law enforcement. The problem was not racist laws, they insisted, it was the lack of federal resources to enforce those laws.

Commissioner Castillo's fears that migrant detention sites would become a target for litigation were soon realized. Immokalee's warden resigned under pressure in February 1980, after a civil rights lawsuit accused him of using physical force against migrants and releasing German shepherds into Haitians' cells.[139] County officials chose their words carefully, stating that Lester's methods "were [not] quite in line with county, state, and federal guidelines." It was a toothless way to describe Black asylum seekers being attacked by dogs, all because the INS suspected them of experiencing insufficient political persecution.[140]

Rather than litigation providing an opportunity to pursue noncarceral alternatives, the INS used abuse as a bargaining chip to push for *more* detention sites in the late 1970s and early 1980s, preferably facilities that the INS would have a greater role in managing. Jails like Immokalee's might be beyond repair, the INS suggested, but the agency could build a new form of detention site, better suited to its needs, if given the opportunity. It was the same familiar argument the agency had used to fuel carceral expansion for nearly fifty years.

The relationship built between the INS and local law enforcement in the 1970s proved foundational for the agency in the 1980s, when it encountered an unprecedented number of people seeking refuge. By the time of the 1980 Mariel Boatlift, during which more than 125,000 migrants from Cuba came to the United States in six months, the INS had a system that it was thoroughly frustrated with. Hundreds of localities charged the INS more than it thought was fair. Towns abandoned their agreements with the INS when detained people brought unwanted attention. Detentions grew longer and longer as legal aid groups organized to ensure due process. Mass migration from the Caribbean generated a pivotal opportunity for the INS to campaign for new federal detention facilities. It also built upon rhetoric the immigration service had been using since the 1970s: that if the federal government was serious about transforming the INS into a law enforcement agency, with a mission that centered on apprehension and deportation, it required more space for incarceration.

6

South Florida and the Local
Politics of the Criminal Alien

ON SEPTEMBER 9, 1980, Murray Meyerson, the mayor of Miami Beach, penned a furious letter to President Jimmy Carter.[1] Four months had passed since Cuban leader Fidel Castro opened the Port of Mariel and announced that anyone who wanted to leave Cuba was free to go. In that time, 125,000 Cubans had fled or been forced out of their homeland, the vast majority ending up in and around Miami's Dade County. The Mariel Boatlift was a "federally created farce," the mayor declared. Miami Beach had almost no housing vacancies and a population whose median age hovered above sixty years old, many of them retirees from the Northeast who sought a quiet, warm place to live out their golden years. It was not, the mayor claimed, a place prepared to take in tens of thousands of new arrivals.[2]

In describing the city's predicament to President Carter, Meyerson called Mariel Cubans "jackals" who prowled the streets, committing crimes and preying on the elderly. While the mayor's letter dripped with racist contempt, he ended with an acknowledgment of how the absence of a social safety net had exacerbated the situation: "Not all refugees are criminals, *yet*. With no hope for even a basic existence, how long will it be before desperation and instinct for survival govern their actions?" The federal government had created a migration catastrophe, Meyerson accused, through both a dearth of social support and inadequate policing, but municipalities were bearing the burden.[3]

Within a year, some of the Cuban migrants Meyerson had criticized were in the Dade County Jail, an aging facility with rows of yellow cellblocks and a few dying palm trees in the yard.[4] Florida Governor Bob Graham's appeals to the federal government echoed those of municipalities: The federal government was "legally and morally bound to assume responsibility for the consequences of its [immigration] policy."[5] To Graham, a crucial element of assuming responsibility was moving Mariel Cubans out of Florida jails and into federal custody.

For the majority of Cubans jailed in Dade County, this was their second experience of incarceration in the United States. Most had previously been detained in refugee resettlement camps on military bases located throughout the country. Some had waited for more than a year to find a community sponsor. Their problems did not end there: Sponsorships fell through, and jobs were hard to come by. For some refugees, Miami's flourishing drug economy beckoned. Others entered the criminal legal system via the heightened policing that people like Meyerson had fought for—programs that put record numbers of cops on Miami streets, instituted stop-and-frisk policies, and criminalized loitering and vagrancy. Regardless of their specific experiences, all Mariel Cubans faced the stigma of being the United States' newest public enemy: the "criminal refugee" or the "criminal alien," a late twentieth-century reinvention of the illegal immigrant.[6]

Cubans were, in many ways, unlikely candidates to become the figureheads for refugee danger. Since 1966, Cubans had enjoyed a privileged position in U.S. immigration policy, as the Cuban Adjustment Act allowed any Cuban arriving in the United States—whether they overstayed a visa or arrived unannounced on American shores—to acquire permanent residency and eventually citizenship. Cuban Americans became a powerful interest group in South Florida: They ran businesses, attained political office, and became a symbol of American success and integration. The Cubans who migrated in the 1980s were primarily young, single, working-class men with limited education, a pronounced contrast to the "Golden Exile" of primarily urban, middle-aged, light-skinned, and white-collar workers who arrived immediately after the revolution.[7] Approximately 20 percent of Mariel Cubans were Black or *mulato*, compared with just 7 percent of the Cubans who arrived between 1960 and 1964.[8] For the first time in two decades of Cuban refugee migration to the United States, the Carter administration refused to grant refugee status to all arriving Cubans. It instead sought to assure Americans that immigration officials were separating the deserving from the undeserving, the threatening from the nonthreatening.

This chapter examines two experiences of incarceration and policing in the early 1980s, each of which reveals a shifting understanding of federalism and who was responsible for immigration law enforcement. The first took place at refugee resettlement camps throughout the United States where Cubans waited to learn their fates. Like each incarnation of migrant incarceration that preceded them, these camps were sites of abuse and violence alongside debilitating monotony and uncertainty. Camp officials promised Cuban migrants that their stay would be temporary. Yet, as weeks stretched into months, migrants' faith in the system withered. The federal government used camp uprisings and protests as evidence that the Mariel Cubans were dangerous and unassimilable—the type of person who needed to be taken off a community's streets.[9] It also used the camps as a space to experiment with granting the military a greater role in policing migrants alongside federal and local law enforcement. Expanding the role of the military in domestic crime control would become a signature of the Reagan administration, making Miami the focus of an interagency task force that mobilized the resources of the military, the police, and even the Internal Revenue Service to stop migrants and narcotics from crossing borders.

The second example of incarceration and policing took place in South Florida. Inflamed by Fidel Castro's claims to have placed the island's prisoners on U.S.-bound boats, local officials used fears about Mariel Cubans to justify a radical remaking of policing in Miami. Dade County municipalities instituted new ordinances and curfews targeting refugees. They explored new ways to share data between law enforcement and the immigration service. And above all, Miami and its suburbs implored the federal government for financial assistance, framing Dade County as driven to the brink of destruction by the federal government's inability to control its borders. In making these claims, Miami leaders fixated on Cuban refugees who had been accused of criminal infractions, mostly misdemeanors and drug offenses, after release from resettlement camps.[10] The vast majority of migrants from Mariel, around 91 percent, were never arrested.[11] Still, the "criminal refugee" became an outsize figure in the local and national imagination. Fear and grievances turned South Florida into a prototype for increased collaboration between the federal immigration service and local law enforcement, capitalizing on refugees' perceived criminality as a rationale for the expansion of police forces and prisons.

In the 1970s, cities and states had expressed frustrations with the Immigration and Naturalization Service's limited resources and deportation capacity, suggesting that it had left localities no choice but to take on immigration control themselves. Miami in the 1980s made an even more aggressive version of this claim: It argued that the federal government *owed* the locality financial compensation to the tune of tens of millions of dollars for its own sovereign impotence. Federal funding for criminal justice expenditures, the Miami county manager wrote, needed to be elevated "to a number one priority, equal to that of health care."[12] Dade County officials declared that refugees were a disaster of the federal government's own making. And the locality did not just want food stamps or social services—it wanted money for bigger jails and more policing.

The Mariel Boatlift had massive ramifications for the future of migrant detention and incarceration writ large: It refocused the agency on removing people with a criminal record, cementing the bureaucracy's image as a branch of law enforcement. The jail became the center of INS deportation activities: It was not just a space to hold migrants the INS sought to remove; it was the filter by which local law enforcement would deliver the INS the most politically symbolic candidates for deportation. Working within the jail, as the INS described in 1982, allowed the agency to claim that it was not just expelling people who had crossed a border without authorization. It was expelling people who had been proven, at best, morally unfit and, at worst, dangerous, by virtue of a criminal conviction. Certainly, the INS had deported people based on criminal offenses before, but by the 1980s this work became the center of the agency's mission and the key metric by which the agency made appeals for its own necessity. Miami also illustrated a shifting local calculus that distinguished migrants detained for immigration offenses from migrants who were convicted of criminal infractions and were, as a result, excludable or deportable. The city claimed that amid an ongoing drug war and local reluctance to build new carceral institutions, its jail space was tremendously valuable. One way to maximize local law enforcement's capacity to incarcerate was to tell the federal government that noncitizens with criminal convictions were not a local responsibility, exerting pressure on the federal government to build its own detention sites for migrants or offer localities more money for use of jails. As federal and local tensions brewed, Miami became a pivotal early episode in a national, interagency "scramble for jail beds" throughout the 1980s and 1990s.[13]

The Boatlift

On April 20, 1980, Fidel Castro opened the Cuban shipping port of Mariel and announced that all dissenters were free to depart. Castro's once iron grip on emigration had loosened over the previous month, as more than ten thousand Cubans crowded onto the grounds of the Peruvian Embassy attempting to file claims for asylum. Peru and Cuba negotiated an agreement that enabled about

7,500 Cubans to fly to Costa Rica and other locations, an episode that became an embarrassment for Castro as the exiles decried his repressive regime. Desperate for a way to diffuse political tension, free up jobs and housing units in a sluggish Cuban economy, and perhaps create some new problems for his American enemies, Castro encouraged Cuban Americans to retrieve their family members.[14] The Cuban government was facing a crisis of legitimacy. Within hours, the Carter administration would face a crisis of its own.

The U.S. State Department warned Cuban Americans that sending boats to Mariel would mean "playing into Castro's hands" and cautioned that there could be criminal consequences for the transportation of Cubans. These warnings did little to deter Cuban Americans who saw a rare, fleeting opportunity to secure loved ones' passage into the United States. Within twenty-four hours of Mariel's opening, a "ragtag armada" of yachts, fishing boats, and cruisers was en route from South Florida to Cuba. By the end of May 1980, an astounding 94,181 Cubans had arrived in the United States.[15] "Although the [INS] has faced a number of contingency emergency programs over the years, none has challenged the Service as did the Mariel Boatlift," the INS wrote in its 1982 Annual Report. "Never had such a massive wave of intending immigrants arrived at our shores unannounced."[16]

Castro refused to allow images of joyful family reunions to dominate "the Yankee press." He used his 1980 May Day speech to undercut the positive reception of the Mariel Cubans.[17] The Cubans arriving in Florida were not dissidents, or patriots, but *lumpen*, declared Castro; they undermined communist ideals and lacked "revolutionary blood."[18] He gestured to the "limp wrists" (*flojito*) of homosexuals and gender-nonconforming people he promised to expel to the United States—a particularly uneasy situation for U.S. policymakers, who had just affirmed in the Hart-Celler Act that queer migrants were "afflicted with . . . sexual deviation" and ineligible for visas.[19] "They are doing an excellent sanitation job for us," Castro bellowed to a roaring audience.[20] Families fleeing for the Port of Mariel faced acts of harassment from neighbors and law enforcement, who decried them as traitors to their homeland.[21] Castro would later equate the expulsion of his regime's dissenters to an act of national "plastic surgery," ridding the nation of its weakest factions.[22] Castro's homophobic taunts, alongside reports that his officials were forcing Cuban prisoners onto boats bound for Florida, caused panic in the United States. Virtually overnight, news stories about how Cubans had stood against communism and "voted with their feet" were replaced by stories focusing on the arrival of Castro's "undesirables."[23]

Racism had already shaped migrants' experiences with policing and punishment in Cuba. Despite Americans' fears of violent criminals among the new arrivals, the majority of migrants who confessed to serving prior jail time had done so under the *ley de peligrosidad*, or the "law of dangerousness." This catchall provision of the Cuban Criminal Code sentenced convicted persons to a four-year imprisonment for an offense against the Cuban socialist state.[24] The *peligrosidad* laws reflected and produced vast racial inequalities. In a 1987 study, historian Alejandro de la Fuente found that though nonwhite Cubans represented 34 percent of the adult population in Cuba, they made up a staggering 87 percent of those deemed socially "dangerous."[25] As U.S. policymakers coalesced around a plan that would filter out Cubans with a criminal record, they were drafting a blueprint that would target and criminalize Afro-Cuban refugees at a disproportionate rate, while maintaining a facade of racial neutrality.[26]

The biggest question facing the Carter administration was whether it should process the Mariel Cubans under the Refugee Act of 1980, a sweeping revision of refugee law passed just a few months prior, or should instead create some new form of ad hoc emergency legislation. The Refugee Act marked a significant expansion of U.S. refugee admissions, providing for the entry of fifty thousand refugees with no restrictions on country of origin—a number almost never met in practice, as the Reagan administration went to great lengths to raise barriers to entry.[27] The law had been premised on the assumption that the United States would send officials to refugee camps abroad, where they would screen potential migrants before granting them permission to travel to the United States. The law "simply did not anticipate" the possibility of thousands of asylum seekers showing up on American shores, a Carter policy memorandum noted.[28] After months of vacillating public responses and behind-the-scenes administrative infighting, the Carter administration settled on the creation of a new legal category for both Cuban and Haitian migrants who arrived in the United States prior to October 11, 1980: a classification of "Cuban-Haitian Entrant," accompanied in official documents with the parenthetical note "status pending."

The new "Cuban-Haitian Entrant" legal category emerged from a range of concerns. Some of them were logistical. The Asylum Unit of the State Department had only fifteen employees, hardly enough to adjudicate tens of thousands of cases. Others were political: In linking the fates of the Cuban and Haitian asylum seekers, the Carter administration hoped to pacify groups such as the Congressional Black Caucus, which had contended that the mass denial of Haitians' asylum claims in the 1970s was blatantly discriminatory.[29] To policymakers' dismay, the Castro administration had also begun drawing attention to the United States' disparate treatment of Cubans and Haitians, endeavoring to sow tension about the racist contradictions of American human rights claims.[30] Above all, the new legal classification bought time for the administration to determine what "status pending" would mean without formally offering Cubans and Haitians the benefits and permanent legal status promised to full-fledged refugees.[31]

Most of the Cubans who arrived from Mariel would eventually regularize their immigration status through the 1966 Cuban Adjustment Act, which allowed Cuban parolees to upgrade to permanent residents after one year in the United States—an avenue to legalization that did not exist for the twenty-five thousand Haitian asylum seekers who arrived on Florida shores concurrently. However, the "entrant" status put Cubans in a legal limbo for the early years of the 1980s and had significant consequences for those who entered the criminal legal system. Because criminal convictions triggered revocation of "entrant" status, migrants could be subject to indefinite detention or deportation after serving jail or prison sentences. But even for those outside the criminal legal system, distancing Cubans from the full status of "refugee" shaped their reception, their access to social services, and their legal rights. Their membership in the nation was precarious and conditional.

Policing Emergency Detention Sites

When Cuban migrants came ashore in Florida, federal officials moved them to temporary holding sites, where they conducted background checks and searched for family members or a community sponsor. As it became clear that the rate of migration was rapidly outpacing officials' ability to find holding spaces in Florida, the Carter administration proposed a new solution: transporting Cubans out of South Florida and to military bases throughout the country, where they would await sponsors and resettlement. The federal government prioritized keeping Cubans who had nearby family at resettlement centers in South Florida. Because of the richer, whiter demographics of Cuban migration in the 1950s and 1960s, this meant that refugees sent to military camps were more likely to be Black and less likely to have close ties to wealth and U.S. citizenship.[32] In total, about 45 percent of Mariel Cubans were detained at military bases at Fort Eglin in the Florida Panhandle, Fort Chaffee in Arkansas, Fort McCoy in Wisconsin, and Fort Indiantown Gap in Pennsylvania from 1980 to 1981.[33]

Communities surrounding these military bases had mixed responses to their new role in refugee resettlement. The federal government did not promise localities financial support but vowed that the detention sites would pose no threat to nearby towns. Opening the first site at Fort Eglin Air Force Base offered a sense of what authorities could anticipate. On May 2, 1980, a local newspaper headline announced "City Fairgrounds Will Be Refugee Camp," with a subheading that read "Who Are Cuban Criminals?"[34] Some residents in nearby Fort Walton Beach complained that the city had already "served" in 1975, when more than ten thousand Vietnamese refugees had been housed at the base. The superintendent of Okaloosa County, Florida, advocated that no Cuban children be allowed in the county school system as a way of deterring refugees from permanently settling in the Panhandle.[35]

The Mariel Cubans arrived in Okaloosa County on May 3, 1980, shouting refrains of "Freedom lives," "Death to Castro," and "Long live Carter" as they boarded buses to the base.[36] On the day of their arrival, a small-engine plane pulling a banner reading "THE KKK IS HERE" flew over the refugees' temporary home. Klansmen in plainclothes would be "monitoring" the activities of Cubans if they left the base, threatened Klansman B. W. Robinson. "We'll follow them around. If they make a mistake or break the law, they're going to get hurt."[37] (Figure 23.) Klan activity was not limited to Florida. When Fort Chaffee in Fort Smith, Arkansas, opened as a resettlement site the following week, Klansmen protested outside the site, with one robed man running onto the tarmac when a plane of Cubans landed.[38] Though the federal government and the Cuban-Haitian Task Force (CHTF), an interagency group created to coordinate the refugee response, rarely mentioned race, racism imbued communities' fears of security, dependency, and demographic change.

At the resettlement camps, the immigration service again confronted thorny issues of policing and jurisdiction. In a departure from prior decades, its central question had little to do with whether it could deputize local law enforcement to police migrants. Instead, the Department of Justice contemplated whether it could deputize an even more powerful arbiter of state order and violence: the U.S. military. In the first two weeks of operation, the tension between Cubans and camp management at Fort Eglin had escalated into a series of minor uprisings over food shortages, cigarette rationing, and the exceptionally sluggish resettlement rate. A May 18, 1980, conflict culminated with Air Force personnel blasting protesting refugees with a fire truck hose. Major General Robert M. Bond of the U.S. Air Force expressed concerns about the optics of the increasingly militarized security mechanisms at the camp. "What

FIGURE 23. Protest in Fort Walton Beach, Florida, attended by both Klansmen and other residents, 1980. Signs at the protest read "The KKK Likes Cubans if They're in Cuba" and "Castro Sent the Cubans to Us. Let's Send Carter to Castro." *Source:* Mark T. Foley, State Archives of Florida, MF1019.

would Eglin and the Air Force look like if the nation were told that Air Police were guarding Cuban Refugees with barbwire, dogs, guns, fire trucks, and clubs?" General Bond asked in a meeting. "These people left Cuba because of the same conditions."[39]

While most of the jurisdictional battles over immigration and policing prior to the 1980s centered on the role of local police in carrying out the work of border enforcement, bureaucrats in the early 1980s asked what it might look like to make more expansive use of federal law enforcement in responding to migration. By framing Mariel as a foreign relations crisis, the federal government gained increased latitude in enlisting the military as well as a range of federal agencies, including the U.S. Park Police, the Federal Protective Service, the Federal Emergency Management Agency, the U.S. Marshals Service, and INS officers.[40] Agencies such as the Federal Protective Service, whose prior tasks were mostly limited to guarding federal buildings, were now asked to do the delicate work of "peacekeeping" among people who did not speak their language and did not understand why they were being held in barbed wire camps.[41] This had often disastrous results. Cases of abuse abounded, from officials forcefully arresting pregnant women to defiant youth being locked in barracks or handcuffed to camp perimeter fences.[42]

On June 1, 1980, protests reached a fever pitch at Arkansas' Fort Chaffee, as more than three hundred Cubans stormed the gates of the camp, throwing rocks and setting fire to two of the guard shacks. Federal police retaliated by opening fire on the refugees. By the end of the conflict, more than one thousand Cubans had been involved, and thirty-seven Cubans had been injured, primarily from gunshot and stab wounds.[43] In theory, the main task of resettlement camps like the one at Fort Chaffee was to locate sponsors and to ensure a smooth transition into American communities. In reality, their main purpose became policing and control—how to prevent people from breaking out of sites that bore names like "Camp Liberty" and "Freedom City."

Similar to General Bond's hesitations about aggressive policing at Eglin, the soldiers at Fort Chaffee made little attempt to stop Cubans from leaving the base because they did not believe that they had the authority to use force to detain migrant civilians.[44] Arkansas Governor Bill Clinton was incensed. He had been furious at President Carter for sending the migrants to Arkansas in the first place and was even more angry that they had breached the confines of the base.[45] In the week following the uprising, the federal government formally expanded the military's authority to conduct preventive patrols within the detention sites and to use "reasonable force" to secure the sites' borders and suppress uprisings. The attorney general declared that the military had legal authority to police civilian refugees on military bases because these sites could not be "rationally segregated" for law enforcement purposes.[46] This distanced Cuban migrants from the category of "civilian," making them something akin to foreign combatants housed on American soil.[47] And with the presidential go-ahead, many military personnel would treat them as such.

The military quickly took on a more active role in policing Fort Chaffee. Nearly two hundred soldiers were flown to Arkansas and organized into two "reaction forces" that would be used in case of an uprising, bringing the total military population to just under four thousand. The reaction forces were equipped with military trucks, body armor, ballistic helmets, riot batons, and pistols.[48] Other soldiers were tasked with building a double-strand concertina wire wall around the camp. While in earlier months the military had been restrained to camp perimeters, after the June 1980 edict, military police patrolled Cuban barracks and recreational areas both on foot and on horseback.[49] However, if migrants left the camp and were found in outside communities, the Joint Security Plan stipulated that they should be picked up by Border Patrol agents, "the only agency authorized by law to arrest illegal aliens"— collapsing asylum seekers into the umbrella category of "illegal immigrant."

By September 1980, five months after the beginning of the boatlift, there were more than five thousand "hard cases" remaining at the four military bases.[50] Eager to downsize the number of detention sites, the CHTF announced that all Cuban migrants awaiting resettlement would be moved to Fort Chaffee. The *Washington Post* wrote that security at the site would be intensified in preparation for the arrival of "hard-core refugees."[51] The phrase "hard-core refugees" exemplified the new nexus of illegality and refugee status. No longer sympathetic anti-communist allies, Mariel Cubans had become a threat for the state to contain. By the time Fort Chaffee initiated plans to close the following summer, status reports indicated that 95 percent of remaining men and 100 percent of remaining women were Black.[52] The consolidation at Fort Chaffee became yet another process to reinforce the criminality of racialized migrants, to both the government and the American public. (Figures 24 and 25.)

In January 1982, the resettlement camp at Fort Chaffee closed for good. The Reagan administration announced plans to transfer the last Cubans at Fort Chaffee to the United States Penitentiary, Atlanta, with a smaller number of those with psychiatric illness sent to the federal prison hospital in Springfield, Missouri.[53] Fort Smith Mayor Jack Freeze expressed little concern about losing the Cubans, despite the jobs and contracts for food, services, and

FIGURE 24. Cubans being resettled from Wisconsin's Fort McCoy, one of the four resettlement camps established at U.S. military bases, after being sponsored by the Hebrew Immigrant Aid Society, 1980. Courtesy of Miguel Tamayo, the *La Crosse Tribune* and Murphy Library Special Collections, University of Wisconsin–La Crosse.

FIGURE 25. One of the last Cuban refugees at Fort McCoy, Wisconsin, waiting to be transferred to Arkansas' Fort Chaffee, September 1980. Three months after the Fort Chaffee consolidation, in January 1981, the government reported that 75 percent of the 5,052 remaining refugees were Black. By the summer of 1981, the population at Fort Chaffee would be 95 percent Afro-Cubans. Courtesy of William J. Lizdas, the *La Crosse Tribune* and Murphy Library Special Collections, University of Wisconsin–La Crosse.

construction they brought his town. "So would prostitution, but is it good for the community?" Freeze retorted.[54] When asked about the optics of sending refugees to prison because of the government's inability to locate sponsors, Arkansas Governor Frank White told reporters that they were splitting hairs. "People knowledgeable about the situation know that Fort Chaffee was a prison, too," the governor candidly replied.[55]

Even though the federal government framed Mariel as an international incident and used it as an experiment in all-hands-on-deck federal policing, it still recognized the importance of local cooperation. Towns had no real power to stop the federal government from using military bases, but they could certainly make the process more difficult. Officials presented the embrace of militarized policing at these sites as a concession to local communities and a way to appease groups such as the National Governors Association, which argued that the federal government had placed an undue burden on states. They *owed it* to nearby towns to keep Cubans inside these camps at whatever cost.[56] As detained migrants grew frustrated and took action, media images of protests and military pushback reinforced the idea that Mariel Cubans, and especially Afro-Cubans, were an out-of-control criminal mob. This made it more difficult to locate sponsors and led municipalities to push for more policing, even after refugees were released. That these events would conclude with the transfer of refugees to federal prisons, with no trial and often little evidence of prior criminal wrongdoing, was a predictable culmination of nearly two years of criminalization and expanding federal authority, alongside decades of using prisons and jails as tools of sovereignty and border control.

In the final issue of the Fort Chaffee camp newspaper, *La Vida Nueva*, employees carefully avoided mentioning what awaited those remaining at the camp—incarceration, this time at "real" prisons rather than makeshift base camps. The last workers at Fort Chaffee praised the Cubans for their cooperation, maintaining the perpetually sunny tone of a state-sponsored newspaper. But one writer, Antonio Dalama Matienzo, who had been a refugee community leader at Fort Chaffee before his release, addressed the future explicitly. He wrote in a letter to the last migrants at the camp:

> Dear Brother: It's difficult for me to describe the pain that I felt, and still feel, upon learning of the decision to transfer the remaining refugees to federal institutions—specifically prison. We all fled our homeland and our loved ones with one objective . . . freedom and a new life in a freedom loving country. Many have been granted the opportunity to realize their dream, but a few sadly were not as fortunate and now find themselves confined to federal prisons, in effect serving their sentences. I beg you with all my heart to not lose faith and to trust in the Lord. . . . I shall never forget you.[57]

"Miami, Refugee City"

Many of the localities that had hosted resettlement camps feared that Cubans would settle permanently in their towns. These anxieties were largely unfounded. Most Cuban refugees, about four of every five, returned to a place where they could be among others who shared their language and history: Miami's Dade County, the Cuban "homeland in absentia."[58] The Mariel Boatlift's impact on Miami was extraordinary. In a month, the city added the population of Tallahassee, Florida.[59] It was a seismic event for schools, hospitals, the labor market, and even the DMV—one that economists would argue about for decades to come.[60] For nearly every South Florida institution, Mariel meant recalibration.[61] For nearly every South Floridian, it meant new neighbors.

What awaited Mariel Cubans after they were freed from resettlement camps? Resettlement brought its share of horror stories. Seven women were released from Fort Eglin to a man who attempted to force them into sex work.[62] Other refugees were released to "phantom sponsors" who immediately disappeared, leaving the migrants with no housing or support.[63] The government had grown laxer in vetting sponsors as it scrambled to empty Fort Chaffee, an expensive political liability.[64] More often, resettlement brought familiar tales of sponsoring families whose patience waned and refugees who struggled to secure jobs in a city where many employers refused to hire Mariel Cubans.[65] Lucas Perez, an unhoused welder who came to the United States from Mariel told *Time*: "I've gone through two pairs of shoes looking for work. There is none."[66] For people whose legal status was in flux, the complexities of resettlement added yet another layer of precarity.[67]

The Florida congressional delegation maintained a clear position to President Carter in the months following the boatlift: The challenges facing South Florida were entirely the result of federal decisions and thus required federal appropriations. If the president failed to address Floridians' concerns, they promised he had little chance of winning the state in the looming presidential election.[68] Policymakers presented the issue as nothing less than a referendum on South Florida's survival. In a letter to the White House, Representative William Lehman, a Miami Democrat, appealed that there were "still ways to save Florida" and blamed the lack of border enforcement for tearing apart what had once been "a viable multiethnic community."[69]

Mariel Cubans came to Miami in a moment of tremendous local tension, one that undercut Representative Lehman's invocations of a multiracial urban utopia. In the first summer after Mariel, the city lodged unhoused refugees in the Miami Orange Bowl, the city's downtown football stadium. While Cuban migrants rested on cots in the strange athletic grounds, Miami was erupting.[70] Arthur McDuffie, a thirty-three-year-old Black insurance salesman, had been brutally beaten by Miami Police Department officers following a traffic incident. Police cracked his skull against the pavement, causing his brain to swell. McDuffie died shortly thereafter. Officials immediately began covering their tracks. Despite a damning autopsy, the law enforcement officers were

charged only with manslaughter, not murder.[71] Following the case's verdict—
an acquittal for the officers at the hands of an all-white jury—Black Miamians
took to the streets to protest the latest in a decades-long pattern of institutional
racism and injustice in the Magic City.

The uprisings, marked by fires and punctuated by eighteen deaths, reached
a few blocks from the football stadium, where the news trickled to the refugees
via Spanish-language radio. Some Afro-Cuban migrants told reporters that
they had heard in Cuba how poorly Black Americans were treated—Was this
true or more of Castro's propaganda?[72] Others skeptically asked journalists
whether police *ever* experienced legal consequences in the United States. The
rebellions bolstered policymakers' perceptions that Miami was a city on
the brink and a city desperately in need of federal intervention.[73]

Dade County's jails were already overtaxed with people apprehended from
drug charges as Miami became a central node in a transnational war on drugs.
Paralleling the watery metaphors used to describe migrants, a representative
from the Drug Enforcement Administration told Congress in 1983 that a relentless "tidal wave of drugs" had inundated South Florida, one that would fill
the jails with a fifteen-year backlog of cases if the government had the capacity
to prosecute all offenders.[74] Miami's geographic relationship to the Americas
gave the city's war on drugs a specific character; officials focused on drug im-
porters and exporters moving through South Florida, as incidents such as a
1979 shoot-out between Colombian drug traffickers at the suburban Dadeland
Mall made the "war" descriptor feel apt.[75]

By the early 1980s, there was bipartisan consensus that crime was a national
security problem, one that required aggressive surveillance of Black youth in
urban areas, as well as aggressive surveillance of the nation's land, air, and sea
borders.[76] South Florida became a testing ground for programs connecting
the military with local law enforcement in shared efforts to seal off the United
States from "undesirable influences" originating in the rest of the Western
Hemisphere.[77] Over the course of two years, South Floridians saw the military
deployed first to police the arrival and resettlement of Cubans, then to provide
reinforcements during the McDuffie uprisings, and finally, to thwart the international drug trade. By 1982, there were Navy surveillance aircrafts operating off the Florida coast, U.S. Army Cobra helicopters tracking smuggling
aircrafts, and U.S. Navy warships interdicting boats suspected of carrying
drugs and migrants.[78] For both local and federal policymakers, the traffic of
drugs and refugees became two intertwined threats to the city's stability and
survival. Both, they suggested, required unprecedented intergovernmental
cooperation in policing.

Despite claims of total abandonment by the federal government, South Florida did receive federal money to support refugees. In the year following Mariel, a $10 million grant was made available to develop refugees' literacy and occupational skills. There was a $4 million Department of Education grant for the thirteen thousand refugee children entering Dade schools, plus a $1 million emergency grant to train teachers who would work with these students. A $6.8 million grant from the Department of Health and Human Services expanded health and mental health care delivery. These funding streams were controversial, as some policymakers feared that any extension of social services would catalyze future movement of migrants.[79] Federal aid, like that provided for by the 1982 Fascell-Stone Amendment, prioritized the most pressing concerns for Cubans' survival: food, shelter, and medical aid, making "entrants" eligible for the same support as those formally designated "refugees."[80]

Yet this was not the money localities desired. While states and municipalities certainly did not reject any checks from the federal government, local leaders made it clear that they did not just want funding focused on integrating refugees into the community. They wanted money that helped them *expel* refugees, to rid them of a group that one Florida congressman coldly described as "surplus."[81] This "help" could take two forms: either in resettlement programs that took Mariel Cubans far from South Florida or in programs that gave the city more money for policing and incarceration—money that brought the additional benefit of increasing the city's firepower against the Black Miamians who had just staged one of the largest urban rebellions in American history. For many Miami officials, an effective response to the refugee "crisis" looked like one that eliminated the refugees altogether.

Allegations of skyrocketing crime went hand in hand with a collapsing social safety net for refugees. As some social services such as access to food stamps and educational services expanded in the first months after the boatlift, other lifelines disappeared. Key among them was housing. Dade County's rental market had a vacancy rate of less than 0.5 percent at the time of the boatlift, and Cubans' demand for housing further drove up the prices of affordable rentals.[82] Initially, Miami Beach housed 1,500 refugees in vacant hotel rooms. But in October 1980, county commissioners abruptly ended the program, even as the CHTF offered more money to sustain the initiative. Hotel owners evicted hundreds of residents, some of whom had children and most of whom had nowhere to go.[83]

Other unhoused refugees found shelter in hundreds of tents set up under an interstate a few blocks from the eastern boundary of Little Havana (Figure 26). The city referred to the site as the "Tent City," while Cubans called it

FIGURE 26. Miami's Tent City, beneath I-95 Highway, 1980. The Tent City was set up in the shadow of Interstate 95, a highway project that had displaced thousands of Black Miamians in the 1950s and 1960s. "A makeshift blowing-in-the-wind tent city in subtropical South Florida in the middle of hurricane season," quipped the *Miami News*. "If there must be a tent city for refugees, it should be on the lawn at 1600 Pennsylvania Avenue." Courtesy of Michael L. Carlebach and Special Collections at the University of Miami Libraries, Michael Carlebach Photography Collection, Coral Gables.

"Campamento del Rio"—the "River Camp." The Tent City, opened in July 1980, was a physical reminder that resettlement was neither an easy nor a straightforward process. Many of the camp's residents had already been detained in the tent cities and barracks of Fort Chaffee, Fort Eglin, and others but now were lodged in a camp operated by the city, rather than the federal government. The camp population plateaued at around six hundred residents, with about three thousand Cubans moving through the site over its two-month life span. Miami officials observed that the Tent City and local jail worked symbiotically, with struggling Cubans cycling between the two sites. Miami Police Captain Martin Green called the Dade County Jail "Tent City North."[84] The city implored voluntary groups to begin searching for sponsors outside of the Miami area, offering nonprofits $2,000 for each Cuban successfully resettled out of state—a substantial increase from the $300 they were paid to resettle arrivals in South Florida immediately following the boatlift.[85]

Both the hotels program and the Tent City were temporary measures, and by the autumn of 1980 both had ended. At the same time Dade County was forcing thousands of refugees onto the streets, municipalities passed a new set of emergency laws that effectively criminalized homelessness. Claiming that the crime rate had soared 36 percent above that of the previous year, Miami Beach passed an anti-loitering ordinance and a stop-and-frisk law, as well as a 10 p.m. curfew for city parks and beaches.[86] The loitering ordinance outlawed sleeping, standing, or gathering in a way that blocked sidewalks and streets or threatened the safety of property or persons. Stop-and-frisk gave police the power to stop and search anyone they deemed suspicious, a law that the *Miami Herald* said "[guaranteed] the harassment of anyone with a Latin accent."[87] The new laws were enforced through a series of "street sweeps," where police deployed into neighborhoods frequented by Mariel Cubans and made apprehensions, typically on loitering charges. Though intended as temporary, many of the loitering provisions stayed on the books after the emergency period expired. County Judge David Gersten reported in 1981 that 25 percent of the defendants on his criminal misdemeanor calendar were Mariel Cubans charged with "Loitering and Prowling" or disorderly conduct.[88]

Much like laws that the Mexican American community had challenged in the 1970s, arguing that the policies made it illegal to "look Mexican," Dade County's laws added a new element of risk to being Cuban and poor in public.[89] Some police officers reported that they had mistaken the "Havana custom" of street corner political debates for violent brawls. One Mariel Cuban was working as a garbage collector in a wealthy Miami neighborhood;

homeowners called the police when he knocked on their door to ask for a glass of water. Miami police arrested another refugee for carrying a small pocket-knife that he used to open boxes at the grocery store where he worked.[90] By the end of 1981, even some law enforcement officials questioned whether the city's crime sweep programs had legalized anti-immigrant harassment.[91]

The city had an obvious interest in linking crime and immigration because it made crime a federal problem requiring federal dollars. "Attempts to pin down the actual number of Mariel refugees being held in Dade County jail yield answers such as 'we estimate,' 'we believe,' 'we think,' 'it must be,'—but no facts," criticized Monsignor Bryan O. Walsh, a longtime ally of Miami's Cuban community.[92] In the absence of reliable records, officials guessed which people at the jail were from Mariel based on self-declaration or by an officer's assumptions about what a "recent arrival" looked like.[93] Some officials based this on whether a "Latin" inmate listed an emergency contact, assuming that recent refugees were less likely to have local connections.[94] Other police officers claimed that they could identify Mariel Cubans from their clothes, particularly if they wore reflective sunglasses and jeans with rolled bottoms.[95] Law enforcement officers from as far away as Charleston, South Carolina, wrote to the INS with information about decoding Cubans' tattoos, which they insisted were evidence of a criminal past.[96] Cops collated this questionable evidence and marked the letter R (for "refugee") in the top right corner of their crime reports.[97]

Despite unreliable data, the Miami Police Department used the Mariel Boatlift and the alleged spike in refugee-related crime as an opportunity to dramatically expand law enforcement presence in the city. The police department had 650 officers in 1980, but by 1985 the force had grown to 1,033. The police budget swelled accordingly, doubling over five years, even as the department faced lawsuits and a federal civil rights investigation.[98] Some localities looked to taxpayers to finance the law enforcement expansion. In Hialeah, a heavily Cuban suburb in Dade County, the city council approved a 2 percent hike in the utility tax, with all funds going to the police department budget.[99] The city of Miami green-lit a special taxing district downtown, which funded the hiring of 186 additional cops.[100] Other localities exerted pressure elsewhere: Even though the federal government had not yet approved any funding for criminal justice expenditures, Miami Beach mailed federal officials itemized bills listing its increased policing expenses.[101]

By the end of 1980, after months of corresponding with outraged Floridian lawmakers and citizens, the federal government agreed to offer states money for "criminal justice/law enforcement costs associated with the recent Cuban-Haitian immigration."[102] The CHTF and the Law Enforcement Assistance Administration—a federal agency that issued block grants to local police departments—agreed to a $5 million program to aid state and local governments. Eighty percent of funding was allocated for states with 2,500 or more "entrants," while the remaining 20 percent of funding went to the five states that had hosted resettlement camps. Florida received about three-quarters of the total funding, which was earmarked to reimburse criminal justice institutions, renovate and expand jails in Dade County, and expedite hearings for detained pretrial migrants.[103] This was the first time in the Law Enforcement Assistance Administration's history that money had gone specifically to address refugee-related expenses.[104] For local leaders, it was evidence that their strategy worked. Blaming immigration policy for rising crime rates could be an avenue to federal resources. Mariel transformed funding for criminal justice expenditures into a component of refugee resettlement and solidified the idea that more asylum seekers necessitated more policing and incarceration.

Dade County Jail and the Criminal Alien

Dade County Jail, the facility Miami police called "Tent City North," was no stranger to problems. It opened its doors in 1961. By the early 1970s, the county had a shortage of public defenders and outdated procedures for handling mounting caseloads. Violence within the institution was rampant, with the death of an incarcerated white seventeen-year-old sparking national attention.[105] Detained people waited weeks or months for legal representation in what the *Miami Herald* described as "unspeakable" conditions—conditions that became the target of legal action and a court-ordered population cap in 1974.[106] Though the jail population caps proliferating in cities throughout the United States may have looked like progress, Melanie Newport writes that they undercut much of the activism of incarcerated people in prior decades—activism that had centered the jail as a site of urban inequality and anti-Black racism. Setting population caps "shifted prisoner rights from a qualitative to a quantitative determination, from the substance of conditions to the number of people in jail."[107] It was this overcrowding and litigation that had led the INS to seek out detention space for Haitian asylum seekers in Immokalee, far from where migrants had landed. Residents of Dade County's growing suburbs fiercely protested county plans to build larger regional jails in their communities.[108] As a result, Cuban migrants encountered an outdated, massively overcrowded facility, where they were segregated from other inmates due to officials' paranoia about a looming "racial trench war."[109]

To the perpetual frustration of Miami officials, the INS had no formal procedure for identifying or assuming responsibility for Mariel Cubans moving through jails and prisons, even though a criminal record jeopardized "entrant" legal status.[110] As part of a 1981 study, the Miami Grand Jury submitted a list of seventy-one noncitizens in the county jail system and asked the INS to report on their status. The INS testified that not one "immigration hold" had been placed on any of the seventy-one defendants.[111] Local leaders used this as evidence of the ineptitude of the immigration service—How could the INS take "criminal aliens" seriously if it had no system to identify them?

When the Tent City was disbanded in September 1980, local authorities observed a predictable outcome: rising rates of homelessness and vagrancy among refugees. With nowhere to go, refugees slept in cars, in city parks, in alleyways behind Little Havana Santería shops.[112] They shined shoes, took on odd jobs, and desperately tried to avoid the cops. In December 1980, the Florida congressional delegation demanded that the Carter administration undertake a massive, almost certainly unconstitutional "sweep" that would bring these unhoused refugees *back* into federal custody.[113] The proposed roundup was controversial at the Miami jail, where officials grumbled that it would add "minor offenders and drunks" to a facility that already had more than three hundred people sleeping on the floor. Their concerns were justified: That same month, Judge Alcee Hastings decreed that the overcrowded Dade County Jail must release two people for each new person it admitted.[114]

The INS demurred on a sweep but agreed to a more measured step: It would take custody of the approximately five hundred Cuban and Haitian migrants who were held in South Florida jails and transfer them to INS detention sites in New York, Texas, and California. It was a strategic use of the growing INS detention network and an acknowledgment that Florida jails had effectively supplanted the Tent City as a place for migrants who could not find work or support in Miami. Just as federal prisons were used to immobilize Cubans who could not be aided by the resettlement process, local jails were used to immobilize Cubans who had been released from federal custody but failed to be "assimilated" into the local community. "They say they are going to pick up bums," said Lazaro Martinez, a forty-year-old refugee who was living on the streets of Little Havana after his sponsorship and construction gig fell through. "How can I be a bum when I'm looking for a job?"[115]

Even this plan for limited federal intervention quickly fell apart. Immigration authorities encountered the same obstacle Miami police had reported: Fearing deportation, people in jail knew better than to say that they were from Mariel. Identifying refugees by their tattoos and denim, the INS conceded, was not a reliable means of settling jurisdiction. Faced with erratic recordkeeping, wavering relations with local police, and countless other refugee-related issues to resolve, the immigration service decided that a "roundup" of jailed refugees exceeded its bureaucratic capacity.[116]

With the threat of further court intervention looming and the INS reluctant to act, both the state and federal governments attempted to reduce the population at the Dade County Jail. The governor of Florida agreed to transfer inmates from local jails to state prisons in order to keep the city facilities afloat.[117] The Bureau of Prisons similarly offered to take custody of Mariel refugees convicted of felonies, but with a major caveat: Florida would need to *reimburse* the BOP, at an average rate of $37 per inmate, per night.[118] This proposal was a total reversal of the prevailing economic arrangement for migrant detention in the twentieth century. Rather than the federal government paying localities for holding noncitizens, the federal government demanded compensation *from* the locality for use of federal facilities.

In February 1981, Governor Bob Graham decided that his state had endured enough. He filed a lawsuit against the federal government, demanding it "accept its responsibilities" for the Cuban entrants and remove them from the jail. Governor Graham's actions built on the complaints made by many localities in the 1970s that had argued the INS was not doing enough, but his actions also represented a clear escalation: He was now asking the courts to *force* the immigration service to do more. If the courts were willing to intervene in the local issue of jail overcrowding, the logic went, they should also be willing to make the federal government do its part.[119] Graham's lawsuit was quickly dismissed, but it marked a high point of federal-local tension over who bore responsibility for incarcerating noncitizens. By the following summer, observing few improvements at Miami's jail, an increasingly exasperated Judge Hastings levied a $2,000 a day fine against the locality for each day the site exceeded its population limit.[120]

Financial penalties spurred the elusive intergovernmental cooperation Miami had sought. With fines accumulating, the federal government transferred seventy-five detained migrants from Dade County Jail to the Federal Correctional Institution in Tallahassee, with a promise to transfer more as soon as possible.[121] Other migrants were sent to the detention center in El

Paso, where officials expressed confusion about why people with legal status were at a facility primarily used for undocumented Mexicans crossing the border. The INS insisted that it was only sending Cubans who had been convicted of crimes. Migrants told different stories. "I was stopped on the street in Miami by police," said Silverio Torres, who had been detained at El Paso for three months. "They checked my papers and took me to court. There were no charges, but they still sent me to Immigration. I hadn't done anything wrong. This is an injustice."[122]

The emphasis on the criminal alien, and on the jail as the central site of immigration law enforcement, signaled a shift in how authorities positioned the problem of illegality. In a 1986 list of talking points for increasing federal appropriations for "deportable criminal aliens," proponents in Congress were encouraged to stress the following point: "Instead of *picking up* convicted felons upon release from prison, INS 'picks on' field hands, dishwashers and janitors who are trying to survive by working long hours at menial jobs."[123] This recast the undocumented worker, typically imagined as Mexican, as a victim of overpolicing. The logic extended to other groups as well. Miami officials complained that the federal government was setting up new federal detention centers to jail Haitians who posed, in the words of the Grand Jury, "no danger" to Dade County.[124] The INS would never have the resources to deport all unauthorized migrants, but this provided a new rationale for how it should allocate resources—one that demanded an even more expansive relationship between local law enforcement and the INS.

———

By the mid-1980s, the jail was not just a staging area for the immigration service to facilitate deportations and removals; it was the arena where the INS identified those whose expulsions it deemed most imperative. Going forward, the INS declared that it planned to "work within the prison system."[125] The immigration service faced a crisis of legitimacy in the wake of Mariel. Aligning with corrections in an era that saw bipartisan embrace of punitive anti-crime policies was a way to salvage the agency's reputation and refine its mission.[126]

With the support of President Reagan, the immigration service denounced previous attempts to draw firm jurisdictional lines between local law enforcement and the INS. Under the 1986 "Meese Directive," passed down from Attorney General Edwin Meese, the federal government promised greater coordination and fewer restrictions on how local law enforcement could aid the immigration service. The new policy "clearly identifies the INS as a criminal justice agency, as well as an integral part of the law enforcement community," wrote the Department of Justice, an affirmation of a rebranding the immigration service had pursued since the 1970s.[127] By 1986, some cities, such as New York City, had effectively given up on notifying the INS about migrants in local custody, while others, such as San Diego, threatened to follow Miami's lead and sue the federal government for financial support related to policing people without U.S. citizenship.[128] The attorney general's directive promised localities that change was coming.

In the 1980s, Congress passed two laws that not only cemented the relationship between the INS and the criminal legal system but redefined the parameters of crime itself. The first came in 1986, with the Immigration Reform and Control Act (IRCA), a law best remembered for providing "amnesty," which enabled tens of thousands of unauthorized migrants to legalize their status. Like virtually all U.S. attempts at immigration reform, a liberalizing gesture was accompanied by punitive counterweights. One counterweight was the federalization of employer sanctions. Throughout the 1970s, states had passed laws imposing criminal penalties on employers who knowingly hired undocumented migrants. Questions soon arose about whether this was an unconstitutional effort by states to create immigration law; IRCA superseded these federalism debates by inscribing the sanctions into federal law.[129] Another counterweight was a provision requiring the attorney general to begin any deportation proceeding "as expeditiously as possible" after a noncitizen was convicted of a deportable offense. To achieve this, the INS piloted a new initiative, the Alien Criminal Apprehension Program (ACAP). ACAP institutionalized collaboration with local law enforcement and the INS, created shared information systems, and encouraged INS investigators to intervene at the point of arrest, rather than after incarceration.[130]

ACAP promised a "unified" INS approach to removing criminal aliens that could still be modified to suit local conditions. Officials in New York and California began channeling noncitizens with criminal convictions into just a few prisons where immigration judges were stationed, effectively segregating noncitizens from the general population.[131] Within several years of ACAP's creation, INS officials were stationed 24/7 at the Los Angeles County Jail to identify migrants for deportation.[132] Internally, the INS descriptions of ACAP's targets read like a list of ethnic stereotypes: Alongside Mariel Cubans, the agency envisioned heavily armed Jamaican drug dealers, Chinese gambling rings, Nigerian credit card scammers, and Italian mobsters.[133] Laws making it easier to deport migrants convicted of crimes had been on the books since 1917, and many of ACAP's purported targets would have seemed awfully familiar to 1917 lawmakers. Still, ACAP transformed the statistic of "criminal aliens removed" into the new measure of efficacy for the INS. In the years to come, the agency would issue a monthly press release touting the number of criminal aliens taken off American streets—nearly every month, the number was declared a new record for the INS.[134]

Ten days after IRCA entered the books, Congress passed the Anti-Drug Abuse Act of 1986, which stipulated that any noncitizen convicted of an "aggravated felony" was subject to deportation. The list of aggravated felonies steadily expanded in the following years, but even at its initiation it included nearly all drug offenses.[135] The INS reported a "rapid deterioration" of relationships with local jails following the passage of the Anti-Drug Abuse Act.[136] Lawmakers had once pitched aggressive deportation efforts as a tool for rectifying prison and jail overcrowding, suggesting that the savings from removing migrants before long incarcerations could fund additional removals. However, new Anti-Drug Abuse Act rules dictated that a noncitizen convicted of an aggravated felony could not be released from custody upon completion of a sentence, essentially forcing states and localities to hold onto people who had already served their time. A Florida INS official wrote in 1989 that the state was on the verge of a "crisis in detention space," even as the INS accelerated transfers of migrants from Florida facilities to jails and detention sites around the country.[137] As a result, between 1987 and 1991, Florida added 27,087 new prison beds; pressure from drug-related arrests alongside prison conditions litigation caused fiscal conservatism to take a backseat to the demand for more carceral space.[138]

As historian Alexander Stephens has argued, the influence of Florida lawmakers on national immigration legislation was difficult to miss. IRCA specifically referred to "Cuban nationals" and "Marielito Cubans convicted of a felony" in a provision allocating funds to reimburse states for costs associated with incarcerating migrants.[139] Cubans were not the sole factor leading the agency to turn toward the "criminal alien," but the overwhelming media coverage, the sudden nature of their arrival, and the protests of South Florida leaders made the risk seem tangible and overwhelming. Local pressure had pushed the federal government to reexamine its immigration choices before. It had propelled the construction of federal jails, the boarding or removal of migrants in local institutions, the siting of new immigration detention sites, and the specifics of raids. Yet Mariel still signaled a new era—one in which localities demanded a total overhaul of INS priorities, technologies, and funding streams. And, remarkably, localities seemed to get what they wanted.

Miami's struggle for federal funding, and its push to move refugees out of its jails, upended how municipalities responded to migrants and what they demanded of the federal government. This had reverberations as other state and local leaders began demanding reimbursement for costs associated with incarcerating noncitizens. California Governor Pete Wilson made federal reimbursement a cornerstone of his push for the notoriously regressive Proposition 187, a 1994 ballot initiative that would deny social services to undocumented Californians.[140] The law also contained enforcement-oriented measures, forbidding local governments from restricting cooperation with immigration authorities and requiring all law enforcement to verify the immigration status of any arrested person.[141] Prop 187 was found unconstitutional, but it prompted copycat legislation around the country, as well as a series of sensational lawsuits by state and local officials seeking federal reimbursements for benefits and services to undocumented migrants.[142]

Many of Prop 187's provisions would eventually be written into federal law. Congress institutionalized federal reimbursements for localities' incarceration expenses in an initiative called the State Criminal Alien Assistance Program (SCAAP), part of the 1994 omnibus crime law. "When people enter the country illegally and commit crimes, it isn't fair to ask the states to bear the entire cost of their imprisonment," President Clinton declared when signing the bill.[143] SCAAP was the culmination of the arguments Miami leaders had spent over a decade making: that they were entitled to federal funds not only for the administrative detention of migrants but also for the criminal incarceration of migrants. Florida's jail beds were "precious," said the special counsel to the governor—if the federal government wanted states and localities to prioritize immigration enforcement, they needed financial incentives.[144]

By the end of the 1980s, provoked by both federal legislation and bureaucratic maneuvering, the INS had effectively ingrained itself in the criminal justice system. This relationship would become even more concrete as the immigration service laid plans to build more prisons of its own, often invoking the fear of the deviant, criminal migrant as a rationale for the agency's move toward incarceration. The legacy of SCAAP would be similarly long-lasting. Despite efforts from both Republican and Democratic presidents to end the program, in 2021, SCAAP dispersed more than $221 million to 507 counties and states.[145] Critics have suggested that the program creates incentives for law enforcement to prioritize noncitizens for arrest and for sheriffs to inflate their numbers of detained migrants.[146] Only about one-third of the 1.8 million local law enforcement referrals for SCAAP funds from 2005 to 2010 were determined to be eligible for funding; more than three hundred thousand of these referrals were filed for U.S. citizens and legal permanent residents, and some of them were intentionally fraudulent.[147] Legal scholar Anjana Malhotra has argued that localities' efforts to secure SCAAP funding has led them to subvert *Miranda* rights, with police failing to inform arrested people of their right to an attorney and their right to remain silent before questioning their citizenship status. At New Jersey's Morris County Jail, individuals who remained silent to immigration-related inquiries were placed in isolation until they responded.[148]

Localities continue to reinvest SCAAP funding into the criminal justice system—paying deputy salaries, renovating jails, and funding rehabilitation programs. Federal revenues have also been used an all-too-familiar way: bankrolling the whims of sheriffs. Broward County, Miami's neighbor to the north, had also claimed that it bore an unfair burden from the migrations of Caribbean refugees in the 1980s, around thirty thousand of whom settled in the county.[149] A 2004 investigation found that the Broward sheriff used SCAAP funds for a $1.82 million renovation of his office, featuring leather furniture, marble countertops, and oak wainscoting. The federal government confirmed that it does not audit, or regulate, how localities use federal grant money.[150] Turning the "criminal alien" into a nexus of federal-local collaboration became one more way for localities to transform the work of immigration law enforcement into few-strings-attached discretionary funds—an enduring legacy of Dade County's response to the Mariel Boatlift.

7

Flexible Space and the
Weaponization of Transfers

"WELCOME TO KROME NORTH—THIS IS an Immigration and Naturalization Service Facility," an INS official recited from a script to a room full of Haitian migrants in 1981. The migrants had just completed the six hundred-mile trek across the Greater Antilles to seek political asylum in Florida, the same journey their compatriots had been making since the *Saint Sauveur* arrived in 1972. They were exhausted. They were anxious. And now they were sitting in a nondescript room in the Florida Everglades, as a uniformed man read them a carefully worded statement. "This is not a prison and you are not under arrest. This will be your home for a short period of time."[1]

The INS officer proceeded to deluge the new arrivals with the necessary information for their stay at Krome Service Processing Center. The official explained how toilets worked and where they would sleep. There were cigarette machines and a limited number of Creole interpreters. Migrants were allowed to walk freely around the premises but should watch out for the construction taking place to convert a onetime missile testing site into makeshift dormitories.[2]

With the Mariel Boatlift demanding almost all of the immigration service's attention, the bureaucracy's other responsibilities fell by the wayside.[3] Though the federal government grouped Haitians together with Cubans in the new legal category of "entrant," they were often viewed as an afterthought to U.S. entanglements with Castro. Between April and October 1980, ten thousand Haitian migrants had traveled across the Straits of Florida, yet the Cuban-Haitian Task Force designated only one of its forty-three employees to work full time on issues facing Haitian refugees.[4] And although Cubans faced hasty, discretion-driven entry proceedings, their prospects remained markedly better than those of Haitian asylum seekers, who beginning in 1981 faced mandatory detention without trial in the United States.

Eager to differentiate himself from his predecessor with a hard-line stance on illegal immigration, President Reagan convened an immigration task force shortly after entering office in 1981.[5] In a memo titled "Cuban/Haitian Enforcement Options," the task force laid out two paths for deterring further migration from the Caribbean: instituting a policy of mandatory detention upon entry or instituting a program to interdict migrants' boats at sea. The memo listed pros and cons for each option. Detention would prevent migrants from disappearing before hearings and would indicate a "major commitment" to enforcement. But what community would want to host these detention centers? The task force also conceded that the optics were not ideal, writing that the "appearance of 'concentration camps' which, at the present time, would be filled largely by blacks, may be publicly unacceptable."[6]

Interdiction, meanwhile, would be less expensive and would not create the same unwanted images, but it still had some political liabilities.[7] Reagan officials questioned its legality and feared that it might result in "ugly incidents" where Haitian migrants jumped overboard and drowned. Still, the report concluded, interdiction would be a highly visible act of law enforcement that would ease the tense political situation in Florida. Perhaps most important, keeping Haitians out of the country meant keeping them away from legal aid and circumventing the courts altogether.[8] If Haitians never made it ashore, they could not connect with Miami's growing community of advocates, and the INS could avoid the contentious legal battles that had plagued its detention program in the late 1970s.[9]

Reagan's task force ultimately suggested a policy that combined detention and interdiction: attempting to stop migrants before they arrived but relying on migrant incarceration for those who managed to make it ashore. Under the resulting 1981 policy, all immigrants and asylum seekers who did not have a "prima facie case for admission"—a legal term meaning based on first impression—would be detained while awaiting immigration hearings.[10] It was the beginning of what scholars have called a "mandatory detention" policy. Where these migrants would be detained, however, was still an open question.

This chapter shows how the federal government took on an expanding role in immigration detention in the 1980s and 1990s, shifting toward a model of sites jointly operated by the Bureau of Prisons and the INS. The logic laid out in the 1981 memo—that stopping migrants before they came ashore would separate them from attorneys and access to the courts—influenced not only the policy of interdiction but also the shape of migrant incarceration. New detention sites were built in remote locations, and the enthusiastic support of locals became central to the site selection process. The creation of these sites generated a tremendous amount of litigation, as migrants' rights groups and attorneys challenged the sites' environmental impact, the ability of the INS to transfer migrants to faraway sites, and the disproportionate rates of detention for Haitian asylum seekers compared with migrants from other countries. Though activists and attorneys registered short-term victories in halting deportations and formalizing ambiguous policies, they failed to stop the expansion of migrant detention, which was empowered through a robust corpus of legal precedents rooted in sovereignty and plenary power.

Even as the federal government formalized its mandatory detention policy and invested unprecedented money in detention, these federal sites housed only a fraction of the total migrants in custody. The federal government lobbied Congress for more construction funds. It built the first "alien detention center" mutually operated with the BOP in Oakdale, Louisiana. It forged new relationships with private contractors. Yet, through it all, city and county jails continued to be central to the enforcement project. Rather than subverting the immigration service's reliance on local jails, the bipartisan embrace of migrant detention in the 1980s solidified the agency's dependence on local carceral infrastructure. By the start of the 1990s, the INS maintained contracts with more than nine hundred state and local prisons and jails for additional bed space, making the financial and political relationship between the immigration service and localities more expansive than ever.[11]

Above all else, the INS in the 1980s and early 1990s came to value *flexibility*, in its approach both to incarceration and to its own bureaucratic autonomy. What the INS called the "emergency nature" of Mariel transformed the agency's perspective on its day-to-day work—at any moment it might need to mobilize against a massive arrival of people from a location it could not predict. Much of the agency's work was already relatively unencumbered by judicial interference, but in the 1980s the agency doubled down, arguing that any adherence to administrative norms and procedures threatened its ability to protect American borders. In creating new detention sites, the agency envisioned that they could be used for short-term detention of Mexican migrants or long-term detention of asylum seekers. The INS collaborated with the BOP to build sites that could be swiftly converted to prisons if the demand for migrant detention space receded. But the ultimate form of flexibility came in maintaining a network of carceral spaces around the United States that the INS could transfer migrants to in politically tense moments. Jails continued to provide the safety valve for the INS: Migrant resistance, congressional investigations, and legal interventions could all be thwarted by temporarily moving detained people to local, nearly invisible, outposts.

Conditions and Controversies at Krome

In the months of 1980 preceding the Mariel Boatlift, Haitians who arrived in South Florida were taken to the Federal Correctional Institution (FCI) in South Dade. Medics gave health screenings, and officials inquired about migrants' asylum claims from within a federal prison. The INS established the FCI Haitian Processing Center "at the request of the White House" and touted it as far superior to the local jails that had detained Haitians in South Florida through the late 1970s.[12] The INS claimed that a centralized facility could have its own clinic and offices for INS officials, ensuring better medical attention and faster processing for migrants. "Compared to Immokalee, the FCI is opulent," a *Miami News* editorial opined. "But it is still a prison."[13]

The INS first opened Krome as a site to house refugees in May 1980, weeks after the Mariel Boatlift began, over the protests of hundreds of Dade County residents.[14] By June 1980, Krome held both Cuban and Haitian migrants— Cuban migrants went to Krome North, Haitian migrants went to Krome South, two camps about a half-mile apart, with widely disparate conditions. While Cubans had recreational facilities, televisions, regular visitors, and educational activities at Krome North, Haitians at Krome South faced excessive overcrowding, long periods of detention, and an absence of social and informational services. Most Cuban migrants were released from Krome within seventy-two hours. Haitian migrants waited at Krome for months.[15] Attorneys struggled to corroborate stories of abuse because they were routinely denied access to the site by the INS.[16] That November, the federal government decided that the slightly better Krome location would be converted to a "permanent" refugee processing center. The dormitories would not be completed until May 1981, leaving the migrants to sleep in tents perched atop the unsteady swampland. The images emerging from Krome invoked a question Congresswoman Shirley Chisholm had posed in the prior decade: Would the government feel comfortable treating any group other than Black migrants in this way?[17]

The conditions at Krome quickly became a point of conflict between the local and federal governments. The city of Miami and the state of Florida emphasized the site's squalor. The federal government insisted that the camps were sparse but safe. In September 1980, the Dade County Health Department made its first effort to close Krome, citing infractions that ranged from padlocked fire exits, to unchlorinated drinking water, to a persistent rat problem. The district spokesperson for the health department declared Miami's detention site "[not] fit for human habitation."[18]

Krome was particularly dangerous for children, whom the United States had failed to address in its provisional detention policy. In October 1980, a group of social workers and religious leaders identified sixty unaccompanied children at Krome. Some of the issues facing minors were similar to those facing adults—abusive administration, the difficulty of being released even to family members, and an arbitrary system of transfers. Other concerns were more specific: One social worker noted in October 1980 that Krome had no food for babies, leaving all Krome residents to eat the same solid foods. Several reports indicated irregular meals and desperately hungry children.[19] Still conceiving of these detentions as short-term, the INS was reluctant to develop infrastructure for extended detention of children at Krome. Dade County Public Schools tried repeatedly to enroll detained children but were given varying excuses by the INS: first, that school board officials could not enter Krome because of recent breakout attempts; second, that the children's immigration forms had been misplaced; and third, that there were few children left at Krome and that they would soon be relocated to Puerto Rico anyway.[20]

Mothers of detained children did not fare much better. Officials looked at women in Krome with suspicion, rooted in racist fears of reproduction and dependency.[21] In its first year of operation, Krome held a significant number of pregnant women; of the 466 Haitian women detained between January and March 1981, about 15 percent (seventy women) were pregnant. Health officials derisively described the situation as "overpregnancy" and suggested that Haitian women might use children as a "bargaining tool" to access food stamps and Medicaid in the United States. Their anxieties invoked the stereotypes of the "welfare queen" that right-wing policymakers wielded against Black women during the Reagan administration.[22] Women's experiences at Krome were worsened by separation from their male partners and, sometimes, from their children. In a 1981 report, a federal official at Krome described "an 'epidemic' of hysterical episodes among Haitian women," exacerbated by witnessing a group of Chinese migrants admitted and quickly discharged from Krome.[23] Miami INS workers called Krome's small number of migrants from China, India, Colombia, Guatemala, Canada, and other nations "OTHs,"

FIGURE 27. Haitian mother and child, detained at Krome Service Processing Center, Miami, 1980. Courtesy of Michael L. Carlebach and Special Collections at the University of Miami Libraries, Michael Carlebach Photography Collection, Coral Gables.

standing for "Other than Haitians"—an indication of the ubiquity of people from Haiti at the detention site.[24] After many months of incarceration, the sight of other migrants being promptly released was psychologically shattering to the Haitian women at Krome. (Figure 27.)

The INS also experimented with sending Haitian women to other facilities, including the Federal Correctional Institution, Alderson, a women's prison in West Virginia. There, too, women encountered deep suspicion and lack of bodily autonomy. In a letter signed from "the imprisoned Haitian refugees of West Virginia," migrants wrote, "[There] were several women among us who were pregnant and they took their babies from their stomachs with pills and injections, telling them that the babies would prevent them from obtaining their freedom and their right to stay in the country."[25] Other women reported being placed in solitary confinement for refusing to do "houseworking chores" in the prison.[26] The women of Alderson went on a twelve-day hunger strike to protest the conditions at the prison; their demands were amplified by the radical women's collective Off Our Backs, which published testimonies from the women as well as first-person accounts of visits to Alderson.[27]

In March 1981, the INS began exclusion hearings for Haitian migrants who had arrived following the October 1980 cutoff for Cuban-Haitian Entrant status. The proceedings swiftly came to mirror the "Haitian Program," declared illegal in the late 1970s, featuring cursory hearings held in rapid succession that made it virtually impossible for Florida attorneys to keep up. "The Haitian Calendar" made up between 75 and 90 percent of all hearings in South Florida, with thirty to forty hearings occurring each day.[28] The INS at Krome instituted methods of distancing Haitians from legal aid that verged on parody. If migrants asked to use a phone to contact a lawyer, for example, Krome officials would only allow them to make calls after 8 p.m., when few lawyers were in their offices.[29] "We have every indication that INS plans to detain future arrivals," warned the Haitian Refugee Center. Just four months later, Reagan's mandatory detention policy enacted their worst-case scenario.[30]

Formalizing Detention

By the summer of 1981, conditions at Krome were on the brink of environmental catastrophe. The makeshift water and sewer systems were collapsing under the stress of use by 1,600 people. The Dade County Fire Department carried water into the camp, while city officials scrambled to transport one hundred thousand gallons of raw sewage per day from the facility precariously located on the edge of a national park. Governor Graham insisted that the site not only was endangering the safety of its prisoners but was relegating them to the "status of chattel" and jeopardizing the health of all Floridians. As he had done months prior, when trying to force the federal government to remove Cuban refugees from Dade County Jail, Governor Graham returned to court, this time to close Krome.[31]

With a lawsuit pending, the INS searched for new locations to move detained Haitians. The agency benefited from the recent expansion of BOP facilities, many of which had been built in rural places around the country. From 1970 to 1979, the BOP added eighteen new prisons, with more than six thousand bed spaces.[32] One such facility was the Federal Correctional Institution, Ray Brook, in Lake Placid, New York.[33] Ray Brook had novel origins: The structure was built as the Olympic Village for the 1980 Winter Olympics, with a plan to convert it to a federal prison when the games concluded. Boosters marketed the prison as an economic engine for the Adirondacks. First, it would bring winter sports tourism; then it would bring more than two hundred new "recession-free" jobs to a region with New York's highest unemployment rates.[34]

In the wake of the 1971 Attica prison rebellion, a deadly standoff in which more than one thousand incarcerated men took prison staff hostage to protest abuse and prison conditions, opponents of the so-called Olympic Prison raised concerns about hiring guards and employees from a nearly all-white community to incarcerate people far from home.[35] Activist groups such as Stop the Olympic Prison feared that the Lake Placid project might replicate the problems and tensions that had simmered at Attica.[36] Critics never anticipated that the Ray Brook facility would soon hold not just a disproportionate number of Black Americans from Northeast cities but also Black *asylum seekers* from across an ocean. Ray Brook officials announced in the summer of 1981 that the prison would detain Haitian migrants as "a favor to the INS," while the agency confronted overcrowding and a lawsuit in Miami.[37] The prison's isolation was devastating. By June 1982, only one of the 150 Haitian migrants at Ray Brook had received a visit from a family member, and only two had legal representation.[38] A group of Haitians petitioned for a change of detention venue, but a judge denied the claim, calling the lack of INS detention space a "strong circumstantial cause" for keeping the asylum seekers in New York's North Country.[39]

The courts ultimately dismissed Governor Graham's lawsuit demanding Krome's closure, and problems at the federal detention site continued to fester. Again and again, the government turned to the same solution: transfers to prisons and jails in rural places. After a September 1981 protest at Krome, the INS announced that 120 Haitian migrants identified as "troublemakers" would be transferred to Otisville, New York, a federal prison fifty miles northwest of New York City. At the end of 1981, the INS announced plans to detain two thousand Haitian asylum seekers at Army barracks in Fort Drum, New York, just miles from the Canadian border, where the windchill factor dipped below negative 70 degrees Fahrenheit in the winter. The *New York Times* equated the decision to exiling refugees to Siberia.[40]

The INS also looked south. Beginning in August 1981, the United States flew Haitian migrants from Miami to Puerto Rico's Fort Allen, a U.S. Army installation that housed 794 Haitian men and women at its peak.[41] Using Fort Allen was not cheap—rather than sending INS employees to the island, the United States contracted private security personnel, which cost $2 million in the first three months alone.[42] But using an overseas site offered political benefits, enabling the Reagan administration to place a controversial detention site in a community where aggrieved citizens could not vote in presidential elections. It also offered pragmatic benefits, as the INS hoped that it could hold "speedy hearings" with minimal interference from the mainland.[43] While the mayor of San Juan had initially encouraged Puerto Ricans to support the effort as humanitarian outreach to their Caribbean neighbors, his feelings on the project soon soured. "The public image of Fort Allen today is one of a Federal government-sponsored prison or concentration camp, with severe environmental problems and living conditions not suitable for human habitation," the mayor wrote to the attorney general in January 1982.[44]

Concurrent with the state's litigation about Krome's conditions was far more sweeping legal action attacking not just individual detention sites but the entire federal policy of "mandatory detention." The policy initiated by Reagan in July 1981 led to the detention of 2,100 Haitian migrants throughout the United States before meeting its first major legal challenge in June 1982. The Haitian Refugee Center's case in *Louis v. Nelson* challenged the plenary authority of the government in creating immigration law through informal channels and raised questions about racial discrimination against Haitians. Administrative procedure became the heart of the *Louis v. Nelson* ruling, exemplifying the opaque ways in which the federal government generated ad hoc immigration policy directed at those it sought to exclude.[45]

The bulk of the courtroom debate involved whether the INS had violated the 1946 Administrative Procedure Act in creating a radically new policy with no warning and no legislative oversight. The Administrative Procedure Act mandated that for an agency to create a "rule" it must provide adequate notice and publication of the proposed policy, allow interested persons to participate in the decision-making process, publish the final rule thirty days before it went into practice, and allow for petition and modification of the rule.[46] In instituting mandatory detention, the INS did none of these things. The agency never documented the policy shift, nor did it establish parameters for detainment. Few Americans were aware that the detention policy had shifted. In court, the INS argued that because the decision dealt with foreign affairs and sensitive information, it bore no obligation to publicize the change.

Aside from the lack of public transparency, federal records show that the detention policy was also remarkably unclear to the agencies enforcing it. The Department of Justice's understanding was that the policy required detention of all excludable migrants pending hearings, regardless of country of origin. Exceptions could be made for minors, pregnant women, and those with medical problems. However, INS officials reported that they had received "no guidelines" for releasing *any* migrants from detention, regardless of circumstance. The DOJ also pointed to several episodes where INS officials had suggested in the media that Haitians could apply for work permits and that their detention was due to a lack of community sponsors—both of which were inaccurate. Reagan's DOJ called the contradictory statements from the INS "inconceivable." It demanded that the INS overhaul its communication strategy and issue more specific directions to its officers.[47]

The ruling in *Louis v. Nelson*, issued on June 18, 1982, ultimately upheld the legality of detention but ruled that the way the INS had created the policy was illegal.[48] The detention mandate marked a dramatic departure from precedent, said Judge Spellman, as "it makes detention the rule, not the exception" and therefore obligated the INS to follow the Administrative Procedure Act's rule-making requirements. *Louis v. Nelson* ordered the release and parole of 1,900 Haitian migrants.

Backlash against the court's decision began immediately, with both federal and local governments arguing that the INS, not the judiciary, best knew how to enforce immigration laws. Robert Bombaugh, the chief DOJ lawyer on the case, told the *Miami Herald* that "we cannot abide by this court's decision. The government is firmly committed to detention."[49] Within a week, Judge Spellman oversaw a hearing on the *Louis v. Nelson* decision in which Florida and federal officials argued that the judiciary had placed the United States at risk with its nullification of Reagan's detention policy. Spellman determined that while the 1,900 Haitians detained under the previous policy still merited release, the federal government had the right to create a new, administratively legal detention policy that accomplished the same thing. The judgment in *Louis v. Nelson* encapsulated the role of the judiciary in 1980s immigration policy: While the court more actively challenged the discretionary decision-making process of the INS, it still granted the president and Congress wide latitude in policing U.S. borders.

The responses of INS leaders did not indicate relief with Judge Spellman's decision. Instead, the INS expressed annoyance that the courts had interfered with the agency's plenary authority at all. In the days following the judge's decision, a DOJ spokesperson obstinately responded, "[W]e're thinking about it," when asked whether the INS would formalize the policy.[50] Even Judge Spellman conceded that the executive branch likely had the power to overrule him and issue an executive order initiated by "national emergency."[51] Before the DOJ published its formal detention rule it solicited comments, as the Administrative

Procedure Act required. The DOJ rejected complaints about the duration, conditions, and legality of detention as "sanctimonious grandstanding" by groups "hostile to the concept of detention of aliens for any reason." A letter from the NAACP emphasizing the racist implementation of the detention policy was annotated by the DOJ general counsel as "useless, strident, conclusory drivel," a characteristically dismissive response to Black civil rights groups by the Reagan administration.[52] On July 9, 1982, the INS published its policy in the *Federal Register* "under protest." Even as it capitulated to the Administrative Procedure Act requirements, the agency reiterated that this entire episode was judicial overreach in the state's sovereign ability to police its borders.[53]

By the time the Haitians were paroled, they were far from the only migrants incarcerated at Krome. In the summer of 1982, Krome held around fifty people who were not Haitian, hailing primarily from Central America and Asia.[54] A detained Russian man kept a world map where he used colored string to mark the nation of origin of each person at the detention site—in the spring of 1983, the map showed migrants from thirty-five countries, Afghanistan to Yugoslavia.[55] The uptick in people fleeing political unrest in Central America was felt even more acutely along the southern border. In 1986, a detention officer in Texas reported that, while his site's population had once been 90 percent Mexican, it was now about 90 percent "Other than Mexican." They primarily detained people from Nicaragua and El Salvador, fleeing the consequences of Reagan's imperialist foreign policy in the region.[56] Exact demographic data were scarce, with reporters relying on anecdotes from workers and detained people to ascertain exactly who was at these sites. Internally, the INS suggested that collecting better data on the nationalities of people detained—data that went beyond the clunky Mexican/Other than Mexican binary—might help the agency refute accusations of racism against Haitians in the future, if it could show that other groups of migrants were being held for similarly long durations.[57] Though in the summer of 1982, the INS may not have predicted the ways in which detention populations would continue to diversify, the early indications that Krome would hold people from beyond the Caribbean added fuel to the INS push for more detention resources.

Oakdale and the Future of Detention

Though the INS ceded to the court's demand that it formalize a detention policy, internal discussions suggested that the agency would continue to rely on "emergency rulemaking." The DOJ insisted that the courts fundamentally misunderstood the situation on the ground—that in Florida and other border states, the rising number of asylum seekers constituted an *emergency*, thus empowering agencies with distinct legal powers. If the INS were to wait for the standard review and comment period of rulemaking, its policies would not take effect until many more individuals had entered the United States.[58] The specter of Mariel hung over the INS in the years to come, as the Reagan administration and the DOJ crafted contingency plans for what they labeled "mass illegal immigration emergencies."[59] They proposed new laws that would allow the president to place the country in lockdown should an immigration emergency arise: stopping approaching vessels; sealing off harbors, airports, and roads; and imposing travel restrictions even on U.S. residents.[60]

Powerful political allies coupled with surging nativist sentiment ensured detention a future in the early 1980s and beyond; *Louis v. Nelson* would be only a minor roadblock. The same week as the *Louis v. Nelson* decision, Associate Attorney General Rudolph Giuliani appeared before Congress and requested $35 million to construct two new permanent detention facilities, in collaboration with the BOP, for migrants awaiting hearings.[61] Giuliani decried the "completely inadequate" Krome and described the Florida site as a lightning rod for costly and time-consuming litigation. For boosters like Giuliani, there was little doubt that detention would be an enduring, long-term solution for the agency.

The DOJ promised that new detention facilities would reduce INS use of local jails, solving both a public relations problem and a logistical challenge for the agency. Competition for jail bed space had become increasingly fierce in the early 1980s amid growing demand from the U.S. Marshals and the BOP.[62] In 1984, Congress passed the Comprehensive Crime Control Act, celebrated by Reagan's attorney general as "the most far-reaching and substantial reform of the criminal justice system in our history."[63] Its highlights included the abolition of federal parole, the reinstatement of the federal death penalty, and the creation of an asset forfeiture system, which incentivized arrests by allowing police to seize cash and property from accused drug dealers— effectively offering law enforcement a major new revenue stream.[64] In the law's first year, the average number of people imprisoned by the federal government rose by 32 percent.[65] Demand for bed space made the INS "a virtual hostage" to localities' limited availability, the DOJ wrote in a memo to Congress, weakening border control and necessitating more relaxed policies of bond and release.[66] The INS accumulated nearly 25,000 days of detention in local jails in the first five months of 1982. In arguing that carceral expansion could be a humane solution, Giuliani drew on an argument that legislators had fine-tuned over the previous decades: that the way to remedy overcrowding, and the prisoner rights litigation it had wrought, was to build more prisons rather than to embrace policies of parole or decarceration.

Perhaps the biggest question for legislators was where the new federal detention sites would be located. Some communities, such as Prince George County, Virginia, initially expressed interest in hosting a site but backed out after community leaders raised concerns that detentions would not be as "short-term" as federal officials suggested. The DOJ assured Prince George County that average detentions would be just two to three days, an estimate that seemed particularly unrealistic given what was occurring at Krome. Communities also voiced anxieties that relatives or friends of detained people would move near the detention center, creating an additional "social burden"—a thinly cloaked fear of demographic change, heightened by the 1982 Supreme Court's decision in *Plyler v. Doe* days prior, ruling that states could not deny funding for the public education of noncitizen children.[67]

The INS experience in Virginia, alongside its history with frustrated communities that hosted Cuban resettlement camps, made the agency's reception in Oakdale, Louisiana, all the more astonishing. On March 4, 1982, INS officials held a community meeting in the central Louisiana parish hoping to gauge community response to a detention center proposal. They were greeted by more than seven hundred enthusiastic Allen Parish residents. Times were tough in Oakdale. A paper mill had just gone out of business, costing the town 381 jobs. Unemployment hovered around 30 percent, among the highest rates in the nation.[68] Within weeks, INS officials were being feted at the mayor's home, as he extolled Oakdale's virtues over dinner. Another evening, immigration officials attended a community crawfish boil, where Cajun music stretched deep into the night.[69] Officials heard about Oakdale churches hosting prayer vigils, asking God to deliver the detention center to their parish. Plainly put, Oakdale was all in.[70]

Local officials saw both economic and symbolic value in the federal detention site. Mayor George Mowad predicted that Oakdale would be the "boomtown of Louisiana," with the detention center poised to create 350 jobs with an annual payroll of $9 million.[71] Beyond its financial impact, the campaign was also seen as a sorely needed unifying project for the community. In December 1982, three white soldiers from a nearby military base were murdered in a predominantly Black Oakdale neighborhood, leading to racist tensions and headlines about Oakdale's decline into a "war zone."[72] The campaign for the detention center, wrote one local pastor, offered an opportunity for reconciliation. "These efforts of Oakdale people, blacks and whites, working for the good of our people are most inspiring," he opined.[73]

The narrative of who the INS would hold in its new detention center changed depending on the audience. In some cases, it was sold as a solution to alleviate problems at Krome; in other cases, it was sold as a site to hold migrants who entered through Mexico.[74] Initially, INS officials told the parish that the primary mission was "to protect U.S. citizens' employment rights," implying that many of those detained would be undocumented migrant workers pending removal rather than asylum seekers awaiting hearings.[75] In negotiations with town leaders, the federal government stressed the need for Oakdale to agree that the location could be used as a "contingency site" in the case of an immigration emergency—the DOJ was particularly concerned about growing numbers of asylum seekers arriving from Central America—or as a federal prison if the demand for migrant detention space waned.[76]

Oakdale's efforts paid off. In February 1983, Oakdale secured the INS contract.[77] "WE GOT IT!!" announced a three-and-a-half-inch red banner headline in the *Oakdale Journal*.[78] Mayor Mowad immediately started thinking bigger: "We're not resting on our laurels with just the alien center. We're trying to get a state prison for the south end of the parish," Mowad told the *New York Times* in October 1984.[79]

Conditions at sites like Krome had been a major impetus for the construction of federal detention centers, yet the first migrants sent to Oakdale were not from Miami. In March 1986, the site officially opened. A few weeks later it received several dozen migrants, primarily from El Salvador and Colombia, whom the INS transferred from their detention facility in El Centro, California.[80] By the following summer, the INS began transferring Salvadorans apprehended in workplace raids on Long Island, 1,300 miles from Oakdale.[81] That autumn, Oakdale welcomed yet another group: Mariel Cubans with criminal records, whom the United States could not deport because Castro refused to take them back. The change in mission was a fulfillment of what INS officials had pushed local leaders to consent to—that Oakdale would be "flexible" space that the INS could use for whatever it deemed most pressing.

Oakdale was a place "that epitomized the production of remoteness," write geographers Jenna Loyd and Alison Mountz, a place meant to accelerate deportations by separating migrants from legal assistance and community connections.[82] The weaponization of remoteness was evident to communities at the heart of the detention business. The year after Oakdale secured its deal, a private contractor called Behavioral Systems Southwest arrived in Roswell, New Mexico, to pitch a short-term detention center for Mexican and Central American migrants. The company made many of the same promises that had worked in Oakdale: dozens of new jobs, millions of dollars invested in the local economy, a safer alternative for migrants than local jails. Roswell would also be a milestone in public-private relations: the first contracting of a "sizeable detention facility" to the private sector.[83]

While visiting the New Mexico town, a representative of the company promised citizens that the detention center would be so discrete and so removed from the public eye that no one would know it was there. This assurance raised red flags in a community where nearly one-third of the population was Latina/o, a markedly different demographic profile than Oakdale's. "Think of the consequences . . . what civil and human rights could be violated without anyone even knowing it?" asked one local observer. "I believe the government wants to choose Roswell, or some such city, precisely because it is relatively isolated and away from the public attention."[84] Roswell's residents raised another related concern: If they allowed a detention center into their community, how could they be sure that the immigration service's growing incarceration power wouldn't be turned against their own noncitizen residents? While the Roswell bid would soon fall apart, the community's question was prescient.

Kromegate and the Violence of Decentralization

As the United States built new federal facilities in the 1980s and 1990s, Krome became one node in a vast detention network. No longer was it the locus of all detention controversies. In an age of multiplying private prison companies, Krome, a facility run by the federal government, could seem almost quaint—the devil Americans knew, rather than the for-profit devil Americans did not.

The attention receded; the abuse remained. Krome roared back into the national news in 1995, when the Congressional Task Force on Immigration Reform visited Miami to investigate allegations of mistreatment and inhumane detention conditions. Overcrowding at Krome had become so dire that fifty-five women slept on cots in the clinic lobby.[85] The site's legal holding capacity was set at 226, yet reports indicated that Krome held almost seven hundred migrants at various points during 1994, with tents again used as supplemental housing.[86] In emails sent that June, Miami District Director Walter Cadman told a colleague, "Krome is bursting at the seams," disparaging the migrants he housed as the "teeming hordes."[87] A prior investigative team told policymakers that they could not rely on INS records for accurate information, as they were largely handwritten and contained too many discrepancies.[88] Thus, Congress sent a delegation on a fact-finding mission to Miami's pioneering detention center.[89]

With Congress's visit looming, the INS went to stunning lengths to obscure the conditions at Krome. The immigration service cleaned up the facility and temporarily transferred about a quarter of the population to Florida jails, as well as to Oakdale and jails in Louisiana. An INS email specified that the detainees were to be "stashed out of sight for cosmetic purposes."[90] Before the task force's visit, the INS abruptly released fifty-eight migrants without medical checks and hid more than one hundred others within the facility. Inspectors at Krome removed their gun holsters and handcuffs in order to portray a "kinder, gentler" vision of detention.[91] The INS undertook these actions "with the explicitly stated intent to deceive the delegation," Congress later concluded.[92] Maintaining a broad network of flexible detention sites not only allowed the agency to thwart organizing and distance migrants from legal aid; it gave the agency the flexibility to thwart and distance Congress.

The 1995 scandal, christened "Kromegate" by the South Florida media, signaled how far the INS would go to avoid congressional or legal intervention— the same defiant attitude that the agency had exhibited when asked to formalize its detention policy was again on display. As its detention mandate grew, bolstered by the agency's politically popular "criminal alien" programs, the INS operated with more staff, more money, and more autonomy.[93] From the INS perspective, congressional oversight threatened to undermine the bureaucracy's management and discretionary power within detention centers. Leaders routinely clashed with politicians who offered even mild criticisms of the agency, claiming that they understood neither the work nor the stakes of border protection.[94] For members of Congress, allowing the INS more autonomy could function as a form of self-preservation: They could pass laws that appeared tough on illegal immigration while maintaining distance from the dirty, litigious work of detention. The INS continued to be protected by its own powers to eliminate. When investigating cases of abuse at Krome throughout the 1990s, policymakers noted that it was challenging to follow up on allegations because many of the complainants and witnesses had been deported by the time inquiries began.[95] The INS use of transfers was often described as arbitrary and capricious; Kromegate showed that this description failed to give the INS enough credit. The agency intentionally used transfers to evade accountability, punish protest, and reduce costs.[96] Minimizing the visibility of detention enabled the INS to behave with what one reporter called "a culture of impunity," while elected officials pled ignorance.[97]

This impunity was heightened by the decentralized bureaucratic organization of the immigration service. Beginning in the 1950s, the INS pursued a reorganization strategy that vested greater power in INS field offices and their accompanying district directors. Virtually all paperwork, including warrants for arrest and deportation, went through the districts rather than the D.C. office.[98] By the 1990s, INS districts like Miami's functioned like fragmented fiefdoms with little oversight. In the words of one legal aid group, decentralization had allowed "33 districts to implement 33 detention policies."[99] The INS headquarters could not report how many jails the agency was using on a given night.[100] Recommendations from INS leaders that certain asylum seekers be released from detention were ignored by some district directors, who used their discretion to make immigration law more punitive.[101] Kromegate exemplified district directors' power over migrants as well as their institutional subordinates. "The culture at INS appears to be such that inspectors . . . would feel that their jobs would be in jeopardy if they failed to obey an order to lie to Congress," observed the Office of the Inspector General.[102]

The INS largely rejected Congress's recommendations for reform in the wake of the Krome scandal. Cadman, the district director accused of conspiracy to mislead Congress, was transferred from Miami to D.C. and temporarily demoted. Two years later, he was named the director of the INS National Security Unit, one of the most senior positions in the bureaucracy.[103] While Kromegate may have been the most visible manifestation of a deeply broken institution, it was also the product of intentional policy choices over the agency's decades-long history. There was not just one INS but many INSes, each operating with its own agendas, partners, and priorities.

————

Transferring detained migrants when Congress was knocking on the door was a scandal. Transferring detained migrants to remote, dangerous jails for any other reason was business as usual. In response to Kromegate's publicity, the Miami district of the INS began more aggressively moving migrants out of the overcrowded service processing center and into Florida jails. Activists in South Florida immediately expressed alarm about the uptick in transfers. Newly drafted federal standards for INS detention facilities did not apply to county jails, and Florida jails writ large had recently been released from court-mandated state oversight.[104] Fears of eroding accountability were well founded. In 1994, Florida state inspectors investigated 586 incidents of abuse in county jails. Two years later, following the end of the state inspection program, the state investigated just nine cases.[105]

The INS needed detention contracts more than ever following the 1996 passage of the Antiterrorism and Effective Death Penalty Act and the Illegal Immigration Reform and Immigrant Responsibility Act, two draconian laws that rang in what scholars have labeled the "modern era" of migrant incarceration.[106] The Antiterrorism and Effective Death Penalty Act increased the number of immigrants subject to mandatory detention by expanding what constituted an "aggravated felony."[107] The Illegal Immigration Reform and Immigrant Responsibility Act broadened the scope of criminal offenses for which migrants could be detained to include minor offenses such as shoplifting, even if committed decades prior to migration. Under the 1996 laws, detention for most migrants was not left up to bureaucratic discretion; it was now *mandatory*. The legislation also dictated that people could be detained for as long as two years before seeing an immigration judge, essentially granting the INS "incontestable authority" in incarcerating those classified as criminal aliens.[108] After decades of the agency claiming underfunding, the new laws brought it a budget of nearly a billion dollars earmarked for detention and deportation. The agency claimed that it would require 21,000 additional beds to enforce the 1996 legislation. Once again, it found many of these beds in jails.[109]

The majority of Krome's residents were distributed among jails in six Florida counties: Bay, Broward, Dade, Jackson, Manatee, and Monroe, stretching from the Panhandle to the Keys. Some jails, such as the correctional center in Bay County, were operated by private companies, blurring the line between local and private control.[110] Conditions at Florida jails varied widely: Access to telephones, law libraries, written communication, and medical treatment depended on which jail a person was transferred to. Other problems cut across all facilities: The barebones INS contracts did not specify a minimum level of care or any provisions about overcrowding. Attorneys reported that representing clients at Krome was extraordinarily difficult. Representing clients moved to Florida's county jails, on the other hand, was "nearly impossible."[111]

Migrants understood the disparities between being a ward of the federal government and being a ward of a locality, with some people in INS custody demanding that they be moved from jails to federal facilities. (Figure 28.) "At every county jail I live, I am by the rules of the State INMATE NOT by the

FIGURE 28. "This Is a Drawing of Our Suffering." Drawing by Alberto Ruiz, Manatee County Jail, Florida, ca. 1990s. This illustration by a detained Cuban migrant was sent to an attorney with the Florida Immigrant Advocacy Center. It takes the shape of a police badge, or perhaps an Immigration and Naturalization Service badge; the left side depicts migration from Cuba, while the right side and the barbed wire border depict incarceration in the United States. At the top is Castro's signature green military cap. Courtesy of Americans for Immigrant Justice Records, David M. Rubenstein Rare Book and Manuscript Library, Duke University.

federal. . . . What is the different between INMATE and DETAINEE?" one man wrote in a 1996 letter.[112] Migrants wore jail uniforms and, at some facilities, were handcuffed and shackled for medical, attorney, and family visits. One Cuban man found this so humiliating that he told his family not to visit.[113] Some migrants asked to return to Krome, both because of their conflicts with other incarcerated people and because they were subjected to even more ambiguous structures of power in the jails. "I am really scared for my life in this facility," wrote a man held in Manatee County: "[W]e are at the mercy of [the] sheriff."[114] Another detained person corroborated in a 1998 affidavit:

There's a big difference between being in jail and being charged with a crime and being in jail not charged with a crime. I feel I should be detained under the standards of the federal government, because INS is a federal institution.... They are endangering our freedom and our lives.... [Jackson] is a county jail and the county jail officials can do whatever they want.[115]

As migrants sat in Florida jails, the INS became an increasingly distant presence. Migrants struggled to reach deportation officers, and their case files and medical records rarely followed them between jails.[116] Still, the power of immigration law was acutely felt. A group at Manatee County signed a petition expressing disbelief that the Antiterrorism and Effective Death Penalty Act, a law purportedly focused on thwarting terrorists in the wake of the Oklahoma City Bombing, had been weaponized by the immigration service against migrants with minor drug charges. "We read and hear about anti-foreigner sentiments rising in the Land, and we shudder in fear," they wrote. "Are we aliens the guinea pigs?"[117]

An episode of abuse at Jackson County Correctional Facility, located in the rural Panhandle community of Marianna, Florida (motto: "The City of Southern Charm"), epitomized the ways that the militarization of policing and imprisonment affected migrants. Jackson County contracted with the INS throughout the 1990s and had been one of the locations used to hide detained migrants during Kromegate. In 1998, migrants at Jackson County reported that, among various other abuses, they had been electrocuted by guards wielding electrified riot shields. (Figure 29.) One detained man called it "common knowledge" that electrocution was used to subdue people in the jail.[118] When the shield was activated, a startling blue arc of electricity appeared. In some cases, jailers activated the shield as a threat or a show of force. Far worse was placing it in contact with a human body, which caused victims to lose muscle control and collapse.[119] Victims experienced excruciating pain, describing a sensation of their muscles being torn from their bones. Officials insisted that it was nothing permanent. The Texas Department of Criminal Justice banned the shields in 1995 after an employee died from being shocked during a training session. In Florida, however, the weapons remained legal.[120]

Electrified weapons were prohibited in INS detention centers like Krome and Oakdale. They were *not* prohibited in Florida jails.[121] Beginning in the 1970s and propelled by the wars on drugs and gangs of the 1980s and 1990s, federal crime control grants enabled police departments to invest in military-grade weaponry. In turn, federal money incentivized manufacturers to develop

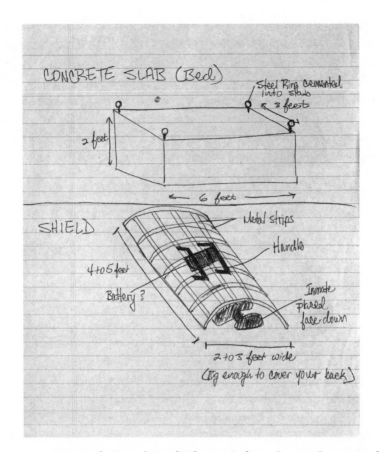

The following text is handwritten within the drawing:

CONCRETE SLAB (Bed)

Steel Ring cemented into slab

← 3 feet

2 feet

← 6 feet →

SHIELD

Metal strips

Handle

4 to 5 feet

Battery?

Inmate placed face-down

2 to 3 feet wide
(Big enough to cover your back)

FIGURE 29. Drawing by Patrick Reed-Johnson, Jackson County Correctional Facility, Marianna, Florida, ca. 1998. This sketch of the electric shields used at Jackson County Correctional Facility was attached to the affidavit of a detained Afro-Cuban migrant. The man described being slammed against a concrete slab, which also served as detainees' beds, and then handcuffed to steel rings at the corners. "After they tied me down, Officer [redacted] brought in a large shield, placed it over me and shocked me once with it. When the electricity ran through my body, I felt paralyzed. . . . I have never seen a device like that shield at any other detention facility." Reed-Johnson testified that he was shackled to the concrete slab for seven or eight additional hours after the electrocution. Courtesy of Americans for Immigrant Justice Records, David M. Rubenstein Rare Book and Manuscript Library, Duke University.

new policing technologies that they argued would modernize American law enforcement—electro-shields and other electrified "riot control" weapons were among these innovations.[122] Despite adamant denials from jail staff, the Civil Rights Division of the DOJ opened an investigation into Jackson County. Investigators found that staff engaged "in excessive and unwarranted use of restraints to control inmates" and said that electro-shields had been "overused for inmate control purposes." In numerous cases, the shields had been a first response when migrants failed to heed verbal warnings. In one particularly horrific incident, jail officials used an electro-shield to threaten a woman who was nine months pregnant.[123] Moving migrants to local carceral facilities, operated by local law enforcement, exposed them to forms of policing they would have been less likely to encounter in INS facilities.

In 1997, more than forty U.S. companies produced electrified weapons like those used against migrants in Jackson County. "Electricity speaks every language known to man. No translation necessary. Everybody is afraid of electricity, and rightfully so," proclaimed Dennis Kaufman, the president of Stun Tech, a company that sold stun belts and shields to numerous Florida counties.[124] Experts at Amnesty International expressed concerns that classifying these weapons as "crime control" products effectively allowed U.S. companies to sell torture devices to nations around the world.[125] In 1995, the U.S. Department of Commerce had approved exports of electrified weapons to countries including Algeria, Bulgaria, China, Lebanon, Russia, Saudi Arabia, South Africa, Sri Lanka, Turkey, and Uruguay—all nations where torture using electro-shock weapons had been reported.[126] There was significantly less attention paid to the ways the weapons were used against noncitizens via the INS reliance on local contracts. Migrants, many of whom were asylum seekers fleeing state violence, confronted tools of torture during their "administrative detention" in American jails. In some cases, these were the same tools of torture the United States had exported to their homelands. It was a vicious cycle: U.S. interventions and counterinsurgency efforts had destabilized many of these asylum seekers' nations of origin, and now, U.S. companies would profit from policing the people these interventions had displaced. Like tear gas, the electro-shield represented a supposedly nonlethal weapon that moved along what historian Stuart Schrader has called an "imperial circuit," crossing borders to ensure an American vision of order abroad and order at home.[127]

Even as the INS made some gestures toward centralization and greater institutional cohesion in the 1980s and 1990s—creating federal detention centers, new standards for detention, and a more formal policy of who was to be detained and released—dispersed local jails remained the backbone of enforcement. The "flexibility" that the INS valued was only possible because it maintained a network of carceral facilities it could turn to in politically precarious moments, whether because of a congressional investigation, a hunger strike, or a lawsuit over environmental impact. As geographer Nancy Hiemstra has argued, the detention system projects a sense of chaos, and that chaos offers peculiar structural advantages to those in power: obscuring the system's functioning, demoralizing its victims, and foreclosing alternatives.[128] While the centralization efforts and the construction of new detention centers from the ground up received the most attention from media and policymakers, the ongoing use of jails meant that "reformed" INS policies and practices would not meaningfully impact the lives of many detained migrants.

The events of the 1980s and 1990s showed that an arrangement of federal, local, and private facilities offered the INS flexibility not just in the physical movement of migrants but also in the explanations for the transfers. If centers like Krome came under fire, the INS could argue that jails were a better alternative. If migrants complained about conditions in jails, the INS could use these frustrations to agitate for more federal funding and construction of new facilities. Transfers, the weaponized mobilization of an immobilized population, were central to insulating the INS detention program from legal and legislative intervention.

8

Sheriffs, Corporations, and the Making of a Late Twentieth-Century Jail Bed Economy

WHAT DID IT look like for communities to financially capitalize on migrant incarceration in the final decades of the twentieth century? With legislation that made vast numbers of migrants susceptible to mandatory detention, the era saw extraordinary opportunities for localities to profit. Sheriffs and local officials throughout the United States explored programs that would, in the words of one Texas sheriff, "transform empty jail beds into tax revenue."[1] By the 1980s, many states and cities faced budget crunches, heightened by the Reagan administration's end of revenue-sharing programs that had provided localities with few-strings-attached federal money.[2] The cuts had an outsized impact on rural communities, which funded a greater percentage of their budgets from federal aid. Towns laid off municipal workers, including firefighters and police officers. They raised taxes and curtailed local services. And amid the financial upheaval, they searched for creative ways to bring back federal dollars.

The jail looked like one of the best products towns had to offer the federal government, particularly as new laws lengthened sentences and expanded mandatory detention and summary removal. Propelled by the 1984 revisions to the criminal code, federal criminal caseloads nearly doubled in the 1980s, growing from 28,921 in 1980 to 47,411 in 1990.[3] Jail capacity increased by 4 percent in the year following the passage of the Comprehensive Crime Control Act of 1984, and jail capacity doubled over the following decade.[4] What arose was a jail bed space market, unprecedented in American history.[5] Fewer people detained by the federal government would be held in federal facilities; most people facing federal charges would await hearings or serve sentences in America's jails.

However, localities were no longer the only game in town for an immigration service that had a vast removal mandate and insufficient space. Local jails now competed with private prisons for detention contracts. Throughout the 1990s, the Immigration and Naturalization Service's growth relied on a concept it called "balanced detention resources," a plan that involved rapidly expanding detention capacity through the use of local jails, contract detention facilities, and government-owned and -operated service processing centers.[6] This model built on the lessons learned over previous decades: It created a far-reaching network of spaces that migrants could be moved between, further obstructing political accountability and legal liability. Privatization was not a radical break from the detention models that preceded it. It built on the devolution of immigration authority, effectively transforming jail workers and private-sector employees into the front line of immigration law enforcement. And it built on the existing notion of federalism that empowered state and local governments as active collaborators in exclusion and deportation.[7]

The rise of private prisons did not foreclose opportunities for localities to profit from migrant incarceration. Early private prisons had a host of liabilities: People escaped, migrants challenged the authority of private companies, poorly compensated guards were abusive in ways the INS struggled to ignore. When these issues arose, jails were there. The INS met every disaster, from a hostage standoff, to a multimillion-dollar lawsuit, to a Category 5 hurricane, with the same solution: take migrants out of the facility under fire and scatter them among jails.[8] The failures of private institutions, and the visibility of these failures, made jails indispensable for the federal government.

In turn, the bed space economy produced what legal scholar Aaron Littman has called "a financial incentive to overbuild."[9] Despite enthusiasm for punitive anti-crime policies, communities were generally reluctant to foot the bill for expanding or renovating jails in the late twentieth century.[10] Both privatization and INS contracts offered more appealing arrangements for financing carceral expansion. In some cases, a private company would fully cover the costs of construction or renovation. In other cases, the federal government intervened. The Reagan administration launched a new Cooperative Agreement Program, which provided capital investment funds to local governments for jail construction in exchange for a guarantee that the federal government could use that jail space.[11] Between 1982 and 2005, the Cooperative Agreement Program paid $285 million to fund localities' jail construction and expansion, effectively allowing communities to increase jail space without requiring community approval for new bonds.[12] When taxpayers did choose to fund jail building, sheriffs could point to their intergovernmental service agreements with the INS or U.S. Marshals as evidence that the jail would quickly pay for itself. Sheriffs argued that they were not only providing a critical service to the federal government; they were also expanding the capacity of the local and state governments to incarcerate.

This chapter first examines Avoyelles Parish, a community that cashed in on a specific population of migrants: Mariel Cubans facing indefinite incarceration as the United States struggled to negotiate their deportation with an uncooperative Cuban government. The prospect of a permanently detained subclass made migrant incarceration look like an even more reliable financial investment, spurring jail growth throughout Louisiana. The chapter then turns to several additional models of migrant incarceration that traversed the public-private division: a Texas detention shed operated by a shipping company; a sprawling New Jersey detention site run by a pioneering private prison company; and the jails of York County, Pennsylvania, which the INS transformed into a hub of migrant detention in the Northeast. As jails and other forms of incarceration grew, communities had incentives to fill beds by any means necessary; citizens and noncitizens alike would suffer under a system that made imprisonment the cornerstone of jobs creation, economic development, and racial control.

The Political Economy of "Undeportables"

On February 4, 1982, the last Mariel Cubans remaining at Fort Chaffee boarded buses to travel from Arkansas to Atlanta. Their destination was the United States Penitentiary, Atlanta, one of the oldest federal prisons still in operation. It was a site with violence so rampant it had warranted an entire congressional hearing in 1978.[13] In months prior, U.S. officials had been eager to convince Cuban migrants that Fort Chaffee was not a prison. Even though refugees could not leave, even though they were surrounded by federal police and barbed wire fences, authorities repeatedly assured refugees that this was a distinct, nonprison place.[14] Most Cubans did not buy it. But as they gazed up at the hulking Victorian penitentiary, some of them may have had second thoughts—maybe this *was* different.

The migrants left at Fort Chaffee were soon joined by other Mariel Cubans who had been convicted of crimes in U.S. courts but could not be deported because of stalled U.S. diplomatic relations with Cuba. They included men such as Anselmo Guerra-Carillo, who had been working as a bartender and was awaiting new fatherhood in Las Vegas. He was arrested for possessing less than a gram of marijuana four years after the boatlift. By the spring of 1987, he was still in the Atlanta prison; the offense had transformed him from a "Cuban-Haitian Entrant" into a criminal alien in the eyes of the law, marked for deportation. "I feel like I'm doing a life sentence," Guerra-Carillo said. "I will do anything to get out of here."[15] In response to criticism of Atlanta Federal Penitentiary, particularly a damning congressional investigation that called the Cubans' incarceration a brutal "form of warehousing," the Department of Justice relocated some Mariel Cubans to the new INS facility at Oakdale, Louisiana. Moving from an eighty-year-old federal prison to a new migrant detention center was presented to the Cubans as an incentive for good behavior.[16] Lawyers called the move "a new way to describe an old procedure"—indefinite detention with little chance of release.[17]

In November 1987, Cuban migrants at Atlanta and Oakdale decided that they had endured enough. Some had been waiting for sponsors for years. Others had already served their criminal sentences and now faced a second, indefinite incarceration. Some were desperate to return to Cuba and escape this legal twilight zone. Others would do anything to avoid deportation, fearing retaliation from Castro. All were frustrated with a system that had promised them parole reviews that never came and exposed them to years of abuse and degradation.[18] Detention in Atlanta had taken an overwhelming psychological toll; in 1986, the warden wrote to a congressman that there had been 158 suicide attempts by Cuban nationals from July 1982 to January 1986, compared with just seven attempts by people serving criminal sentences.[19] And so, first at Oakdale and then at Atlanta, Cubans rose up against prison guards, wielding makeshift weapons, setting fires, and taking dozens of workers hostage. "It looks like a war zone out there with buildings burned out," observed Oakdale Mayor George Mowad, who, just years prior, had spearheaded the campaign to locate the United States' first Immigration and Naturalization Service–Bureau of Prisons detention center in his town.[20]

The impasse between hostage negotiators and the Cubans lasted eleven days, the longest prison standoff in U.S. history.[21] Amid the chaos, a young, politically ambitious sheriff named Bill Belt received a call from the INS. Would he be willing to hold some of these Cubans in the Avoyelles Parish Jail? The jail was located in the rural town of Marksville, Louisiana, about fifty miles from Oakdale. The INS could offer him $45 per person, per night. Sheriff Belt was already in the business of contracting out his jail space, but he was accustomed to much lower rates. The parish received just $8.00 to house men whom the state had sent after instituting a population cap at the notorious Louisiana State Penitentiary, known colloquially as "Angola."[22] To Belt, this sounded like the deal of the century.[23]

Avoyelles Parish was desperate for the cash. Belt's embrace of jails as a local industry was driven in part by the national shift away from President Richard Nixon's "New Federalism" and the federal revenue-sharing allocations it had brought to communities such as Avoyelles. Revenue sharing, Nixon said in 1972, would "reverse the flow of power and resources from the States and communities to Washington"; his advisors were quick to add that it would also reduce local taxation.[24] The program was an effort to cement Nixon's "silent majority" of working-class and suburban white voters. Revenue sharing allowed local elected officials to continue dodging and decrying property tax increases—a massively popular position among Nixon's base—while using federal funds to keep local budgets afloat.[25] The money had minimal strings attached and totaled $30 billion over the first five years, making it the largest federal grant-in-aid ever enacted.[26] For towns with fewer than ten thousand residents, revenue sharing typically represented the only federal assistance they received. Avoyelles used these funds to pay for raises for parish teachers, bus drivers, and law enforcement; to operate the parish courthouse; and to maintain roads and bridges.[27]

But there were signs that, in the words of the parish manager, "the federal gravy" might not flow forever.[28] As inflation rose over the 1970s, deficit hawks grew louder. And post-Watergate, members of Congress were eager to eliminate initiatives they viewed as "pet programs" of the now disgraced Nixon.[29] Reagan came to office preaching a *new* New Federalism—one that would radically reimagine federal fiscal structures, replacing general revenue sharing with block grants as a step toward eliminating the vestiges of New Deal and Great Society social programs.[30] In the 1983 budget, Congress cut the Avoyelles revenue-sharing allocation by 68 percent and, in 1986, ended federal revenue sharing altogether.[31] The diminishing federal resources were matched by catastrophic budget problems on the state level. Oil prices, previously the largest single source of income for the state, plummeted in the 1980s.[32] Some Louisiana parishes were on the verge of bankruptcy and were considering terminating vital services.[33] At the time of the prison uprisings, the state of Louisiana suffered from massive budget deficits and the nation's highest unemployment rate.[34]

When Belt took office in 1980, the sheriff's office had an annual budget of $750,000. By 1988, the budget had *more than septupled* to $5.5 million, despite a parish population of just over 41,000 residents.[35] Once the sheriff got his foot in the door, he aggressively pursued INS business by expanding old jails and building new ones. In 1986, Belt spearheaded a $3.3 million expansion to increase the parish jail's capacity, turning the facility into what the sheriff declared the nation's "most modern" jail.[36] As the federal money grew, Belt saw opportunity in the parish's 1988 federal desegregation order, which had consolidated nineteen schools down to a dozen.[37] He proposed that three Avoyelles schools could be transformed into detention centers for migrant women, a population the parish had not yet been able to accommodate. Avoyelles had five detention facilities, with a total bed space of 1,326, by the end of the 1990s.[38]

By 1988, Belt's jail held more Cubans in detention than any other local facility in the country. The sheriff had transformed incarceration into a jobs creation initiative and a reinvention of Nixon's revenue-sharing program—a new way to move federal money into a rural place.[39] Using revenue generated from detaining migrants, the parish funded a range of community services, including free ambulances, a youth summer camp, and an upgraded police radio system. It also hired an enormous number of Avoyelles residents to work for the sheriff's office. Belt employed more than four hundred deputies by the end of the decade, remaking the landscape of policing and employment in Avoyelles. It was "enough deputies to start an army," one resident remarked.[40]

When detained Cubans learned about these economic arrangements, many suspected a conspiracy. Surely they were trapped in the bayou forever if powerful people were getting rich off of their incarceration.[41] A 1989 hunger strike generated national attention, with some onlookers wondering whether another hostage situation was on the horizon. Media reports attributed the conflict to a jailer turning off a television. Cubans in Avoyelles told a more complicated story about negligence and overcrowding, noting that they had not even been informed when one of their fellow refugees died in a local hospital.[42] During the hunger strike, one guard brought in his pet pit bull to "help with the situation." "These people treat us like pigs. They treat us like animals," a detained man named Pedro Horta told a reporter.[43]

Other migrants drew links between slavery and incarceration as shared projects of racial subordination and capitalism. These connections were particularly potent in Avoyelles, a hub of the plantation economy and the onetime home of *Twelve Years a Slave* author Solomon Northrup. Pedro A. Carvajal told a judge in 1990, "I did not know our pain and suffering brought a gain to these people who only think about the money they are making from us. I thought that the trade of human beings ended hundreds of years ago, but I see that it still exists."[44] Father Isidore Vicente, a priest who visited the parish jails, concurred: "It's human commerce. It's trading human beings for financial gain."[45] Racism was deeply embedded in how jailers treated the people they incarcerated. In 1991, two Black Americans lodged a lawsuit documenting the horrific abuse they had encountered at the hands of Belt's deputies. The case alleged that deputies held the men at gunpoint, put a noose around one man's neck, and wrote "KKK" on one man's forehead.[46] Just as they had been at Angola, the legacies of Jim Crow were very much alive at the Avoyelles Parish Jail.

At first glance, Belt's prison expansion did not appear to be making him rich. The INS money went to the parish, and the sheriff's salary was set by the state. It did, however, transform Belt into a local power broker: One newspaper speculated that he could be the most powerful elected official in Avoyelles history.[47] He clashed with citizens, commissioners, federal judges, and even the governor over how he ran his jails, but no one successfully hindered his carceral empire.[48] Belt's insistence on expansion puzzled some observers. "WHY would someone keep making his job tougher and tougher if he ain't getting a bigger salary?" the parish's anonymous gossip column implored.[49]

In 2007, the question appeared to have an answer. When Belt was in his remarkable twenty-seventh year as sheriff, he was indicted by a Grand Jury for profiting from phone calls placed by the people incarcerated in his jails. An FBI investigation alleged that Belt, along with his wife and sister, had received more than half a million dollars in kickbacks from a company called Cajun Callers, the sole telephone service provider for Avoyelles jails. Making a phone call from jail, the Grand Jury alleged, meant putting money in the sheriff's pocket.[50] The investigation claimed that Belt had been defrauding the people he incarcerated since 1988.[51] The indictment did not mention it, but the allegations dated to a few months after the uprisings at Oakdale and Atlanta delivered dozens of Mariel Cubans to his parish.[52]

Though the nationalities of detained migrants had changed, the basic calculus of immigration detention mirrored the logic that had persisted since the Chinese exclusion era: Racialized migrants were a commodity that could sustain cash-strapped communities and enrich local leaders. But there were some key differences. In the first half of the twentieth century, communities considered European migrants who could not be deported a liability, as their extended detentions often attracted unwanted media attention and rising federal costs. In the late twentieth century, however, many cities saw Cuban "undeportables" as a sustainable source of revenue. In Jackson County, Illinois, Gene

Truitt, a twenty-year veteran of local corrections, told the *Southern Illinoisan* that his jail had long cooperated with the INS in detaining Mexican workers awaiting deportation. Cubans, however, were a special population. "We usually held [Mexicans] about 15 days in the county jail," Truitt said. "But now it's just forever."[53]

This economic arrangement stretched beyond the Gulf South; counties around the country cashed in on migrant incarceration. In the wake of the Oakdale and Atlanta uprisings, forty-seven local jails and corrections institutes housed Mariel Cubans.[54] Belt became a model for how to transform jails into revenue-producing properties on the backs of some of the nation's least protected people. Some counties followed his lead: Fond du Lac County, on the southern tip of Wisconsin's Lake Winnebago, used its INS contract, which brought in $24,000 a month, to fund a $1.5 million jail expansion.[55] Other counties complained that Belt had cornered the market. When migrants were removed from Mississippi's Harrison County Jail, local officials protested that "Louisiana sheriffs wanted all the Cubans for themselves."[56] In the next several years, Belt inked contracts to incarcerate people from Washington, D.C., and from Puerto Rico, further diversifying his jail's sources of revenue.[57]

Sheriffs and city commissioners were not the only ones noticing the potential for profit. In 1989, Belt signed a contract for a controversial "super prison" project in Evergreen, Louisiana, which would be funded and operated by a New Orleans–based company called Maximum Securities Properties, Inc.[58] Funding prison expansion with bonds had been a challenge for Belt in previous projects—voters rejected plans, and banks sued Belt over his financing schemes.[59] Maximum Securities Properties offered a new "creative financing" model, in which a private corporation would build the jail and would then lease it back to the county, with the lease payments used to pay investors.[60] A month after the super prison deal, a Texas-based company called RTDS, Inc., appeared at a meeting of an Avoyelles city council with a proposal to build and operate yet *another* prison. It was evident that others, both in and outside of Acadiana, recognized that Belt's model was a lucrative one. Private prison companies smelled blood in the water—they wanted in.

Privatizing Corrections

In many ways, privatization seemed like a perfect embodiment of Reagan-era economic ideas: an evangelical belief in efficiency, a faith in the free market, a distrust of unions. It was neoliberalism at its purest, transforming the work of the government into the work of the private sector.[61] In 1982, Reagan enlisted

150 top executives to form the President's Private Sector Survey on Cost Control, known as the Grace Commission. Reagan demanded that the group "work like tireless bloodhounds" to root out waste in the federal government, via a survey on cost control that would leave no agency unexamined.[62] The executives heard the president's directive and returned with a less-than-manageable 2,500 recommendations they claimed would eliminate $424.4 billion from the federal budget. Four years later, the President's Commission on Privatization carried the torch from the Grace Commission, with recommendations for how to "[increase] private sector participation" in nearly every government service. The commission was bullish about private prisons, which it suggested could be built cheaper, faster, and with less community buy-in; INS facilities, it noted, were particularly ripe for "experimentation."[63]

Congress held its first hearing on the rise of privatized prisons in 1985. The BOP made inroads into privatization in 1981, when it contracted out operation of halfway houses for people in federal custody. The agency already contracted out for education, food service, and medical services at federal institutions but was cautious about privatizing the more "visible" elements of its work, such as the management of entire prisons.[64] Even in an era that glorified the free market, prison privatization drew an unlikely alliance of skeptics: The National Sheriffs' Association, the American Civil Liberties Union, the American Bar Association, and union representatives from the American Federation of Government Employees all raised serious doubts about delegating corrections to companies. Their concerns ranged from the material—the status of federal workers and the undercutting of wages by private prison companies—to the ideological: What did it mean for the state to turn its most essential functions over to the private sector?

The question of how profit-seeking companies would reshape incarceration in the United States often obscured the ways that communities like Avoyelles were *already* profiting from imprisonment. The National Sheriffs' Association's statement to Congress asked whether paying a fixed amount for each incarcerated person would provide incentives for companies to keep jails full for as long as possible.[65] Unions made a similar case; the American Federation of Government Employees declared that "for the first time, it is in someone's *self-interest* to foster and encourage incarceration."[66] These groups presented privatization as a major departure from the corrections systems of the past.[67] Yet migrant incarceration was profitable for a wide variety of actors—local governments, contractors, and sheriffs—for decades before a language of "privatization" emerged. It was profitable at Ellis Island in the 1900s. When

Ellis Island's newly elected commissioner attempted to remove "private interests" from the detention site, congressmen with financial stakes in Ellis Island's dining contract launched a campaign for his impeachment.[68] It was profitable seventy years later at Fort Chaffee and the resettlement camps. Local businesses received massive contracts for food, clothing, and construction, deals that made some locals reluctant to see Cubans resettled at all.[69] What was different by the end of the twentieth century was that companies would no longer just provide a service: They would run the entire carceral operation.

Animated by the Grace Commission's suggestions, alongside pervasive ideas about detained migrants being less dangerous and less litigious than other incarcerated persons, the INS became an early laboratory for privatization. In 1980, the chairman of the Tennessee Republican Party, together with the corrections commissioners of Tennessee and Virginia, founded what would become the nation's largest private incarceration company: Corrections Corporation of America (CCA).[70] In 1984, CCA secured its first governmental contract to operate detention centers for the INS in Houston and Laredo, Texas. When CCA won the Houston contract it had not yet built a facility to hold migrants. To fulfill its obligations, it detained 125 migrants in a run-down motel surrounded by barbed wire gates.[71] That same year, Texas, Florida, and Tennessee passed laws allowing private companies to administer corrections and detention facilities. Within months, CCA operated all jails in Hamilton County, Tennessee, which the company parlayed into a bid to take over all Tennessee prisons.[72] CCA's aggressive approach to expansion suggested that it was not just looking to supplement the work of the state in incarceration; it was ready to replace the state altogether.[73]

The INS initially embraced privatization not only for financial reasons but for the speed with which new facilities could be constructed. While the federal government decided that CCA had done a satisfactory job operating the Houston detention site, the BOP noted that it had not seen substantial cost savings. The major advantage of private-sector facilities, BOP Director Norman Carlson wrote, "is that during a period of unprecedented growth in the Federal inmate population, they can provide additional options for the confinement of selected categories of inmates. Specifically, that group is the illegal alien serving short sentences and requiring low security custody."[74] As space in both long-term federal prisons and short-term local jails became increasingly sought after, the years-long negotiations around Oakdale did not look like a promising model for rapid expansion. To carry out its detention mandate, the INS wanted beds, fast. Companies rose to the challenge. Wackenhut, Inc., a pioneer of private corrections, built and opened a 150-bed immigration detention facility in just ninety days from when the government signed the contract.[75]

The federal government's private prison boosters also had another hope: that private facilities might help the government evade some of the legal liability that had ensnared the nation's jails and prisons throughout the previous decades. Whether private companies would be liable under Section 1983 of the Civil Rights Act of 1871 was an open question throughout the 1980s.[76] Section 1983 created a cause of action against any person who, acting under color of state law, deprived someone of a right guaranteed by federal or constitutional law. Attorneys concerned about the growing power of private prisons anticipated that this could be a route to defending the constitutional rights of people incarcerated by private companies.[77]

One of the first tests of the law came in 1984 in the case of *Medina v. O'Neill*, in the Federal District Court of Southern Texas.[78] The case illustrated the practice of ad hoc detention privatization—though major companies like CCA and Wackenhut had been the core of attention and debate, the INS had quietly relied on other private companies to detain migrants for years before the first official INS contract with CCA.[79] In February 1981, the vessel *Cartagena de Indios* docked in the Port of Houston, carrying twenty-six stowaways, whom workers had discovered on the voyage from Colombia to Texas. The police brought some stowaways to the local jail and brought others to Danner's, Inc., a maritime security company based in Houston—notably not a private prison company.[80] Danner's maintained two cells at its offices for "temporary detention purposes." Within two days of the arrival of the *Cartagena de Indios*, twenty of its passengers were held in Danner's office building, with sixteen people incarcerated in the two cells. After forty-eight hours trapped in windowless rooms, several men tried to escape; a Danner's employee with no formal firearms training used a shotgun as a prod to force them back into the facility. The gun went off, killing Ramon Garcia and injuring another migrant.[81]

To successfully lodge a Section 1983 claim, the plaintiffs needed to show that the private party was acting "under color of state law," making the company liable under the Fifth and Fourteenth Amendments.[82] The core of the *Medina* case centered on whether the actions of a private company providing detention space constituted "state action." The court ultimately concluded that because regulating immigration and detention had typically been the exclusive prerogative of a sovereign state, the actions of Danner's constituted actions on behalf of the U.S. government. It held that the INS had violated the constitutional rights of the migrants by failing to ensure their confinement in conditions that met constitutional requirements.[83] The family of the deceased could press charges against *both* the INS and the private company; the immigration service could not relinquish legal responsibility merely by handing migrants over to a private company.

Richard G. Crane, a vice president of CCA, conceded that the state would not fully immunize itself from liability by contracting out, but he maintained that privatization would reduce the risk of legal action. Because private firms could build quickly, private prison executives argued that they could promptly reduce overcrowding at existing facilities, making them less likely to come under further court injunctions. While CCA insisted that it never claimed the state would completely evade legal liability through privatization, other companies reportedly distributed promotional literature to investors suggesting that privatization would diminish or eliminate the government's liability under Section 1983.[84]

Both the BOP and the INS warmed to privatization under the Clinton administration. Clinton made reducing the size of the federal government an oft-invoked campaign promise, and his administration fervently believed that most government programs could be improved by more closely emulating markets.[85] In 1993, Clinton introduced legislation to reduce the federal workforce by 273,000 people over the next five years.[86] The law established caps on federal hiring for the remainder of the 1990s. Perhaps unsurprisingly, the DOJ had grown faster than any other federal agency from 1985 to 1995, adding 37,600 employees for a 60 percent increase over the decade.[87] In the 1996 DOJ budget, the agency announced plans for the privatization of all new low- and minimum-security prisons and pretrial detention facilities operated by the BOP—a move it claimed would eliminate four thousand federal jobs.[88] CCA executives argued that introducing market incentives into corrections would reform prisons in a way that judicial intervention alone could not. Because the courts could not "fire" the state for mismanagement of prisons, there was no real pressure to change, Crane claimed. Under privatization, companies would have multiple incentives to maintain acceptable conditions: Their contract could be revoked, their reputation could be harmed, and their shareholders could revolt. Privatization was positioned as a rational reform for a broken system that the courts had been unable to tame.

As the federal government moved toward privatizing federal facilities, it encountered resistance from municipalities that had been enthusiastic about hosting a federal prison but now balked at the prospect of a *privatized* federal prison. In Forrest City, Arkansas, a predominantly African American town with a largely white political class, both residents and politicians welcomed a new federal institution as a solution to the Mississippi Delta's double-digit unemployment.[89] In 1995, the Office of Management and Budget submitted a proposal that would privatize the under-construction prison in Forrest City. Mayor Danny Ferguson wrote an anxious letter to President Clinton, emphasizing the town's "tremendous sacrifices and investments to get this Federal prison complex," including the town's $5 million investment in purchasing the land for the project.[90] He implored the president to reconsider the privatization plan, fearing that privatization meant lower-paid, less desirable jobs than the stable federal jobs Forrest City was promised.[91] Local pressure ultimately moved the Clinton administration to a more gradual shift toward privatization.[92] By the end of 1999, fourteen corporations operated more than 150 private correctional facilities for adults in the United States, earning combined annual revenues over a billion dollars. Most of these facilities were state and local prisons and jails, rather than federal prisons.[93]

Private immigration detention centers proved similarly contentious throughout the 1990s.[94] In the summer of 1992, the INS began accepting bids to build a new facility to detain asylum seekers and migrants who arrived through JFK and Newark airports. Esmor Correctional Services Corporation, a company that went from operating some of New York City's most notorious welfare hotels to operating some of its first privatized halfway houses, pledged that it could manage a facility on a shoestring budget. It won the federal contract to build in Elizabeth, New Jersey, in 1993. Its bid was so low that even other private prison companies called it unrealistic and dangerous to operate the site at such a price point.[95]

By 1995, the Esmor Detention Facility held 315 asylum seekers from more than thirty countries, a reflection of the diverse populations seeking refuge through the United States' busiest airports.[96] When investigators visited Elizabeth, they found a site with operators willing to cut costs in big ways: understaffing the facility, paying workers poverty wages, and refusing to perform medical care in-house. They also found operators desperate to cut costs in even the most minor ways, for example, by fining migrants for lost kitchen utensils and drinking cups.[97] Investigators described a total breakdown in communication between the INS and its contractor. Esmor regularly withheld information about the site's operation from the immigration service, a move that paralleled the agency's own behavior during Kromegate—the center's administrator, Willard Stovall, called Esmor "my house" and suggested that the INS should not interfere in its operation.[98]

Physical abuse, religious repression, and racism fueled an uprising at Esmor in June 1995. Fifty detained persons shattered glass and overturned tables, as police launched flash and percussion grenades into the private prison. The INS published a shocking postmortem of the uprising, documenting an institutional culture in which guards regularly beat and stole from detained migrants, locked them in solitary confinement, and hazed them in ways intended to humiliate and degrade. The INS condemned its contractor and the conditions in Elizabeth, eager to distance itself from abuse so rampant even the immigration bureaucracy could not ignore it.[99] The Esmor Detention Facility promptly became the symbol of everything migrants and their advocates had feared about privatized detention centers: little oversight, no formal standards, and companies incentivized to cut corners for profit.[100]

York County and the Persistence of Federal-Local Partnership

In the aftermath of the Esmor uprising, the federal government turned back to jails, dispersing migrants from Esmor between local lockups in eight nearby counties. Once again, the protests and resistance of detained migrants remade the landscape of incarceration. At the center of the new arrangement was York, Pennsylvania, a town of 43,000 people and only one immigration lawyer, one hundred miles west of Philadelphia.[101]

By the end of 1995, with doubts growing about the reliability of private contractors like Esmor, the INS transformed York County Prison (which, despite its name, is a jail rather than a prison) into its detention hub of the Northeast.[102] The INS established a permanent office in the jail and converted a nearby two hundred-year-old farmhouse into a federal immigration court.[103] Migrants from all parts of the world entered the old Pennsylvania house in handcuffs to plead their cases for asylum or for relief from deportation. In exchange, York County received $45 nightly for each person in INS custody, a windfall that officials suggested might be enough to eliminate personal property tax for county residents.[104] Migrants understood the financial throughlines between the two sites: Fauziya Kassindja, a Togolese asylum seeker, wrote of her transfer to York, "It was like Esmor all over again. All that money."[105] (Figure 30.)

York County had found itself at the center of a migrant incarceration controversy before. It first established itself as a go-to partner for the INS in June 1993, when the *Golden Venture*, a ship smuggling Chinese migrants, ran aground in the middle of a New York City summer night. Chinese migrants dove into the freezing ocean and swam for the Queens shoreline. They were

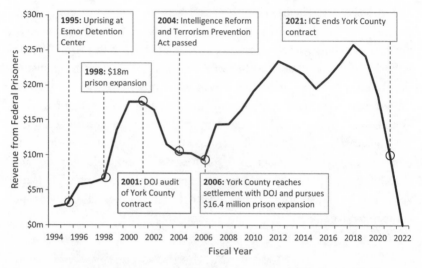

FIGURE 30. Graph of revenue from federal prisoners at York County Prison, Pennsylvania, 1994–2022. ICE = Immigration and Customs Enforcement; DOJ = Department of Justice. *Source:* York County Budgets, York County Municipal Archives.

desperate for an end to a 130-day voyage that had cost all of them tens of thousands of dollars (paid to human smugglers known as "snakeheads") and had cost some of them their lives. The emaciated men and women aboard the ship had suffered unthinkable atrocities. Some had spent three years in transit to the United States, moving through smuggling networks in Southeast Asia and Africa, before eventually boarding the decrepit cargo vessel.[106] And now, the surreal culmination: jail in southern Pennsylvania.

York was at the right place at the right time. The county had signed a contract with the INS in 1992, it was close enough to New York City, and it had ample empty space in its recently expanded jail. The Clinton administration chose to detain all *Golden Venture* passengers in an effort to deter future asylum seekers from China—a move torn straight from Reagan's playbook for Haitian refugees.[107] Suddenly, migrants were an in-demand population for the sheriffs and city councils of Greater Pennsylvania. At Perry County, located along Pennsylvania's Susquehanna River, the jail faced layoffs and budget shortfalls. "We tried like the dickens to get some of those Chinese," County Commissioner Joseph A. Conrad sighed.[108] Perry County officials watched enviously as York County reaped $1,650 per day from holding the *Golden Venture* passengers—they, too, wanted a piece of the pie. The INS heard their pleas and sent an intriguing response: It would be happy to work with Perry County, but it would need a bigger jail.[109] Carceral expansion became a condition of working with the immigration service, incentivizing communities to invest in more jail beds.

In York County, the incarceration of the *Golden Venture* refugees was met with mixed reactions. As in Avoyelles Parish, local leaders stressed the material ways citizens benefited from the incarceration of noncitizens, namely, through the elimination and reduction of various taxes. They also insisted that incarceration was responsible municipal fiscal policy. The average county investment of surplus funds yielded somewhere between a 4.8 and 5.2 percent return per year. INS detainees netted York County an enormous 56 percent return.[110] However, the *Golden Venture* migrants were a highly publicized group at the center of a humanitarian crisis. Left-leaning churches saw their plight as an extension of the Sanctuary movement, in which religious communities had mobilized to aid and house asylum seekers from Central America.[111] Right-leaning churches saw *Golden Venture* as a referendum on China's oppressive family planning policies, drawing particular attention to the plight of detained women.[112] Public interest was substantial; the York community, led by the local paper, took the INS to court to force the agency to move asylum hearings out of the jail so that the press and public could attend.[113] Clinton's decision to detain incurred bipartisan censure. "[We] are balancing our county budget on the backs of people who are being incarcerated with no indication as to what their future will bring them," said Representative William Goodling, a longtime Republican congressman from Pennsylvania.[114]

Much of this controversy would dissipate as the detention mandate grew and the stories of migrants faded. The timing of the Esmor uprisings could hardly have been better for York County officials, who worried about revenue loss as more *Golden Venture* passengers secured their freedom.[115] With the 1996 passage of the Antiterrorism and Effective Death Penalty Act and Illegal Immigration Reform and Immigration Responsibility Act, Pennsylvania's jails became even more central to the immigration service's labor. Every day, green-and-white INS buses sped down Interstate 78, bringing new rounds of migrants from New York City to southern Pennsylvania. The jails held what the INS called a broad "cross section of detainees": asylum seekers, migrants apprehended at New York City's airports and in workplace raids, and people passed into INS custody after arrest for criminal offenses.[116] It was the "criminal aliens" that the INS most emphasized in its public relations efforts, reinforcing its bona fides as a law enforcement agency actively engaged in crime control. "We need to remember that these criminal alien statistics represent more than just numbers," the INS declared in a 1997 press release. "Each time INS removes one of those criminal aliens, we take another dangerous person off the streets and out of our communities."[117]

All the people classified as criminal aliens had, of course, their own individual story and set of circumstances. Cecilia Jeffrey, a woman incarcerated at York, was one of the noncitizens whose detention and expulsion the 1996 legislation had mandated. Jeffrey was originally from Liberia and had been a legal U.S. resident since 1989. She worked as a home health aide and cofounded a church for Liberian migrants in New York. In 1992, with civil war escalating, she returned to Liberia to search for family members. Her trip lasted longer than expected, and her return ticket expired. Jeffrey was stuck in London when a man asked whether she would be willing to bring a bag on board in exchange for a ticket. When airport workers discovered heroin in the luggage, Jeffrey was sentenced to a twenty-two-month prison sentence in Connecticut, followed by a stint in INS custody in Elizabeth, New Jersey. After the Esmor facility shuttered, the INS transferred Jeffrey to York. She was incarcerated for four additional years before winning an appeal to suspend her deportation.[118]

Once again, the immigration service's contracts propelled carceral growth.[119] In 1998, York County commissioners voted to take on substantial debt to fund a $19.9 million expansion of the county jail, with the understanding that the INS would continue filling beds.[120] With the DOJ's announcement that the 1999 INS budget would top $4.2 billion, doubling the agency's allotment in just five years, York County leaders felt more confident than ever that they had made a sound long-term investment—they were a pivotal local partner of what was now the largest federal law enforcement agency in the United States.[121] Like communities across the United States, York County reinvested some of the INS revenue back into law enforcement, purchasing stun guns, shields, new vans, and other equipment for corrections officers.[122] The county anticipated that INS demand for bed space was so high it would pay off the bond for prison construction in just three years.

By 2002, the INS contract brought more than $17 million into York County annually.[123] But tensions were rising. An independent audit indicated that the county had overcharged the federal government by an annual $6.1 million. When York County refused to reduce its nightly rates, the DOJ dissolved the partnership. Residents were stunned to see their property tax increase by 33 percent following the loss of the immigration service's business.[124] Teamsters Local 430, the union that represented York County Prison guards, warned that they would lose ninety jobs if the INS left for good.[125] "Why [counties] aren't allowed to make a profit, I don't know. Lockheed Martin and Boeing certainly make a profit," a York County attorney mused.[126] The local newspaper declared the county "addicted" to money from immigration contracts—trapped in a perpetual cycle of taking immigration prisoners, reinvesting the money into jail expansion, and then detaining even more people. Ending the contract might be a form of federally forced rehab, the paper suggested, a chance for the county and its budget to take a long, hard look in the mirror.[127]

Alarm around the decline in immigration revenue was palpable, even if local officials suspected that they could find American prisoners to fill many of their empty beds. York County was optimistic that the 2003 outset of the Iraq War, along with the immigration service's recategorization under the newly created Department of Homeland Security (DHS), would make its jail space more essential.[128] Almost immediately after the 9/11 attacks, the FBI initiated a massive investigation to identify the men who had hijacked the airplanes, as well as any of their associates. The federal government embarked on a devastating campaign of racial and religious profiling against Muslim, Arab, and South Asian people throughout the United States.[129] About 1,200 people were detained in the two months following 9/11, 762 of whom were added to an INS Custody List and held indefinitely until the FBI cleared them. The federal government charged most people in custody with minor violations of immigration law—very few faced criminal charges or received a trial. They were detained in familiar locations: Krome Service Processing Center; the Federal Detention Center in Oakdale; and a range of state and local facilities already under contract with the INS, primarily jails in the Northeast.[130] In the months that followed, the Bush administration embraced spectacles of national security that targeted noncitizens. It invested more money in border walls and a vast system of "virtual fences," towers along the border that used radar and sensor signals, much of which the DHS enthusiastically outsourced to private companies and military contractors.[131]

York County's prediction that an expanding immigration–national security apparatus would require its jail space proved correct. Two days before the U.S. invasion of Iraq began, the DHS initiated "Operation Liberty Shield," a program mandating detention of asylum seekers from nations where al-Qaeda or other terrorist groups were known to have operated. The DHS refused to specify which nations this included.[132] In 2004, the Intelligence Reform and Terrorism Prevention Act authorized forty thousand new immigrant detention beds, tripling the total bed space available to Immigration and Customs Enforcement. York County agreed to a settlement with ICE in 2006, and within months, residents voted to expand the jail yet again. In 2008, York County's facility averaged seven hundred migrants a night.[133]

The post-9/11 demand for detention space was a boon for private prison companies that had struggled in the 1990s as the INS favored local sites, like York County Prison, over privately run facilities, like Esmor.[134] In 2000, independent auditors expressed uncertainty that CCA would even stay in business after the company suffered a net loss of $203 million, due mainly to an inability to fill private prison beds after a series of high-profile escapes, uprisings, and abuse allegations.[135] George W. Bush entered the White House with a legacy of privatization behind him; *The American Prospect* called Bush's Texas "the world capital of the private-prison industry."[136] President Bush dramatically recast the role of the state in national security, with immigration detention serving as one small part of a larger national turn toward outsourcing. The private prison industry immediately noted the shifting winds: The month following the 9/11 attacks, an executive of a private prison contractor called Cornell Companies, Inc., told investors, "[It] is clear that since September 11 there's a heightened focus on detention. More people are going to get caught. . . . The federal business is the best business for us, and September 11 is increasing that business."[137] In 2006, the Bush administration awarded a $6 million contract to a subsidiary of Halliburton, the oil and gas conglomerate formerly run by Vice President Dick Cheney, to create immigration detention sites in the case of another "emergency" like the Mariel Boatlift. CCA's revenue grew by 88 percent between 2001 and 2011, as Bush hired massive numbers of new Border Patrol officials and declared a switch from a "catch and release" to a "catch and return [deport]" policy.[138] Private prison companies' financial struggles were quickly becoming a fading memory.

Private companies received a growing proportion of detention contracts post-9/11, but localities went to great efforts to show that they, too, could be highly efficient incarcerators. By the 2010s, York County had initiated an "innovative jail diversion program" to keep people accused of criminal offenses *out* of the York County Prison, "thereby creating space for additional ICE detainees."[139] Policies that could appear progressive at first glance—reducing incarceration for Pennsylvanians who should never have been jailed in the first place—were, in fact, just work-arounds for the county to pursue more profitable incarcerations. The jail was understood, first and foremost, as a money-making project.

———

Throughout the 1980s and 1990s, sheriffs and city commissioners expanded jails for reasons that had nothing to do with community safety. They were remarkably transparent about why they were building: Adding beds was an economic decision, one that linked their communities' budgets to the rapidly expanding deportation machine. These linkages enabled communities to locate new modes of funding outside of the typical model of municipal debt, using financing from the state and federal governments or from private prison companies. As Bill Belt's trajectory indicates, sheriffs who built more jail space for the federal government were rewarded. They became powerful local figures as their payroll surged, and they often found ways to personally profit. However, tying the local economy to federal prisoners also made localities highly dependent on the whims of the federal government: If the federal government chose to change courses or take its business elsewhere, as briefly occurred in York, communities were left with empty beds and towering debt.[140]

The legislative history and financial interests at the heart of the late twentieth-century detention business matter enormously: They show how the United States turned its immigration system into a law enforcement project fixated on removing criminal aliens, how American communities tethered their financial fortunes to incarceration, and how this system became quickly and quietly ubiquitous by the turn of the new millennium. But each so-called detention bed also represented a life and a story, a set of circumstances that led a person to leave their homeland for an unknown life in the United States. Activists on the inside and outside of jails have pushed to make these stories visible.

One of the most well-known migrants incarcerated by ICE post-9/11 was Hiu Lui (Jason) Ng, who arrived in New York City with his family in 1992 as a seventeen-year-old. He built a life, a career, and a family in the city. In 2007, Ng was apprehended by ICE because of an overstayed visa and a missed immigration hearing—years prior, ICE had sent notice of the hearing to the wrong address. ICE detained Ng at Wyatt Detention Facility in Rhode Island's Blackstone Valley, a publicly owned site operated by the private Central Falls Detention Facility Corporation. Thirteen months later, Ng was dead at age thirty-four, his body overrun with liver cancer that had gone undiagnosed in detention, along with a fractured spine from being forced into an ICE van. His case was prominently featured in the *New York Times* and was taken up by the ACLU, which secured a significant financial settlement for his wife and children.[141]

Ng's case was seen by many reporters and activists as an indictment of private prison operations and of ICE: Wyatt staff and ICE officials had subjected Ng to physical violence and lied to him about court proceedings, pressuring him to consent to a voluntary departure. Less acknowledged was how Ng's case showed the precarity of jail-based incarceration and the flexible system of transfers. After an initial 175 days in Wyatt, Ng was transferred to the Franklin County Jail and House of Corrections in Greenfield, Massachusetts, a remote jail four hours from Boston. Four months later, in April 2008, ICE moved Ng to Franklin County Jail in St. Albans, Vermont. Both jails had intergovernmental service agreements to house ICE detainees. Ng's medical records did not follow him. ICE did not alert his family or legal counsel about the transfers. Neither the Greenfield jail nor the St. Albans jail had medical facilities. There was a particular irony to Ng's incarceration in Vermont. The physical building had changed, but Ng, a Chinese national, was incarcerated in the same county jail that had detained dozens of Chinese migrants a century prior, when St. Albans had been a depot for the Canadian Pacific Railway.[142]

Multiple American communities and companies profited from jailing Ng's dying body. Two years before his death, the St. Albans sheriff had reported that his rural community could not afford to keep its jail open without its ICE contract. The Greenfield jail suffered budget shortfalls of nearly $2.8 million when the federal government chose to remove migrants following Ng's death.[143] The Wyatt detention center had been sold to the Rhode Island town in the 1990s as a solution to the region's economic woes and as a chance to be on the cutting edge of private corrections. It instead became a financial drain, with far more money going to investors than to the locality.[144] The jail was a source of terror in the majority-Latino town.[145] Counties had built systems of incarceration that relied on the immigration service; when ICE left, they had to find other solutions, by either incarcerating more local people or contracting out jail space to other agencies and states. In the ACLU's lawsuit, ICE again tried to distance itself from the contractors that it had long relied on. "The United States is not liable for the acts of Wyatt, Franklin House of Corrections, and the Franklin County Jail because they are contractors," read ICE's Motion to Dismiss.[146] The court did not accept this rationale, but it showed how the federal government envisioned these relationships. Contractors were central to exclusion and removal, yet the federal government did not see itself as having an obligation, or perhaps even the ability, to oversee them. Over and over, immigration officials claimed that they were merely "guests" in America's jails, regrettably unable to influence the policies at individual facilities.[147] The government's priority was reducing costs and obscuring visibility. People like Ng paid the price.

Getting ICE out of Jails

Statistics can prove that foreigners have not been living off the system.
It's the system that has been living off foreigners.

—LETTER FROM MIGRANTS INCARCERATED AT
MANATEE COUNTY JAIL, FLORIDA, 1998

FOR EVERY YORK COUNTY OR Avoyelles Parish, where detention became a
pillar of the local economy, there are localities pushing back against the immigration service's calls for collaboration. In the past decade, immigration
law enforcement has become an exemplar of what scholars have called "uncooperative federalism," with cities and states challenging forceful, but ultimately voluntary, federal requests for cooperation.[1] These tensions came to a
head under the Trump administration's family separation policies, as communities throughout the United States reckoned with what it meant to be a
partner of Immigration and Customs Enforcement in an age of resurgent nativism and unprecedented removals.

In some ways, detention appears to be more ingrained in immigration
law and policy than ever before. Since the creation of ICE in 2003 under
the Department of Homeland Security, the agency's budget has more than
doubled; this was driven by the conflation of migrants with potential terrorists,
a connection that had particularly shattering consequences for both citizens
and noncitizens perceived to be Arab or Muslim.[2] Beginning with the passage
of the 2004 Intelligence Reform and Terrorism Prevention Act, Congress required ICE to add eight thousand additional detention beds each year.[3] Things
escalated in 2009, when Congress introduced a national bed quota in the annual appropriations bills, a policy shift fueled by conservative critiques that
parole had become a "catch and release policy" for dangerous noncitizens.[4]

Today, ICE maintains a minimum of 34,000 detention beds per night, which the government pays for regardless of whether they are filled.[5] These beds can be used interchangeably by various institutions and agencies and are justified as ways of fighting wars on crime, illegal immigration, and terrorism.[6] Like many of the immigration service's enforcement powers, these quotas, too, have devolved: Localities and private companies have sought to include "guarantees" in their contracts, requiring ICE to pay for a certain number of beds even if demand wanes.[7]

Despite detention's proliferation, the years since the creation of ICE have also been marked by remarkable local activism and resistance. These actions build on long lineages of organizing and questioning detention's legitimacy and have been critical in severing decades-long relationships between the deportation state and local governments. Local resistance has made detention's cruelty visible and has documented the negligence, abuse, and profiteering that define the system. This epilogue offers a snapshot of migrant incarceration today: where it takes place, who it entraps, and what is being done to end it.

———

As this book has shown, detention has long been, and remains, a national phenomenon—one that takes place both near and far from the nation's land borders. Though today federal ICE facilities are concentrated in states such as Texas, California, Florida, New York, and Arizona, the immigration service maintains at least one detention site in each of the fifty states.[8] Sites range from isolated rural jails to unmarked urban office buildings.[9] Most sites bear the usual hallmarks of prisons: government uniforms, a regimented schedule, and the constant threat of greater punishment if one disobeys.[10]

ICE has several methods for acquiring detention space, each with its own sets of obstacles for the agency and distinct hazards for the people detained at these sites. In FY 2022, ICE authorized the use of 181 sites for detention exceeding seventy-two hours.[11] While this section will focus on this group of facilities, it is worth noting that this is only a fraction of the total contracts and agreements ICE maintains. A set of data released in 2017 showed that ICE had around 850 contracts between local and federal authorities to detain migrants in 669 counties.[12] Some of these agreements are with jails ICE has not used in years; others are jails that ICE uses only for very brief periods before moving migrants to larger facilities. Still, these data show the immigration service's expansive reach and capacity.

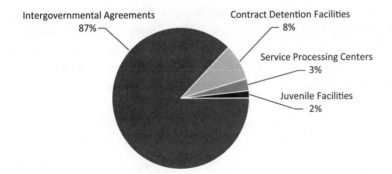

Intergovernmental Agreements
87%

Contract Detention Facilities
8%

Service Processing Centers
3%

Juvenile Facilities
2%

FIGURE 31. Graph of Immigration and Customs Enforcement detention facilities by contract type, October 2022. These data represent Immigration and Customs Enforcement (ICE) dedicated and nondedicated facilities. The category "Intergovernmental Agreements" includes intergovernmental service agreements signed by ICE, as well as those signed by the U.S. Marshals Service (USMS) with riders allowing ICE to use USMS facilities. "Contract Detention Facilities" also includes two sites that have contracts with the USMS, which ICE can use under a similar arrangement. *Source:* All data are from Immigration and Customs Enforcement, Enforcement and Removals Operations Custody Management Division, last updated Oct. 11, 2022, https://www.ice.gov/doclib/facilityInspections/dedicatedNonDedicatedFacilityList.xlsx.

ICE acquires most of its facilities—roughly 87 percent of all detention sites—through intergovernmental service agreements (IGSAs).[13] (Figure 31.) IGSAs are signed agreements that formalize the type of collaboration between federal and local governments documented throughout this book, notably the detention of people in local institutions at the request of the federal government. Today, the federal government uses IGSAs for education, Medicaid, and disaster relief, with ICE using them largely for jailing and policing. There are few consistent policies for negotiating, executing, and modifying IGSAs, granting ICE tremendous discretion.[14] At first glance, IGSAs look like straightforward arrangements between the local and federal governments, the same type of arrangement that the immigration service has relied on since the end of the nineteenth century. They document nightly rates, standards of care, and processes of federal oversight. However, privatization has added another layer to these already ambiguous delegations of power. ICE has insisted that IGSAs are not a cooperative agreement but, rather, a procurement contract to obtain a commodity: bed space.[15] IGSAs allow ICE to access private prison space while evading the more cumbersome rules governing federal contracting, such as soliciting bids or auditing companies' past performance. When using an IGSA, the agency does not contract with a company directly. It simply signs an agreement with a locality. The locality can then either operate a detention site itself *or* outsource to a third party. These agreements create the illusion that ICE is working with a local government when, in reality, it is often working with private contractors.

In one particularly egregious example, ICE modified an IGSA with Eloy, Arizona, in September 2014 to create the South Texas Family Residential Center, a privately operated detention site more than nine hundred miles away in Dilley, Texas.[16] ICE signed an agreement with Eloy, and Eloy then signed a contract with the Corrections Corporation of America. The town pocketed $438,000 annually for detention services. Eloy became, in the words of a federal audit, an "unnecessary middleman" that allowed ICE to acquire beds quickly and circumvent the procurement process. Once again, ICE praised the flexibility that these agreements granted the immigration service, arguing that this was a justified response to the rising number of families and unaccompanied minors crossing the southern border. There are countless more mundane examples as well, wherein localities have brought in private companies to manage their local jails.[17] Privatization has not replaced the federal government's dependence on localities. Instead, it has made federal-local collaboration even more central to migrant incarceration.

As criticisms of ICE lead more counties to reexamine their IGSAs, the immigration service has a backup plan: contracting directly with private companies to create what the agency calls "contract detention facilities." In Williamson County, Texas, the city commissioners ended their IGSA with ICE in 2016 after significant public pressure. However, this did not actually eliminate detention in the county. ICE signed a new contract with the private prison company CoreCivic (formerly Corrections Corporation of America), which had been operating the detention center under the now-terminated IGSA.[18] Direct contracting is not the immigration service's first choice. However, in states such as Texas, which are unlikely to pass legislation limiting migrant incarceration broadly, private contracting remains a viable strategy for cementing detention's future in spite of local resistance. ICE embraced the local middleman for its expediency, but it can just as easily purge the middleman as the political winds shift.

The smallest percentage of current ICE facilities are service processing centers (SPCs), facilities owned and operated by the federal government specifically for migrant incarceration. These facilities are, in some sense, a relic of a bygone era. SPCs were once pitched to Congress as the solution to get migrants *out of jails* and consolidate them in safer, healthier spaces designed for administrative detention rather than punitive control. As evidenced by the immigration service's use of space in the last twenty years, this idea has been all but abandoned. Two of the SPCs, El Paso and Port Isabel, date to the height and aftermath of Operation Wetback. Another two, Krome and an SPC in Florence, Arizona, date to the early 1980s.[19] The most recent site, located in Batavia, New York, originated during the Clinton administration.[20] The DHS has *closed* four SPCs in recent years—perhaps surprising given detention's meteoric expansion.[21]

Deterred by migrant organizing and uprisings, as well as critical media coverage of SPCs following events such as Kromegate, the immigration service determined that centralization was *not* what it wanted for detention and removal operations. A decentralized system gave the agency far more power, both over migrants and over the public perception of its detention system—a lesson the agency learned over the century of detention experiments documented in this book. Decentralization created a moving target for its critics: a landscape of incarceration constantly in flux, making it harder to challenge or even to see. "[Much] could be said for a fully government-owned and government-operated detention model, if one were starting a new detention system from scratch," the DHS opined in a 2016 report. "But of course we are not starting anew."[22]

How do people enter ICE detention today? The paths to incarceration look quite different than they did one hundred, or even forty, years ago. In the twenty-first century, the federal government has invested heavily in interior enforcement and in programs that claim to prioritize the removal of "criminal aliens," an escalation of initiatives forged in the 1980s and 1990s.[23] Most migrants enter detention via one of two routes. The first is through community arrests and raids, where ICE apprehends noncitizens at home, at work, or in the wider community. The second is through "nonimmigration-related minor offenses," such as traffic or drug infractions, after which noncitizens are passed from local law enforcement custody to ICE custody.[24] With the expansion of expedited removal programs since 1996, immigration officials have wide latitude to deport unauthorized migrants if they are apprehended within two weeks of arrival or within one hundred miles of a U.S. land border. Because migrants in expedited removal proceedings have very few legal rights, they typically do not face detentions as long as those encountered by longer-term U.S. residents or asylum seekers.[25] The United States also continues to detain people who arrive at the border or at U.S. airports seeking asylum; under Biden administration policy, ICE has been more likely to release family units into communities, with the use of curfews and ankle monitor bracelets, whereas single adult asylum seekers are more likely to be detained.[26]

In recent years, the immigration service's collaboration with local law enforcement has become an even more integral component of the agency's work. One hundred forty sheriff's offices around the United States now maintain 287(g) arrangements with ICE, which deputize local law enforcement to carry out certain functions of federal immigration officials.[27] So-called 287(g) officers have access to federal immigration databases and may arrest and interrogate anyone suspected of violating federal immigration law. Granting law enforcement this discretionary power has created a form of racialized social control that targets Latina/o people regardless of immigration status.[28] Sheriffs have justified this system of localized immigration enforcement by promoting the myth of migrant criminality, even as roughly half of all 287(g) arrests come from routine traffic stops. When an ICE official pitched the program to Congress in 2005, he assured policymakers that it would target criminals and not "landscaping type of individuals."[29]

The immigration service has long seen sheriffs as a potential partner and a way to amplify its own power. The 287(g) program formalized these relationships.[30] The Trump administration aggressively recruited sheriffs, bringing 111 new offices into the 287(g) program; many of these sheriffs became outspoken anti-immigrant pundits. Though President Biden pledged to end 287(g) during the 2020 presidential campaign, the program has persisted. Alejandro Mayorkas, the head of the DHS, has encouraged mayors to resume collaborating with ICE, promising that it is "not the agency of the past."[31] In 2021, President Biden nominated a sheriff to be the new director of ICE.[32] Deportation and detention have been, and continue to be, a bipartisan project—the details may change, but leaders of all political affiliations have sought to expand the immigration service's roster of collaborators.

This book has shown how inconsistency in information-sharing with local police has been a recurring frustration for the immigration service. In the 1920s, immigration officers complained that police only occasionally passed information about deportable arrested persons to the immigration service. In the 1970s and 1980s, immigration officers in Miami argued that they had no way to keep track of how many asylum seekers were in Florida jails, proposing software that could cross-reference between immigration and police databases. Under the Obama administration, this technology came to fruition through the Secure Communities Program. The program provided police and corrections officers with access to the DHS immigration database, where they could cross-check fingerprints after arrest. Secure Communities further eroded the boundary between federal immigration law enforcement and local policing, placing the two in technological lockstep and creating yet another path into detention. Secure Communities, in the words of one ICE official, "[created] a virtual ICE presence at every local jail."[33] This data-sharing program has also continued under the Biden administration, rebranded as the ICE Criminal Apprehension Program.[34]

As decades of data and scholarship attest, Black and Latina/o people face dramatically disproportionate rates of incarceration, criminal arrests, and interactions with law enforcement through police actions such as traffic stops.[35] Because any of these interactions can be a path to detention and deportation, overpolicing makes Black and Latina/o migrants more vulnerable to the vagaries of immigration law, with migrants being targeted for infractions as minor as open carrying alcohol or urinating in public. On two occasions, the DOJ sued sheriffs' offices, alleging that they used the 287(g) program to target Latinos. Patterns of overpolicing are especially stark for Black migrants: A recent report by a coalition of immigrants' rights organizations found that 76 percent of Black migrants are deported because of contact with the police and the criminal legal system.[36] They also face disproportionate abuse within detention, something that decades of archival documents can similarly confirm: Though Black migrants make up just 6 percent of all people in ICE custody, they constitute about 28 percent of all abuse-related reports and 24 percent of migrants in solitary confinement.[37] Federal-local collaboration has always been most politically popular when it means containing and expelling racialized groups—this continues to be true today.

———

Throughout the United States, local activism has been critical in directing public attention to the web of financial connections linking ICE to local governments. One early anti-ICE success story occurred in Santa Ana, California. Santa Ana signed a contract allowing ICE to use its local jail in 2006, under what is now an all-too-familiar story: The city had millions of dollars of debt; it built an oversized jail with $107.4 million in bonds in the 1990s; ICE promised to turn that jail into a place that could produce revenue for the town. It raised eyebrows that Santa Ana, a 78 percent Latina/o city, had partnered with the immigration service; this, too, reflected a growing trend of ICE pursuing agreements with municipalities with large Latina/o populations.[38] Five years later, in 2011, ICE announced plans to create a specialized unit of the Santa Ana jail to detain gay, bisexual, and transgender migrants—the first of its kind in the country.

Grassroots activism against the ICE presence in Santa Ana grew over several years, bringing together groups focused on immigrants' rights and queer liberation. In a 2015 LGBT Pride Month event at the White House, an undocumented transgender woman named Jennicet Gutiérrez interrupted a speech by President Obama to draw attention to the plight of trans people in the Santa Ana County Jail.[39] In 2016, a Santa Ana high school student, Deyaneira García, went on a hunger strike in a tent pitched outside the jail.[40] Attorneys joined the fight, as well, filing lawsuits about sexual assaults and unnecessary strip searches of detained women.[41] It was all the more significant that this activism was taking place in Orange County, California, the county that earned the single highest amount of revenue for jailing migrants for ICE. In 2018, the county brought in $36,707,946 from ICE agreements, about $15 million more than the second-highest earner: York County, Pennsylvania.[42]

In December 2017, after months of disruption and national media coverage, Santa Ana city commissioners announced plans to begin phasing ICE out of their jail. A few weeks later, ICE beat them to the punch, terminating the contract with the county. "Santa Ana is just one city, but we just showed that it is possible to get [ICE] out of our communities," said Hairo Cortes, an organizer with Orange County Immigrant Youth United.[43]

Santa Ana became one of the first dominoes to fall in California. By 2022, not a single California jail held migrants for ICE, with most localities ending their agreements in 2018 and 2019. It was a stunning turnaround in a place where many jails had worked with the immigration service for decades. California's last jail housing detained migrants, Yuba County, had signed a contract with ICE that extended until 2099. Local protests, coupled with COVID outbreaks, sealed the fate of the state's holdout. On October 27, 2021, ICE told Ricardo Vasquez Cruz to pack his bags. He was driven out of the sixty-year-old jail to an office where his family was waiting. "I cried, and they cried with joy," he said. Cruz was the final migrant detained by ICE in a California jail.[44]

A surge of state-level legislation has curtailed localities' collaboration with ICE. New Jersey, California, Washington, Nevada, and Illinois have all passed laws that limit or bar migrant incarceration.[45] In the summer of 2021, Governor Phil Murphy signed a bill that banned new or renewed agreements between ICE and public or private entities in New Jersey, the product of years of activism in and outside of jails. A man writing under the pseudonym "Lautaro" offered a first-person account of a hunger strike he organized inside the Hudson County Jail in Kearny, New Jersey, just months before the legislation was signed. "I come from a family that was marked by dictatorship. My grandfather was tortured, my uncle was murdered," Lautaro wrote. "[When] powerful people try to take advantage of the weak, you have to do something about it. You can't just stand there with your arms crossed. If we don't take care of ourselves, no one is going to take care of us." Migrants in Hudson County were allowed out of cells for only thirty minutes a day as COVID swept throughout the jail. More than sixty migrants engaged in a hunger strike, despite authorities' threats that their deportations would be expedited or that they would be sent to faraway jails if they protested. Lautaro said of his refusal to eat: "It's the only way that people will listen. It's a cry of desperation."[46] As of this book's publication, the U.S. District Court sided with private prison company CoreCivic in declaring the New Jersey law illegal, calling the detention statute "a dagger aimed at the heart of the federal government's immigration enforcement mission and operations."[47] The future of these laws remains to be seen.[48]

In both California and New Jersey, migrants whom ICE has removed from local jails have typically been transferred to other detention centers rather than released. ICE has argued that by reducing the agency's access to jails, activists are forcing migrants farther away from networks of support.[49] Even today, ICE is not required to notify family members of a loved one's transfer. Attorneys do receive notice, which does little to benefit the 70 percent of migrants in detention who do not have legal representation.[50] Still, the agency's narrative suggests that, prior to these changes, ICE strove to keep migrants in geographic locations that served their best interests—something that has never been true about the agency's incarceration practices. Other reformers have advocated that ICE use tools of "e-carceration," such as pretrial electronic ankle monitors and app-based geolocation tracking, to keep migrants out of jails. Though some liberal think tanks and advocacy groups have praised these alternatives, they bear many of the same problems as supervisory parole in the 1950s and 1960s: infringing on civil liberties, stigmatizing migrants, and turning homes and workplaces into prisons. These programs do not signal an emancipation from carceral control but, rather, a reinvention of it.[51]

Local officials have cited various rationales for terminating their contracts with ICE. Some have framed the decision in moral terms, a particularly potent claim during the 2018 peak of family separations. As images of children sobbing behind fences and sleeping beneath tinfoil-esque emergency blankets flooded the news, more and more citizens questioned local relationships with ICE. "It just felt inherently unjust for Sacramento to make money from dealing with ICE," said Phil Serna, a Sacramento County supervisor, who voted to end an IGSA that brought $6.6 million to the county. "For me, it came down to an administration that is extremely hostile to immigrants. I didn't feel we should be part of that."[52]

Other local leaders stressed logistics, suggesting that working with ICE had become more trouble than it was worth. New Jersey sheriffs announced that they would shift to holding people detained by the U.S. Marshals Service, who were not administratively detained and thus would not need to be segregated from the general jail population.[53] A commissioner in conservative Williamson County, Texas, called dealing with ICE "distracting" from the business of running the county, a distraction made worse when five hundred migrant women who had been separated from their children were moved to Williamson County's T. Don Hutto Residential Center. "The federal government made their bed with its policies, so let them sleep in it," the Texas commissioner grumbled. His comment invoked decades of local skepticism toward becoming the foot soldiers of laws and policies municipalities had no role in creating. Many localities determined that migrant incarceration was a desirable deal if it could be done quietly. It was a far worse deal if activists, media, and policymakers started asking questions.

Under the Biden administration, political intervention and sustained public attention have continued to require the most horrific of circumstances. In 2020, nurse Dawn Wooten filed a formal complaint about "jarring medical neglect" she had witnessed at Irwin County Detention Center (ICDC) in rural southeast Georgia.[54] The complaint noted systemic purging and fabricating of medical records, inadequate COVID policies, and most shockingly, a pattern of forced hysterectomies of Black migrant women. The Biden administration ended detention at ICDC the following year. A Senate investigation in 2022 confirmed that women at ICDC were subjected to "excessive, invasive, and often unnecessary gynecological procedures."[55] ICE had received complaints about medical abuse as early as 2018 and had done little to address them. Though ICDC was run by a private company and had a population of virtually all federal detainees, it had once been the local jail. ICE began acquiring beds through an IGSA with Irwin County in 2006, and a few years later, Irwin County brought in LaSalle Corrections to run the site. Once again, understanding detention meant looking beyond a binary of public or private and toward the entity that bridged both worlds: the local government.

———

The enduring idea that deportation and border control are federal powers has obscured the ways in which the detention and removal of migrants has always been a local project. Federal agents have worked closely with local officials to keep the gears of the deportation machine turning, both because of the potential for financial rewards and because many communities and their constituents saw unauthorized immigration as criminal and as a violation of local, as well as national, sovereignty. Examining the history of the local deportation landscape shows how the immigration service worked around its limited budget and resources for much of the twentieth century—it effectively deputized local officials as immigration agents, adjusting their exact responsibilities and authority as activists and lawsuits intervened. Understanding the deportation system as local also encourages us to rethink how illegality is constructed, not just through law but through the physical and symbolic spaces of punishment. It raises ongoing questions about how migrants confront a fractured, unstable state, where they can move between local and federal jurisdictions multiple times over the course of one removal proceeding. As local practices have deviated from federal norms, as local officials have been intermittently vested with and then stripped of immigration authority, and as the immigration service has relied on an ever-expanding number of jails, prisons, and private carceral facilities, the trajectory of detention has produced an immigration system where jurisdiction is perpetually up for grabs rather than a settled fact. This has created even greater vulnerability for migrants and has empowered the state with a fluid, wide-ranging network of control.

Detention and its reliance on local jails set devastating precedents for American democracy. On the local level, the transformation of jails into revenue-making institutions has meant that towns can evade the will of voters: If state and local governments access revenue bonds and alternative forms of financing, then municipalities no longer need voter approval to build or expand jails.[56] When localities enter into IGSAs, these agreements are rarely public, even though they function as a tool of public law. When asked in a 2014 deposition about whether ICE maintained a formal list of all its contracts and intergovernmental agreements, an ICE official responded, "I believe we do somewhere. It's not a formal list."[57] His ambivalent response spoke to a longstanding lack of public data and transparency in the immigration service's deals. To this day, ICE does not track the amount of money localities collect from private prison companies when they subcontract detention services.[58]

By creating a nesting doll of agreements, contracts, and subcontracts, ICE makes it nearly impossible for any observer to gain a comprehensive picture of the nation's detention practices. Decentralization, as well as the agency's actions in purging records and thwarting oversight, has led to a lack of historical memory about the reach and nature of detention in the past.[59] It has led even experts to think that the immigration service's reliance on jails is a new outgrowth of mass incarceration, rather than a highly malleable, century-long strategy for policing borders and engineering the nation's population. Lack of oversight is further exacerbated by an aggressive system of transfers, constantly moving migrants across localities and states. By creating an interstate "trade" in detained persons, contracting delocalizes detention, provides incentives to overbuild, and makes it more difficult for detained people to demand accountability.[60] Across the twentieth century and into the twenty-first, jail growth has been motivated by a dangerous mix of market opportunity, racism, and in the case of migrant detention, persistent nativism.[61]

Beyond bureaucracy and financing, detention destabilizes communities by creating a precarious subclass of the American public. This subclass is incentivized to distance itself from institutions—schools, hospitals, law enforcement—as any interaction with the state can become a means of exposure to immigration officials. By any reasonable metric, ICE has been a tremendous failure: It has terrorized communities, it has wasted billions of dollars, and it has not improved compliance with immigration laws.[62] Despite this, the agency has been given more money and more resources, another chapter in a long history of the immigration service's failures serving to further enshrine the agency's "necessity."

Migrant incarceration, and the criminalization of migration, has propelled mass incarceration and turned sheriffs into distinctly powerful actors. This book has argued that the federal government sought to build more prisons and jails not solely in response to longer criminal sentences and antidrug laws but because of immigration laws and the ability to profit from contracting bed space. As immigration policies made rising numbers of noncitizens subject to mandatory detention and made nearly any criminal offense grounds for deportation, jail space was transformed into a commodity. This increased the influence of sheriffs, who have campaigned on their successes in bringing revenue from federal prisoners to their counties. In some cases, incarceration of migrants has enabled jails to stay open when criminal justice reform efforts have undercut local demand. In other cases, federal prisons have closed, only to reopen months later as migrant detention centers.[63]

Even if today's protests do not immediately achieve freedom or abolition, they signal an evolving understanding of who controls immigration policy. The movement Abolish ICE has recognized the centrality of the local. In the winter of 2020, "Free Them All" was scrawled in spray paint outside the home of the Bergen County sheriff amid fights to end the New Jersey county's agreements with the immigration service. Hand-wringing about vandalism aside, actions like this reveal an understanding that the sheriff functions as an extension of ICE. These protests, which have occurred throughout the United States in the form of sit-ins, strikes, and civil disobedience, suggest that local officials' ability to hide behind the cloak of federalism is waning. Constituents are demanding accountability for deportation and detention decisions not just from immigration bureaucrats or from members of Congress but from the local officials who are making mass removals possible. The devolution of plenary power is becoming more and more visible. It is becoming harder to pass the buck.

———

What are the stakes of this history? Where does this leave us? In a 1988 panel discussion, a woman named Jane Ochoa discussed the experiences of her husband, Mario, a Mariel Cuban indefinitely detained at the United States Penitentiary, Atlanta.[64] The Ochoas were among the countless families whose lives had been ruptured by the deportation system. "The real question is, are we going to learn from this injustice, or will it happen again 40 years from now when there will be a new group of people detained in this country?" Ochoa asked an audience. "The real problem for me is not so much how history will judge it. History will condemn it. They will say it was partially the Cubans' fault, and partially the government's fault."[65] Assigning blame was only half the battle.

What mattered, Ochoa said, was how her husband would make sense of this history: How would he return to society after the ways he had suffered? How would she, an American citizen who believed that her nation would never incarcerate without due process, make sense of this history? What did it mean to be an imperfect victim of an unjust system—someone who had committed a crime that would have been a minor event for a citizen but a life-altering mistake for a noncitizen? She offered no answers to these questions, but she concluded with a declaration of ownership: that this story, in all its complexity, was theirs. "That is my history. I am not ashamed of that history."[66]

More than thirty-five years after Ochoa questioned whether anyone would learn from detentions of the past, migrant incarceration has expanded in ways that neither its 1900s pioneers nor its 1980s boosters could have anticipated. Every day, hundreds of adults and children make long journeys across deserts and oceans. Some flee violence, and others hope for work and opportunity, only to find themselves in the surreal horror of American jail cells. This, too, is our history, the history of the self-declared nation of immigrants. It belongs to all Americans and all of those who have traversed the nation's borders. The roots of migrant incarceration are deep, yet its persistence is a constant choice.

ARCHIVES AND MANUSCRIPT COLLECTIONS

Barry University Archives and Special Collections—Miami Shores, FL
   William Lehman Papers
C. L. Sonnichsen Special Collections Department, University of Texas–El Paso—El Paso, TX
   Chris P. Fox Papers
   El Paso County Records
   UTEP Institute of Oral History Transcripts
California Historical Society—San Francisco, CA
   American Civil Liberties Union of Northern California Records
Cuban Heritage Collection, University of Miami—Miami, FL
   Alberto Muller Papers
   Cuban Refugee Center Records
   Fort Chaffee Collection
   Mirta Ojito Papers
Florida International University Special Collections—Miami, FL
   La Vida Nueva Newspapers
Gerald Ford Presidential Library—Ann Arbor, MI
   James M. Cannon Papers
Harvard Law School Library, Historical and Special Collections—Cambridge, MA
   Felix Frankfurter Papers
Jimmy Carter Presidential Library—Atlanta, GA
   Louis Martin Papers
   Office of Staff Secretary Papers
Louisiana State University Special Collections—Baton Rouge, LA
   J. Bennett Johnston Papers
   John B. Breaux Papers
Museum of Chinese in America—New York, NY
   Port Henry Jail Ledgers
National Archives and Records Administration—Chicago, IL
   Chinese Exclusion Case Files (Record Group [RG] 85)
National Archives and Records Administration—College Park, MD
   Records of the Bureau of Prisons (RG 129)
   Records of the Cuban-Haitian Task Force (RG 220)
   Records of the Department of Justice (RG 60)
   Records of the United States Sentencing Commission (RG 539)

National Archives and Records Administration—New York, NY
Chinese Exclusion Case Files (RG 85)
National Archives and Records Administration—San Bruno, CA
Immigration and Deportation Case Files (1300), 1944–1955 (RG 85)
National Archives and Records Administration—Washington, D.C.
Records of the Immigration and Naturalization Service (RG 85)
New York Public Library, Schomburg Center for Research in Black Culture—New York, NY
Ira Gollobin Collection
Ira Gollobin Haitian Refugee Collection
Princeton University Library, Department of Rare Books and Special Collections—Princeton, NJ
American Civil Liberties Union Records
Ronald Reagan Presidential Library—Simi Valley, CA
James W. Cicconi Files
Kenneth T. Cribb Files
Martin Anderson Files
David M. Rubenstein Rare Book and Manuscript Library, Duke University—Durham, NC
Americans for Immigrant Justice Records
Caribbean Sea Migration Collection
National Coalition for Haitian Rights Records
Tamiment Library/Robert F. Wagner Labor Archives, New York University—New York, NY
American Committee for Protection of Foreign Born Records
Ira Gollobin Papers
University of California San Diego Special Collections and Archives—San Diego, CA
Herman Baca Papers
University of Chicago Special Collections Research Center—Chicago, IL
American Civil Liberties Union, Illinois Division, Records
University of Miami Special Collections and University Archives—Miami, FL
Dante Fascell Papers
Michael Carlebach Photography Collection
University of Michigan Library, Special Collections Research Center—Ann Arbor, MI
American Committee for Protection of Foreign Born Records
University of New Mexico Center for Southwest Research and Special Collections—Albuquerque, NM
Frank I. Sanchez Papers
United States Marshal (New Mexico) Records
U.S. Citizenship and Immigration Services History Office and Library—Camp Springs, MD
Vertical Files
William J. Clinton Presidential Library—Little Rock, AR
Domestic Policy Council Records
Wisconsin Historical Society—Madison, WI
Robert W. Kastenmeier Papers
York County Municipal Archives—York, PA
County Budgets
Online Repositories
Digital Library of the Caribbean
Gale U.S. Supreme Court Records and Briefs, 1832–1978
Proquest History Vault

APPENDIX

TABLE 2. Migrants Detained in Service and Nonservice
Immigration and Naturalization Service Facilities, 1962–1996

Year	Service	Nonservice	Total
1962	21,505	13,007	34,512
1963	17,119	16,571	33,690
1964	11,426	19,372	30,798
1965	17,041	26,918	43,959
1966	35,027	43,041	78,068
1967	37,621	56,427	94,048
1968	53,796	73,965	127,761
1969	59,771	89,477	149,248
1970	94,053	121,670	215,723
1971	111,627	145,562	257,189
1972	148,839	125,710	274,549
1973	171,559	120,985	292,544
1974	132,382	154,444	286,826
1975	109,138	103,888	213,026
1976	100,805	101,178	201,983
1977	—	—	294,699
1978	211,750	128,547	340,297
1979	204,079	112,312	316,391
1980	147,730	95,357	243,087
1981	170,005	98,576	268,581
1982	143,616	85,519	229,135
1983	149,072	84,813	223,885
1984	81,144	87,926	169,070
1985	68,691	77,298	145,989

(*continued*)

TABLE 2. (*continued*)

Year	Service	Nonservice	Total
1986	75,114	62,218	137,332
1987	48,336	34,325	82,660
1988	51,527	41,272	92,799
1989	74,925	60,075	104,639
1991	50,706	36,463	87,169
1992	46,589	35,757	82,346
1993	31,153	41,611	72,764
1994	31,510	42,969	74,479
1995*	31,510	45,919	77,429
1996*	40,787	69,750	110,537

* Projected.
Source: Data compiled from U.S. Department of Justice appropriations and Immigration and Naturalization Service annual reports.

TABLE 3. Average Daily Population in Immigration and Naturalization Service/
Immigration and Customs Enforcement Custody, 1947–2022

Year	Average Daily Population	Year	Average Daily Population
1947	2,946	1985	4,045
1948	2,306	1986	3,938
1949	2,105	1987	3,472
1950	1,840	1988	3,844
1951	2,000*	1989	6,438
1952	3,254	1991	6,571
1953	2,790	1992	5,928
1954	4,054	1993	4,642
1955	2,448	1994	6,785
1956	1,387	1995	7,475
1957	1,170	1996	9,011
1958	1,228	1997	11,871
1959	968	1998	15,447
1960	821	1999	17,772
1961	791	2000	19,458
1962	836	2001	20,429
1963	819	2002	20,282
1964	906	2003	21,133
1965	1,178	2004	22,812
1966	1,500	2005	19,718
1967	1,732	2006	22,975
1968	1,969	2007	30,295
1969	2,016	2008	31,662
1970	2,504	2009	32,098
1971	2,853	2010	30,885
1972	2,564	2011	33,330
1973	2,346	2012	34,260
1974	2,548	2013	33,788
1975	1,854	2014	33,227
1976	2,131	2015	28,449
1977	2,418	2016	34,376
1978	2,466	2017	38,106
1979	2,371	2018	42,188
1980	1,624	2019	49,403
1981	2,659	2020	33,724
1982	2,868	2021	19,461
1983	2,972	2022	22,630
1984	3,380		

* Projected.

Source: Data compiled from U.S. Department of Justice appropriations, U.S. Department of Homeland Security appropriations, and Immigration and Naturalization Service annual reports.

NOTES

Introduction

1. Prison Association of New York, *Annual Report of the Prison Association of New York* (Albany: J. B. Lyon Company Printers, 1926), 20.

2. Stuart Alfred Queen, *The Passing of the County Jail* (Menasha, Wisc.: George Banta Publishing Company, 1920), 1.

3. I use *migrant* as a flexible, inclusive term that encompasses people crossing national borders as short-term laborers, permanent residents, asylum seekers, refugees, and so forth. At the moment of crossing, as well as in the liminal space of detention, many people did not know whether their stay would be a permanent one, nor did they know how the U.S. state might legally classify them. *Migrant* gestures to the many unknowns of leaving and settling and to the considerable fluidity between state-imposed legal categories. While this book primarily uses the terms "detained migrants" or "migrants in detention," I occasionally use the terms "detainee" or "prisoner" for brevity. In particular, when speaking to the broad category of people incarcerated under the custody of the federal government, I use "federal prisoner" in lieu of "person incarcerated on federal charges."

I use the phrase *immigration service* to refer to the federal bureaucracy that managed entry and exclusion in the United States; the agency went by several different names from the late nineteenth to the early twenty-first century. In 1891, Congress created the Office of Superintendent of Immigration and placed it in the Treasury Department. Four years later the agency became the Bureau of Immigration, which would soon be transferred to the Department of Commerce and Labor. In 1924, the U.S. Border Patrol was created as a branch of the Bureau of Immigration. In 1933, the Bureau of Immigration and the Bureau of Naturalization merged into a single entity, the Immigration and Naturalization Service (INS). In 1940, the federal government moved the INS to the Department of Justice. In 2003, the INS became Immigration and Customs Enforcement, housed in the newly created Department of Homeland Security.

4. "Denies Lurid Tale of Britons in Jails," *New York Times*, Dec. 19, 1929; "Repeats We Hold Britons in Prison," *New York Times*, Dec. 23, 1929.

5. "Jails Again Filled with U.S. Prisoners," *Plattsburgh Sentinel*, Aug. 19, 1930.

6. On the political economy of jailing in Louisiana, see Lydia Pelot-Hobbs, *Prison Capital: Mass Incarceration and Struggles for Abolition Democracy in Louisiana* (Chapel Hill: University of North Carolina Press, 2023).

7. Bryn Stole, "In North Louisiana, Sheriff and Private Prison Operator Trade Prisoners for ICE Detainees," *New Orleans Times-Picayune*, Oct. 21, 2019.

8. In 2017, Louisiana Governor John Bel Edwards signed bipartisan legislation aimed at lowering the prison population by reducing sentences for people convicted of nonviolent offenses. The reforms were desperately needed. Louisiana imprisoned more people per capita than any other state or country in the world. Just before the new laws took effect, there were about 35,500 people under the Louisiana Department of Corrections' jurisdiction, held in prisons or local jails. By the summer of 2022, that number had fallen by nearly a quarter to about 27,000; the number of people in Louisiana prisons and jails for nonviolent offenses was effectively cut in half. See Michelle Russell, "5 Years In, 5 Things to Know about Louisiana's Justice System," Pew Charitable Trusts, Nov. 1, 2022.

This pattern of using migrant detainees to fill jail beds emptied by criminal justice reform efforts was not limited to Louisiana. For example, reductions in prison population following the implementation of New Jersey's 2017 bail reform laws were partly counteracted by renting beds to ICE. See Deirdre Conlon and Nancy Hiemstra, "'Unpleasant' but 'Helpful': Immigration Detention and Urban Entanglements in New Jersey, USA," Urban Studies 59, no. 11 (2022): 2179–98.

9. Noah Lanard, "Louisiana Decided to Curb Mass Incarceration. Then ICE Showed Up," Mother Jones, May 1, 2019.

10. Norman Merchant, "Louisiana Becomes New Hub in Immigrant Detention under Trump," Associated Press, Oct. 9, 2019.

11. These cases include Chy Lung v. Freeman, 92 U.S. 275 (1876); and Henderson v. Mayor of City of New York, 92 U.S. 259 (1875). Much of the scholarship on immigration federalism focuses on the relationship between states and the federal government; for example, in their book Citizenship Reimagined, Allan Colbern and S. Karthick Ramakrishnan emphasize that the Constitution and courts gave states leeway in granting citizenship rights that they did not give to local governments. By contrast, my work shows that in immigration law enforcement, and especially in migrant incarceration, the federal immigration service has spent far more time negotiating with city and county-level officials. One reason for this is relatively straightforward: Localities controlled the jails. While the immigration service could have used (and occasionally did use) state prisons, this created even more troubling optics and raised further questions about the lack of due process—jails, after all, already held many people who had not been convicted of crimes. However, there are other reasons localities may have been more sympathetic to the federal government. As legal scholar Spencer E. Amdur notes, localities have tighter budgets, more constrained authority, and fewer litigation resources to resist federal pressure—all of which make them less likely to challenge federal requests, even if they do have a constitutionally protected "right of refusal." Allan Colbern and S. Karthick Ramakrishnan, Citizenship Reimagined: A New Framework for State Rights in the United States (Cambridge: Cambridge University Press, 2021); Spencer E. Amdur, "The Right of Refusal: Immigration Enforcement and the New Cooperative Federalism," Yale Law and Policy Review 35, no. 1 (2016): 116.

12. César Cuauhtémoc García Hernández, "Creating Crimmigration," Brigham Young University Law Review 2013, no. 6 (2013): 1457–515; Juliet Stumpf, "The Crimmigration Crisis: Immigrants, Crime, and Sovereign Power," American University Law Review 56 (2006): 367–420.

13. Paulina D. Arnold, "How Immigration Detention Became Exceptional," Stanford Law Review 75, no. 2 (Feb. 2023): 282–87.

14. The Florida Supreme Court claimed in 1952 that a county jail and courthouse were "an absolute and indispensable county necessity," without which "a county government could not

exist." Today, jails are operated by 82 percent of the nation's 3,144 counties. Aaron Littman, "Jails, Sheriffs, and Carceral Policymaking," *Vanderbilt Law Review* 74, no. 1 (2021): 931.

15. *Wong Wing v. United States*, 163 U.S. 228 (1896); *Fong Yue Ting v. United States*, 149 U.S. 698 (1893). In 1893, the government ordered the deportation of Fong Yue Ting, a Chinese migrant who had refused to register for a certificate of residence as part of a larger civil disobedience campaign spearheaded by the Chinese Six Companies. The Geary Act, passed in 1892, mandated that all Chinese residents carry a resident permit at all times, with failure to do so punishable by deportation or a year of hard labor. "All Chinese in the district who do not possess a registration certificate will be arrested," a revenue collector in San Francisco said of the new law: "[As] fast as the Chinese are arrested they will be lodged in county jails, and when these are filled arrangements can easily be made for accommodating more of them on Angel Island, or any other place the Government may designate." The Supreme Court ultimately ruled that deportation, and by extension, detention, was not a punishment for a crime. *Fong Yue Ting* created one of the fundamental paradoxes of immigration detention—migrants held in American jails, with extremely limited rights and freedoms, were not technically criminals. See Kelly Lytle Hernández, *City of Inmates: Conquest, Rebellion, and the Rise of Human Caging in Los Angeles, 1771–1965* (Chapel Hill: University of North Carolina Press, 2017), 76–81.

16. Celeste Menchaca shows that some immigration stations along the southern border also featured "detention rooms," which were frequently insufficient for the number of apprehensions the Bureau of Immigration made—the site in El Paso, for example, was designed to hold only six migrants in 1906. Celeste R. Menchaca, "'The Freedom of Jail': Women, Detention, and the Expansion of Immigration Governance along the US–Mexico Border, 1903–1917," *Journal of American Ethnic History* 39, no. 4 (2020): 29. Elliott Young shows that early twentieth-century detention space was often in federal prisons, such as the McNeil Island Penitentiary, rather than in immigration stations, particularly for Chinese migrants who encountered criminalization for forged paperwork and unauthorized presence. Elliott Young, *Forever Prisoners: How the United States Made the World's Largest Immigrant Detention System* (New York: Oxford University Press, 2021), 23–54.

17. Political geographer Lauren L. Martin writes that detention does not commodify migrants' bodies as property but, instead, commodifies their routines and biological needs as services, thus making these economic relationships reconcilable with liberal democratic regimes and international human rights frameworks. Lauren L. Martin, "Carceral Economies of Migration Control," *Progress in Human Geography* 45, no. 4 (2021): 752. On detention as a process, see Alison Mountz, Kate Coddington, R. Tina Catania, and Jenna M. Loyd, "Conceptualizing Detention: Mobility, Containment, Bordering, and Exclusion," *Progress in Human Geography* 37, no. 4 (2013): 522–41.

18. Many legal scholars have suggested that local officials had no legal obligation to do the immigration service's bidding; the Tenth Amendment provides for the separation of federal and state powers, emphasizing that localities cannot be coerced or conscripted into enforcing federal laws. In practice, this has been a contentious claim that has continued to play out in recent battles over state efforts to protect residents from federal immigration enforcement. See *United States v. California*, No. 18-16496 (9th Cir. 2019). Still, throughout history, the immigration service has typically presented cooperation as an invitation rather than a command.

19. In detention's earliest years, it often served to financially enrich sheriffs, who received fees for each person held in the jail. By the 1910s, most counties had discontinued the fee system,

with surplus money from the jail going back into the county budget. As this book shows, sheriffs and local officials found creative ways to profit from migrant incarceration long after the fee system ended.

20. In re co-operation, received from officials of states, cities, municipalities, etc. in connection with the enforcement of the immigration laws, Oct. 8, 1923, File 549451/General-A, Subject Correspondence, Record Group (RG) 85, National Archives and Records Administration (NARA), Washington, D.C. (hereafter NARA1).

21. Juliet Stumpf argues that federal immigration law has evolved from "a stepchild of foreign policy into a national legislative and regulatory scheme that intersects with the triumvirate of state power: criminal law, employment law, and welfare." While Stumpf identifies this shift as beginning in the mid-1980s, I show that county and city officials were weighing these factors much earlier, particularly when considering what forms their collaboration with the immigration service would take. Juliet P. Stumpf, "States of Confusion: The Rise of State and Local Power over Immigration," *North Carolina Law Review* 86, no. 6 (2008): 1557–618.

22. Scholars have noted that even as the subfederal role in immigration law was restricted, states and localities still maintained considerable authority over "alienage law," laws pertaining to how migrants are treated once they enter the United States. Alienage laws could act as de facto admission and removal policies in states, as they affected migrants' access to welfare, education, employment, health services, free movement within the nation, and other rights and services to which citizens are entitled. State laws varied widely, creating what historian Brendan Shanahan has described as "disparate regimes of citizen-only rights encountered by immigrants on a state-by-state basis." Observers have also noted that alienage laws and immigration laws are deeply interconnected, both because noncitizens live under the perpetual shadow of deportation and removal and because anti-migrant alienage laws are often created to deter migration. See Jennifer M. Chacón, "Immigration Federalism in the Weeds," *UCLA Law Review* 66 (2019): 1330; Brendan A. Shanahan, "A 'Practically American' Canadian Woman Confronts a United States Citizen-Only Hiring Law: Katharine Short and the California Alien Teachers Controversy of 1915," *Law and History Review* 39, no. 4 (2021): 621–47; Linda Bosniak, *The Citizen and the Alien: Dilemmas of Contemporary Membership* (Princeton, N.J.: Princeton University Press, 2008); Sarah R. Coleman, *The Walls Within: The Politics of Immigration in Modern America* (Princeton, N.J.: Princeton University Press, 2021); Pratheepan Gulasekaram and S. Karthick Ramakrishnan, *The New Immigration Federalism* (Cambridge: Cambridge University Press, 2015); Cybelle Fox, *Three Worlds of Relief: Race, Immigration, and the American Welfare State from the Progressive Era to the New Deal* (Princeton, N.J.: Princeton University Press, 2012).

23. Historical scholarship that examines immigration law enforcement from the perspective of localities includes Adam Goodman, *The Deportation Machine: America's Long History of Expelling Immigrants* (Princeton, N.J.: Princeton University Press, 2020); Ethan Blue, *The Deportation Express: A History of America through Forced Removal* (Oakland: University of California Press, 2021); Hernández, *City of Inmates*; Emily Pope-Obeda, "'When in Doubt Deport!' U.S. Deportation and the Local Policing of Global Migration during the 1920s" (Ph.D. diss., University of Illinois at Urbana-Champaign, 2016). This topic has also received careful attention from sociologists. See Amada Armenta, *Protect, Serve, and Deport: The Rise of Policing as Immigration Enforcement* (Oakland: University of California Press, 2017); Felicia Arriaga, *Behind Crimmigration: ICE, Law Enforcement, and Resistance in America* (Chapel Hill: University of North Carolina Press, 2023).

NOTES TO INTRODUCTION   241

All of this work builds upon scholars who established the "federal story," an enormous undertaking in itself. See Mae M. Ngai, *Impossible Subjects: Illegal Aliens and the Making of Modern America* (Princeton, N.J.: Princeton University Press, 2004); Daniel J. Tichenor, *Dividing Lines: The Politics of Immigration Control in America* (Princeton, N.J.: Princeton University Press, 2002); Aristide R. Zolberg, *A Nation by Design: Immigration Policy in the Fashioning of America* (Cambridge, Mass.: Harvard University Press, 2006); Daniel Kanstroom, *Deportation Nation: Outsiders in American History* (Cambridge, Mass.: Harvard University Press, 2007).

24. There are countless examples of this in the history of migration control. Mae Ngai points to liberal efforts to reform deportation policy in the 1930s, which highlighted cases where deportation separated families or exacted other hardships. These reforms focused on the experiences of Europeans and Canadians, whose unauthorized presence was reimagined as a "technical irregularity" rather than a criminal infraction. See Mae M. Ngai, "The Strange Career of the Illegal Alien: Immigration Restriction and Deportation Policy in the United States, 1921–1965," *Law and History Review* 21, no. 1 (2003): 69–107.

25. Carl J. Bon Tempo, *Americans at the Gate: The United States and Refugees during the Cold War* (Princeton, N.J.: Princeton University Press, 2008); Jeffrey S. Kahn, *Islands of Sovereignty: Haitian Migration and the Borders of Empire* (Chicago: University of Chicago Press, 2019); Carl Lindskoog, *Detain and Punish: Haitian Refugees and the Rise of the World's Largest Immigration Detention System* (Gainesville: University Press of Florida, 2018).

26. Gulasekaram and Ramakrishnan, *New Immigration Federalism*.

27. Coleman, *Walls Within*, 5–6.

28. Harold T. Toal to James Giganti, Sept. 24, 1980, Box 19, Folder 4, Cuban Refugee Center Papers, Cuban Heritage Center, University of Miami (hereafter CRC).

29. "Police Pick Up Suspected Aliens," *The Dispatch* (Moline, Ill.), Sept. 6, 1975.

30. See historical work on detention in the late twentieth century by scholars including Kristina Shull, Perla Guerrero, Carl Lindskoog, Jeffrey Kahn, Alexander Stephens, Alison Mountz, Jenna Loyd, Jana K. Lipman, and Patrisia Macías-Rojas. Historians who examine migrant incarceration in the first half of the twentieth century include Ana Raquel Minian, Elliott Young, Kelly Lytle Hernández, Ethan Blue, Celeste Menchaca, and Emily Pope-Obeda. Work by Jessica Ordaz, Judith Dingatantrige Perera, and Jennifer Cullison illuminates the mid-century history of migrant incarceration, particularly in the Southwest.

31. Lucy E. Salyer, *Laws Harsh as Tigers: Chinese Immigrants and the Shaping of Modern Immigration Law* (Chapel Hill: University of North Carolina Press, 1995).

32. Melanie D. Newport, "Jail America: The Reformist Origins of the Carceral State" (Ph.D. diss., Temple University, 2016), xvi; Ram Subramanian, Christian Henrichson, and Jacob Kang-Brown, *In Our Own Backyard: Confronting Growth and Disparities in American Jails* (New York: Vera Institute of Justice, 2015), 4.

33. Wendy Sawyer and Peter Wagner, "Mass Incarceration: The Whole Pie 2023," Prison Policy Institute, March 14, 2023, https://www.prisonpolicy.org/reports/pie2023.html. There is certainly overlap in these numbers, as many people move from jails into state and federal prisons. However, they still indicate that far more people will interact with a jail, rather than a prison, in their lifetimes.

34. On the variety in jail system scale, see Littman, "Jails, Sheriffs, and Carceral Policymaking," 870–71.

35. Melanie Newport, *This Is My Jail: Local Politics and the Rise of Mass Incarceration* (Philadelphia: University of Pennsylvania Press, 2022).

36. Littman, "Jails, Sheriffs, and Carceral Policymaking," 869.

37. Historian Kelly Lytle Hernández calls migrant detention a process of "mass elimination," which builds on legacies of slavery, colonialism, and segregation. A recent edited volume has taken up the interconnection of racial oppression in what it describes as the "overlapping carceral regimes" of immigration detention and criminal incarceration—this is particularly well articulated in the contribution of David Manuel Hernández. Robert T. Chase, ed., *Caging Borders and Carceral States: Incarcerations, Immigration Detentions, and Resistance* (Chapel Hill: University of North Carolina Press, 2019). Other scholars have interrogated the links between plenary power's usage in Indian law and its usage in immigration law, emphasizing how settler-colonialism undergirds migration policy: Julian Lim, "Immigration, Plenary Powers, and Sovereignty Talk: Then and Now," *Journal of the Gilded Age and Progressive Era* 19, no. 2 (2020): 217–29.

38. A. Naomi Paik, *Bans, Walls, Raids, Sanctuary: Understanding U.S. Immigration for the Twenty-first Century* (Oakland: University of California Press, 2020), 79.

39. Joseph Pugliese describes the process of writing "constitutively incomplete scholarship," which he describes as "an incompleteness determined by the power of the state to impose fundamental omissions of information through the redaction of key documents, through the legal silencing of its agents and through the literal obliteration of evidence." Joseph Pugliese, *State Violence and the Execution of Law: Biopolitical Caesurae of Torture, Black Sites, Drones* (New York: Routledge, 2013), 27. I find this a useful way of thinking about detention scholarship, particularly in the era of ICE. On the archival challenges of immigration detention, see also Mary Rizzo, "Reading against the Grain, Finding the Voices of the Detained," *Museums and Social Issues* 12, no. 1 (2017): 26–32.

40. A. Naomi Paik has written extensively on how to interpret affidavits and other sources of testimony in such collections, suggesting that we should see the legal archive as both storytelling and truth-telling. See A. Naomi Paik, *Rightlessness: Testimony and Redress in U.S. Prison Camps since World War II* (Chapel Hill: University of North Carolina Press, 2016); A. Naomi Paik, "Testifying to Rightlessness: Haitian Refugees Speaking from Guantánamo," *Social Text* 28, no. 3 (104): 39–65.

41. *Sa K'pase*, Edition 44, March 1, 1992, Box 2, Caribbean Migration Collection, David M. Rubenstein Rare Book and Manuscript Library, Duke University. The U.S. government responded to this letter, writing: "God has blessed our country. His favors have helped us through the good times and the bad times. History has made us a superpower. As such we can do good or we can do evil. We try to do good but we have limits. We cannot receive every person in the world that would prefer to live in Miami rather than his own country."

42. Letter from Mario Medina Mora, St. Martinville Parish Jail, Box 13, Folder "County Jails—Florida PENDING," Americans for Immigrant Justice Records, David M. Rubenstein Rare Book and Manuscript Library, Duke University (hereafter AIJ).

43. Letter from Manatee County Jail, 1998, Box 14, Folder "County Jail Supplement 2 of 3," AIJ.

44. Emma Kaufman, "Segregation by Citizenship," *Harvard Law Review* 132, no. 5 (2019): 1383.

45. Justin Driver and Emma Kaufman, "The Incoherence of Prison Law," *Harvard Law Review* 135, no. 2 (2021): 536; *Turner v. Safley*, 482 U.S. 78 (1987). There has been considerable debate about whether pretrial custodial institutions can have "penological interests." In 2015, a case

challenging an immigration detention center's decision to put hunger striking women in solitary confinement invoked the *Turner* standard in arguing that their isolation served the "legitimate penological interest" of repressing potential insurrections. Alina Das, "Immigration Detention and Dissent: The Role of the First Amendment on the Road to Abolition," *Georgia Law Review* 56, no. 4 (2022): 1468–69.

46. *Chae Chan Ping v. United States*, 130 U.S. 581 (1889).

47. Hiroshi Motomura, "Immigration Law after a Century of Plenary Power: Phantom Constitutional Norms and Statutory Interpretation," *Yale Law Journal* 100, no. 3 (1990): 547.

48. Peter H. Schuck, "Taking Immigration Federalism Seriously," *University of Chicago Legal Forum* 7, no. 3 (2009): 57–58.

49. See Mary Sarah Bilder, "The Struggle over Immigration: Indentured Servants, Slaves, and Articles of Commerce," *Missouri Law Review* 61, no. 4 (1996): 743–824; Gerald L. Neuman, *Strangers to the Constitution: Immigrants, Borders, and Fundamental Law* (Princeton, N.J.: Princeton University Press, 1996); Hidetaka Hirota, *Expelling the Poor: Atlantic Seaboard States and the Nineteenth-Century Origins of American Immigration Policy* (New York: Oxford University Press, 2017). Hirota shows how Irish migrants were overrepresented in civil confinement facilities, including almshouses, workhouses, and state hospitals, throughout Massachusetts and New York. In her groundbreaking article, legal scholar Paulina D. Arnold suggests that we should see these forms of civil confinement as part of a nascent migrant detention system that linked immigration and poverty-based confinement and built on long-standing precedents of confinement without full criminal process. Arnold notes that the late nineteenth-century Supreme Court cases that invalidated passenger taxes, and thus laid the foundation for the federalization of immigration, were particularly potent because they destroyed states' ability to use migrants to fund these "charitable" confinement institutions. Arnold, "How Immigration Detention Became Exceptional."

50. On the recent historical scholarship on federalism, see Sara Mayeux and Karen Tani, "Federalism Anew," *American Journal of Legal History* 56, no. 1 (2016): 128–38; Brent Cebul, Karen Tani, and Mason B. Williams, "Clio and the Compound Republic," *Publius: The Journal of Federalism* 47, no. 2 (2017): 235–59.

51. This remains true today. While local "sanctuary" policies are often seen as rooted in human rights claims or a desire to protect migrants from federal overreach, the primary rationale cited by localities for noncooperation is that immigrant communities may not work with law enforcement if it risks exposing them to ICE. Amdur, "Right of Refusal"; David A. Harris, "The War on Terror, Local Police, and Immigration Enforcement: A Curious Tale of Police Power in Post-9/11 America," *Rutgers Law Journal* 38, no. 1 (2006): 1–60.

52. Miriam Wells notes that much of this contracting is done through the immigration service's regional and district administrators, as the INS is an "exceptionally" decentralized federal agency that has granted significant autonomy to lower-level bureaucrats. Miriam J. Wells, "The Grassroots Reconfiguration of U.S. Immigration Policy," *International Migration Review* 38, no. 4 (2004): 1326. My work builds on a rich body of scholarship about the history of the immigration agency and its functioning. See Kitty Calavita, *Inside the State: The Bracero Program, Immigration, and the I.N.S.* (New York: Routledge, 1992); S. Deborah Kang, *The INS on the Line: Making Immigration Law on the US-Mexico Border, 1917–1954* (New York: Oxford University Press, 2017); Kelly Lytle Hernández, *Migra! A History of the U.S. Border Patrol* (Berkeley: University of California Press, 2010).

53. Sawyer and Wagner, "Mass Incarceration."

54. Emily Ryo and Ian Peacock, "Jailing Immigrant Detainees: A National Study of County Participation in Immigration Detention, 1983–2013," *Law and Society Review* 54, no. 1 (2020): 67.

55. "Northern Jails Crowded May Boost U.S. Prisoners' Board," *Chateaugay Record*, Oct. 2, 1925.

1. Policing and Profits in New York's Chinese Jails

1. Frederick J. Seaver, *Historical Sketches of Franklin County and its Several Towns* (Albany: J. B. Lyon Co. Printers, 1918), 1.

2. Stuart Pratt Sherman, *The Main Stream* (New York: Charles Scribner's Sons, 1927), 96.

3. Poultney Bigelow, "The Chinaman at Our Gates," *Collier's*, Sept. 12, 1903.

4. Prison Association of New York, *Annual Report of the Prison Association of New York for the Year 1902* (Albany: Argus Co. Printers, 1903), 69.

5. Quoted in Erika Lee, *America for Americans: A History of Xenophobia in the United States* (New York: Basic Books, 2019), 75. The imagined threat was multifaceted: Anti-Chinese politicians accused migrants of bringing foreign diseases, of undercutting Americans' wages, and of disrupting the gender order—either by the assumption that they participated in sex work, in the case of Chinese women, or by pursuing and corrupting innocent white women, in the case of Chinese men.

6. Llana Barber notes that state-level policies banned Black migrants in the antebellum era, decades prior to the Chinese exclusion law. See Llana Barber, "Anti-Black Racism and the Nativist State," *Journal of American Ethnic History* 42, no. 4 (2023): 16–20.

7. Beth Lew-Williams, *The Chinese Must Go: Violence, Exclusion, and the Making of the Alien in America* (Cambridge, Mass.: Harvard University Press, 2018).

8. "For Sheriff: Earnest A. Douglass," *The Sun* (Fort Covington, N.Y.), Aug. 3, 1899.

9. Despite their distinct legal status as administratively detained migrants, both media and federal officials generally lumped people in immigration proceedings into the category of "federal prisoner" in the first half of the twentieth century. "Federal prisoners" included both pretrial defendants held for federal offenses and people convicted of federal crimes. The term "federal prisoners" was used interchangeably with "United States prisoners," a term that indicated federal custody rather than the citizenship of the accused person.

10. Neighboring Clinton County also cited $20,000 as the expected income of the sheriff, noting that "[if] the Chinese business holds good for the coming three years the next sheriff of Clinton County can rest comfortably on the sunny side of easy street for the remainder of his days." *Malone Farmer*, Aug. 28, 1901.

11. *United States v. Wong Kim Ark*, 169 U.S. 649 (1898).

12. Bigelow, "Chinaman at Our Gates."

13. On the centrality of local power in generating and carrying out immigration law in the nineteenth century, see Hidetaka Hirota, "The Moment of Transition: State Officials, the Federal Government, and the Formation of American Immigration Policy," *Journal of American History* 99, no. 4 (2013): 1092–108; Neuman, *Strangers to the Constitution*.

14. On the state's production of "legibility," see James C. Scott, *Seeing like a State: How Certain Schemes to Improve the Human Condition Have Failed* (New Haven, Conn.: Yale University Press, 1998).

15. The use of "commodity" to describe human beings is most commonly encountered in the historiography on Atlantic slavery. Migrants' experiences in jails paled in comparison to the violence experienced by enslaved people: Migrants were generally not forced to labor; they were not vested with a permanent, heritable status of subordination; and their personhood was not erased in law, or in society, to nearly the same extent. Stephanie Smallwood writes about commoditization as a "representational act," most visible in discursive forms such as ledgers and bills of sale. Her work links the violence of slavery with an experience of dehumanization, characterizing commoditization as "probing the limits up to which it is possible to discipline the body without extinguishing the life inside." Nicholas Rinehart has challenged this interpretation, suggesting that "people as commodities" has become an "unproductive cliché" that obscures the lived experience of enslavement—one in which being human was central to the forms of suffering and exploitation enslaved people endured. Rinehart suggests a view of commoditization based on Igor Kopytoff's concept of "commodity-as-process," which I find useful. Rather than a more static understanding of "person as commodity," he suggests seeing the individual as "a social figure that moves through various phases of expulsion, marginality, and incorporation." I borrow his phrase "potential commodity" here, and I note that migrants were only seen as fulfilling this "potential commodity" role at certain, specific points in migrant detention's history. Stephanie E. Smallwood, *Saltwater Slavery: A Middle Passage from Africa to American Diaspora* (Cambridge, Mass.: Harvard University Press, 2007); Nicholas T. Rinehart, "The Man That Was a Thing: Reconsidering Human Commodification in Slavery," *Journal of Social History* 50, no. 1 (2016): 28–50; Igor Kopytoff, "The Cultural Biography of Things: Commoditization as Process," in *The Social Life of Things: Commodities in Cultural Perspective*, ed. Arun Appadurai (Cambridge: Cambridge University Press, 1986), 64–94. I thank Max Mishler for bringing this point to my attention.

16. On the multiple strategies of resistance employed by Chinese migrants, see Estelle T. Lau, *Paper Families: Identity, Immigration Administration, and Chinese Exclusion* (Durham, N.C.: Duke University Press, 2006).

17. Aaron Korthuis, "Detention and Deterrence: Insights from the Early Years of Immigration Detention at the Border," *Yale Law Journal* 129 (2019): 238–57. There were certainly exceptions, most notably the case of Lee Puey You, who was detained on Angel Island for twenty months as her case underwent a series of legal appeals. Judy Yung, "'A Bowlful of Tears' Revisited: The Full Story of Lee Puey You's Immigration Experience at Angel Island," *Frontiers: A Journal of Women Studies* 25, no. 1 (2004): 1–22.

18. *Annual Report of the Commissioner General of Immigration for the Fiscal Year Ending June 30, 1904* (Washington, D.C.: Government Printing Office, 1904), 102.

19. "Wants Detention Station Built," *SF Chronicle*, Nov. 18, 1902.

20. There was some precedent for the immigration service using county jails. In 1891, four Japanese women were detained by immigration authorities in the Alameda County Jail, located across the bay from San Francisco. The Japanese consul protested the women's incarceration, arguing that being held in a jail did not constitute being "properly housed" under the 1891 immigration law. "[It] is not claimed nor does it appear that the women have been guilty of any offense that would warrant their confinement in jail," wrote the consul to a U.S. Circuit Court judge. "Japan's Protest," *SF Chronicle*, June 21, 1891.

21. Ledger from Port Henry Chinese Jail, Vols. 1 and 2, July 1901–Dec. 1903, Moriah Historical Society, Port Henry, N.Y., digitized by the Museum of Chinese in America, 2018.017; Robert

Barde and Gustavo J. Bobonis, "Detention at Angel Island: First Empirical Evidence," *Social Science History* 30, no. 1 (2006): 103–36. Judy Yung and Erika Lee also note occasional longer stays at Angel Island, notably that of Quok Shee, the wife of a Chinese merchant, who was detained nearly two years. Judy Yung and Erika Lee, *Angel Island: Immigrant Gateway to America* (New York: Oxford University Press, 2010), 70.

22. *Annual Report of the Commissioner General of Immigration for the Fiscal Year Ending June 30, 1903* (Washington, D.C.: Government Printing Office, 1903), 76.

23. Adam McKeown, *Melancholy Order: Asian Migration and the Globalization of Borders* (New York: Columbia University Press, 2008), 269.

24. *Fong Yue Ting v. United States*, 149 U.S. 698.

25. On Chinese migration through Canada, see Erika Lee, *At America's Gates: Chinese Immigration during the Exclusion Era, 1882–1943* (Chapel Hill: University of North Carolina Press, 2004); Elliott Young, *Alien Nation: Chinese Migration in the Americas from the Coolie Era through World War II* (Chapel Hill: University of North Carolina Press, 2014); McKeown, *Melancholy Order*; Kornel S. Chang, *Pacific Connections: The Making of the U.S.-Canadian Borderlands* (Berkeley: University of California Press, 2012).

26. Young, *Alien Nation*, 170.

27. There is a growing field of scholarship examining the intersections of settler-colonialism, Native dispossession, and immigration. See Evan Taparata, "No Asylum for Mankind: The Creation of Refugee Law and Policy in the United States, 1776–1951" (Ph.D. diss., University of Minnesota, 2018); Carl D. Lindskoog, "Migration, Racial Empire, and the Carceral Settler State," *Journal of American History* 109, no. 2 (2022): 388–98; Roxanne Dunbar-Ortiz, *Not "a Nation of Immigrants": Settler Colonialism, White Supremacy, and a History of Erasure and Exclusion* (New York: Beacon Press, 2021).

28. Audra Simpson, *Mohawk Interruptus: Political Life across the Borders of Settler States* (Durham, N.C.: Duke University Press, 2014), 136.

29. "Dispatch from *New York Journal*," *Chateaugay Record*, Nov. 30, 1900.

30. *Annual Report of the Commissioner General of Immigration for the Fiscal Year Ending June 30, 1903*, 97.

31. William H. Siener, "Through the Back Door: Evading the Chinese Exclusion Act along the Niagara Frontier, 1900 to 1924," *Journal of American Ethnic History* 27, no. 4 (2008): 53.

32. Lee, *At America's Gates*, 153.

33. *Annual Report of the Commissioner General of Immigration for the Fiscal Year Ending June 30, 1903*, 94.

34. "Porter Discharged," *Malone Farmer*, Jan. 24, 1900.

35. Martin L. Friedland, *The Death of Old Man Rice: A True Story of Criminal Justice in America* (New York: New York University Press, 1996), 105.

36. *Annual Report of the Commissioner General of Immigration for the Fiscal Year Ending June 30, 1903*, 96.

37. Lee, *At America's Gates*, 156.

38. *Annual Report of the Commissioner General of Immigration for the Fiscal Year Ending June 30, 1904*, 164. The Bureau of Immigration deported a total of 704 Chinese migrants, including 307 from the eastern region of the northern boundary. The deportations cost the bureau a total of $80,375.45, with about $65,000 going toward the deportation of people from

communities along the U.S.-Canada border. Deporting migrants from New York and the U.S.-Canada borderlands represented about 25 percent of the entire operating budget for Chinese exclusion. Torrie Hester, *Deportation: The Origins of U.S. Policy* (Philadelphia: University of Pennsylvania Press, 2017), 22.

39. Habeas corpus, sometimes referred to as "The Great Writ," tests the grounds for constraint and detention. Latin for "that you have the body," habeas corpus requires detained persons to be brought before a court to assess the validity of their custody. It has a deep history in Anglo-American jurisprudence, with the Supreme Court declaring it "the fundamental instrument for safeguarding individual freedom against arbitrary and lawless state action." *Harris v. Nelson*, 394 U.S. 286, 290–91 (1969). See Salyer, *Laws Harsh as Tigers*; Christian G. Fritz, "A Nineteenth Century 'Habeas Corpus Mill': The Chinese before the Federal Courts in California," *American Journal of Legal History* 32, no. 4 (1988): 347–72; Gerald L. Neuman, "Habeas Corpus, Executive Detention, and the Removal of Aliens," *Columbia Law Review* 98, no. 4 (1998): 961–1067.

40. John L. Lott to Attorney General, Sept. 28, 1903, *Series A: Subject Correspondence Files, Part I* (National Archives Microfilm Publication, Roll 18, Image 2), RG 85, NARA1.

41. U.S. House of Representatives, Committee on Foreign Affairs, *Compilation from the records of the Bureau of Immigration of facts concerning the enforcement of the Chinese-exclusion laws* (Washington, D.C.: Government Printing Office, 1906), 100.

42. John L. Lott to Attorney General, Sept. 28, 1903.

43. Rebecca M. McLennan, *The Crisis of Imprisonment: Protest, Politics, and the Making of the American Penal State, 1776–1941* (Cambridge: Cambridge University Press, 2008), 202–3.

44. "Most of the County Jails of the Empire State are Sadly Behind the Age from Several Points of View," *New-York Tribune*, June 28, 1903; National Prison Association of the United States Congress, *Proceedings of the Annual Congress of the National Prison Association of the United States* (Chicago: Knight & Leonard, 1889), 244.

45. State of New York Commission of Prisons, *Sixth Annual Report of the State Commission of Prisons* (Albany: State of New York Commission of Prisons, 1900), 147.

46. Hastings H. Hart, *United States Prisoners in County Jails: Report of the Committee of the American Prison Association on Lockups, Municipal and County Jails* (New York: Russell Sage Foundation, 1926), 8.

47. State of New York Commission of Prisons, *Sixth Annual Report of the State Commission of Prisons*, 146.

48. State of New York Commission of Prisons, *Sixth Annual Report of the State Commission of Prisons*, 151.

49. "Detention Shed is Up to City," *Tacoma Daily Ledger*, Nov. 23, 1910.

50. Young, *Forever Prisoners*, 23–29.

51. Ethan Blue shows how these institutions, many of which blurred the lines between carceral and charitable, worked together throughout the early years of detention and how migrants, especially women, moved between them. See Blue, *Deportation Express*, 84–86.

52. "The Influx of Chinese," *Malone Palladium*, Nov. 22, 1900.

53. The longest detentions recorded in the Essex County ledger books are for Hoo Fing and Lee Cheung Gin, both of whom spent 563 days in detention.

54. "The Chinese Must Go—to Plattsburgh," *Chateaugay Record*, Sept. 28, 1900.

55. "Herding Chinese Malone's Monopoly," *Chateaugay Record*, Nov. 23, 1900.

56. In a dispatch from Malone, a journalist for the *New York Journal* observed, "[That] the Chinese Exclusion law is being violated by shrewd men bent on making money cannot be doubted." "Dispatch from *New York Journal*."

57. "Alleged Illegal Entry into the United States of Chinese Persons," Senate Document No. 167, 55th Cong., 1st sess., 1897.

58. "Trouble over Chinamen," *Ogdensburg Advance and St. Lawrence Weekly Democrat*, Sept. 27, 1900; "Chinese Must Go—to Plattsburgh."

59. *Ogdensburg Journal*, July 15, 1901.

60. "Dispatch from *New York Journal*." The $50,000 amount is noted in "How the Chinese Boldly Evade the Exclusion Act," *New York Herald*, Dec. 9, 1900.

61. "Chinese Matters," *Malone Palladium*, Dec. 13, 1900.

62. "Commissioner Paddock's Statement of the Chinese Situation," *Malone Palladium*, Dec. 13, 1900.

63. *Plattsburgh Sentinel*, May 24, 1901.

64. "To Restrict Immigration Through Canadian Ports," *Brooklyn Daily Eagle*, April 13, 1901.

65. State of New York Commission of Prisons, *Seventh Annual Report of the State Commission of Prisons* (Albany: State of New York Commission of Prisons, 1901), 66–67.

66. "Of Local Interest," *Malone Farmer*, May 8, 1901.

67. I have not found any evidence of Chinese women or girls detained in Northern New York during this period.

68. David L. Eng, *Racial Castration: Managing Masculinity in Asian America* (Durham, N.C.: Duke University Press, 2001); Sang Hea Kil, "Fearing Yellow, Imagining White: Media Analysis of the Chinese Exclusion Act of 1882," *Social Identities* 18, no. 6 (2012): 663–77. The term "coolie" was a racialized term for workers, typically Asians, coerced into migration and unfree labor. Moon-Ho Jung writes that coolies "were never a people or a legal category. Rather, coolies were a conglomeration of racial imaginings that emerged worldwide in the era of slave emancipation, a product of the imaginers, rather than the imagined." Moon-Ho Jung, *Coolies and Cane: Race, Labor, and Sugar in the Age of Emancipation* (Baltimore, Md.: Johns Hopkins University Press, 2006), 5.

69. "Invasion of Chinese," *Ogdensburg Journal*, March 5, 1901.

70. "Of Local Interest," *Elizabethtown Post*, April 4, 1901.

71. "Uncle Sam's Chinese Inn," *Boston Globe*, April 24, 1904.

72. "Orientals' Jail Life," *St. Lawrence Republican and Ogdensburg Weekly Journal*, Oct. 9, 1901.

73. "How the Chinese Boldly Evade the Exclusion Act."

74. "The Chinese Situation," *Malone Farmer*, Dec. 5, 1900.

75. Lew-Williams, *Chinese Must Go*, 25.

76. The Rev. S. L. Baldwin, "Chinese and Other Exclusion," *Western Christian Advocate* 68, no. 3 (1902): 10.

77. The Chinese business was "giving [Malone] as unsavory a reputation abroad as any border Texas and Mexican greaser town ever had," a newspaper opined in 1900. "Chinese Smugglers Busy," *Malone Palladium*, March 1, 1900.

78. In the nineteenth century, Northern New York had a number of Black families, many of whom had arrived via philanthropist Gerrit Smith's land grants to poor Black men in the 1850s.

The region developed a reputation for abolitionist activity, highlighted by the actions of John Brown, who lived in Timbuctoo, N.Y., a farming community of African American homesteaders. Sally E. Svenson, *Blacks in the Adirondacks: A History* (Syracuse, N.Y.: Syracuse University Press, 2017), 19–29. By the twentieth century few Black families remained. In the 1920s, the region would see a powerful resurgence of the Ku Klux Klan. Historian Edward Berenson has also noted the history of anti-Semitism in Northern New York, which became the center of blood libel accusations against the Jewish community of St. Lawrence County in the 1920s. Edward Berenson, *The Accusation: Blood Libel in an American Town* (New York: W. W. Norton and Company, 2019).

79. When an inspector toured Essex County's Chinese jail in 1901, he reported that "such herding together of any Chinaman in any of the prisons is contrary to decency. It is simply a question of money consideration for the keeper." State of New York Commission of Prisons, *Seventh Annual Report of the State Commission of Prisons*, 155.

80. State of New York Commission of Prisons, *Seventh Annual Report of the State Commission of Prisons*, 155.

81. See Evelyn Ruggles-Brise, "An English View of the American Penal System," *Journal of the American Institute of Criminal Law and Criminology* 2, no. 3 (1911): 366.

82. "Want Chinese with Them," *Commercial Advertiser*, Jan. 8, 1902.

83. Bigelow, "Chinaman at Our Gates."

84. Rick Ruddell and Ken Leyton-Brown, "All in the Family: The Role of the Sheriff's Wife in 20th-Century Mom and Pop Jails," *Women and Criminal Justice* 23, no. 4 (2013): 269.

85. See Raymond Moley, "The Sheriff and the Constable," *ANNALS of the American Academy of Political and Social Science* 146, no. 1 (1929): 28–33.

86. On the move away from the fee system, see Michael Willrich, *City of Courts: Socializing Justice in Progressive Era Chicago* (Cambridge: Cambridge University Press, 2003); Nicholas R. Parrillo, *Against the Profit Motive: The Salary Revolution in American Government, 1780–1940* (New Haven, Conn.: Yale University Press, 2013).

87. Critics at the time noted that sheriffs were particularly inclined to fining and arresting tourists and noncitizens to maximize fees, while reducing alienation of potential voters. See Moley, "Sheriff and the Constable"; Frances A. Kellor, "Justice for the Immigrant," *ANNALS of the American Academy of Political and Social Science* 52, no. 1 (1914): 159–68.

88. Philip Klein, *Prison Methods in New York State* (New York: Columbia University Press, 1920), 164–65.

89. *Commercial Advertiser*, Feb. 5, 1902. Clinton County followed suit, making sheriff a salaried position at the end of 1902. *Chateaugay Journal*, Dec. 18, 1902.

90. "Annual Meeting," *Elizabethtown Post and Gazette*, Jan. 12, 1905.

91. Erika Lee, "Enforcing the Borders: Chinese Exclusion along the U.S. Borders with Canada and Mexico, 1882–1924," *Journal of American History* 89, no. 1 (2002): 77.

92. *Annual Report of the Commissioner General of Immigration for the Fiscal Year Ending June 30, 1903*, 101.

93. Adam McKeown, *Chinese Migrant Networks and Cultural Change: Peru, Chicago, and Hawaii 1900–1936* (Chicago: University of Chicago Press, 2001), 28.

94. Ledger from Port Henry Chinese Jail, Vols. 1 and 2, July 1901–Dec. 1903.

95. *United States v. Sing Tuck*, Petition for Writ of Certiorari to the Circuit Court of Appeals for the Second Circuit, 1903.

96. *United States v. Sing Tuck*, 194 U.S. 161 (1904).

97. "Saint Paul and Sing Tuck," *The Nation* 79, no. 2045 (1904): 191.

98. On one of Moore's notable criminal trials, see Friedland, *Death of Old Man Rice*. When Moore died in 1921, his representation of Chinese clients was barely referenced in the extensive media coverage of his passing.

99. *United States v. Sing Tuck*, Petition for Writ of Certiorari, 6.

100. *United States v. Sing Tuck*, Petition for Writ of Certiorari, 4–5.

101. "The Yellow Peril Here," *Malone Palladium*, March 3, 1904.

102. "Smuggling in Chinese," *New-York Tribune*, Nov. 22, 1903.

103. *United States v. Sing Tuck*, Petition for Writ of Certiorari, 7; *United States v. Sing Tuck*, Motion to Advance, No. 591.

104. Gabriel J. Chin, "Regulating Race: Asian Exclusion and the Administrative State," *Harvard Civil Rights–Civil Liberties Law Review* 37 (2002): 41.

105. *United States v. Sing Tuck*, 194 U.S. 161, 165.

106. *United States v. Sing Tuck*, 194 U.S. 161, 178.

107. *United States v. Sing Tuck*, 194 U.S. 161, 162.

108. *United States v. Sing Tuck*, 194 U.S. 161, 169. There was extensive legal precedent for civil detention of citizens, in institutions including workhouses, mental asylums, and almshouses, which Paulina D. Arnold suggests were seen as "appropriate exercises of benevolent state power," even as they granted people little to no due process. In the case of *Wong Wing v. United States*, the Supreme Court compared immigration detention with pretrial detention, calling time in jail a "usual feature of every case of arrest . . . even when an innocent person is wrongfully accused." Arnold, "How Immigration Detention Became Exceptional," 273, 290.

109. Owen M. Fiss, *Troubled Beginnings of the Modern State, 1888–1910*, History of the Supreme Court of the United States, vol. 8 (New York: Macmillan, 1993), 318.

110. Fiss writes that "little of the promise" of *Sing Tuck's* more liberal notes was realized, particularly as the following year's Supreme Court decision in *United States v. Ju Toy* solidified that an administrative ruling on the claim of nativity must be final. Fiss, *Troubled Beginnings of the Modern State*, 318; *United States v. Ju Toy*, 198 U.S. 253 (1905).

111. *Malone Farmer*, June 22, 1904.

112. *Annual Report of the Commissioner General of Immigration for the Fiscal Year Ending June 30, 1904*, 140.

113. Salyer, *Laws Harsh as Tigers*, 108–13.

114. "Fighting Yellow Men," *Ogdensburg Journal*, June 24, 1904.

115. "The County Legislature," *Malone Farmer*, Dec. 7, 1904; "What it Costs to Run the County," *Massena Observer*, Nov. 23, 1905.

116. A jail ledger from Essex County shows that the jail held 151 Chinese men between January 1904 and May 1907. While apprehensions were less frequent, detentions continued to be quite long, regularly stretching to three or four months. Port Henry Jail Logbook, Jan. 1904–May 1907, Museum of Chinese in America, 2022.040.001.

117. "General News Items," *Madrid Herald*, Nov. 21, 1907.

118. "Essex County Board of Supervisors Meeting," *Elizabethtown Post*, Jan. 10, 1907. The landlord's appeal did not work, and the county cancelled the lease at the beginning of 1907. "Resolution—Chinese Jail," *Elizabethtown Post*, Jan. 17, 1907.

119. *Annual Report of the Commissioner General of Immigration for the Fiscal Year Ended June 30, 1910* (Washington, D.C.: Government Printing Office, 1910), 138. The immigration service proposed an arrangement where all Chinese passengers would be processed and examined at Vancouver, thus saving excludable Chinese "the expensive and useless trip across Canada." Railroad companies argued that this plan would be economically ruinous to their business: If Chinese migrants could not be examined within the United States, they could not access the U.S. courts and would "certainly choose to land at San Francisco where they would have at least a limited protection in the Courts of the United States." The immigration service countered that the right to habeas corpus had already been so severely restricted by recent legal rulings such as *Sing Tuck* that landing in the United States would make an "infinitesimal" difference in the migrant's likeliness of staying in the country. "The opportunity for [judicial review], by recent decisions of the Supreme Court been so reduced as to be practically destroyed," the commissioner-general assured a railroad executive in September 1909. Daniel J. Keefe to Lucius Tuttle, Sept. 11, 1909, *Series A: Subject Correspondence Files, Part I: Asian Immigration and Exclusion* (National Archives Microfilm, Roll 15, Image 14), RG 85, NARA1.

120. *United States v. Wong You*, 223 U.S. 67 (1912). For immigration officials' discussions about the rise in Northern New York migration, see File 52541/27, Subject Correspondence, RG 85, NARA1.

2. Negotiating Freedom in an Era of Exclusion

1. "Jailed Chinamen Celebrate Holiday," *Saint Paul Globe*, Feb. 6, 1905.

2. "Funeral of a Poor Chink," *Brownsville Herald*, Oct. 26, 1909.

3. "Chinamen Took to their Knees," *Democrat and Chronicle*, March 27, 1903.

4. *Deming Headlight*, July 26, 1907.

5. "Ordered Deported," *Montgomery Advertiser*, May 30, 1903.

6. "Marshal Removed," *Buffalo Enquirer*, Oct. 15, 1903.

7. Attached letters from detained Chinese migrants, translated by the Bureau of Immigration, July 11, 1908, File 52165/1, Subject Correspondence, RG 85, NARA1.

8. Shoba Sivaprasad Wadhia, "Discretion and Disobedience in the Chinese Exclusion Era," *Asian American Law Journal* 29 (2022): 49–90.

9. "Herding Chinese Malone's Monopoly." There is robust scholarship on medical nativism in this era, much of which focuses on cities—Franklin County Jail shows how these same anxieties could also be transposed to rural places, particularly when the congestion of jails reproduced the conditions of tenements. See Nayan Shah, *Contagious Divides: Epidemics and Race in San Francisco's Chinatown* (Berkeley: University of California Press, 2001); Natalia Molina, *Fit to Be Citizens? Public Health and Race in Los Angeles, 1879–1939* (Berkeley: University of California Press, 2006).

10. Lew-Williams, *Chinese Must Go*, 225.

11. Letter from detained Chinese migrants, File 14/3905, Chinese Exclusion Case Files, NARA, New York City (hereafter CECF-NYC).

12. Illness was common in Northern New York jails, though it is difficult to ascertain the exact number of migrant deaths. The Essex County ledgers indicate two migrants "discharged by death" between July 1901 and December 1903. Newspaper mentions of deaths are typically

imprecise. For example, during a December 1903 lawsuit about Chinese at Malone, the *Massena Observer* wrote that the Chinese in custody "comprised a large party, some of whom died in the summer months." "Chinese to be Liberated," *Massena Observer*, Dec. 10, 1903. A 1903 report of the St. Lawrence Purchasing Committee listed "Casket for Chinese" as a budgetary line item. "Report of Purchasing Committee," *Courier and Freeman* (Potsdam, N.Y.), Nov. 25, 1903.

13. U.S. House of Representatives, Committee on Foreign Affairs, *Compilation from the records of the Bureau of Immigration of facts concerning the enforcement of the Chinese-exclusion laws*, 99.

14. File 14/3945, CECF-NYC.

15. "Home Matters," *Malone Farmer*, Jan. 13, 1904.

16. R. J. Wilding, M.D., to E. V. Skinner, Jan. 18, 1904, *Series A: Subject Correspondence Files, Part I* (National Archives Microfilm Publication, Roll 18, Image 259), RG 85, NARA1.

17. "Home Matters."

18. File 14/3653, CECF-NYC.

19. Letter to Mr. Berkshire, 1904, File 14/3653, CECF-NYC.

20. The 1900 Census indicated three Chinese men living in Malone outside of the jail, all laundrymen.

21. "The Chinese Must Go," *Malone Farmer*, Nov. 28, 1900; "Something New: A Chinese Restaurant to be Opened in Plattsburgh," *Plattsburgh Sentinel*, April 12, 1901.

22. Billy effectively offered to become an informant for the immigration service if it let him out of jail, writing: "[I]f, Mr. Berkshire, you can help me for to get to the United States where I can earn some money to send home to my family I will in return for its promise, at any time you feel like calling upon me, to look up any information that you or your officers may not be able to find." Letter to Mr. Berkshire, 1904.

23. "I really had quite a little confidence in this Chinaman, and had reason to believe that, from talks I had with him, he could give very valuable information regarding the Chinese situation," wrote Chinese Inspector Thomas D'Arcy to his superior. File 14/3653, CECF-NYC.

24. F. W. Berkshire to Commissioner-General, Feb. 4, 1904, File 14/3653, CECF-NYC.

25. Ark Toy Interview, File 14/3945, CECF-NYC.

26. Lew-Williams, *Chinese Must Go*, 225–26; Sue Fawn Chung, "An Ocean Apart: Chinese American Segregated Burials," in *Till Death Do Us Part: American Ethnic Cemeteries as Borders Uncrossed*, ed. Allan Amanik and Kami Fletcher (Jackson: University Press of Mississippi, 2020), 93.

27. Robert A. Doremus to W. R. Morton, May 8, 1904, File 14/3918, CECF-NYC.

28. Chinese Inspector to F. W. Berkshire, May 31, 1904, File 14/3945, CECF-NYC.

29. F. W. Berkshire to Commissioner-General S. H. Howes, May 27, 1904, File 14/3945, CECF-NYC.

30. Rachel St. John, *Line in the Sand: A History of the Western U.S.-Mexico Border* (Princeton, N.J.: Princeton University Press, 2011), 104.

31. U.S. House of Representatives, Committee on Foreign Affairs, *Compilation from the records of the Bureau of Immigration of facts concerning the enforcement of the Chinese-exclusion laws*, 10.

32. Lee, "Enforcing the Borders," 59.

33. Lee, "Enforcing the Borders," 80.

34. St. John, *Line in the Sand*, 1–2.

35. "Deportation of Chinamen Costs $18,000," *El Paso Times*, July 8, 1908.

36. An inspector in El Paso wrote to his boss in 1910 that though a new regulation in the Chinese Exclusion Act authorized the bureau to arrest Chinese migrants on departmental warrants, he intended to defer strict enforcement of the rule until satisfactory detention quarters were built. F. W. Berkshire to Commissioner-General of Immigration, Jan. 28, 1910, *Series A: Subject Correspondence Files, Part I: Asian Immigration and Exclusion* (National Archives Microfilm, Roll 16, Images 91–93), RG 85, NARA1.

37. "Report of the Special Committee in Charge of the Investigation to the Treatment of Chinese Residents and Immigrants by U.S. Immigration Officers," *Series A: Subject Correspondence Files, Part I: Asian Immigration and Exclusion* (National Archives Microfilm, Roll 26, Image 809), RG 85, NARA1.

38. Genevieve Carpio, *Collisions at the Crossroads: How Place and Mobility Make Race* (Oakland: University of California Press, 2019), 62.

39. Hernández, *City of Inmates*, 86.

40. See forthcoming work from Heather R. Lee, exploring how the New York Office of the Chinese Inspector worked with both the New York Police Department and the immigration service to target sites of Chinese entrepreneurship: Heather R. Lee, *Gastrodiplomacy: Chinese Exclusion and the Ascent of New York's Chinese Restaurants* (University of Chicago Press, forthcoming).

41. "Chinks will be Deported," *Billings Gazette*, April 8, 1903. On the use of local police power in Geary Act raids, see K. Scott Wong, "'The Eagle Seeks a Helpless Quarry': Chinatown, the Police, and the Press. The 1903 Boston Chinatown Raid Revisited," *Amerasia Journal* 22 (1996): 81–103; Mark T. Johnson, *The Middle Kingdom under the Big Sky: A History of the Chinese Experience in Montana* (Lincoln: University of Nebraska Press, 2022).

42. On California ordinances targeting Chinese, see Shah, *Contagious Divides*.

43. "Her Brother Has Feast," *Los Angeles Times*, July 28, 1907.

44. "Get Rich in County Jail," *Los Angeles Times*, March 10, 1907.

45. On deportation parties, see Goodman, *Deportation Machine*; Blue, *Deportation Express*. Deportation parties became more standardized and frequent after 1914.

46. Long Chong Casefile 52331/1, *Series A: Subject Correspondence Files, Part I: Asian Immigration and Exclusion* (National Archives Microfilm, Roll 13, Image 110), RG 85, NARA1.

47. "Poor Pang Sho Yin," editorial, *Morning Journal-Courier* (New Haven, Conn.), June 13, 1907.

48. Historian Ethan Blue has called the rural county jail a "legal and informational black hole" for migrants in this era, who often attempted to accelerate their removals when hope seemed lost. Ethan Blue, "Strange Passages: Carceral Mobility and the Liminal in the Catastrophic History of American Deportation," *National Identities* 17, no. 2 (2015): 180.

49. "Three Months Behind Bars," *Butte Miner*, Aug. 3, 1903.

50. Pang Sho Yin Testimony, Sept. 9, 1914, File 2005/238, Chinese Exclusion Case Files, NARA, Chicago.

51. Examination of Pang Sho Yin, July 2, 1906, File 2616A, Chinese Exclusion Case Files, NARA, Chicago.

52. "Pang Sho Yin Free at Last," *Detroit Free Press*, June 7, 1907.

53. "Pang Sho Yin Finds Friend," *Detroit Free Press*, March 24, 1907. On the Denby family's connections to China, see Jedidiah Joseph Kroncke, *The Futility of Law and Development: China and the Dangers of Exporting American Law* (New York: Oxford University Press, 2015), 64; Lew-Williams, *Chinese Must Go*, 169–78.

54. "Poor Pang Sho Yin."

55. *Pang Sho Yin v. United States*, 154 F. 660 (1907).

56. "Immigrant Star Chamber Checked," *Detroit Free Press*, March 9, 1909.

57. Concerns about the Boards of Special Inquiry proliferated in the early twentieth century. The U.S. Industrial Commission wrote that members of the boards were "sometimes without very much legal or judicial qualifications, but they are placed in the position where they are, for the time being, judges." When appeals did occur, the Department of Commerce and Labor reversed the decisions made by the Boards of Special Inquiry in nearly 50 percent of all cases. Critics believed that this was further evidence of their incompetence. U.S. Congress, House of Representatives, *Reports of the Industrial Commission on Immigration and Education*, 57th Cong., 1st sess., 1901, 661; Salyer, *Laws Harsh as Tigers*, 156.

58. Some of these bail practices were instituted by states rather than the federal government. In 1874, California began requiring ship captains to post a $500 bond for any immigrant passenger who could be classified as undesirable, including any "convicted criminal" or "lewd or debauched woman." Alina Das, "Inclusive Immigrant Justice: Racial Animus and the Origins of Crime-Based Deportation," *UC Davis Law Review* 52, no. 1 (2018): 184. Daniel Wilsher notes that these bonds also provided "a power to re-detain in the event of [migrants who] become destitute." Even after migrants had passed through border control, their legal presence in the nation was precarious and revocable. Daniel Wilsher, *Immigration Detention: Law, History, Politics* (Cambridge: Cambridge University Press, 2011), 17–18.

59. Andrew Urban, *Brokering Servitude: Migration and the Politics of Domestic Labor during the Long Nineteenth Century* (New York: New York University Press, 2018), 208–9.

60. The law generally cited around bail was Section 5 of the Geary Act, which stated that "on an application to any judge or court of the United States in the first instance for a writ of habeas corpus, by a Chinese person seeking to land in the United States to whom that privilege has been denied, no bail shall be allowed and such application shall be heard and determined promptly without unnecessary delay." Mary Roberts Coolidge, *Chinese Immigration* (New York: H. Holt and Co., 1909), 214.

61. "Three Arrested on Perjury Charge," *Buffalo Evening News*, July 21, 1902.

62. Daniel Bronstein, "Segregation, Exclusion, and the Chinese Communities in Georgia, 1880s–1940," in *Asian Americans in Dixie: Race and Migration in the South*, ed. Jigna Desai and Khyati Y. Joshi (Champaign: University of Illinois Press, 2013), 107–30.

63. "Exclusion Laws of the United States; Judge Speer Ruled Against Contention that Chinese from Hong Kong are British Subjects," *Augusta Chronicle*, June 20, 1904.

64. *United States v. Fah Chung*, 132 F. 109 (U.S.D.C. Ga., 1904).

65. Ariana Lindermayer, "What the Right Hand Gives: Prohibitive Interpretations of the State Constitutional Right to Bail Note," *Fordham Law Review* 78 (2009): 267–310.

66. *United States v. Fah Chung*, 132 F. 109, 110.

67. *United States v. Fah Chung*, 132 F. 109, 112.

68. *United States v. Kol Lee*, 132 F. 136 (U.S.D.C. Ga., 1904).

69. *United States v. Fah Chung*, 132 F. 109, 112.

70. "Peculiar Case of Chinese Boy Appeals to The Supreme Court for Bail," *Baltimore American*, Feb. 4, 1911.

71. "Peculiar Case of Chinese Boy Appeals to The Supreme Court for Bail."

72. For correspondence between Jem Yuen's attorney and the Court, see File 15/5232, Box 81, Straight Numerical Files, 1904–1974, RG 60, NARA, College Park, Md. (hereafter NARA2).

73. *Chin Ying Don v. Billings*, 220 U.S. 629 (1911).

74. *Chin Ying Don v. Billings*, 220 U.S. 629, Transcript of Record, Oct. 4, 1910, *U.S. Supreme Court Records and Briefs, 1832–1978*, Gale, Cengage Learning, 34.

75. Oliver Wendell Holmes to Warren Ozro Kyle, Aug. 20, 1910, *Chin Ying Don v. Billings*, Brief in Behalf of Appellants on Motion for Admission of Appellant to Bail Pending the Determination of Bail, *U.S. Supreme Court Records and Briefs, 1832–1978*, Gale, Cengage Learning, 8.

76. Benjamin S. Cable to Warren Ozro Kyle, Jan. 16, 1911, *Chin Ying Don v. Billings*, Brief in Behalf of Appellants on Motion for Admission of Appellant to Bail Pending the Determination of Bail, *U.S. Supreme Court Records and Briefs, 1832–1978*, Gale, Cengage Learning, 9.

77. "Chinese Want Bail," *Morning Oregonian*, Sept. 9, 1910; "Chinese Prisoner Cannot Get Bail," *Morning Oregonian*, Oct. 5, 1910; "Bail Case Puzzles," *Morning Oregonian*, Oct. 12, 1910.

78. *Chin Wah v. Colwell*, 187 F. 592, 594–95 (1911).

79. Daniel J. Keefe, Commissioner-General, to Inspector in Charge, Portland, Oreg., Jan. 24, 1911, File 52028/6, Subject Correspondence, RG 85, NARA1.

80. Daniel J. Keefe, Commissioner-General, to Inspector in Charge, Portland, Oreg., Oct. 29, 1910, File 52028/6, Subject Correspondence, RG 85, NARA1.

81. *In re: Ah Tai*, 125 F. 797 (U.S.D.C. MA, 1903).

82. "Poor Pang Sho Yin."

83. *Annual Report of the Commissioner General of Immigration for the Fiscal Year Ended June 30, 1913* (Washington, D.C.: Government Printing Office, 1914), 174; File No. 52116/22, File 52028/6, Subject Correspondence, RG 85, NARA1.

3. A Kaleidoscopic Affair: Rethinking the Progressive-Era Migrant Jail

1. "Lots of Deer All over the Adirondacks," *Chateaugay Record and Franklin County Democrat*, Sept. 25, 1924.

2. "Youths Were Unsuspecting of Cronk," *The Republican-Journal* (Ogdensburg, N.Y.), Nov. 11, 1924.

3. On Edward Cronk, see Allan Seymour Everest, *Rum across the Border: The Prohibition Era in Northern New York* (Syracuse, N.Y.: Syracuse University Press, 1978), 77.

4. Cronk was apprehended shortly thereafter, while trying to pass a bad check in Vermont in December 1924. He was sentenced to four years and nine months in the United States Penitentiary, Atlanta. "Edward Cronk, Ex-Trooper Sent to Atlanta," *Gouverneur Free Press*, Dec. 17, 1924.

5. Peter Andreas, *Smuggler Nation: How Illicit Trade Made America* (Oxford: Oxford University Press, 2013), 223. Daniel Kanstroom has called this a shift from "entry control" to "post-entry social control." Daniel Kanstroom, "Deportation, Social Control, and Punishment: Some Thoughts about Why Hard Laws Make Bad Cases," *Harvard Law Review* 113, no. 8 (2000): 1890–935.

6. Jessica R. Pliley, *Policing Sexuality: The Mann Act and the Making of the FBI* (Cambridge, Mass.: Harvard University Press, 2014); Grace Peña Delgado, "Sexual Self: Morals Policing and the Expansion of the U.S. Immigration Bureau at America's Early Twentieth-Century Borders," in *Entangling Migration History*, ed. Benjamin Bryce and Alexander Freund (Gainesville: University Press of Florida, 2015), 100–119.

7. Bruno Ramirez, *Crossing the 49th Parallel: Migration from Canada to the United States, 1900–1930* (Ithaca, N.Y.: Cornell University Press, 2001).

8. Libby Garland, *After They Closed the Gates: Jewish Illegal Immigration to the United States, 1921–1965* (Chicago: University of Chicago Press, 2014); Ashley Johnson Bavery, *Bootlegged Aliens: Immigration Politics on America's Northern Border* (Philadelphia: University of Pennsylvania Press, 2020).

9. "Many Hang on Rim of U.S. Melting Pot," *Detroit Free Press*, Sept. 2, 1929.

10. While the BOP declared its federal jail projects to be the nation's first, the United States did establish jails in Indian Territory in the late nineteenth century, in what would later become the states of Oklahoma and Arkansas. As these sites detained both Indigenous and non-Indigenous people convicted in the federal courts of Indian Territory, federal officials viewed them as a separate system of incarceration—officials were not transferring prisoners from federal courts in the rest of the United States to these sites, as they would with the jails that originated in 1930. Still, it would be most accurate to describe the BOP's jails as "the first federal jails established outside a territory." For more on how Indigenous people interacted with federal jails and prisons, see Sara M. Benson, *The Prison of Democracy: Race, Leavenworth, and the Culture of Law* (Oakland: University of California Press, 2019), 34–56.

11. Lisa McGirr, *The War on Alcohol: Prohibition and the Rise of the American State* (New York: W. W. Norton and Company, 2016), 201.

12. Young, *Forever Prisoners*, 44–49.

13. New York State Commission of Correction, *Annual Report of the New York State Commission of Correction for the Year 1930* (Albany: New York State Commission of Correction, 1931), 42.

14. Dr. George W. Kirchwey said that the "problem of the county jail is primarily a problem of classification and of individual treatment. The task of ridding our State of the shame of the county jail is ours." "The Problem of the County Jail," in *Seventh Annual Report of the New York State Probation Commission for the Year 1923* (Albany: J. B. Lyon Company, 1924), 212.

15. There is a robust field of scholarship on this era in both carceral state history and immigration history. On "expertise" in policing and incarceration, see Khalil Gibran Muhammad, *The Condemnation of Blackness: Race, Crime, and the Making of Modern Urban America* (Cambridge, Mass.: Harvard University Press, 2010); Kali N. Gross, *Colored Amazons: Crime, Violence, and Black Women in the City of Brotherly Love, 1880–1910* (Durham, N.C.: Duke University Press, 2006); Cheryl D. Hicks, *Talk with You like a Woman: African American Women, Justice, and Reform in New York, 1890–1935* (Chapel Hill: University of North Carolina Press, 2010). On immigration, see Katherine Benton-Cohen, *Inventing the Immigration Problem: The Dillingham Commission and Its Legacy* (Cambridge, Mass.: Harvard University Press, 2018).

16. Joseph F. Fishman, *Crucibles of Crime: The Shocking Story of the American Jail* (New York: Cosmopolis Press, 1923), 13.

17. "[These] people have no special fear of imprisonment on account that their lives within the prison is easier than freedom in their own country," said one immigration inspector about detained Mexicans in Arizona in 1923. File 54933/351B, Subject Correspondence, RG 85, NARA1.

18. Hester, *Deportation*, 30.

19. Torrie Hester notes that the caveat about procedural challenges had little impact on the overall rate of deportation. Hester, *Deportation*, 29.

20. Hester, *Deportation*, 30.

21. Hyung-chan Kim, ed., *Asian Americans and the Supreme Court: A Documentary History* (Westport, Conn.: Greenwood Press, 1992), 93.

22. Hester, *Deportation*, 33.

23. See Pliley, *Policing Sexuality*; W. P. Dillingham, Committee on Immigration, *Importing Women for Immoral Purposes: A Partial Report from the Immigration Commission on the Importation and Harboring of Women for Immoral Purposes* (Washington, D.C.: Government Printing Office, 1909).

24. Randy William Widdis, *With Scarcely a Ripple: Anglo-Canadian Migration into the United States and Western Canada, 1880–1920* (Montreal: McGill-Queen's University Press, 1998), 207.

25. Map: "Sanborn Fire Insurance Map from Watertown, Jefferson County, New York," Sanborn Map Company, June 1890, https://www.loc.gov/item/sanborn06332_002/.

26. "A Serious Charge," *Watertown Re-union*, Oct. 4, 1911.

27. "Held for the U.S. Grand Jury," *Ogdensburg Journal*, Oct. 19, 1911; "Are Sent Back to Canada," *Ogdensburg Journal*, Jan. 12, 1912.

28. A similar pattern occurred on the southern border, where both Mexican and European women spent months in jail pending the trials of men accused of trafficking. See Grace Peña Delgado, "Border Control and Sexual Policing: White Slavery and Prostitution along the U.S.-Mexico Borderlands, 1903–1910," *Western Historical Quarterly* 43, no. 2 (2012): 157–78.

29. Anne E. Bowler, Chrysanthi S. Leon, and Terry G. Lilley, "'What Shall We Do with the Young Prostitute? Reform Her or Neglect Her?' Domestication as Reform at the New York State Reformatory for Women at Bedford, 1901–1913," *Journal of Social History* 47, no. 2 (2013): 458–81.

30. Commissioner-General Memorandum for the Secretary, April 15, 1915, File 53678/155A, Subject Correspondence, RG 85, NARA1.

31. The report recognized that this might not always be possible. It included a caveat that if girls and women had to be detained in jails or immigration stations, it was critical that the bureau hire female employees to oversee them. See Jessica Pliley, "The Petticoat Inspectors: Women Boarding Inspectors and the Gendered Exercise of Federal Authority," *Journal of the Gilded Age and Progressive Era* 12, no. 1 (2013): 95–126; *Annual Report of the Commissioner General of Immigration for the Fiscal Year Ended June 30, 1915* (Washington, D.C.: Government Printing Office, 1915), 14.

32. For an in-depth discussion of the policy change, see Eva Payne, "Deportation as Rescue: White Slaves, Women Reformers, and the US Bureau of Immigration," *Journal of Women's History* 33, no. 4 (2021): 40–66.

33. Memorandum for the Bureau of Immigration, March 8, 1917, File 53678/155B, Subject Correspondence, RG 85, NARA1.

34. See Robert Cassanello, *To Render Invisible: Jim Crow and Public Life in New South Jacksonville* (Gainesville: University Press of Florida, 2013).

35. Payne, "Deportation as Rescue," 57.

36. Menchaca, "Freedom of Jail," 34.

37. See Savitri Maya Kunze, "The Undeportables: Diplomatic Nonrecognition and the Periphery of Rights in the United States" (Ph.D. diss., University of Chicago, 2021).

38. Jane Perry Clark, *Deportation of Aliens from the United States to Europe* (New York: Columbia University Press, 1931), 17. Emily Pope-Obeda offers a rich analysis of the foreign policy

implications of deportation, highlighting the "interlocking scales of space in which deportation was negotiated" in the 1920s; see Pope-Obeda, "When in Doubt Deport!" 36, 44–97.

39. "Ten Aliens Are Being Held in Jail for Deportation," *The Republican-Journal* (Ogdensburg, N.Y.), Oct. 15, 1925. The 1924 Immigration Act charged that immigrants from colonies would fall under the quota of the metropole but gave the U.S. consul significant power in determining how visas would be distributed. This dramatically restricted routes to legal migration for people from the British Caribbean. Barber, "Anti-Black Racism and the Nativist State," 23.

40. "Insane Alien Brought to City," *The Republican-Journal* (Ogdensburg, N.Y.), Nov. 22, 1926. In 1926, one New York newspaper claimed that the state paid $4,400,000 for the maintenance of "the alien insane." "Alien Convicts," *Plattsburgh Sentinel*, March 19, 1926. Elliott Young argues that many migrants in the early twentieth century were incarcerated in insane asylums, requiring us to look "beyond jails, prisons, and immigration detention centers" to gain a full picture of detention in this era. Young, *Forever Prisoners*, 7, 54–85. The early twentieth century was a period of rapid expansion for psychiatric institutions; many of these institutions reported that they were housing a disproportionate number of noncitizens. States called for greater federal intervention to reduce the burden on subfederal budgets. Arnold, "How Immigration Detention Became Exceptional," 296–98.

41. Clark, *Deportation of Aliens from the United States to Europe*, 17.

42. *United States ex rel. Ross v. Wallis*, 279 Fed. 401 (C.C.A. 2d, 1922).

43. *Schlimm v. Howe*, 222 Fed. 96 (S.D.N.Y. 1915).

44. On eugenics in immigration law, see Alexandra Minna Stern, "From 'Race Suicide' to 'White Extinction': White Nationalism, Nativism, and Eugenics over the Past Century," *Journal of American History* 109, no. 2 (2022): 348–61; Douglas C. Baynton, *Defectives in the Land: Disability and Immigration in the Age of Eugenics* (Chicago: University of Chicago Press, 2016).

45. In 1917, Congress created the "barred Asiatic zone," encompassing the entire area from Afghanistan to the Pacific, minus Japan and the Philippines. People from this zone were excluded from immigration. In 1924, the Johnson-Reed Act excluded "persons ineligible to citizenship." This extended the exclusion to Japanese immigrants, as the Nationality Act of 1790 only permitted naturalization of "free white persons." Ngai, *Impossible Subjects*, 37.

46. "Report on County Jail," *Adirondack News*, Aug. 16, 1924.

47. "State Takes Action to Close Overcrowded Clinton Co Jail," *Plattsburgh Sentinel*, Sept. 11, 1925. Risk of suicide is much higher in jails than in prison, in part because it is often mental health crises and trauma that cause people to be arrested in the first place. While migrants were in a somewhat different position, it is worth noting that they were sharing a space notorious for high rates of self-harm. See Littman, "Jails, Sheriffs, and Carceral Policymaking," 874–75.

48. "Northern Jails Crowded May Boost U.S. Prisoners' Board."

49. Simpson, *Mohawk Interruptus*, 134–37. Some immigration officials arbitrarily decided whether and when to allow Mohawks to cross, despite the Supreme Court's ruling, leading some Mohawks to cross the border at unofficial entry points. Gerald F. Reid, "Illegal Alien? The Immigration Case of Mohawk Ironworker Paul K. Diabo," *Proceedings of the American Philosophical Society* 151, no. 1 (2007): 68. On the history of Indigenous people in Northern New York, see Melissa Otis, *Rural Indigenousness: A History of Iroquoian and Algonquian Peoples of the Adirondacks* (Syracuse, N.Y.: Syracuse University Press, 2018).

50. "State Takes Action to Close Overcrowded Clinton Co Jail."

51. Alden Whitman, ed., *American Reformers: An H. W. Wilson Biographical Dictionary* (Bronx, N.Y.: H. W. Wilson Company, 1985), 407–8.

52. The topic of jails had been entirely absent from the American Prison Association's annual meetings from 1915 to 1920. Sanford Bates, *Prisons and Beyond* (New York: Macmillan, 1936), 38.

53. U.S. Congress, House, *Federal Penal and Reformatory Institutions: Hearings before the Special Committee on Federal Penal and Reformatory Institutions*, 70th Cong., 2d sess., Jan. 7–15, 1929, 157. Melanie Newport has shown that in the first decade of the twentieth century, much of reformers' energy centered on centralizing jails under state control, an idea that grew out of anxieties about local corruption in jailing. By the 1910s and 1920s, as the number of Black people incarcerated in urban jails expanded exponentially, the enthusiasm for abolition waned. Newport, *This Is My Jail*, 28–35.

54. U.S. Congress, House, *Federal Penal and Reformatory Institutions*, 158.

55. In 1928, John Boylan, a New York congressman, contacted the Department of Justice for a complete list of rates paid to New York county jails and statistics on how many federal prisoners were held at each site; he was told that no such information existed. Hart noted in 1924 that the federal government paid eleven different rates to jails in New York alone. U.S. Congress, House, Committee on Rules, *Federal Prison Bill: Hearings before the Committee on Rules*, 70th Cong., 1st sess., 1928; Hart, *United States Prisoners in County Jails*, 3.

56. Hart, *United States Prisoners in County Jails*, 1.

57. Hart, *United States Prisoners in County Jails*, 3.

58. U.S. Congress, House, Committee on Rules, *Federal Prison Bill*, 23.

59. "Asks Jail Inquiry by Federal Bench," *New York Times*, Jan. 25, 1926.

60. Nina Kinsella, "County Jails and the Federal Government," *Journal of Criminal Law and Criminology* 24, no. 2 (1933): 428–39.

61. U.S. Congress, House, *Federal Penal and Reformatory Institutions*, 8.

62. Hernández, *Migra!* 80. Daniel Kanstroom writes of budget limitations: "Tens of thousands of Chinese workers were now subject to deportation for failure to register. The secretary of the treasury, with a budget of $25,000, faced a task that was estimated to cost $7,310,000." Kanstroom, *Deportation Nation*, 120.

63. U.S. Congress, House, Committee on Immigration and Naturalization, *Deportation: Hearings before the Committee on Immigration and Naturalization, House of Representatives*, 69th Cong., 1st sess., 1926, 13.

64. U.S. Congress, House, Committee on Immigration and Naturalization, *Deportation*, 14.

65. "Alien Convicts."

66. "An Act to amend the county law, in relation to the commitment of prisoners by United States courts," *Laws of the State of New York*, 149th sess. (Albany: J. B. Lyon Company, 1926), 389.

67. New York State Commission of Correction, *Annual Report of the New York State Commission of Correction for the Year 1930*, 60.

68. "Jails Again Filled with U.S. Prisoners."

69. "'Your Bill, Sir,' Says City to Uncle Sam," *New York Times*, Jan. 17, 1921.

70. This problem persisted into the 1930s, with jails in Texas, Illinois, and California claiming that the federal government had long-overdue outstanding payments for board of federal prisoners. See "U.S. Owes Jails $20,00 for Its Prisoners' Keep," *Chicago Daily Tribune*, Jan. 11, 1933; "Dispute on Prisoners' Keep Ends," *Los Angeles Times*, Aug. 1, 1934.

71. "Sheriff Duns U.S. for Ludlow Bills," *New York Herald*, Jan. 17, 1921.

72. "Jail Order Causes Stir," *New York Times*, Nov. 27, 1927; Ned Mcintosh, "U.S. Prisoners Costing City $25,000 Yearly," *New York Herald Tribune*, Dec. 25, 1926.

73. "U.S. Court Faces Problem: Practically No Place to Send Federal Prisoners," *Boston Daily Globe*, Oct. 21, 1925.

74. "Baltimore Jail Turns Away U.S. Prisoners," *Washington Post*, April 27, 1927.

75. Hon. Joseph C. Hutcheson Jr., "United States Prisoners in Jails," speech, Jackson, Miss., Nov. 10, 1925.

76. Hutcheson, "United States Prisoners in Jails."

77. Congress approved the bill to build the first three federal prisons on March 3, 1891. These sites were used for any person convicted of a federal crime whose imprisonment was a year or more. An appropriation of $500,000 was made for the construction of each of the three institutions. Charles B. Fields, "Three Prisons Act 1891," in *Encyclopedia of Prisons and Correctional Facilities*, 2 vols., ed. Mary Bosworth (Thousand Oaks, Calif.: SAGE Publications, Inc., 2005), 963–64. The United States' nineteenth-century territorial jails had been incredibly contentious in their own right. In an 1898 visit, Frederick Howard Wines declared the territorial jails "fouler, crueler, and more destructive of morals, minds, and bodies than any of the places of confinement in Cuba or Mexico," while Anna Dawes, daughter of Senator Henry Dawes, called a territorial jail in Fort Smith, Arkansas, "a veritable hell upon earth." "A Republic of Criminals," *New York Times*, Feb. 6, 1898; Anna L. Dawes, "A United States Prison," *Lend a Hand: A Journal of Organized Philanthropy* 1 (1886): 3–6.

78. U.S. Congress, House, *Federal Penal and Reformatory Institutions*, III.

79. R. E. Sims, Superintendent of Arizona State Prison, to Governor of Arizona, Aug. 16, 1923, File 54933/351-C, Subject Correspondence, RG 85, NARA1.

80. U.S. Department of Labor, *Eleventh Annual Report of the Secretary of Labor* (Washington, D.C.: Government Printing Office, 1923), 106.

81. Act of March 4, 1929 (45 Stat. 1551).

82. Lew-Williams, *Chinese Must Go*, 51.

83. Ngai, "Strange Career of the Illegal Alien," 76. Elliott Young notes that while this is often credited as the law that "criminalized" migration, there were plenty of ways to be charged criminally for border crossing before this law, particularly for Chinese migrants charged with "unlawful presence" or "violation of restriction act." Young, *Forever Prisoners*, 29–30.

84. U.S. Department of Labor, *Seventeenth Annual Report of the Secretary of Labor* (Washington, D.C.: Government Printing Office, 1929), 62.

85. "Act Puts Teeth in Immigration Law," *North Countryman* (Rouses Point, N.Y.), March 28, 1929.

86. Ngai, "Strange Career of the Illegal Alien," 84.

87. Kang, *INS on the Line*, 57.

88. On perceptions of criminality, see Kelly Lytle Hernández, *Bad Mexicans: Race, Empire, and Revolution in the Borderlands* (New York: W. W. Norton and Company, 2022); Francisco A. Rosales, ¡Pobre Raza! *Violence, Justice, and Mobilization among México Lindo Immigrants, 1900–1936* (Austin: University of Texas Press, 1999).

89. Hernández, *City of Inmates*, 137.

90. Ngai, *Impossible Subjects*, 25.

91. Doug Keller, "Re-thinking Illegal Entry and Re-entry," *Loyola University Chicago Law Journal* 44 (2013): 77.

92. Kang, *INS on the Line*, 57, 65.

93. U.S. Department of Justice, *Report of the Attorney General for the Fiscal Year 1931* (Washington, D.C.: Government Printing Office, 1931), 77.

94. S. 5094 county jail data, File 55639/73, Subject Correspondence, RG 85, NARA1.

95. As previously noted, this was not the first time migrants had faced criminal prosecution for migration-related offenses. However, the 1929 law did create a criminal charge for illegal entry that could be broadly applied and did not require, for example, evidence that a person had been engaged in smuggling.

96. Under Section 1, defendants had to be held for a grand jury, further extending pretrial detention and government costs. Office of Inspector in Charge to District Director, El Paso, Aug. 14, 1929, File 55601/816, Subject Correspondence, RG 85, NARA1.

97. "To Enforce New Deportation Act," *Chateaugay Reporter*, March 29, 1929.

98. "Favor Malone for Detention House to End Jail Crowding," *The Republican-Journal* (Ogdensburg, N.Y.), Sept. 20, 1930; "Jails Again Filled with U.S. Prisoners."

99. New York State Commission of Correction, *Annual Report of the New York State Commission of Correction for the Year 1929* (Albany: New York State Commission of Correction, 1930), 277.

100. The detention of children in a county jail was a violation of the Children's Court Act, a 1922 law that forbade holding children under the age of sixteen in jails or lockups. See John P. Woods, "New York's Juvenile Offender Law: An Overview and Analysis," *Fordham Urban Law Journal* 9, no. 1 (1980): 1–50. The immigration service was eager to distance itself from these sorts of prosecutions—in the 1932 annual report, the commissioner-general wrote that the agency was focusing on pursuing repeat offenders rather than individuals who had entered illegally only once. He also noted that immigration officers would take "extenuating factors, such as the youth or sex of the offenders" into account, given the congested conditions of jail in border districts. *Annual Report of the Commissioner General of Immigration for Fiscal Year Ended June 30, 1932* (Washington, D.C.: Government Printing Office, 1932), 3.

101. New York State Commission of Correction, *Annual Report of the New York State Commission of Correction for the Year 1929*, 277.

102. "Denies Lurid Tale of Britons in Jails"; "Repeats We Hold Britons in Prison."

103. "Consul Tells of Difficulty," *Tucson Daily Star*, April 27, 1931. The Mexican consul also inquired about conditions in jails; see Evren John Turan, "South Texas Media Representations of Rio Grande Valley Mexican Deportation Drives and Repatriation, 1928–1930" (M.A. thesis, University of Texas Rio Grande Valley, 2019), 62–67.

104. "Why?" editorial, *The Leader-Post* (Regina, Canada), April 15, 1932.

105. Ngai, *Impossible Subjects*, 57.

106. Hernández, *City of Inmates*, 138–39.

107. U.S. Congress, House, *Federal Penal and Reformatory Institutions*, 144.

108. U.S. Congress, House, *Departments of State, Justice, Commerce, and Labor Appropriation Bill for 1931: Hearing before the Subcommittee of House Committee on Appropriations*, 71st Cong., 2d sess., Dec. 14–16, 1929, 39.

109. New York State Commission of Correction, *Annual Report of the New York State Commission of Correction for the Year 1930*, 42.

110. From July to December 1930, county jails in New York held 1,187 people for immigration charges and 1,148 for Prohibition charges. The report noted that many Prohibition cases were not counted in these numbers because the violators were bailed or fined. New York State Commission of Correction, *Annual Report of the New York State Commission of Correction for the Year 1931* (Albany: New York State Commission of Correction, 1932), 50.

111. Bureau Circular, Sept. 27, 1923, File 54951/General, Subject Correspondence, RG 85, NARA1.

112. Migrants identified in these institutions were likely eligible for deportation under the public charge law, but few deportations would actually be carried out—fewer than 1,500 individuals were deported on the public charge doctrine between 1906 and 1932. Fox, *Three Worlds of Relief*, 132.

113. Ethan Blue describes this as the "two axes" of integration, one vertical, one horizontal. Blue, *Deportation Express*, 17.

114. In re co-operation, received from officials of states, cities, municipalities, etc. in connection with the enforcement of the immigration laws, Oct. 8, 1923; Seattle District to Commissioner-General, Oct. 2, 1923, File 549451/General, Subject Correspondence, RG 85, NARA1.

115. San Francisco District to Commissioner-General, Oct. 5, 1923, File 549451/General, Subject Correspondence, RG 85, NARA1; Portland District to Commissioner-General, Oct. 3, 1923, File 549451/General, Subject Correspondence, RG 85, NARA1.

116. In re co-operation, received from officials of states, cities, municipalities, etc. in connection with the enforcement of the immigration laws, Oct. 8, 1923.

117. Los Angeles District to Commissioner-General, Oct. 2, 1923, File 549451/General, Subject Correspondence, RG 85, NARA1.

118. Kaufman, "Segregation by Citizenship," 1371.

119. S. Deborah Kang writes that the United States instituted the first Passport Act in 1918 to police the entry and departure of suspected enemy aliens during wartime; the law made providing migrants with false documents or smuggling them into the country a criminal act punishable by fines and jail time. In 1920, Congress authorized a Passport Act outside the auspices of emergency wartime measures. Kang, *INS on the Line*, 12–35; Garland, *After They Closed the Gates*, 93.

120. Washington County Jail detainees to Secretary of Labor, July 31, 1924, File 54933-351-D, Subject Correspondence, RG 85, NARA1.

121. In re co-operation, received from officials of states, cities, municipalities, etc. in connection with the enforcement of the immigration laws, Oct. 8, 1923.

122. James L. Long, Superintendent of New York Prisons, to John H. Clark, Commissioner of Immigration, Aug. 13, 1924, File 54933/351-D, Subject Correspondence, RG 85, NARA1.

123. Samuel H. Sibley, U.S. District Judge, to E. J. Hunning, Assistant Secretary of Labor, July 14, 1923, File 54933/351B, Subject Correspondence, RG 85, NARA1.

124. E. J. Hunning, Assistant Secretary of Labor, to Samuel H. Sibley, U.S. District Judge, July 18, 1923, File 54933/351B, Subject Correspondence, RG 85, NARA1.

125. Office of Supervisor, El Paso District, to Commissioner-General of Immigration, Oct. 9, 1923, File 5002/983, Subject Correspondence, RG 85, NARA1.

126. Historian Nora Krinitsky calls this the rise of "crime control politics," characterized by concern about urban crime and deviancy from a broad coalition of officials, residents, and institutions of differing political stripes. Krinitsky argues that the term "law-and-order politics" is an

imperfect fit for much of the twentieth century, as it connotes a conservative turn to punitive policies and obscures the range of reformers and municipal leaders concerned with imposing urban order and defending the urban color line. Khalil Gibran Muhammad's work highlights the role of the social sciences in cementing an association between race and criminality. Even as cities fretted about the lawbreaking of immigrants, social scientists suggested that white city dwellers were still more reformable and less innately criminal than their Black counterparts. Nora C. Krinitsky, "The Politics of Crime Control: Race, Policing, and Reform in Twentieth-Century Chicago" (Ph.D. diss., University of Michigan, 2017); Muhammad, *Condemnation of Blackness*.

127. Ashley Johnson Bavery, "'Crashing America's Back Gate': Illegal Europeans, Policing, and Welfare in Industrial Detroit, 1921–1939," *Journal of Urban History* 44, no. 2 (2018): 242.

128. "Many Hang on Rim of U.S. Melting Pot."

129. "Many Hang on Rim of U.S. Melting Pot."

130. "Agents of U.S. Sweep City in Alien Roundup," *Detroit Free Press*, July 22, 1932.

131. Bavery, "Crashing America's Back Gate," 250. On the relationship between local law enforcement, immigration officials, and the policing of noncitizens in the first decades of the twentieth century, see Matthew Guariglia, *Police and the Empire City: Race and the Origins of Modern Policing in New York City* (Durham, N.C.: Duke University Press, 2023); Krinitsky, "Politics of Crime Control," 237–83; Edward J. Escobar, *Race, Police, and the Making of a Political Identity* (Berkeley: University of California Press, 1999).

132. "Where Is the Deportation Report?" *Detroit Free Press*, Aug. 7, 1931.

133. "Doak Raps Slogan of 'America Last,'" *Detroit Free Press*, July 17, 1931.

134. "Asks Speedier Deportations," *Detroit Free Press*, Feb. 2, 1931.

135. "Looking Over the Day's News," *Battle Creek Enquirer*, Feb. 3, 1932.

136. "Boy, 'Lost' in Jail 8 Months, Rescued," *Detroit Free Press*, May 16, 1931.

137. "Woman Held 5 Days after Release Order," *Detroit Free Press*, Feb. 1, 1930.

138. John V. Watts, "German's Dream of America Shattered as He Reposes in Dade County Jail," *Miami Daily News*, July 25, 1925.

139. "Alien Crews Held in Jail as Ships Dock," *Miami Daily News*, July 26, 1925. There were earlier precedents for this practice: In the nineteenth century, so-called Negro Seamen Acts mandated the detention of free Black sailors to prevent the "contagion of liberty" from spreading to states' enslaved populations. See Michael Schoeppner, "Peculiar Quarantines: The Seamen Acts and Regulatory Authority in the Antebellum South," *Law and History Review* 31, no. 3 (2013): 559–86.

140. Aliens smuggling through Florida, 1921, File 55086/55, Subject Correspondence, RG 85, NARA1.

141. Letter from deportees in Mobile County Jail, July 14, 1940, File 55853/262, Subject Correspondence, RG 85, NARA1.

142. Response to deportees in Mobile County Jail, Sept. 21, 1940, File 55853/262, Subject Correspondence, RG 85, NARA1.

143. Letter from deportees in Mobile County Jail, July 14, 1940.

144. On countries of origin, see File 55599/137-A, Subject Correspondence, RG 85, NARA1. This distinction appeared to be more of a guideline than a firm rule, as Galveston incarcerated migrants from Mexico, Australia, and Brazil in the years that followed.

145. Description of County Jail, Galveston, Tex., File 55599/137-A, Subject Correspondence, RG 85, NARA1. This episode is part of a longer history of violence against Mexican women incarcerated by the immigration service; see Menchaca, "Freedom of Jail," 35–37.

146. Alvin M. Johnson, Immigrant Inspector, to U.S. Immigration Service District Director, April 26, 1928, File 55599/137-A, Subject Correspondence, RG 85, NARA1.

147. "Y.W.C.A. May Aid in Deportees' Care," Galveston Daily News, April 12, 1929.

148. League of Women Voters to Morris Sheppard, U.S. Senate, Aug. 13, 1925, File 55591/137, Subject Correspondence, RG 85, NARA1.

149. Galveston Chamber of Commerce to Henry E. Hull, Commissioner of Immigration, Aug. 22, 1925, File 55599/137, Subject Correspondence, RG 85, NARA1.

150. McGirr, War on Alcohol, xxi.

151. "For a Federal Jail," Plattsburgh Sentinel, Aug. 5, 1930; "Favor Malone for Detention House to End Jail Crowding."

152. Eric W. Rise, "Crime, Comity and Civil Rights: The NAACP and the Extradition of Southern Black Fugitives," American Journal of Legal History 55, no. 1 (2015): 121.

153. Walter White to James Cobb, Jan. 3, 1930, Part 11, Series A, Folder: Federal Prisoners 1930, National Association for the Advancement of Colored People Papers, Proquest History Vault.

154. Sanford Bates wrote to the NAACP that they were not violating convict leasing policies, because there was a distinction between "leasing" and "boarding"—namely, that there was no private interest involved and that the federal government was paying the locality for the convicted men's care. Internally, the NAACP noted that this distinction seemed designed to appease labor unions worried about competition, not to indicate a difference in conditions for incarcerated people. Sanford Bates to Walter White, Nov. 7, 1929, Part 11, Series A, Folder: Federal Prisoners, Oct.–Nov. 1929, National Association for the Advancement of Colored People Papers, Proquest History Vault.

155. Attorney General to the NAACP, Feb. 3, 1930, Part 11, Series A, Folder: Federal Prisoners 1930, National Association for the Advancement of Colored People Papers, Proquest History Vault.

156. Despite requests by the New York State Commission of Correction, Northern New York did not receive a federal jail. Instead, the federal government chose to place a Federal Detention Farm in Milan, Michigan, outside of Detroit. Newspapers reported a smattering of immigration offenders moving through Milan in its early years. Many were "extreme" cases, such as Joseph Alphonse Courteau, a Canadian the United States had deported seven times in seven years before sentencing him to eight months in jail for illegal entry. "Courteau Gets 8-Month Term," Windsor Star, July 22, 1933.

157. "El Paso Sheriff's Forces Will Be Drastically Cut," El Paso Times, July 27, 1932.

158. "Federal Prisoners Are Transferred to County Jail," El Paso Times, March 10, 1933; Francisco E. Balderrama, Decade of Betrayal: Mexican Repatriation in the 1930s (Albuquerque: University of New Mexico Press, 2006), 64–71.

159. Henry Cohen to Frances Perkins, June 9, 1938, File 55599/137-C, Subject Correspondence, RG 85, NARA1.

160. U.S. Department of Justice, Bureau of Prisons, Federal Offenders 1934–1935 (Fort Leavenworth, Kans.: Federal Prison Industries, Inc. Press, 1936), 24.

161. U.S. Department of Justice, Bureau of Prisons, Federal Offenders 1938–1939 (Fort Leavenworth, Kans.: Federal Prison Industries, Inc. Press, 1940), 24.

162. William M. Tuck, "The Jail and the People," in *Proceedings of the Annual Congress of the American Prison Association* (Indianapolis: W. B. Burford, 1940), 411–42.

163. Harry Elmer Barnes, "The Kindergarten of Crime," *Jail Association Journal* 2, no. 1 (1940): 25–44.

4. "A Concentration Camp of Their Own": Detention in and after War

1. This was all the more egregious as the United States repeatedly denied special admissions programs for Jewish refugees, including children. Historian Rafael Medoff writes that between 1933 and 1945, nearly two hundred thousand quota places for people living in Nazi Germany and later Nazi-occupied nations went unused, largely because of the difficulty of securing visas. Assistant Secretary of State Breckinridge Long was a critical driver of a program to, in his own words, "delay and effectively stop for a temporary period of indefinite length the number of immigrants into the United States." Rafael Medoff, *The Jews Should Keep Quiet: Franklin D. Roosevelt, Rabbi Stephen S. Wise, and the Holocaust* (Lincoln: University of Nebraska Press, 2019), 65. See Tara Zahra, *The Lost Children: Reconstructing Europe's Families after World War II* (Cambridge, Mass.: Harvard University Press, 2011), 69; Medoff, *Jews Should Keep Quiet*, 61–70.

2. *Annual Report of the Immigration and Naturalization Service 1941–1942* (Washington, D.C.: Government Printing Office, 1942), 5.

3. For more information on each of these groups, see Rachel Ida Buff, *Against the Deportation Terror: Organizing for Immigrant Rights in the Twentieth Century* (Philadelphia: Temple University Press, 2017).

4. Buff, *Against the Deportation Terror*, 44.

5. On the long connections between white supremacy and national security, as well as the ways U.S. empire targeted and racialized Asians as seditious threats, see Moon-Ho Jung, *Menace to Empire: Anticolonial Solidarities and the Transpacific Origins of the US Security State* (Oakland: University of California Press, 2022).

6. On the legal strategies pursued by attorneys representing clients excluded on ideological grounds, see Smita Ghosh, "'The Worst Kind of Prison in the World': The Executive Power to Detain and Exclude Noncitizens, 1950–1996" (Ph.D. diss., University of Pennsylvania, 2020). Ghosh notes that the use of "concentration camp" at the mid-century would not necessarily have invoked the Holocaust. Americans were more likely to think of the camps that had held noncitizens and Japanese Americans during the war: "[C]oncentration camps were tools that any government—totalitarian or democratic—could use to isolate citizens or subjects without trial." Ghosh, "Worst Kind of Prison in the World," 37. On another use of "concentration camp" to describe the Department of Justice's work at the mid-century, see Anna Pegler-Gordon, *Closing the Golden Door: Asian Migration and the Hidden History of Exclusion at Ellis Island* (Chapel Hill: University of North Carolina Press, 2021), 165–93.

7. Jared Keller, "The Legacy of Japanese Internment Lives on in Migrant Detention," *Pacific Standard*, June 13, 2019, https://psmag.com/ideas/the-legacy-of-japanese-internment-lives-on-in-migrant-detention.

8. "Japs Evicted on Terminal Isle," *Los Angeles Times*, Feb. 3, 1942.

9. Tetsuden Kashima, *Judgment without Trial: Japanese American Imprisonment during World War II* (Seattle: University of Washington Press, 2003), 55.

10. Anna Pegler-Gordon, "'New York Has a Concentration Camp of Its Own': Japanese Confinement on Ellis Island during World War II," *Journal of Asian American Studies* 20, no. 3 (2017): 377–78.

11. Kashima, *Judgment without Trial*, 55.

12. Interview with Sadaichi Asai, Dec. 12, 1994, Terminal Island Life History Project, Japanese American National Museum.

13. "Fish Harbor like Deserted Town," *Los Angeles Times*, March 1, 1942.

14. The War Relocation Authority oversaw far more Japanese and Japanese Americans than the enemy aliens program: Japanese enemy aliens in INS custody formed only about 11 percent of all ethnic Japanese incarcerated during World War II. Pegler-Gordon, "New York Has a Concentration Camp of Its Own," 375.

15. Kashima, *Judgment without Trial*, 106.

16. Kashima, *Judgment without Trial*, 235n37.

17. Ngai, *Impossible Subjects*, 175–76.

18. Kashima, *Judgment without Trial*, 107.

19. Kashima, *Judgment without Trial*, 378; Blue, *Deportation Express*, 54.

20. "County Jail Now Concentration Camp," *Daily News* (Los Angeles), Dec. 12, 1941. On the history of the Los Angeles County Jail, see Hernández, *City of Inmates*; Jonathan van Harmelen, "Los Angeles County Jail (Detention Facility)," *Densho Encyclopedia*, 2021, https://encyclopedia .densho.org/Los%20Angeles%20County%20Jail%20(detention%20facility) (accessed June 20, 2023).

21. Kashima, *Judgment without Trial*, 94–95.

22. Inter-American Commission on Human Rights, Report No. 26/20, Case 12.545, Merits Report (Publication), Isamu Carlos Shibayama, Kenichi Javier Shibayama, and Takeshi Jorge Shibayama, United States, April 22, 2020, 6, https://www.oas.org/en/iachr/decisions/2020/US _12.545_EN.PDF.

23. Stephen Seng-hua Mak, "'America's Other Internment': World War II and the Making of Modern Human Rights" (Ph.D. diss., Northwestern University, 2009), 104.

24. Inter-American Commission on Human Rights, Report No. 26/20, 7.

25. Alexandra Minna Stern, "Buildings, Boundaries, and Blood: Medicalization and Nation-Building on the U.S.-Mexico Border, 1910–1930," *Hispanic American Historical Review* 79, no. 1 (1999): 45.

26. Julia Rose Kraut, *Threat of Dissent: A History of Ideological Exclusion and Deportation in the United States* (Cambridge, Mass.: Harvard University Press, 2020), 152–53.

27. Ellen Schrecker, "Immigration and Internal Security: Political Deportations during the McCarthy Era," *Science and Society* 60, no. 4 (1996): 393–426.

28. Schrecker, "Immigration and Internal Security," 401.

29. Schrecker, "Immigration and Internal Security," 403.

30. U.S. Congress, House, Committee on the Judiciary, *Supervision and Detention of Certain Aliens: Hearings before Subcommittee No. 2*, 77th Cong., 1st sess., 1941, 103.

31. In the 1950 case of *Wong Yang Sung v. McGrath*, the Supreme Court ruled that the Administrative Procedure Act did apply to the INS. *Wong Yang Sung v. McGrath*, 339 U.S. 33 (1950); Joanna Grisinger, *The Unwieldy American State: Administrative Politics since the New Deal* (New York: Cambridge University Press, 2012), 83.

32. The American Committee for Protection of Foreign Born adamantly denied being communist-affiliated—it began as a branch of the ACLU, founded in 1933. Rachel Ida Buff argues that though the ACPFB defended members of the Communist Party USA, it also "worked . . . to defend a democratic vision of the United States that was the creation of a broad coalition that included many foreign-born activists," some of whom were fleeing communism. Buff, *Against the Deportation Terror*, 14.

33. Kraut, *Threat of Dissent*, 95.

34. Internal Security Act of 1950, 64 Stat. 987 (Pub. L. 81-831).

35. "127 Now Held on Ellis Island under New Security Act," *New York Times*, Oct. 10, 1950.

36. Masumi Izumi, "Prohibiting 'American Concentration Camps,'" *Pacific Historical Review* 74, no. 2 (2005): 169–70; *Korematsu v. United States*, 323 U.S. 214 (1944).

37. Kraut, *Threat of Dissent*, 127.

38. Recent scholarship by Katherine Reed examining graffiti in Ellis Island detention buildings compellingly argues against dismissing pre-1924 Ellis Island detention as "marginal," despite the relatively low number of migrants affected. Katherine Reed, "'The Prison, by God, Where I Have Found Myself': Graffiti at Ellis Island Immigration Station, New York, c. 1900–1923," *Journal of American Ethnic History* 38, no. 3 (2019): 8.

39. For example, "Consul Tells of Difficulty."

40. Frances W. Kerr, *Immigration and Naturalization Service Monthly Review*, Ellis Island, May 1949; Brianna Nofil, "Ellis Island's Forgotten Final Act as a Cold War Detention Center," *Atlas Obscura*, Feb. 2, 2016, https://www.atlasobscura.com/articles/ellis-islands-forgotten-final-act-as-a-cold-war-detention-center.

41. Blake Ehrlich, "Inside Ellis Island," *New York Herald Tribune*, Nov. 26, 1950.

42. "Germans Raise Clamor as Press Sees Ellis Island," *New York Herald Tribune*, March 19, 1948; Joseph J. Ryan, "Ellis Island Myth Exploded in Tour," *New York Times*, April 8, 1949.

43. Letter to Tom Clark, Feb. 25, 1948, Box 20, American Committee for Protection of Foreign Born Papers, University of Michigan Library, Special Collections Research Center (hereafter ACPFB).

44. "U.S. Judge Frees 4 Accused Aliens on Bail of $3,500," *New York Times*, March 7, 1948.

45. "U.S. Judge Frees 4 Accused Aliens on Bail of $3,500."

46. See Buff, *Against the Deportation Terror*, 27–52.

47. Political scientist V. O. Key would also note the pattern of Southern support for legislation like the Hobbs bill, identifying the Hobbs bill as one of three "nonrace issues . . . that set the South against the rest of the country." Key writes that the South, a region with few immigrants, "lacked sympathy for the alien ordered deported," while the bill faced resistance from non-Southern Democrats and Republicans. Valdimer Orlando Key Jr., *Southern Politics in State and Nation* (New York: Alfred A. Knopf, 1949), 373.

48. Eisler was joined in his strike by Jamaican immigrant Ferdinand Smith; a circular produced by the hunger strike's supporters called him "labor's most prominent Negro leader." Gerald Horne, *Red Seas: Ferdinand Smith and Radical Black Sailors in the United States and Jamaica* (New York: New York University Press, 2009), 203.

49. Letter from Claudia Jones, *Daily Worker*, Nov. 8, 1950.

50. C.L.R. James, *Mariners, Renegades, and Castaways: The Story of Herman Melville and the World We Live In* (Hanover, N.H.: University Press of New England, 2001), 54.

51. For an examination of James's and Jones's intellectual work while in deportation proceedings, see Joseph Keith, *Unbecoming Americans: Writing Race and Nation from the Shadows of Citizenship, 1945–1960* (New Brunswick, N.J.: Rutgers University Press, 2013).

52. Fred Jerome, *The Einstein File: J. Edgar Hoover's Secret War against the World's Most Famous Scientist* (New York: Macmillan, 2003), 108–9.

53. Pfeiffer escaped Europe after nearly seven years in a Soviet-run forced labor camp in Poland, which primarily detained former Nazi affiliates. Though a member of the Hitler Youth, Pfeiffer had been placed in the gulag at around eleven years old. See CIA Information Report, Escape of German Prisoner from Forced Labor Camp (Declassified), June 18, 1952, Report No. 00-8-52155.

54. "Ellis Island—So Near Yet So Far for Aliens," *Los Angeles Times*, July 12, 1953.

55. Charles D. Weisselberg, "The Exclusion and Detention of Aliens: Lessons from the Lives of Ellen Knauff and Ignatz Mezei," *University of Pennsylvania Law Review* 143, no. 4 (1995): 985.

56. *Knauff v. Shaughnessy*, 338 U.S. 537, 539 (1950).

57. *Knauff v. Shaughnessy*, 338 U.S. 537, 540.

58. The charges against Knauff were never made explicitly clear. However, the gist of the allegations was that Knauff was formerly a paid agent of the Czechoslovak government and had reported on American personnel assigned to the Civil Censorship Division in Germany. Weisselberg, "Exclusion and Detention of Aliens," 960.

59. *Knauff v. Shaughnessy*, 338 U.S. 537, 540.

60. Ellen Raphael Knauff, *The Ellen Knauff Story* (New York: W. W. Norton, 1952), xiii.

61. *Knauff v. Shaughnessy*, 338 U.S. 537, 542; *Nishimura Ekiu v. United States*, 142 U.S. 651 (1892).

62. *Knauff v. Shaughnessy*, 338 U.S. 537, 544.

63. Andrea Friedman, *Citizenship in Cold War America: The National Security State and the Possibilities of Dissent* (Amherst: University of Massachusetts Press, 2014), 49.

64. U.S. Congress, House, Committee on the Judiciary, *Exclusion of Ellen Knauff: Hearings before Subcommittee No. 1, Committee on the Judiciary*, 88th Cong., 2d sess., 1950; Knauff, *Ellen Knauff Story*, xv.

65. "Mrs. Knauff Leaves Ellis Island after Winning Fight to Enter U.S.," *New York Times*, Nov. 3, 1951.

66. Weisselberg, "Exclusion and Detention of Aliens," 964.

67. "Federal Jail to Open Today," *Los Angeles Times*, May 26, 1938.

68. Each of these individuals had a rich personal history of activism beyond the scope of this case. Of the four, David Hyun has received the most scholarly attention. See Cindy I-Fen Cheng, *Citizens of Asian America: Democracy and Race during the Cold War* (New York: New York University Press, 2013), 127–35; Buff, *Against the Deportation Terror*, 150–68.

69. Justice Frankfurter to Justice Jackson, Feb. 23, 1952, Box 49, Felix Frankfurter Papers, Harvard Law School Library, Historical and Special Collections.

70. Justice Jackson to Justice Frankfurter, Feb. 25, 1952, Box 49, Felix Frankfurter Papers, Harvard Law School Library, Historical and Special Collections.

71. *Carlson v. Landon*, 342 U.S. 524, 538 (1952).

72. Schrecker, "Immigration and Internal Security," 411.

73. See Brianna Nofil, "Notes on Detention Camp," *Topic*, July 5, 2017.

74. Ellen D. Wu, *The Color of Success: Asian Americans and the Origins of the Model Minority* (Princeton, N.J.: Princeton University Press, 2013), 111–44.

75. Pegler-Gordon, *Closing the Golden Door*, 204–5.

76. "More Room for Immigrants, Sept. 25, 1948," Box 481, American Civil Liberties Union of Northern California Records, California Historical Society.

77. "Immigration Check Will Be Speeded," *SF Chronicle*, Sept. 4, 1947.

78. Jack Foisie, "Chinese Immigration—Wixon Gives Admission Figures," *SF Chronicle*, Sept. 25, 1948.

79. Xiaojian Zhao, *Remaking Chinese America: Immigration, Family, and Community, 1940–1965* (New Brunswick, N.J.: Rutgers University Press, 2002), 85.

80. I. F. Wixon to W. F. Kelly, Sept. 21, 1948, File 1300/078976, Immigration and Deportation Investigation Case Files, 1944–1955, RG 85, NARA, San Francisco.

81. Jack Foisie, "Chinese Side of the Immigration Problem," *SF Chronicle*, Sept. 26, 1948.

82. "Chinese Bride of Ex-GI Kills Self," *SF News*, Sept. 21, 1948.

83. "Reunion in S.F.," *SF Chronicle*, June 3, 1948.

84. George Draper, "Suicide Leap Is Prevented," *SF Chronicle*, June 2, 1948.

85. Chinese News Service Special Release, Sept. 28, 1948, quoting *Chinese Pacific Weekly*, Sept. 25, 1948, Box 481, Folder "Aliens/INS Detention and Registration," American Civil Liberties Union of Northern California Records, California Historical Society.

86. "Immigrants Go on Hunger Strike," *SF Chronicle*, Sept. 22, 1948.

87. I. F. Wixon to W. F. Kelly, Sept. 21, 1948.

88. U.S. Immigration and Naturalization Service, "Manual of Instructions for Detention Officers," 1955, 4–12, U.S. Citizenship and Immigration Services Library (hereafter USCIS Library).

89. Ngai, *Impossible Subjects*, 237.

90. Zolberg, *Nation by Design*, 311.

91. For example, César Cuauhtémoc García Hernández, *Migrating to Prison: America's Obsession with Locking Up Immigrants* (New York: New Press, 2019), 17; Wilsher, *Immigration Detention*, 64–65.

92. Mary L. Dudziak, *Cold War Civil Rights: Race and the Image of American Democracy* (Princeton, N.J.: Princeton University Press, 2011).

93. Arnold, "How Immigration Detention Became Exceptional," 312. On deinstitutionalization, see Anne E. Parsons, *From Asylum to Prison: Deinstitutionalization and the Rise of Mass Incarceration after 1945* (Chapel Hill: University of North Carolina Press, 2018).

94. U.S. Congress, House, President's Commission on Immigration and Naturalization, *Hearings before the President's Commission on Immigration and Naturalization*, 82nd Cong., 2d sess., 1952, 997; Rene de la Pedraja, *A Historical Dictionary of the U.S. Merchant Marine and Shipping Industry* (Westport, Conn.: Greenwood Press, 1994), 178.

95. The 1891 Immigration Act stated "[that] all aliens who may unlawfully come to the United States shall, if practicable, be immediately sent back on the vessel by which they were brought in. The cost of their maintenance while on land, as well as the expense of the return of such aliens, shall be borne by the owner or owners of the vessel on which such aliens came." See Ethan Blue, "Finding Margins on Borders: Shipping Firms and Immigration Control across Settler Space," *Occasion: Interdisciplinary Studies in the Humanities* 5 (2013), https://arcade

.stanford.edu/occasion/finding-margins-borders-shipping-firms-and-immigration-control
-across-settler-space.

96. Prescott Farnsworth Hall, *Immigration and Its Effects Upon the United States* (New York: Henry Holt, 1906), 227.

97. "Steamship Companies Protest," *New York Times*, Dec. 19, 1894.

98. "1¼ Years on Ellis Island," *New York Times*, Aug. 12, 1953.

99. Harry S. Truman, "Veto of Bill to Revise the Laws Relating to Immigration, Naturalization, and Nationality," June 25, 1952, online by Gerhard Peters and John T. Woolley, American Presidency Project, https://www.presidency.ucsb.edu/node/231060.

100. Ghosh, "Worst Kind of Prison in the World," 73.

101. Immigration and Nationality Act of 1952, Pub. L. No. 82-414, § 242(d) (1952).

102. Immigration and Naturalization Service San Francisco Speech, Box 47, Folder 16, ACPFB.

103. Supervisory Parole, Box 1, Folder 2, Records of the American Committee for Protection of Foreign Born, Tamiment Library/Robert F. Wagner Labor Archives, New York University.

104. Clara Gelman to Abner Green, Box 47, Folder 16, ACPFB. The most severe elements of supervisory parole were reined in over the coming years. In 1956, the Supreme Court heard the case of Antonia Sentner. Under her initial parole sanction, Sentner was forbidden to speak to anyone with a Communist Party affiliation, including her husband. In its ruling, the Court reaffirmed that supervisory parole was constitutional as an auxiliary to deportation power but that it could not supervise a person's political activities, associations, or communications. Sentner's case came soon after another similar Supreme Court decision regarding George I. Witkovich, who had been held under criminal charges for willful failure "to give information" to the INS. *Barton v. Sentner*, 353 U.S. 963 (1957); *United States v. Witkovich*, 353 U.S. 194, 209 (1957).

105. *Annual Report of the Immigration and Naturalization Service 1953–1954* (Washington, D.C.: Government Printing Office, 1954), 36.

106. Herbert Brownell Jr., "Humanizing the Administration of the Immigration Law," speech, New York City, Jan. 26, 1955, U.S. Department of Justice, https://www.justice.gov/sites/default/files/ag/legacy/2011/09/12/01-26-1955.pdf.

107. Brownell was also careful to note that migrants were generally not being detained in jails but, instead, in "a Service or hotel facility." Statement of Honorable Herbert Brownell Jr., Attorney General of the United States, prepared for delivery before Subcommittee on Immigration of Committee on the Judiciary, April 13, 1956, https://www.justice.gov/sites/default/files/ag/legacy/2011/09/12/04-13-1956%20pro.pdf.

108. Deportation: Detention in Prisons, 1954, American Civil Liberties Union Records: Subgroup 2, Subject Files Series, Box 830, Folder 13, Public Policy Papers, Department of Rare Books and Special Collections, Princeton University Library; Edward Shaughnessy, letter to the editor, *New York Times*, Nov. 24, 1954.

109. "Ends Detention Pact," *New York Times*, Nov. 27, 1954.

110. Joseph J. Ryan, "Detained Aliens Lodged in Hotel as U.S. Ends Housing Them in Jail," *New York Times*, Dec. 10, 1954.

111. Goodman, *Deportation Machine*, 52.

112. Discourses of security on the southern border were long-standing. In the wake of the Mexican Revolution, concern about displaced persons fleeing over the border led to new

passport controls and inspections in the 1917 immigration law. In the 1930s and 1940s, authorities targeted the Mexican "illegal alien" as a criminal threat who required extensive policing and, ultimately, removal via mass roundups and repatriations. Julian Lim, *Porous Borders: Multiracial Migrations and the Law in the U.S.-Mexico Borderlands* (Chapel Hill: University of North Carolina Press, 2017), 162; Max Felker-Kantor, "Latinx Criminality," in *Oxford Research Encyclopedia of American History*, June 20, 2022, https://doi.org/10.1093/acrefore/9780199329175.013.651.

113. Kang, *INS on the Line*, 133.

114. The INS reported that detention length went from an average of 5.2 days in 1953 to 2.5 days in 1954. *Annual Report of the Immigration and Naturalization Service 1953–1954*, 37. There were certainly exceptions where detentions stretched on for much longer periods; see Jessica Ordaz, *The Shadow of El Centro: A History of Migrant Incarceration and Solidarity* (Chapel Hill: University of North Carolina Press, 2021), 21. For a granular account of how many migrants were detained and deported in one border city, see Immigration U.S. Prisoners, Jail Registers, Records of El Paso County Sheriff, El Paso County Records, C. L. Sonnichsen Special Collections Department, University of Texas at El Paso Library. Particularly striking in these logbooks is the number of migrants who were apprehended, booked into a detention site, and deported in the same day.

115. Goodman, *Deportation Machine*, 53.

116. Judith Irangika Dingatantrige Perera, "From Exclusion to State Violence: The Transformation of Noncitizen Detention in the United States and Its Implications in Arizona, 1891–Present" (Ph.D. diss., Arizona State University, 2018), 116–17.

117. Brownell, "Humanizing the Administration of the Immigration Law."

118. On the Bracero Program, see Mireya Loza, *Defiant Braceros: How Migrant Workers Fought for Racial, Sexual, and Political Freedom* (Chapel Hill: University of North Carolina Press, 2016); Deborah Cohen, *Braceros: Migrant Citizens and Transnational Subjects in the Postwar United States and Mexico* (Chapel Hill: University of North Carolina Press, 2011); Calavita, *Inside the State*.

119. Richard Gage, "County Jailers, with Big Don Lemme as Chief Handle 2,600 Prisoners per Year," *Rock Island Argus*, Nov. 18, 1953; Lyle Downing, "Agents Caught Them in Secret Raids on Ranches, Camps, Hobo Jungles," *Herald and News* (Klamath Falls, Oreg.), Oct. 28, 1953.

120. On Jamaican guest workers and farm labor in the Pacific Northwest, see Cindy Hahamovitch, *No Man's Land: Jamaican Guestworkers in America and the Global History of Deportable Labor* (Princeton, N.J.: Princeton University Press, 2011); Erasmo Gamboa, *Mexican Labor and World War II: Braceros in the Pacific Northwest, 1942–1947* (Austin: University of Texas Press, 1990).

121. Ngai, *Impossible Subjects*, 155.

122. Ngai, *Impossible Subjects*, 156.

123. Hernández, *Migra!* 156.

124. This was a 160 percent increase over the previous year. *Annual Report of the Immigration and Naturalization Service 1953–1954*, 36.

125. Alan Eladio Gómez, *The Revolutionary Imaginations of Greater Mexico: Chicana/o Radicalism, Solidarity Politics, and Latin American Social Movements* (Austin: University of Texas Press, 2016), 32–34; Kang, *INS on the Line*, 96–97.

126. Gladwin Hill, "'Wetback' Influx near the Record," *New York Times*, Nov. 22, 1953. Despite this rhetoric, from the 1950s to the 1970s "criminal aliens" accounted for only 5 percent of all

272 NOTES TO CHAPTER 4

deportations. Jennifer Cullison, "Valle de inmigrantes enjaulados: Castigo, protesta y la aparición del Centro de Detención Puerto Isabel," *Tabula Rasa* 33 (2020): 235.

127. Bera Casey, "County Jails along Mexican Border," *Prison World* 11, no. 5 (Sept.–Oct. 1949): 8.

128. Dwight D. Eisenhower, "Annual Message to the Congress on the State of the Union," Jan. 6, 1955, online by Gerhard Peters and John T. Woolley, American Presidency Project, https://www.presidency.ucsb.edu/node/233954.

129. On Chinese incarceration in New Mexico's jails, see Box 1, Folder 10, United States Marshal (New Mexico) Records, University of New Mexico Center for Southwest Research and Special Collections, Albuquerque; on earlier incarceration in Pima County, see Perera, "From Exclusion to State Violence," 89–90.

130. Ben A. Parker, interview by Douglas V. Meed, July 25, 1984, Interview 661, Transcript, University of Texas at El Paso Institute of Oral History.

131. Judith Irangika Dingatantrige Perera has done remarkable work collating receipts from several Arizona counties to illustrate how their revenue from migrant incarceration changed over time. Perera shows that by 1974 Pima County was making $457,896.12 for the keep of federal prisoners. Perera, "From Exclusion to State Violence," 148–50.

132. S. C. Warman, "Current Campaign Takes Heavy Toll in This Area," *Tucson Citizen*, June 16, 1953.

133. Sheriff Fletcher to U.S. Marshal, Jan. 4, 1936, Box 21, Folder 18, United States Marshal (New Mexico) Records, University of New Mexico Center for Southwest Research and Special Collections, Albuquerque.

134. "County Heads to Discuss Jail Changes," *Corpus Christi Caller-Times*, April 10, 1951.

135. Guy McNamara to Chris P. Fox, July 8, 1941, Box 3, Folder 51, Chris P. Fox Papers, C. L. Sonnichsen Special Collections Department, University of Texas at El Paso Library.

136. "Sheriff Issues Request to Eliminate Alien Camp," *Brownsville Herald*, Dec. 9, 1957.

137. "Fleming Gets Commendation on County Jail," *Brownsville Herald*, July 24, 1952.

138. "Court Okehs $18,000 for Jail Expansion," *The Monitor* (McAllen, Tex.), April 19, 1949.

139. *Corpus Christi Caller-Times*, July 27, 1956.

140. Lim, *Porous Borders*, 172.

141. U.S. Congress, House, Department of Justice, Subcommittee of House Committee on Appropriations, *Appropriation Bill for 1937*, 74th Cong., 2d sess., 1936, 208.

142. U.S. Department of Justice, *Federal Offenders—1940* (Fort Leavenworth, Kans.: Federal Prison Industries, Inc. Press, 1941), 186.

143. Hernández, *City of Inmates*, 141.

144. Bern Berard, "Detention Facilities along the Mexican Border," *INS Monthly Review* 9, no. 3 (Sept. 1951): 32–33.

145. "Alien Detention Camp Site Announced at Brownsville," *Austin Statesman*, June 17, 1952.

146. "Proposed Alien Camp Draws Fire," *Brownsville Herald*, June 4, 1952; "You Name 'Em for Five Bucks," *Valley Morning Star* (Harlingen, Tex.), June 11, 1952; "Construction on Rancho Rooney to Begin Thursday," *Brownsville Herald*, June 24, 1952.

147. "Prizes Coming Up," *Brownsville Herald*, June 15, 1952.

148. "Bentsen Raps Airlift as Useless," *The Monitor* (McAllen, Tex.), June 10, 1952.

149. Third Supplemental Appropriation Bill, 1952, H.R. 2017, 82d Cong., 2d sess., *Congressional Record* 98, pt. 5 (1952): 6632.

150. "Texas Revolution," *Odessa American*, June 18, 1952.

151. John Weber, *From South Texas to the Nation: The Exploitation of Mexican Labor in the Twentieth Century* (Chapel Hill: University of North Carolina Press, 2015), 210; Kang, *INS on the Line*, 125–27.

152. Sen. Rooney speaking on H.R. 2017, June 5, 1952, 82d Cong., 2d sess., *Congressional Record* 98, pt. 5 (1952): 6633.

153. *Annual Report of the Immigration and Naturalization Service 1952–1953* (Washington, D.C.: Government Printing Office, 1953), 48.

154. Young, *Forever Prisoners*, 86–118.

155. Selfa A. Chew, *Uprooting Community: Japanese Mexicans, World War II, and the U.S.-Mexico Borderlands* (Tucson: University of Arizona Press, 2015), 156.

156. Pete Wittenberg, "Detention Center Awaits End as Barracks Stand Deserted," *The Monitor* (McAllen, Tex.), Aug. 22, 1965. El Centro Immigration Detention Camp was constructed from structures originally part of the Fort Stanton Internment Camp, which had held Germans and, briefly, Japanese Americans. Japanese American detainees were employed in tearing down and moving the camp. Ordaz, *Shadow of El Centro*, 11–18.

157. "Officials Won't Talk on Rumors," *The Monitor* (McAllen, Tex.), July 16, 1954.

158. David V. Blackwell, Oral History Interviews, Border Patrol Museum, https://borderpatrolmuseum.com/oral-history-interviews/; Goodman, *Deportation Machine*, 81.

159. Goodman, *Deportation Machine*, 83.

160. Goodman, *Deportation Machine*, 80.

161. Ordaz, *Shadow of El Centro*, 57.

162. "Wetbacks Pay for Deportation," *The Monitor* (McAllen, Tex.), July 18, 1954.

163. "Wetbacks Pay for Deportation."

164. Jennifer L. Cullison, "The Growth of Immigrant Caging in Postwar America: National Immigration Policy Choices, Regional Shifts toward Greater Carceral Control, and Continuing Legal Resistance in the US and South Texas" (Ph.D. diss., University of Colorado Boulder, 2018), 351–54.

165. Department of Justice Circular No. 2124, Rules and Regulations of the Maintenance of Federal Prisoners in State and County Institutions, Box 21, Folder 7, United States Marshal (New Mexico) Records, University of New Mexico Center for Southwest Research and Special Collections, Albuquerque.

166. See Lan Cao, "Made in the USA: Race, Trade, and Prison Labor," *New York University Review of Law and Social Change* 43 (2019): 1.

167. "Don't Pay Your Wetbacks; The Border Patrol Doesn't," editorial, *Brownsville Herald*, March 3, 1955.

168. Cullison, "Valle de inmigrantes enjaulados," 243.

169. E. V. Ayala, interview by Rodolfo Mares, April 28, 1976, Interview 230, Transcript, University of Texas at El Paso Institute of Oral History.

170. Ordaz, *Shadow of El Centro*, 30.

171. Knauff, *Ellen Knauff Story*, 42.

172. "New Crime Plan Step toward Detention Camps?" *Baltimore Afro-American*, Feb. 11, 1969.

173. The Bail Reform Act of 1984, Pub. L. No. 98-473, 98 Stat. 1985 (codified at 18 U.S.C. §§ 3142[f]).

174. Wittenberg, "Detention Center Awaits End as Barracks Stand Deserted."

175. On Port Isabel's origins and early years of operation, see Cullison, "Valle de inmigrantes enjaulados."

176. Cullison, "Growth of Immigrant Caging in Postwar America," 311–14.

5. Disorderly Expansion: Resisting Detention in the 1970s

1. "65 Haitian Refugees Make It to the U.S.," *Washington Post*, Dec. 13, 1972.

2. Pat Gurosky, "Haitian Refugees May Be Freed Soon," *Miami News*, Oct. 3, 1973.

3. Kristina Shull, *Detention Empire: Reagan's War on Immigrants and the Seeds of Resistance* (Chapel Hill: University of North Carolina Press, 2022); Lindskoog, *Detain and Punish*; Jenna M. Loyd and Alison Mountz, *Boats, Borders, and Bases: Race, the Cold War, and the Rise of Migration Detention in the United States* (Oakland: University of California Press, 2018).

4. Tichenor, *Dividing Lines*, 222–23.

5. On the relationship between racism and the war on drugs, see Elizabeth Hinton, *From the War on Poverty to the War on Crime: The Making of Mass Incarceration in America* (Cambridge, Mass.: Harvard University Press, 2016); Donna Murch, "Crack in Los Angeles: Crisis, Militarization, and Black Response to the Late Twentieth-Century War on Drugs," *Journal of American History* 102, no. 1 (2015): 162–73; Julilly Kohler-Hausmann, "'The Attila the Hun Law': New York's Rockefeller Drug Laws and the Making of a Punitive State," *Journal of Social History* 44, no. 1 (2010): 71–95; David Farber, ed., *The War on Drugs: A History* (New York: New York University Press, 2022).

6. Gulasekaram and Ramakrishnan, *New Immigration Federalism*, 68.

7. Donald F. Kettl, *The Divided States of America: Why Federalism Doesn't Work* (Princeton, N.J.: Princeton University Press, 2020), 175.

8. On the bipartisan consensus over crime policy across the second half of the twentieth century, see Naomi Murakawa, *The First Civil Right: How Liberals Built Prison America* (New York: Oxford University Press, 2014).

9. Lee, *America for Americans*, 223–24.

10. Lee, *America for Americans*, 224.

11. Jane Hong, "The Law that Created Illegal Immigration," *Los Angeles Times*, Oct. 2, 2015.

12. Ngai, *Impossible Subjects*, 227–28.

13. Leonard F. Chapman, commissioner of the INS, used the phrase "silent invasion" in a 1976 article in *Reader's Digest*. He wrote, "When I became commissioner of the Immigration and Naturalization Service (INS) in 1973, we were out-manned, under-budgeted, and confronted by a growing, silent invasion of illegal aliens. . . . At least 250,000 to 500,000 more arrive each year. Together they are milking the U.S. taxpayer of $13 billion annually by taking away jobs from legal residents and forcing them into unemployment; by illegally acquiring welfare benefits and public services; by avoiding taxes." Leonard F. Chapman, "Illegal Aliens: Time to Call a Halt!" *Reader's Digest*, Oct. 1976, 188–89. Sociologist Douglas Massey notes that Chapman's numbers were "entirely made up" but politically useful. See Douglas S. Massey, Jorge Durand, and Karen A. Pren, "Why Border Enforcement Backfired," *American Journal of Sociology* 121, no. 5 (2016): 1557–600.

14. Lee, *America for Americans*, 255.

15. The budget cut was recommended to Congress by the Office of Management and Budget in October 1974. Concurrently with the budget cuts, President Ford established a Domestic Council Committee on Illegal Aliens. In March 1975, Congress made a $1.3 million appropriation to the INS after cities, including Los Angeles and Houston, reported bringing their migrant apprehensions to a standstill due to lack of funding. See Frank del Olmo, "Alien Arrests to Be Resumed," *Los Angeles Times*, March 12, 1975. On the Ford administration's immigration policy, see Daniel J. Tichenor, "Strange Bedfellows: The Politics and Pathologies of Immigration Reform," *Labor* 5, no. 2 (2008): 47–49.

16. U.S. Congress, House, Committee on the Judiciary, *Oversight of INS Programs and Activities: Hearings before the Subcommittee on Immigration, Citizenship, and International Law*, 95th Cong., 1st and 2d sess., 1978, 102.

17. Elizabeth Hinton, *America on Fire: The Untold History of Police Violence and Black Rebellion since the 1960s* (New York: Liveright Publishing, 2021).

18. Newport, "Jail America," 168.

19. See, e.g., *Slavik v. Miller*, 89 F. Supp. 575, 576 (W.D. Pa. 1950).

20. Felker-Kantor, "Latinx Criminality," 15–16; Nicholas P. De Genova, "Migrant 'Illegality' and Deportability in Everyday Life," *Annual Review of Anthropology* 31 (2002): 419–47.

21. U.S. Congress, House, Committee on the Judiciary, *Oversight of INS Programs and Activities*, 146.

22. "Vegas Stops Jailing Aliens; Out of Funds," *Los Angeles Times*, Jan. 3, 1975.

23. "Illegal Alien Arrests Rise Despite Fund Cut," *The Times* (San Mateo, Calif.), Feb. 13, 1975.

24. Mark Oliva, "O'Callaghan Hits Halt on Alien Deportation," *Reno Gazette-Journal*, Jan. 3, 1975.

25. In California, the attorney general issued a statement saying that local police could arrest for misdemeanors even if they were federal violations. Thus, some California officers arrested immigrants based on Section 275 of 18 U.S.C. 1325, which made unlawful entry a misdemeanor—a precedent that dated back to 1929. Mary Barber, "Illegal Aliens Problem Clouded by Legal, Moral Maze," *Los Angeles Times*, Oct. 28, 1976.

26. Coleman, *Walls Within*, 145–46.

27. "Police Pick Up Suspected Aliens."

28. *IMC v. David Vandersall*, Complaint, Box 447, Folder 3, American Civil Liberties Union, Illinois Division Records, Special Collections Research Center, University of Chicago Library.

29. Julie Kracke, "Terminology Works against Migrants," *The Dispatch* (Moline, Ill.), Aug. 15, 1976.

30. Frank del Olmo, "Bell Will Remind Police Not to Overstep Authority," *Los Angeles Times*, June 22, 1979.

31. Barber, "Illegal Aliens Problem Clouded by Legal, Moral Maze."

32. Max Felker-Kantor, *Policing Los Angeles: Race, Resistance, and the Rise of the LAPD* (Chapel Hill: University of North Carolina Press, 2018), 162–63.

33. U.S. Congress, Senate, Committee on Public Works, *Repairs and Alterations Prospectuses: Hearing before the Subcommittee on Buildings and Grounds*, 95th Cong., 1st sess., 1977, 83.

34. Toussaint Losier, "Against 'Law and Order' Lockup: The 1970 NYC Jail Rebellions," *Race and Class* 59, no. 1 (2017): 28.

35. U.S. Congress, House, Committee on the Judiciary, *Oversight of INS Programs and Activities*, 143.

36. U.S. Congress, House, Committee on the Judiciary, *Oversight of INS Programs and Activities*, 124.

37. On policing and Philadelphia, see Timothy J. Lombardo, *Blue-Collar Conservatism: Frank Rizzo's Philadelphia and Populist Politics* (Philadelphia: University of Pennsylvania Press, 2018).

38. The INS district office in Boston elaborated on the "hostility" in a 1974 report: "During a recent operation in the New England area agents of INS who apprehended 24 illegal aliens and returned with them to the Boston district office at 6 o'clock in the evening were still there at 4 o'clock the following morning because they were trying to make arrangements for the detention of the aliens. These same agents were reporting back to work at 8 o'clock that morning." U.S. Congress, House, Committee on Government Operations, *Interim Report on Immigration and Naturalization Service Regional Office Operations*, 93rd Cong., 2d sess., 1974, 47.

39. U.S. Congress, House, Committee on the Judiciary, *Oversight of INS Programs and Activities*, 130.

40. U.S. Congress, House, Committee on the Judiciary, *Oversight of INS Programs and Activities*, 102.

41. Jeff South, "Government Shuns Jump in Jail Fee," *Lubbock Avalanche-Journal*, Sept. 28, 1977.

42. This arrangement was likely created because the Border Patrol threatened that its office might be forced to close if Lubbock could not find appropriate detention space. See Jeff South, "U.S. Border Patrol May Close Local Station," *Lubbock Avalanche-Journal*, July 12, 1977.

43. *Ortega v. Rowe*, 796 F.2d 765, 766 (5th Cir. 1986).

44. Debra Whitney Stalter, "Inmate Tells of Filth in Jail," *Lubbock Evening Journal*, Sept. 20, 1983.

45. *Ortega v. Rowe*, 796 F.2d 765, 769.

46. *Ortega v. Rowe*, 796 F.2d 765, 769.

47. On litigation against detention conditions, see Margaret H. Taylor, "Detained Aliens Challenging Conditions of Confinement and the Porous Border of the Plenary Power Doctrine," *Hastings Constitutional Law Quarterly* 22, no. 4 (1995): 1087–158.

48. For data on coyote usage, see Massey et al., "Why Border Enforcement Backfired."

49. U.S. Congress, House, Committee on the Judiciary, *Oversight of INS Programs and Activities*, 39.

50. Jeffrey Kaye, "Illegal Aliens in Jail for Weeks as Witnesses, Not Criminals," *Washington Post*, Aug. 12, 1979. Though the federal government prioritized placing material witnesses in federal facilities where possible, it still used more than ninety county jails to hold witnesses, particularly those apprehended in rural areas. John M. Crewdson, "Border Sweeps of Illegal Aliens Leave Scores of Children in Jails," *New York Times*, Aug. 4, 1980.

51. Narda Zacchino, "INS Locks Up Illegal Aliens in Dark Warehouse," *Los Angeles Times*, Nov. 11, 1977.

52. U.S. Congress, House, Committee on the Judiciary, *Bureau of Prisons Pre-trial Detention Program: Hearings before the Subcommittee on Courts, Civil Liberties, and the Administration of Justice*, 95th Cong., 2d sess., 1978; U.S. Department of Justice, *Federal Bureau of Prison Annual Report 1975* (Washington, D.C.: Government Printing Office, 1975), 8–10.

53. Crewdson, "Border Sweeps of Illegal Aliens Leave Scores of Children in Jails." On migrant children as material witnesses, see Ivón Padilla-Rodriguez, "'A Violation of the Most Elementary

Human Rights of Children': The Rise of Migrant Youth Detention and Family Separation in the American West," in *The North American West in the Twenty-first Century*, ed. Brenden W. Rensink (Lincoln: University of Nebraska Press, 2022), 199–219; Erin Mysogland, "'Where's Your Birth Certificate, Pilgrim?' Analyzing Double Age in Immigration Policing and Chicano Community Organizing, 1975–1985," *Journal of the History of Childhood and Youth* 15, no. 3 (2022): 422–33.

54. Herman Baca to Jimmy Carter, Feb. 28, 1980, Box 25, Folder 1, Herman Baca Papers, University of California San Diego Special Collections.

55. "Kids in Prison, April 1980," Box 25, Folder 1, Herman Baca Papers, University of California San Diego Special Collections.

56. U.S. Congress, House, Committee on the Judiciary, *Oversight of INS Programs and Activities*, 141–42.

57. U.S. Commission on Civil Rights, *Immigration Policy and Procedure, Volume II: Exhibits, Hearing before the United States Commission on Civil Rights* (Washington, D.C.: Government Printing Office, 1978), 374.

58. Immigration and Naturalization Service Investigations Division, "A Briefing Paper: Alien Absconders: Strategies for Service Adoption," Dec. 11, 1984, USCIS Library. The INS did note as a drawback that "this amendment may be perceived as too stringently enforcement minded."

59. Bon Tempo, *Americans at the Gate*, 1.

60. Bon Tempo, *Americans at the Gate*, 60–85.

61. Gil Loescher and John A. Scanlan, *Calculated Kindness: Refugees and America's Half-Open Door* (New York: Free Press, 1986), 41.

62. Bon Tempo, *Americans at the Gate*, 5.

63. Lindskoog, *Detain and Punish*, 16.

64. Bon Tempo, *Americans at the Gate*, 86–87.

65. On the origins and evolution of the Tonton Macoute, see Elizabeth Abbott, *Haiti: The Duvaliers and Their Legacy* (New York: Touchstone, 1991); Jeb Sprague, *Paramilitarism and the Assault on Democracy in Haiti* (New York: New York University Press, 2012); Alex Dupuy, *The Prophet and Power: Jean-Bertrand Aristide, the International Community, and Haiti* (New York: Rowman and Littlefield Publishers, 2006).

66. U.S. Congress, House, Committee on the Judiciary, *Caribbean Refugee Crisis: Cubans and Haitians*, 96th Cong., 2d sess., 1980, 55.

67. Homer Bigart, "U.S. Envoy Favors More Aid to Haiti," *New York Times*, April 26, 1971.

68. Benjamin Welles, "U.S. Cautiously Seeking Better Haitian Relations," *New York Times*, Aug. 15, 1971.

69. Amnesty International Report 1976—Plaintiff's Exhibit 331, Box 9, Folder 9, Ira Gollobin Haitian Refugee Collection, Manuscripts, Archives, and Rare Books Division, Schomburg Center for Research in Black Culture, New York Public Library (hereafter IGHRC).

70. *Haitian Refugee Center v. Civiletti*, 503 F. Supp. 442, 509 (1980).

71. "All aliens without proper documentation evidencing prior authorization to enter the United States—excludable aliens—are initially detained if they come to the attention of INS. Some aliens volunteer to leave; others apply for admission and either are further detained or paroled into the United States until a decision is made by INS as to their admissibility." U.S. Government Accountability Office, "Detention Policies Affecting Haitian Nationals," Report No. GAO/GGD-83-68, June 16, 1983, 6.

72. "Haitian Refugee Ruling Expected to Cause Ripples," *Orlando Sentinel*, July 3, 1980.

73. Susan L. Marquis, *I Am Not a Tractor! How Florida Farmworkers Took on the Fast Food Giants and Won* (Ithaca, N.Y.: ILR Press, 2017), 7.

74. Mary Paluch, "Reveal Poor Conditions at Collier County Stockade," *Naples Daily News*, March 23, 1971.

75. Bill Whiting, "Haitians Crowd Stockade, Yield Handsome Profit," *Miami Herald*, Sept. 19, 1975.

76. Pat Gurosky, "Haitians Ordered out of Jail," *Miami News*, June 28, 1973. The Rev. Gérard Jean-Juste spoke to the unpredictable behavior of the agency in 1979, telling the *Palm Beach Post*, "Sometimes they released refugees without our knowledge or their attorney's knowledge. They have even released refugees without anyone signing for them." Some of the refugees, he said, were released "in the middle of the streets—totally at a loss to where they were—and I cannot believe it, but three of them got work permits." (This occurred during a period when the INS was not technically issuing work permits.) Lorna Archer Stanley and Jeffrey Kahn, "24 Haitians, Jailed in Texas, NY," *Palm Beach Post*, March 25, 1979.

77. Pat Gurosky, "Haitian Fight 'Only Begun,'" *Miami News*, June 29, 1973.

78. Frank Greve, "Justice Urged for Haitians by Sponsors," *Miami Herald*, April 25, 1974.

79. Pat Gurosky, "Haitians' Plea Rejected," *Miami News*, Oct. 5, 1973. One lawyer told the *Miami Herald* that of the previous seventy Haitians released from jail in June 1973, fourteen had failed to show up to their hearings. See Gayle Pollard, "U.S. Asked to Unlock 48 Haitians," *Miami Herald*, Oct. 5, 1973.

80. Joe Broadus, "Haitians Protest Exclusion of Countrymen from U.S.," *Miami Herald*, Jan. 4, 1974.

81. John Arnold and Dorothy Gaiter, "County Eyes Ousting Haitians," *Miami Herald*, Oct. 7, 1975.

82. "Food Strike to Continue, Haitians Say," *Miami Herald*, Oct. 5, 1975.

83. Jaclyn Dalrymple, "Haitian Jail Protest Seen as Cause for Move," *Tampa Tribune*, Oct. 10, 1975.

84. "From Fear in Haiti to Jails of America," *The News-Press* (Fort Myers, Fla.), Dec. 23, 1979.

85. Whiting, "Haitians Crowd Stockade, Yield Handsome Profit."

86. "Grant Sought for Immokalee Study," *The News-Press* (Fort Myers, Fla.), July 7, 1978.

87. "U.S. Still Wants Stockade," *The News-Press* (Fort Myers, Fla.), Oct. 10, 1975.

88. See photograph by Ken Steinhoff, a photojournalist for the *Palm Beach Post*. Ken Steinhoff, "You'll Have No Name Except Deportee," May 9, 2010, https://www.capecentralhigh.com/florida/youll-have-no-name-except-deportee (accessed July 26, 2023).

89. Marquis, *I Am Not a Tractor!* 8.

90. Frank Rinella, "Stockade Ships Aliens Home," *Naples Daily News*, Nov. 18, 1977.

91. Bob Morris, "146 Illegal Aliens Are Rounded Up," *The News-Press* (Fort Myers, Fla.), Nov. 13, 1976.

92. Martha Coleman to the Rev. Jack Cassidy, May 1, 1976, Box 31, Folder 5, Ira Gollobin Papers, Manuscripts, Archives, and Rare Books Division, Schomburg Center for Research in Black Culture, New York Public Library.

93. *Haitian Refugee Center v. Civiletti*, 503 F. Supp. 442, 515. For a detailed discussion on the litigation undertaken by lawyers to forestall Haitians' removal, see Kahn, *Islands of Sovereignty*, 55–98; Lindskoog, *Detain and Punish*, 26–33.

94. *Haitian Refugee Center v. Civiletti*, 503 F. Supp. 442, 517.

95. *Haitian Refugee Center v. Civiletti*, 503 F. Supp. 442, 532.

96. U.S. Congress, House, Committee on the Judiciary, *Caribbean Migration: Oversight Hearings before the Subcommittee on Immigration, Refugee, and International Law*, 96th Cong., 2d sess., 1980, 143.

97. Charles C. Sava to Mario T. Noto, July 14, 1978, Box 11, Folder 5, IGHRC.

98. *Haitian Refugee Center v. Civiletti*, 503 F. Supp. 442, 513.

99. Kang, *INS on the Line.*

100. Jeffrey Kahn further explores the racialized construction of "disorder"; Kahn, *Islands of Sovereignty*, 99–134.

101. Kahn, *Islands of Sovereignty*, 79.

102. Memorandum from Richard Gullage to all INS employees, Aug. 23, 1978, Box 10, Folder 6, IGHRC.

103. *Knauff v. Shaughnessy*, 338 U.S. 537, 544.

104. Jack Anderson, "A Shepherd-Policeman for New Americans," *Parade*, Nov. 5, 1978, 4. See U.S. Congress, House, Committee on Appropriations, *Departments of State, Justice, and Commerce, the Judiciary, and Related Agencies Appropriations for 1980: Hearings before a Subcommittee of the Committee on Appropriations*, 96th Cong., 1st sess., 1979, 183–88; on Castillo's legacy, see also Goodman, *Deportation Machine*, 116–18.

105. "EP Alien Center Renamed, Expanded," *El Paso Times*, Dec. 23, 1977; "Alien Detention Standards Told," *Santa Fe New Mexican*, Feb. 10, 1978.

106. Anderson, "Shepherd-Policeman for New Americans."

107. See, for example, *Holt v. Sarver II*, 309 F. Supp. 362 (1970). *Holt v. Sarver II* found that conditions in the Arkansas prison system violated prisoners' constitutional rights by inflicting cruel and unusual punishment. For a broader discussion of court intervention in prison systems throughout the 1970s, see Malcolm M. Feeley and Edward L. Rubin, *Judicial Policy Making and the Modern State: How the Courts Reformed America's Prisons* (New York: Cambridge University Press, 2000).

108. Ordaz, *Shadow of El Centro*, 64.

109. U.S. Congress, House, Committee on the Judiciary, *Caribbean Refugee Crisis*, 247.

110. Anderson, "Shepherd-Policeman for New Americans." On comparisons between Vietnamese refugees and asylum seekers from the Caribbean, see Jana K. Lipman, "A Refugee Camp in America: Fort Chaffee and Vietnamese and Cuban Refugees, 1975–1982," *Journal of American Ethnic History* 33, no. 2 (2014): 57–87; Perla M. Guerrero, *Nuevo South: Latinas/os, Asians, and the Remaking of Place* (Austin: University of Texas Press, 2017); "Immigration Service to Release Haitians," *El Paso Times*, Nov. 10, 1977.

111. In June 1978, the government of the Bahamas began deporting Haitians without proper documentation, in a move it claimed was intended to ease Bahamian unemployment. A substantial number of Haitians expelled from the Bahamas subsequently came by boat to Florida. Concurrently, several thousand Haitians who had been long-term undocumented residents of Florida were arriving at INS offices after the INS general counsel announced that he would be offering work authorizations. "The Haitians in Miami: Current Immigration Practices in the United States," Box 43, Folder "Haiti," Papers of Louis Martin, Jimmy Carter Presidential Library.

112. Jeffrey Kahn calls this the "racialized pathologization of Haitians," which he dates back to nineteenth-century tropes of Haitian contagion. Kahn, *Islands of Sovereignty*, 55–98.

113. Cecilio Ruiz, an INS deportation officer, described a fairly informal process for finding Haitians accommodations in South Florida. Immokalee was the agency's first choice, as it charged the INS a third of the price of jails near Miami. On October 10, 1979, a boat of 103 Haitian asylum seekers landed on Key West; Ruiz planned to send seventy-eight to the Immokalee jail but conceded that it would put the facility fifty-seven people over capacity. If Immokalee rejected the INS, he would get back on the phone and try to find available jail space in Orlando and Leesburg, Florida. Steve Fishman, "78 Haitians on Way as Room Runs Out," *Miami Herald*, Oct. 11, 1979.

114. Fishman, "78 Haitians on Way as Room Runs Out."

115. *Haitian Refugee Center v. Civiletti*, 503 F. Supp. 442, 532.

116. Earni Young, "Haitians Beaten, Gassed, Refugee Center Charges," *Miami News*, Feb. 28, 1979.

117. Haitian Refugee Attempts Suicide, Jailed since March 1976—Press Release from Rescue Committee for Haitian Refugees, Feb. 14, 1977, Box 48, Folder 15, ACPFB.

118. Frank Greve, "Haitian Refugee Found Hanged in Dade Stockade," *Miami Herald*, March 15, 1974.

119. "More Illegal Haitian Refugees Face Deportation," *Miami Times*, Oct. 26, 1973. Thank you to Daniel Rivero for bringing this to my attention.

120. Bill Douthat, "Haitian Died Unaware of Deport Delay," *Miami News*, March 15, 1974.

121. "Model City" is also known as Liberty City. See N.D.B. Connolly, *A World More Concrete: Real Estate and the Remaking of Jim Crow South Florida* (Chicago: University of Chicago Press, 2014).

122. On the politics of Black mourning throughout the twentieth century, see David Wallace McIvor, *Mourning in America: Race and the Politics of Loss* (Ithaca, N.Y.: Cornell University Press, 2016); Samuel Ng, *Assemblies of Sorrow: The Politics of Black Mourning in the United States, 1917–1955* (forthcoming).

123. Funeral Program, Box 34, Folder 5, IGHRC.

124. Coleman, *Walls Within*, 62.

125. Peggy Peterman, "Sailing to Sorrow," *Floridian* (*Tampa Bay Times*), June 23, 1974, 27.

126. Pat Gurosky, "Refugee Issue Offers Challenge to Dade's Black Community," *Miami News*, June 18, 1973.

127. Cornelius J. Leary to Chalmers P. Wylie, Feb. 6, 1979, Box 48, Folder 17, ACPFB.

128. Even in the case of the jailed eight-year-old the INS insisted that it was more humane to incarcerate than to release: An INS representative wrote that they had not wanted to release "her or any of the members of the group without assurances of food or shelter, INS officers determined that the best interest of the aliens . . . would be served by having them housed in the West Palm Beach city jail." Cornelius J. Leary to Chalmers P. Wylie, Feb. 6, 1979.

129. Lorna Archer Stanley and Jeffrey Kahn, "Black Leaders Refused Tour of WPB Jail," *Palm Beach Post*, Jan. 18, 1979.

130. Lorna Archer Stanley and Jeffrey Kahn, "Haitians' Move OK'd," *Palm Beach Post*, Jan. 19, 1979.

131. Gary Blankenship, "Haitians to Benefit from New Jail Contract," *Palm Beach Post*, June 26, 1979.

132. Affidavit of Lucien Calixte, April 18, 1979, Box 43, Folder "Haiti," Papers of Louis Martin, Jimmy Carter Presidential Library.

133. Steve Petrow, "What Did the Haitians Do?" *Floridian* (*Tampa Bay Times*), Nov. 11, 1979.

134. Petrow, "What Did the Haitians Do?"

135. "From Fear in Haiti to Jails of America."

136. Kevin Krajick, "Refugees Adrift: Barred from America's Shores," *Saturday Review*, Oct. 27, 1979.

137. Petrow, "What Did the Haitians Do?"

138. On prison organizing, see Dan Berger, *Captive Nation: Black Prison Organizing in the Civil Rights Era* (Chapel Hill: University of North Carolina Press, 2014); Amanda Hughett, "A 'Safe Outlet' for Prisoner Discontent: How Prison Grievance Procedures Helped Stymie Prison Organizing during the 1970s," *Law and Social Inquiry* 44, no. 4 (2019): 893–921; Robert T. Chase, *We Are Not Slaves: State Violence, Coerced Labor, and Prisoners' Rights in Postwar America* (Chapel Hill: University of North Carolina Press, 2019).

139. Bella English, "Warden Named in Lawsuit for Striking Haitians," *Miami Herald*, March 2, 1979.

140. Steve Fishman, "Hafner Fires Warden Lester," *Miami Herald*, Feb. 2, 1980. The firing took place after a three-month-long investigation of the Collier County Stockade, which found that the extreme overcrowding had led to several "near riots." The report indicated that as many as eighty Haitians had been jammed into quarters intended to house forty. See David Henry, "Stockade Remedies Established," *Miami Herald*, Feb. 6, 1980.

6. South Florida and the Local Politics of the Criminal Alien

1. "Florida Sues U.S. on Cuban, Haitian Problem," *Palm Beach Post*, Feb. 7, 1981.

2. Murray Meyerson to President Carter, Sept. 9, 1980, Box 47, Folder 357A, William Lehman Papers, Barry University Archives and Special Collections, Miami Shores, Fla. (hereafter WLP).

3. Murray Meyerson to President Carter, Sept. 9, 1980.

4. Celia W. Dugger, "Many Prisoners Dread Deportation," *Miami Herald*, Dec. 23, 1984.

5. Associated Press, "Refugee Suit: Florida Wants Uncle Sam to Face 'Its Responsibilities,'" *Fort Lauderdale News and Sun-Sentinel*, Feb. 7, 1981.

6. See Hernández, *Migra!* 207–13; Felker-Kantor, *Policing Los Angeles*, 162–89; Alexander M. Stephens, "Making Migrants 'Criminal': The Mariel Boatlift, Miami, and U.S. Immigration Policy in the 1980s," *Anthurium* 17, no. 2 (2021), https://anthurium.miami.edu/articles/10.33596/anth.439.

7. María Cristina García, *Havana USA: Cuban Exiles and Cuban Americans in South Florida, 1959–1994* (Berkeley: University of California Press, 1996), 110.

8. Jorge Duany, "Cuban Migration: A Postrevolution Exodus Ebbs and Flows," *Migration Information Source*, July 6, 2017, https://www.migrationpolicy.org/article/cuban-migration-postrevolution-exodus-ebbs-and-flows.

9. There is a robust body of scholarship on the social dynamics of the resettlement camps that goes beyond the scope of my discussion here. See Melissa Hampton, "'A Tent City Is Not a Place for a Family': Mariel Cuban Women and Gendered Disorder at Regional Resettlement Facilities," *Anthurium* 17, no. 2 (2021), https://anthurium.miami.edu/articles/10.33596/anth.447; Lipman, "Refugee Camp in America"; Guerrero, *Nuevo South*.

10. Extent of Hispanic crime in Miami Beach Report to Mayor's Task Force on Crime, Box 49, Folder 395, WLP.

11. Eleventh Judicial Circuit of Florida, "Final Report of the Grand Jury," May 11, 1982, 14, http://miamisao.com/wp-content/uploads/2021/02/gj1981f4.pdf.

12. Memorandum from M. R. Stierheim, County Manager, to the Honorable Mayor and Members, Board of County Commissioners, Feb. 1985, Box 5, Folder 27, WLP.

13. Patrisia Macías-Rojas, *From Deportation to Prison: The Politics of Immigration Enforcement in Post–Civil Rights America* (New York: New York University Press, 2016), 54–61.

14. Kate Dupes Hawk, *Florida and the Mariel Boatlift of 1980: The First Twenty Days* (Tuscaloosa: University of Alabama Press, 2014), 32–33.

15. Marlise Simons, "Cuba Approves Refugees' Departure in Florida-Chartered Flotilla of Boats," *Washington Post*, April 22, 1980.

16. *INS Reporter*, Fall/Winter 1982/1983 (Washington, D.C.: U.S. Department of Justice, 1983), 10.

17. Fidel Castro, "International Workers Day Rally Speech," speech, Havana, May 1, 1980, University of Texas Castro Speech Data Base, http://lanic.utexas.edu/project/castro/db/1980/19800501-1.html.

18. *Lumpen* was a derivative of the Marxist term *Lumpenproletariat*. See Julio Capó Jr., "Queering Mariel: Mediating Cold War Foreign Policy and U.S. Citizenship among Cuba's Homosexual Exile Community, 1978–1994," *Journal of American Ethnic History* 29, no. 4 (2010): 78–106.

19. Margot Canaday, *The Straight State: Sexuality and Citizenship in Twentieth-Century America* (Princeton, N.J.: Princeton University Press, 2011), 247–54.

20. Castro, "International Workers Day Rally Speech."

21. Abel Sierra Madero, "'Here, Everyone's Got Huevos, Mister!' Nationalism, Sexuality, and Collective Violence in Cuba during the Mariel Exodus," in *The Revolution from Within: Cuba, 1959–1980*, ed. Michael J. Bustamante and Jennifer L. Lambe (Durham, N.C.: Duke University Press, 2019), 251–54.

22. Madero, "Here, Everyone's Got Huevos, Mister!" 258.

23. Brian Hufker and Gray Cavender, "From Freedom Flotilla to America's Burden: The Social Construction of the Mariel Immigrants," *Sociological Quarterly* 31, no. 2 (1990): 321–35. Monika Gosin's work offers a close analysis of *El Miami Herald*, the preeminent Spanish-language newspaper in Miami, showing how the paper initially framed the Mariel Cubans as "compatriots" worthy of citizenship, before shifting to a focus on criminality and deviance that emphasized racial difference. Gosin also notes a third theme, where the paper emphasized that the Mariel Cubans were imperfect immigrants but were capable of reform. Monika Gosin, *The Racial Politics of Division: Interethnic Struggles for Legitimacy in Multicultural Miami* (Ithaca, N.Y.: Cornell University Press, 2019), 57–90.

24. Resettlement Camps Overview, Box 1, Folder 1, Fort Chaffee Collection, Cuban Heritage Collection, University of Miami (hereafter FCC).

25. Alejandro de la Fuente, "A Lesson from Cuba on Race," *New York Times*, Nov. 17, 2013. Alexander Stephens similarly argues that scholars have overstated the race neutrality of U.S. Mariel policy in his master's thesis: Alexander Stephens, "'I Hope They Don't Come to Plains': Race and the Detention of Mariel Cubans, 1980–1981" (M.A. thesis, University of Georgia, 2016).

26. On Afro-Cubans in Mariel, see Gosin, *Racial Politics of Division*; Devyn Benson and Danielle Clealand, "Re-narrating Mariel: Black Cubans, Racial Exclusion, and Building Community in Miami," *Anthurium* 17, no. 2 (2021), https://anthurium.miami.edu/articles/10.33596/anth.462.

27. Bon Tempo, *Americans at the Gate*, 167.

28. David Wells Engstrom, *Presidential Decision Making Adrift: The Carter Administration and the Mariel Boatlift* (Lanham, Md.: Rowman and Littlefield, 1997), 149–55.

29. Alex Stepick, "Haitian Boat People: A Study in the Conflicting Forces Shaping U.S. Immigration Policy," *Law and Contemporary Problems* 45, no. 2 (1982): 79.

30. Hawk, *Florida and the Mariel Boatlift of 1980*, 33.

31. Susan Eva Eckstein, *Cuban Privilege: The Making of Immigrant Inequality in America* (Cambridge: Cambridge University Press, 2022), 128–33.

32. Stephens, "I Hope They Don't Come to Plains," 43.

33. Lipman, "Refugee Camp in America," 71.

34. "City Fairgrounds Will Be Refugee Camp," *Playground Daily News* (Fort Walton Beach, Fla.), May 2, 1980.

35. Dick Donovan, "Security Tight at Exiles' Tent City," *Palm Beach Post*, May 5, 1980.

36. Sheila Welsh, "Emotions Run High as Exiles Find New Home," *Playground Daily News* (Fort Walton Beach, Fla.), May 4, 1980.

37. "Klan Officer Organizing Anti-Cuban Activities," *Playground Daily News* (Fort Walton Beach, Fla.), May 1, 1980.

38. Department of Defense and Department of Justice, *Task Force Resettlement Operation: After Action Report, Fort Chaffee, Arkansas, 7 May 1980–19 February 1982* (Fort Sill, Okla.: Department of the Army, 1982), 13, Ike Skelton Combined Arms Research Library Digital Library, https://cgsc.contentdm.oclc.org/digital/collection/p4013coll11/id/1299/ (accessed Feb. 10, 2024).

39. Federal Control Center Operational Ceremony, May 21, 1980, Box 1, Folder 7, FCC. Bond emphasized that he would not, under any circumstance, order military personnel to arrest or detain Cubans who attempted to escape, as the military did not have jurisdiction to police civilians.

40. Mario A. Rivera, *Decision and Structure: U.S. Refugee Policy in the Mariel Crisis* (Lanham, Md.: University Press of America, 1991), 43.

41. Status Report—Fort Chaffee—June 1981, Resettlement Camp vs. Holding Camp, Box 1, Folder 5, FCC.

42. Dan Williams, "FBI Probing Rights Charges by Indiantown Gap Cubans," *Miami Herald*, Aug. 7, 1980.

43. Department of Defense and Department of Justice, *Task Force Resettlement Operation*, 112.

44. Tom Fielder and Guy Gugliotta, "Why Resettlement Is So Botched Up," *Philadelphia Inquirer*, June 8, 1980.

45. Guerrero, *Nuevo South*, 96–103.

46. Memorandum for the President: Use of Military Personnel to Maintain Order among Cuban Detainees on Military Bases, 6/5/1980, Box 1, Folder 6, Mirta Ojito Papers, Cuban Heritage Collection, University of Miami.

47. Kristina Shull suggests that we see migrant incarceration in the 1980s as a form of counterinsurgency, "a strategy of preemptive warfare targeting those deemed enemies of the state."

Holding migrants on military bases, with the policing of the U.S. military, further reinforced the notion that migrants were a foreign threat, rather than citizens-in-waiting. Shull, *Detention Empire*, 1.

48. Department of Defense and Department of Justice, *Task Force Resettlement Operation*, 277.

49. Department of Defense and Department of Justice, *Task Force Resettlement Operation*, 109.

50. Lipman, "Refugee Camp in America," 72.

51. Andrew Cuadrado, "Mariel Cubans and U.S. Refugee Camps, 1980–1982" (M.A. thesis, College of Charleston, 2014), 23; Charles Babcock, "Ft. Chaffee Strengthened for 'Hard-Core' Refugees," *Washington Post*, Sept. 4, 1980.

52. Status Report—Fort Chaffee—June 1981, Resettlement Camp vs. Holding Camp.

53. Termination of Ft. Chaffee Operations Memorandum, Box 10, Folder "Immigration Policy: Cubans and Haitians," James W. Cicconi Files, Ronald Reagan Presidential Library. The decision to use Atlanta Federal Penitentiary was a complicated and contested process; see Loyd and Mountz, *Boats, Borders, and Bases*, 63–71.

54. Bob Drummond, "Fort Chaffee Empty Again after Cuban Refugees Depart," *Daily Oklahoman* (Oklahoma City), Jan. 31, 1982.

55. Drummond, "Fort Chaffee Empty Again after Cuban Refugees Depart."

56. On the role of the National Governors Association in amplifying the demands of Governor Clinton, see Guerrero, *Nuevo South*, 84–86.

57. Letter from Antonio Dalama Matienzo, *La Vida Nueva*, Jan. 27, 1982, Florida International University Special Collections.

58. Emily Skop notes that these resettlement patterns looked quite different for white and nonwhite Mariel Cubans—whereas 73.1 percent of white Mariels resided in Miami by 1990, only 28.1 percent of nonwhite Mariels did. Nonwhite Mariels were significantly more likely to live in other Florida cities or in New York City. Emily H. Skop, "Race and Place in the Adaptation of Mariel Exiles," *International Migration Review* 35, no. 2 (2001): 449–71. Dade County was 38 percent Hispanic at the time of the Mariel Boatlift. George J. Church, "The Welcome Wears Thin," *Time*, Sept. 1, 1980, 8–10.

59. Eleventh Judicial Circuit of Florida, "Final Report of the Grand Jury," 8.

60. David Card, "The Impact of the Mariel Boatlift on the Miami Labor Market," *Industrial and Labor Relations Review* 43, no. 2 (1990): 245; George J. Borjas, "The Wage Impact of the Marielitos: A Reappraisal," *Industrial and Labor Relations Review* 70, no. 5 (2017): 1077–110.

61. Guillermo Martinez, "Crush of Refugees Has Built a Whole City within a City," *Miami Herald*, April 12, 1981.

62. "Tricked by Sponsor, Refugee Women Say," *Miami Herald*, June 20, 1980.

63. Robert Pear, "Many Cuban Exiles Left in the Lurch," *New York Times*, Nov. 26, 1980.

64. "Government Desperately Trying to Place Cuban Refugees," *Cincinnati Enquirer*, July 10, 1981.

65. Ana Veciana-Suarez, "Study Finds Refugees Face Bias Even from Their Own," *Miami News*, Sept. 11, 1981.

66. Church, "Welcome Wears Thin."

67. The Cuban-Haitian Task Force estimated that 3–5 percent of the resettled Cubans had broken sponsorships. Local officials put the number much higher, estimating that about one in four sponsorships had broken down in the Miami area. Paul L. Montgomery, "Many Cubans Remain Hard to Place in U.S.," *New York Times*, Dec. 18, 1980.

68. Sen. Jack Gordon to Carter Chief of Staff, Aug. 20, 1980, Box 48, Folder 377, WLP.

69. Open letter from William Lehman to President Carter, Sept. 25, 1980, Box 47, Folder 374, WLP.

70. On the events leading up to the police killing of Arthur McDuffie, particularly Miami's history of police brutality and the devastating economic setbacks experienced by Black Americans in the 1970s, see Hinton, *America on Fire*, 201–28.

71. Porsha Dossie, "The Tragic City: Black Rebellion and the Struggle for Freedom in Miami, 1945–1990" (M.A. thesis, University of Central Florida, 2018), 109.

72. Castro had been vocal about racism in the United States since coming to power, seeing African Americans as a group of potential allies. He hosted prominent African American intellectuals and public figures in Cuba and claimed that Cuba's desegregation efforts had been remarkably successful compared with those of the United States. He was particularly invested in portraying Cuba as "a racially harmonious, discrimination-free society," compared with a violent, racist Miami—a claim that became easier to make as Miami erupted against racist law enforcement in 1980. Alejandro de la Fuente, *A Nation for All: Race, Inequality, and Politics in Twentieth-Century Cuba* (Chapel Hill: University of North Carolina Press, 2001), 296–307.

73. On the colliding political and social events of 1980 Miami, see Nicholas Griffin, *The Year of Dangerous Days: Riots, Refugees, and Cocaine in Miami 1980* (New York: 37 Ink, 2020).

74. U.S. Congress, House, Committee on the Judiciary, *Federal Initiatives on Crime Control: Hearings before the Subcommittee on Crime*, 97th Cong., 1st sess., 1981, 310–12.

75. Eliott Rodriguez, "Terror Reigned in Dadeland as Drug War Rained Bullets," *Miami Herald*, July 12, 1979.

76. Hinton, *From the War on Poverty to the War on Crime*, 310–11.

77. Hinton, *From the War on Poverty to the War on Crime*, 311.

78. U.S. Congress, House, Select Committee on Narcotics Abuse and Control, *Federal Drug Law Enforcement Coordination*, 97th Cong., 2d sess., 1982, 30. On the Miami Action Plan and changes to the law of posse comitatus, see Shull, *Detention Empire*, 115–17.

79. Rivera, *Decision and Structure*, 94–103.

80. Interpretation of the Fascell-Stone Amendment: Memorandum for Edward C. Schmults, July 8, 1982, Box 52, Folder "Fascell Stone," Subject Files of the Associate Attorney General Rudolph W. Giuliani, General Records of the U.S. Department of Justice, RG 60, NARA2 (hereafter SF-RWG).

81. Representative Claude Pepper said, "We've now got some real progress in our effort to get these, surplus vagrant vagabonds off our street." Tom Fielder and Dan Williams, "U.S. Will Assume Custody of Refugees Held in Jails," *Miami Herald*, Dec. 11, 1980. On the concept of "surplus" labor and carcerality, see Ruth Wilson Gilmore, *Golden Gulag: Prisons, Surplus, Crisis, and Opposition in Globalizing California* (Berkeley: University of California Press, 2007).

82. Hector Fernando Burga, "The Mariel Boatlift and Comprehensive Planning: Humanitarian Crisis, Demographic Data, and Cuban-American Community Development," *Planning Perspectives* 36, no. 3 (2021): 443.

83. Ellen Bartlett, "Beach Halts Free Housing for Refugees," *Miami Herald*, Oct. 22, 1980.

84. "Little Havana Struck by Boatlift Communities," Box 1, Folder 3, Mirta Ojito Papers, Cuban Heritage Collection, University of Miami.

85. Marilyn A. Moore, "Miami Folds Downtown Cuban Camp," *Miami News*, Sept. 25, 1980.

86. Kathy McCarthy, "Beach Police Enforcing New Anti-crime Stop and Frisk Law," *Miami News*, Oct. 29, 1980.

87. "Stop and Frisk Law Does Not Hold Up," editorial, *Miami News*, Oct. 9, 1980.

88. Extent of Hispanic crime in Miami Beach Report to Mayor's Task Force on Crime.

89. Perhaps unsurprisingly, those in Miami law enforcement were often quite explicit about their anti-immigrant views. An article in *Police Magazine* described a "cultural awareness conference" for Miami Police Department officers. When asked about the event, one officer responded, "It was a joke. We sat around with a couple of shrinkheads who told us that the Haitians were oppressed people. Well, I don't give a damn. What the hell does that have to do with me? They still aren't welcome in my house." Philip B. Taft Jr., "Policing the New Immigrant Ghettos," *Police Magazine*, July 1983, 18.

90. Ana Veciana-Suarez, "Are New Arrivals Victimizers or Scapegoats?" *Miami News*, Dec. 29, 1980.

91. "Dade Begins Crime Sweep," *Florida Today* (Cocoa), Dec. 20, 1981.

92. Bryan O. Walsh, "Mariel, Crime, and 'Scapegoats,'" *Miami Herald*, Dec. 29, 1980.

93. "Beach Sees Crime Rise since Refugee Influx," Box 1, Folder 3, Mirta Ojito Papers, Cuban Heritage Collection, University of Miami; Guillermo Martinez, "Mariel Refugees: A City within a City," *Miami Herald*, Dec. 14, 1980.

94. "Little Havana Struck by Boatlift Communities."

95. Philip B. Taft Jr., "The Cuban Crisis in Miami's Jails," *Corrections Magazine* 8, no. 2 (April 1982): 37.

96. Detective David Dickens to Jeff Marsico, Department of Justice, Sept. 3, 1981, VF: Cubans—U.S.—Crime, USCIS Library.

97. "Beach Sees Crime Rise since Refugee Influx."

98. "Impact of the Refugee Boatlift on the City of Miami Police Department," Box 371, Folder "Mariel Criminal Deportations, 2 of 2," Digital Library of the Caribbean.

99. "Hialeah Hikes Tax to Pay for Cops," *Miami News*, June 10, 1981.

100. "Miami OKs Police Tax," *Miami Herald*, May 16, 1981.

101. Harold T. Toal to James Giganti, Sept. 24, 1980.

102. David Pingree to Marta Goldman, Oct. 30, 1980, Box 47, Folder 357A, WLP.

103. John G. Burke, Director, to Mr. Merrett R. Stierheim, Dec. 30, 1980, Box 49, Folder 397, WLP.

104. On the history of the Law Enforcement Assistance Administration, see Hinton, *From the War on Poverty to the War on Crime*.

105. "A Runaway Youth Died in Miami Jail," *New York Times*, Jan. 28, 1971. On the politicization of white death in jails, see Newport, *This Is My Jail*, 109–13.

106. Charles Whited, "New Dade Jail a Crying Need before Mariel," *Miami Herald*, Dec. 19, 1980.

107. Newport, *This Is My Jail*, 168.

108. By the time the Mariel Boatlift began, the jail had not increased its number of beds in nearly fifteen years. This mirrored national trends; local jail capacity had grown by less than 1 percent each year between 1978 and 1983. Jacob Kang-Brown and Jack Norton, "America's Hidden Gulag," *New York Review of Books*, Feb. 19, 2021.

109. Taft, "Cuban Crisis in Miami's Jails," 35.

110. Memorandum from Dave Johnson to Representative William Lehman, June 30, 1983, Box 49, Folder 393, WLP.

111. Eleventh Judicial Circuit of Florida, "Final Report of the Grand Jury," 16.

112. Dan Williams and Liz Balmaseda, "City Pleads for Help with Vagrant Refugees," *Miami Herald*, Dec. 7, 1980.

113. Fielder and Williams, "U.S. Will Assume Custody of Refugees Held in Jails."

114. Bill Lazarus, "Judge Lifts Order to Ease Jail Overcrowding," *Miami Herald*, Jan. 1, 1981.

115. Dan Williams and Zita Arocha, "Roundup of Homeless Refugees Flops," *Miami Herald*, Dec. 12, 1980.

116. Williams and Arocha, "Roundup of Homeless Refugees Flops."

117. Bill Lazarus, "Florida, U.S. Pledge to Help Dade Jail," *Miami Herald*, Dec. 31, 1980.

118. Lazarus, "Judge Lifts Order to Ease Jail Overcrowding."

119. "Overcrowding and the Jails," editorial, *Miami Herald*, June 8, 1981.

120. "Dade's Jail Crisis," editorial, *Miami Herald*, May 26, 1982.

121. Neil Chethik, "Local Prison Takes Runover from Dade Jail," *Tallahassee Democrat*, Aug. 1, 1981.

122. Steve Brewer, "Cubans Held in Texas after Miami Arrests," Associated Press, April 8, 1981.

123. Talking Points for Mckay Amendments, 1986, Box 53, Folder 443, WLP.

124. Eleventh Judicial Circuit of Florida, "Final Report of the Grand Jury," 24.

125. Cited in Kaufman, "Segregation by Citizenship," 1395.

126. Loyd and Mountz, *Boats, Borders, and Bases*, 129.

127. Memorandum: Revision of AG's guidelines on INS cooperation with other law enforcement agencies, VF: Detention and Deportation—Statistics, USCIS Library.

128. Peter H. Schuck and John Williams, "Removing Criminal Aliens: The Pitfalls and Promises of Federalism," *Harvard Journal of Law and Public Policy* 22, no. 2 (1999): 426–27.

129. Rick Su, "The States of Immigration," *William & Mary Law Review* 54, no. 4 (2013): 1364–69.

130. Schuck and Williams, "Removing Criminal Aliens," 428.

131. Dec. 1986—Alien Criminal Apprehension Program, VF: Interagency Cooperation, USCIS Library.

132. Immigration and Naturalization Service News Release, Sept. 28, 1995, VF: Detention and Deportation—Statistics, USCIS Library.

133. Memorandum: Guidelines for Criminal Alien Policy Implementation, Appendix 2, VF: Interagency Cooperation, USCIS Library.

134. See, broadly, VF: Detention and Deportation—Statistics, USCIS Library.

135. Schuck and Williams, "Removing Criminal Aliens," 387–88.

136. "Additional Criminal Alien Movement," Memorandum to the Southern Regional Office, Oct. 25, 1989, Appendix of State of the District Assessment, Miami District, 1989, USCIS Library.

137. "Additional Criminal Alien Movement."

138. Heather Schoenfeld, *Building the Prison State: Race and the Politics of Mass Incarceration* (Chicago: University of Chicago Press, 2018), 114.

139. Stephens, "Making Migrants 'Criminal,'" 12.

140. Schuck and Williams, "Removing Criminal Aliens," 444–47. A federal program for state reimbursement of costs associated with incarcerating migrants would first be green-lit under

the Immigration Reform and Control Act, but it would not receive congressional funding until the FY 1995 budget. Lawsuits and pressure exerted by Governor Wilson, as well as new litigation from Florida, were instrumental in securing this funding.

141. Su, "States of Immigration," 1370.

142. Su, "States of Immigration," 1373.

143. William J. Clinton, "Statement on the State Criminal Alien Assistance Program," April 22, 1994, online by Gerhard Peters and John T. Woolley, American Presidency Project, https://www.presidency.ucsb.edu/node/219184.

144. Mark Bradley, "6 Inmates Get Tickets for Home," *Pensacola News Journal*, Oct. 25, 1994.

145. "BJA FY 2021 State Criminal Alien Assistance Program (SCAAP) Award Details," Bureau of Justice Assistance, U.S. Department of Justice, https://bja.ojp.gov/funding/SCAAP-FY2021-Awards.pdf.

146. Lee Fang and Ali Winston, "Trump Threatens Funding for California Cops over 'Sanctuary State' Bill. Maybe That's a Good Thing," *The Intercept*, Aug. 22, 2017.

147. Anjana Malhotra, "The Immigrant and *Miranda*," *Southern Methodist University Law Review* 66, no. 1 (2013): 331–32.

148. Malhotra, "Immigrant and *Miranda*," 335.

149. William E. Gibson, "County Pleads for Refugee Aid," *Fort Lauderdale News*, Feb. 4, 1982.

150. Christy McKerney, "Tax Dollars Serve to Beautify Offices for Sheriff, Aides," *South Florida Sun-Sentinel* (Fort Lauderdale), June 22, 2004.

7. Flexible Space and the Weaponization of Transfers

1. Memorandum: Orientation, Feb. 26, 1981, Box 25, Folder 152, CRC.

2. On Krome's history as a military site before the 1980s, see Jana K. Lipman, "'The Fish Trusts the Water, and It Is in the Water That It Is Cooked': The Caribbean Origins of the Krome Detention Center," *Radical History Review* 2013, no. 115 (2013): 118–19.

3. Alex Larzelere, *The 1980 Cuban Boatlift* (Washington, D.C.: National Defense University Press, 1988), 384.

4. Lipman, "Fish Trusts the Water, and It Is in the Water That It Is Cooked," 121.

5. Thomas R. Maddux, "Ronald Reagan and the Task Force on Immigration, 1981," *Pacific Historical Review* 74, no. 2 (2005): 195–236.

6. Meeting of the President's Task Force on Immigration and Refugee Policy, May 19, 1981, Box 19, Folder "Immigration and Refugee Policy, Task Force on," Martin Anderson Files, Ronald Reagan Presidential Library.

7. Interdiction was one way of "offshoring" migration control, a practice that has received significant scholarly attention in recent years. The United States had already experimented with this practice in the early twentieth century, for example, by giving medical inspections to migrants in their country of origin before they set sail for the United States. But the practice took on a new intensity in the 1980s, as the United States breached the sovereignty of other nations to create a "buffer zone" against unwanted migrants and asylum seekers. See Ana Raquel Minian, "Offshoring Migration Control: Guatemalan Transmigrants and the Construction of Mexico as a Buffer Zone," *American Historical Review* 125, no. 1 (2020): 89–111.

8. Meeting of the President's Task Force on Immigration and Refugee Policy, May 19, 1981.

9. For analysis of the Haitian interdiction program, see Kahn, *Islands of Sovereignty*; Shull, *Detention Empire*, 64–103.

10. *Jean v. Nelson*, 472 U.S. 846 (1985).

11. U.S. General Accounting Office, *Immigration Management: Strong Leadership and Management Reforms Needed to Address Serious Problems. Report to the Congress* (Washington, D.C.: Government Printing Office, 1991), 38.

12. Haitian Processing Center, Box 20, Folder 48, CRC.

13. "Political Asylum Haitians' First Need," editorial, *Miami News*, Feb. 22, 1980.

14. Marilyn Weeks, "Residents Angrily Oppose Refugee Center," *Fort Lauderdale News*, April 22, 1980.

15. U.S. Congress, House, Committee on the Judiciary, *Caribbean Migration*, 266.

16. Ira Kurzban to Ambassador Victor H. Palmieri, Aug. 28, 1980, Box 31, Folder 9, IGHRC.

17. U.S. Congress, House, Committee on the Judiciary, *Caribbean Migration*, 144.

18. Mike Clary and Jane Daugherty, "Krome Refugee Camps Ordered to Shut Down," *Miami Herald*, Sept. 10, 1980.

19. Ivy Goldstein, "Specific Incidents Relating to Children at Krome South and North," Oct. 31, 1980, Box 20, Folder 56, CRC.

20. Haitian Refugee Center Press Release, Jan. 8, 1981, Box 20, Folder 59, CRC.

21. Dorothy E. Roberts, *Killing the Black Body: Race, Reproduction, and the Meaning of Liberty* (New York: Pantheon Books, 1997).

22. Haitian Women's Pregnancy Rate/Problems, April 1, 1981, Box 20, Folder 41, CRC. On the restriction of welfare and the racialized trope of the "welfare queen," see Premilla Nadasen, "From Widow to 'Welfare Queen': Welfare and the Politics of Race," *Black Women, Gender + Families* 1, no. 2 (2007): 52–77; Julilly Kohler-Hausmann, "'The Crime of Survival': Fraud Prosecutions, Community Surveillance, and the Original 'Welfare Queen,'" *Journal of Social History* 41, no. 2 (2007): 329–54.

23. Memorandum: Mental Health Conditions Ft. Allen and Krome North, March 29, 1982, Box 52, Folder "Krome—INS," SF-RWG.

24. This was also a regional departure from INS detention statistics that categorized detention populations into Mexican and "Other than Mexican." In the summer of 1982, Krome held around fifty non-Haitian migrants, and observers noted a particular uptick in refugees from Central America. Nery Ynclan, "Non-Haitians Also Expect to Be Freed," *Miami Herald*, June 30, 1982.

25. Alderson Women's Prison to Haitian Refugee Project, April 2, 1982, Box 36, Folder 8, IGHRC.

26. Statement of Lawyers Committee for International Human Rights on the Haitian Detention Program, July 1, 1982, Box 51, Folder "INS—Detention—BOP," SF-RWG.

27. Shull, *Detention Empire*, 94–96.

28. Statement of Haitian Refugee Center, March 25, 1981, Box 20, Folder 50, CRC; "Processing Center Planned for Haitian Refugees," *Miami Herald*, Feb. 19, 1980.

29. American Committee for Protection of Foreign Born Press Release: New Repressive Measures Started against Haitian Boat People, Box 48, Folder 15, ACPFB.

30. Statement of Haitian Refugee Center, March 25, 1981; "Processing Center Planned for Haitian Refugees."

31. *Bob Graham v. William French Smith*, No. 81-1497-Civ. JE.

32. Clarence Jefferson Hall Jr., *A Prison in the Woods: Environment and Incarceration in New York's North Country* (Amherst: University of Massachusetts Press, 2020), 67.

33. See Brianna Nofil, "The Forgotten Tale of How America Converted Its 1980 Olympic Village into a Prison," *Atlas Obscura*, Aug. 16, 2016, https://www.atlasobscura.com/articles/the -time-that-the-us-turned-an-olympic-village-into-a-prison; Hall, *Prison in the Woods*, 51–92.

34. U.S. Congress, House, Committee on the Judiciary, *Bureau of Prisons Fiscal Year 1980 Authorization: Hearing before the Subcommittee on Courts, Civil Liberties, and the Administration of Justice*, 96th Cong., 1st sess., 1979, 73.

35. Heather Ann Thompson, *Blood in the Water: The Attica Prison Uprising of 1971 and Its Legacy* (New York: Pantheon Books, 2016).

36. Hall, *Prison in the Woods*, 67–68.

37. Stephen J. Roberts, "40 Haitian Refugees Housed at Ray Brook Federal Prison," *Lake Placid News*, July 23, 1981.

38. U.S. Congress, House, Committee on the Judiciary, *Detention of Aliens in Bureau of Prison Facilities: Hearing before the Subcommittee on Courts, Civil Liberties, and the Administration of Justice*, 97th Cong., 2d sess., 1982, 72.

39. Petition to Judge Gordon W. Sacks, Sept. 9, 1981, Box 4, Folder 23, IGHRC.

40. "Why Send Haitians to Siberia?" editorial, *New York Times*, Nov. 11, 1981; Box 4, Folder 22, IGHRC.

41. Lipman, "Fish Trusts the Water, and It Is in the Water That It Is Cooked," 131.

42. Doris Meissner to Rudy Giuliani, re: Start-Up Contracts in Support of Fort Allen, Puerto Rico, Sept. 8, 1981, Box 52, Folder "INS—Fort Allen," SF-RWG.

43. Rudolph Giuliani to Hernan Padilla, Feb. 5, 1982, Box 52, Folder "INS—Fort Allen," SF-RWG.

44. Hernan Padilla to AG Smith, Jan. 12, 1982, Box 52, Folder "INS—Fort Allen," SF-RWG.

45. In October 1978, Haitian advocates won a case against the U.S. government for not open- ing the Haitian Program for public comment and for not ensuring due process for asylum claims, both of which violated the Administrative Procedure Act. Judge King also heard this case and ordered a stay of exclusion proceedings until the regulations were revised. Thus, this case followed a similar pattern as *Louis v. Nelson* in ruling the process, but not the outcome, illegal. See *Sannon v. United States*, 460 F. Supp. 458 (S.D. Fla. 1978).

46. *Louis v. Nelson*, 544 F. Supp. 973, 994 (1982).

47. *Louis v. Nelson*, 544 F. Supp. 973, 994.

48. *Louis v. Nelson*, 544 F. Supp. 973, 1004.

49. Anders Gyllenhaal and Alice Klement, "If Spellman Won't Budge, Appeal by U.S. Is Vowed," *Miami Herald*, June 30, 1982.

50. Alice Klement and Guillermo Martinez, "U.S. Given 10 Days to Define a New Policy," *Miami Herald*, July 1, 1982.

51. Klement and Martinez, "U.S. Given 10 Days to Define a New Policy."

52. Public Comments on Interim Detention and Parole Regulations, Aug. 13, 1982, Box 51, Folder "INS—Detention Rules," SF-RWG. On the anti-Blackness of the Reagan administration, see Shull, *Detention Empire*, 8–9.

53. 8 CFR Parts 212 and 235, Detention and Parole of Inadmissible Aliens, Box 51, Folder "INS—Detention Rules," SF-RWG.

54. Ynclan, "Non-Haitians Also Expect to Be Freed."

55. Joseph Cosco, "Aliens in the Land of the Free," *The Sun-Sentinel* (Fort Lauderdale, Fla.), March 6, 1983.

56. Jim Jones, "Central Americans Jam Texas Camp," *Fort Worth Star-Telegram*, Nov. 2, 1986. On Central Americans and detention, see María Cristina García, *Seeking Refuge: Central American Migration to Mexico, the United States, and Canada* (Berkeley: University of California Press, 2006); Robert S. Kahn, *Other People's Blood: U.S. Immigration Prisons in the Reagan Decade* (Boulder, Colo.: Westview Press, 1996).

57. Lisa Duperier, Special Assistant to Commissioner of INS, to Renee Szybala, Special Assistant, AAG, Re: Nationality Breakdown for Aliens in Detention, April 30, 1982, Box 51, Folder "INS—Detention Facilities," SF-RWG.

58. Maurice C. Inman Jr., General Counsel, to Alan C. Nelson, Commissioner, Advisability of Emergency Rulemaking regarding INS Detention Policy, Box 51, Folder "INS—Detention Rules," SF-RWG.

59. "Decision Memorandum Site Selection for a 1,000 Bed Detention Facility," Box 53, Folder "INS—Oakdale," SF-RWG.

60. Attorney General to the Speaker of the House, Proposed Omnibus Immigration Act, Oct. 20, 1981, Box OA 4821, Folder "Immigration Control (3)," Kenneth T. Cribb Files, Ronald Reagan Presidential Library. This legislation did not make it out of subcommittee hearings.

61. U.S. Congress, House, Committee on the Judiciary, *Detention of Aliens in Bureau of Prison Facilities*, 3.

62. In 1982, two-thirds of all federal prisoners resided in nonfederal institutions, with the government spending $26 million annually to house its inmates in local facilities. "Unfortunately for the federal prison system, such agreements have fallen on hard times," reported the U.S. Advisory Commission on Intergovernmental Relations. The number of local contracts had dropped from more than 1,000 to 733, including 167 "major use contracts" in cities that housed federal courts. The Intergovernmental Relations Commission pointed to multiple issues contributing to the closing of local doors: The Reagan administration's drug and organized crime initiatives had rapidly expanded the number of federal offenders, prisoner litigation meant that many facilities were under court order to cap the number of inmates, and municipalities were concerned about federal prisoners bringing civil rights actions against strained facilities. U.S. Advisory Commission on Intergovernmental Relations, *Jails: Intergovernmental Dimensions of a Local Problem* (Washington, D.C.: U.S. Advisory Commission on Intergovernmental Relations, 1984), 155, University of North Texas Digital Library, https://digital.library.unt.edu/ark:/67531/metadc1322/ (accessed June 5, 2019).

63. Hinton, *From the War on Poverty to the War on Crime*, 312.

64. Hinton, *From the War on Poverty to the War on Crime*, 312–13.

65. Kang-Brown and Norton, "America's Hidden Gulag."

66. Additional Background for the House/Senate Conferees on the need for two detention centers proposed by the DOJ in the FY 1982 supplemental request, Box 51, Folder "INS—El Reno/Petersburg," SF-RWG.

67. John W. Warner Jr., et al. to AG William French Smith, Box 51, Folder "INS—El Reno/Petersburg," SF-RWG; *Plyler v. Doe*, 457 U.S. 202 (1982). On the prehistory of the *Plyler* decision, and the ways that border-crossing youth were denied legal rights and access to social services,

see Ivón Padilla-Rodriguez, "Undocumented Youth: The Labor, Education, and Rights of Migrant Children in Twentieth Century America" (Ph.D. diss., Columbia University, 2021).

68. Shull, *Detention Empire*, 199.

69. Lilith Quinlan, "Welcoming Strangers: Oakdale's New Prosperity and Ethical Challenge," MSS 612 BC, Box 22, Folder 13, Frank I. Sanchez Papers, University of New Mexico Center for Southwest Research.

70. Frances Frank Marcus, "Louisianans Wait for Alien Center," *New York Times*, Oct. 7, 1984.

71. "Allen May Overcome Unemployment," *Town Talk* (Alexandria, La.), Jan. 28, 1984.

72. Tom Edwards, "Ballard Road: 'Please God, Don't Go There at Night,'" *Town Talk* (Alexandria, La.), Jan. 3, 1982.

73. Rev. Charles L. Soileau, "Letter to Editor: Contrary to Image, There's No 'War Zone' in Oakdale," *Town Talk* (Alexandria, La.), Jan. 8, 1983.

74. Dorothy Lejune, "Oakdale Mayor Refutes Criticism of Alien Center," *Town Talk* (Alexandria, La.), Sept. 27, 1983.

75. Jim Jeggett, "Officials Seeking Alien Detention Center Site Greeted Enthusiastically in Oakdale," *Town Talk* (Alexandria, La.), March 5, 1982.

76. Wade B. Houk, Asst. Director, Bureau of Prisons, to Renee L. Szybala, Special Assistant to the AAG, Re: Proposed Alien Detention Center, Feb. 3, 1983, Box 53, Folder "INS—Oakdale," SF-RWG.

77. Dorothy Lejune, "Shouts of Joy in Oakdale over Alien Center Decision," *Town Talk* (Alexandria, La.), Feb. 11, 1983. While media reports, as well as scholarly accounts, have stressed the universal approval of the town of Oakdale, skeptics of the detention center raised both ethical and political concerns. "I have nothing against the alien detention center except I don't think putting poor Mexicans behind a barbed wire fence is any way to make a living," wrote Anna Starken of Oakdale. Others were less sympathetic: Vera Lashley wrote to the *Town Talk* that Oakdale would soon have "Angola in [their] back yard" and that an escape or riot was inevitable. Anne Starken, "Letter to the Editor: Curing Symptoms," *Town Talk* (Alexandria, La.), Aug. 29, 1982; Vera Lashley, "Letter to the Editor: Asking for Trouble?" *Town Talk* (Alexandria, La.), Feb. 19, 1983.

78. Quinlan, "Welcoming Strangers," 6.

79. Marcus, "Louisianans Wait for Alien Center."

80. "First Aliens Arrive at Center," *Town Talk* (Alexandria, La.), April 9, 1986.

81. Rex Smith and Gwen Young, "LI Firms Raided; Aliens Sent to La.," *Newsday*, June 21, 1986.

82. Loyd and Mountz, *Boats, Borders, and Bases*, 110.

83. Behavioral Systems Southwest to Del Heiney, Oct. 22, 1983, Box 22, Folder 2, Frank I. Sanchez Papers, University of New Mexico Center for Southwest Research.

84. Letter from Fr. Forest McAllister, Nov. 27, 1983, Box 22, Folder 2, Frank I. Sanchez Papers, University of New Mexico Center for Southwest Research.

85. Susana Barciela, "Covering the INS in South Florida," *Nieman Reports* 56, no. 4 (2002): 15–18.

86. U.S. Department of Justice and Office of the Inspector General, *Alleged Deception of Congress: The Congressional Task Force on Immigration Reform's Fact-Finding Visit to the Miami District of INS in June, 1995* (Washington, D.C.: Government Printing Office, 1996), sec. III, https://oig.justice.gov/special/9606/index.htm.

87. U.S. Department of Justice and Office of the Inspector General, *Alleged Deception of Congress*, sec. III.

88. U.S. Department of Justice and Office of the Inspector General, *Alleged Deception of Congress*, sec. II.

89. The questionable recordkeeping practices of the INS have often been cited as an example of the agency's bureaucratic secrecy. Calavita, *Inside the State*, 12–13.

90. U.S. Department of Justice and Office of the Inspector General, *Alleged Deception of Congress*, sec. III.

91. U.S. Department of Justice and Office of the Inspector General, *Alleged Deception of Congress*, sec. IV.

92. Women's Commission for Refugee Women and Children, "Behind Locked Doors: Abuse of Refugee Women at the Krome Detention Center" (New York: Women's Commission for Refugee Women and Children, 2000), 10.

93. The INS commissioner reported in 1998 that over the prior four years, the agency had received a 172 percent increase in funding and a 75 percent increase in staffing. U.S. Congress, Senate, Committee on the Judiciary, *INS Reform: The Service Side*, 105th Cong., 2d sess., 1998, 117.

94. Joel Brinkley, "At Immigration, Disarray and Defeat," *New York Times*, Sept. 11, 1994.

95. Barciela, "Covering the INS in South Florida."

96. In another example of how transfers protected the INS, Robert Kahn notes that, in the mid-1980s, immigration officials at Port Isabel Service Processing Center beat a Guatemalan asylum seeker and then "transferred the victim to a county jail until the bruises went away." Kahn, *Other People's Blood*, 60.

97. Despite this, the brazenness of Kromegate incurred bipartisan censure. Criticisms grew even louder as the agency bestowed promotions and bonuses on many of the agents involved in the cover-up. See Bob Norman, "Admitting Terror, Part 3," *New Times Broward–Palm Beach*, Nov. 1, 2001.

98. *Annual Report of the Immigration and Naturalization Service 1949–1950* (Washington, D.C.: Government Printing Office, 1950), 8–9.

99. U.S. Congress, Senate, Committee on the Judiciary, *INS Reform*, 138.

100. "Locked Away: Immigration Detainees in Jails in the United States," *Human Rights Watch* 10, no. 1 (1998): 23, https://www.hrw.org/reports/ins989.pdf.

101. In 1992, the INS commissioner launched an initiative called the Asylum Pre-Screening Officer Program, which allowed INS offices to release asylum seekers with "credible cases" from detention, a program that was in part a response to INS detention space constraints. The result was a staggeringly inconsistent system of release, with nearly identical asylum cases treated differently depending on the district office they encountered: The New York district released a mere 2.4 percent of its asylum seekers, while Miami released many more. Some districts required thousands of dollars in bonds for parole; others granted asylum seekers parole as long as they could identify a local family member. Mirta Ojito, "Inconsistency at INS Complicates Refugees' Asylum Quest," *New York Times*, June 22, 1998; Michele R. Pistone, "Justice Delayed Is Justice Denied: A Proposal for Ending the Unnecessary Detention of Asylum Seekers," *Harvard Human Rights Journal* 12 (1999): 197–265.

102. U.S. Department of Justice and Office of the Inspector General, *Alleged Deception of Congress*, sec. IV.

103. Norman, "Admitting Terror, Part 3."

104. Cheryl Little, "Continuing Problems at Krome Service Processing Center," *In Defense of the Alien* 20 (1997): 148. When the INS formally adopted detention standards in 2001, they applied to both local jails and INS-run facilities. This, of course, did not mean that jails complied with them. Chris Hedges, "Policy to Protect Jailed Immigrants Is Adopted by U.S.," *New York Times*, Jan. 2, 2001.

105. Chad Terhune, "State Must Inspect Jails, Corrections Officials Say," *Wall Street Journal*, Aug. 12, 1998. In Vermont, the state passed legislation that put county jails used for detention by the INS under the purview of the Department of Corrections, in an effort to address the lack of oversight. See Detention Watch Network Strategy Session, April 26–28, 1997, Box 16, Folder "INS Detention 1996–1997," AIJ.

106. María Cristina García, "National (In)Security and the Immigration Act of 1996," *Modern American History* 1, no. 2 (July 2018): 233–36. On the "modern-era" periodization, see Emily Ryo and Ian Peacock, "A National Study of Immigration Detention in the United States," *Southern California Law Review* 92, no. 1 (2018): 7.

107. Sarah Gryll, "Immigration Detention Reform: No Band-Aid Desired," *Emory Law Journal* 60, no. 5 (2011): 1218.

108. Michael Welch, *Detained: Immigration Laws and the Expanding I.N.S. Jail Complex* (Philadelphia: Temple University Press, 2002), 59.

109. Mirta Ojito, "Change in Laws Sets Off Big Wave of Deportations," *New York Times*, Dec. 15, 1998.

110. John F. Heenehan, "County Prisons to Go Private," *Tampa Tribune*, Feb. 29, 1988.

111. Cheryl Little, "INS Detention in Florida," *University of Miami Inter-American Law Review* 30, no. 3 (1999): 566.

112. "11-16-96 Affidavit of Cuban Detainee in Bay Co. Jail Annex," in Cheryl Little and Joan Friedland, "Florida County Jails: INS's Secret Detention World," Box 13, Folder "Florida County Jails: INS's Secret Detention World, 1997 Nov.," AIJ.

113. Little and Friedland, "Florida County Jails," 14.

114. Anonymized letter to Cheryl Little, Aug. 19, 1998, Box 14, Folder "County Jail Supplement 2 of 3," AIJ.

115. Affidavit of F.R., July 14, 1998, Box 14, Folder "Jackson County Jail Affidavits," AIJ.

116. Little and Friedland, "Florida County Jails," 12–13.

117. Manatee County Jail Detainees Class Action Move/Plea, Box 14, Folder "County Jail Supplement 1998," AIJ.

118. Affidavit of F.R., July 14, 1998.

119. Bill Lann Lee, Acting Assistant AG, to J. Milton Pittman, Chair, Board of County Commissioners, Jackson County, March 30, 2000, re: Jackson Co. Correctional Facility, Box 14, Folder "Jackson County Jail," AIJ.

120. Anne-Marie Cusac, "Stunning Technology," *The Progressive*, July 1, 1996.

121. Richard B. Cravener, DOJ, to Javier Zuniga, Amnesty International, Nov. 18, 1998, Box 14, Folder "Jackson County Jail," AIJ.

122. Hinton, *From the War on Poverty to the War on Crime*, 145–46.

123. Bill Lann Lee, Acting Assistant AG, to J. Milton Pittman, Chair, Board of County Commissioners, Jackson County, March 30, 2000.

124. Quoted in Amnesty International, "Cruelty in Control? The Stun Belt and Other Electro-shock Equipment in Law Enforcement," June 1999, 3, https://www.amnesty.org/en/wp-content/uploads/2021/06/amr510541999en.pdf.

125. William F. Schulz, "Cruel and Unusual Punishment," *New York Review of Books*, April 24, 1997.

126. Amnesty International, "Arming the Torturers: Electro-shock Torture and the Spread of Stun Technology," March 4, 1997, 22, https://www.amnesty.org/en/documents/act40/001/1997/en/.

127. Stuart Schrader, *Badges without Borders: How Global Counterinsurgency Transformed American Policing* (Oakland: University of California Press, 2019), 129–213.

128. Nancy Hiemstra, *Detain and Deport: The Chaotic U.S. Immigration Enforcement Regime* (Athens: University of Georgia Press, 2019), 84–85.

8. Sheriffs, Corporations, and the Making of a Late Twentieth-Century Jail Bed Economy

1. Yvette Craig, "Tarrant Approves Contract to House Illegal Immigrants," *Fort Worth Star-Telegram*, Dec. 16, 1995.

2. Lindsey Gruson, "End of Federal Revenue Sharing Creating Financial Crises in Many Cities," *New York Times*, Jan. 31, 1987; Omer Kimhi, "Reviving Cities: Legal Remedies to Municipal Financial Crises," *Boston University Law Review* 88, no. 3 (2008): 641–42.

3. Jack Norton and Jacob Kang-Brown, "If You Build It: How the Federal Government Fuels Rural Jail Expansion," Vera Institute of Justice, Jan. 10, 2020, https://www.vera.org/in-our-backyards-stories/if-you-build-it.

4. Kang-Brown and Norton, "America's Hidden Gulag."

5. Sarah Lopez notes a late twentieth-century rhetorical shift in INS documents from describing deportation expenses in terms of "average cost per man-day of detention" and "average cost of detention per alien" to using language of "Beds per Day." She writes, "[This] synecdoche, symptomatic of the dehumanization of migrant persons, is also evidence of the central role of architecture and its beds in ICE and industry's imagination, used as a rhetorical device to distance the engineers of detention space from their involvement in incarcerating largely innocent people." Sarah Lopez, "From Penal to 'Civil': A Legacy of Private Prison Policy in a Landscape of Migrant Detention," *American Quarterly* 71, no. 1 (2019): 130.

6. U.S. Department of Justice, Immigration and Naturalization Service, "The Elizabeth, New Jersey Contract Detention Facility, Operated by ESMOR Inc., Interim Report," July 20, 1995, digitized by Chris Kirkham, *Huffington Post*, 2013, https://archive.org/details/758481-ins-report-esmor/mode/2up.

7. Privatization created what David Rubenstein and Pratheepan Gulasekaram have called an "asymmetrical accountability scheme," in which private prison companies, as private actors, operate outside of the bounds of constitutional and administrative law yet are performing public functions on behalf of the federal government, thus potentially protecting such companies from certain liabilities. David S. Rubenstein and Pratheepan Gulasekaram, "Privatized Detention and Immigration Federalism," *Stanford Law Review (Online)* 71 (2019), https://www.stanfordlawreview.org/online/privatized-detention-immigration-federalism/.

8. When the devastating Hurricane Andrew hit Miami in 1993, migrants were removed from Krome and sent to jails in central Florida; as was all too common, their attorneys received no warning of the transfers. Migrants later aided in the hurricane cleanup at Krome. See Lisa Ocker, "Aliens Returning to Krome," *Fort Lauderdale Sun-Sentinel*, Sept. 16, 1993.

9. Littman, "Jails, Sheriffs, and Carceral Policymaking," 896.

10. Tara Herivel and Paul Wright, *Prison Profiteers: Who Makes Money from Mass Incarceration* (New York: New Press, 2009), 37.

11. U.S. Marshals Service, "Making a Reservation at the Local Jail—CAP Holds Bedspace," *The Pentacle* 7, no. 1 (1987): 13–14.

12. Loyd and Mountz, *Boats, Borders, and Bases*, 190.

13. U.S. Congress, Senate, Committee on Governmental Affairs, *Organized Criminal Activities: South Florida and U.S. Penitentiary, Atlanta, GA. Hearings before the Permanent Subcommittee on Investigations*, 95th Cong., 2d sess., 1978.

14. In 1981, a homemade sign appeared on the barracks at Fort Chaffee declaring, "[We] prefer being prisoners in Cuba rather than here." A Cuban American federal worker named Siro del Castillo gave a rousing speech to the remaining Cubans, denying that Fort Chaffee was a prison. "The person who wrote that doesn't know what freedom is, and we would venture to say that he was never imprisoned in Cuba, in the 'dungeons' of the Island, in the 'hell-holes' of the Cabana prison, in the 'cages' of the Boniato prison or in the 'trenches' of the Nuevo Amanecer prison. In short, the person who wrote that didn't come to the United States for the same reasons that I did or that many of you did." See Siro del Castillo, "One Day More or One Day Less," Box 1, Folder 1, FCC.

15. Daniel Golden, "US No Haven for These Cuban Refugees," *Boston Globe*, March 29, 1987.

16. U.S. Congress, House, Committee on the Judiciary, *Federal Prison Policy: Oversight Hearing before the Subcommittee on Courts, Civil Liberties, and the Administration of Justice*, 110th Cong., 1st sess., 1987, 14.

17. Cuban Review Plan: An Analysis, Box 3, Folder "Plan Review 1987," Alberto Muller Papers, Cuban Heritage Collection, University of Miami.

18. About one in five Cubans at Atlanta Federal Penitentiary had been prosecuted for a drug offense. Under federal guidelines, most individuals with drug charges were barred from parole. However, as many as four hundred of the 1,855 Cubans at Atlanta Federal Penitentiary should have been parole-eligible—this included migrants held for a range of offenses, from "halfway house rules violations" (forty detainees) to "unauthorized use of an auto" (eight detainees) to "aiding food stamp violators" (one detainee). Scott Thurston and Ann Woolner, "Many Detainees Are Eligible for Release Program," *Atlanta Journal-Constitution*, June 22, 1986.

19. Jack A. Hanberry, Warden of Atlanta Federal Penitentiary, to Congressman Robert W. Kastenmeier, Feb. 28, 1986, Box 20, Folder 57, Robert W. Kastenmeier Papers, Wisconsin Historical Society.

20. "Cuban Inmates Hold 24," *Tampa Tribune*, Nov. 23, 1987.

21. Several scholars have produced excellent accounts of the Atlanta and Oakdale uprisings. See Mark S. Hamm, *The Abandoned Ones: The Imprisonment and Uprising of the Mariel Boat People* (Boston: Northeastern University Press, 1995); Shull, *Detention Empire*, 186–231; Young, *Forever Prisoners*, 119–57.

22. By 1994, Louisiana held 33.5 percent of state prisoners in local jails, a higher percentage than any other state. On legal intervention at Angola, see Dennis Childs, *Slaves of the State: Black*

Incarceration from the Chain Gang to the Penitentiary (Minneapolis: University of Minnesota Press, 2015); Liam Kennedy, "'Longtermer Blues': Penal Politics, Reform, and Carceral Experiences at Angola," *Punishment and Society* 15, no. 3 (2013): 304–22; Lydia Pelot-Hobbs, "Scaling Up or Scaling Back? The Pitfalls and Possibilities of Leveraging Federal Interventions for Abolition," *Critical Criminology* 26, no. 3 (2018): 423–41.

23. Despite Belt's enthusiasm, he did eventually reach a limit and began rejecting further INS offers when his jail reached 196 Cubans. Stacy V. Sullivan, "Sheriff Belt: Officials Should Look Somewhere Besides Parish Jails to House Cubans," *Town Talk* (Alexandria, La.), Nov. 25, 1987.

24. Robert Mason, *Richard Nixon and the Quest for a New Majority* (Chapel Hill: University of North Carolina Press, 2004), 123.

25. Brent Cebul, *Illusions of Progress: Business, Poverty, and Liberalism in the American Century* (Philadelphia: University of Pennsylvania Press, 2023), 171–73.

26. Andrew Karch and Shanna Rose, *Responsive States: Federalism and American Public Policy* (Cambridge, Mass.: Cambridge University Press, 2019), 110.

27. "Bus Drivers Near $5,000 Pay Raise," *Bunkie Record*, Oct. 13, 1977.

28. Raymond L. Daye, "Pending Demise of Revenue Sharing Worries Officials," *Town Talk* (Alexandria, La.), May 4, 1986.

29. Karch and Rose, *Responsive States*, 119–23.

30. Cebul, *Illusions of Progress*, 273–74.

31. "Federal Revenue Sharing for Avoyelles Cut $82,899," *Weekly News* (Marksville, La.), Sept. 30, 1982.

32. Gregory B. Upton Jr., "Oil Prices and the Louisiana Budget Crisis: Culprit or Scapegoat?" Louisiana State University Center for Energy Studies, Oct. 24, 2016, https://www.lsu.edu/ces /publications/2016/Upton_10-2016_Oil_and_Gas_and_the_Louisiana_Economy_FINAL .pdf.

33. I. Jackson Burson Jr., "Not Endowed by Their Creator: State Mandated Expenses of Louisiana Parish Governing Bodies," *Louisiana Law Review* 50, no. 4 (1990): 636.

34. Loren C. Scott, "Louisiana in the 1990s: A Different Decade," in *The Southwest Economy in the 1990s: A Different Decade: Proceedings of the 1989 Conference on the Southwest Economy Sponsored by the Federal Reserve Bank of Dallas*, ed. Gerald P. O'Driscoll and Stephen P. A. Brown (Boston: Springer U.S., 1991), 139–46.

35. Kathy Calongne, "Cuban Inmates Good Business for Jail," *Town Talk* (Alexandria, La.), July 25, 1988; population data from the U.S. Census Bureau.

36. Peggy Mulligan, "Belt Promises Jail to Be Run 'like a Modern Penitentiary,'" *Town Talk* (Alexandria, La.), Dec. 14, 1986.

37. On desegregation in Avoyelles, see Susan Plauché, "*Brown*, the Civil Rights Act of 1964, and the NAACP's Impact on Avoyelles Parish Public Schools: 1954–1988," *Louisiana History: The Journal of the Louisiana Historical Association* 54, no. 2 (2013): 172–99.

38. Andrew Griffin, "Avoyelles Losing 100 INS Inmates," *Town Talk* (Alexandria, La.), May 5, 2000.

39. Gary Leshaw, one of the legal aid attorneys defending the Cubans held at Atlanta Federal Penitentiary, made this point in 1991: "Cuban detainees [became] the 1990s version of revenue sharing. In some sense, Bill Belt is a king of revenue making." Kathy Calongne, "Cuban Detainees Tough to Handle," *Town Talk* (Alexandria, La.), July 1, 1991.

40. "Alphonse Sez . . . ," *Greater Avoyelles Journal*, June 10, 1980.

41. U.S. Congress, House, Committee on the Judiciary, *Mariel Cuban Detainees: Hearing before the Subcommittee on Immigration, Refugees, and International Law*, 100th Cong., 2d sess., 1988, 92.

42. Kathy Calongne, "Avoyelles Hunger Strike," *Town Talk* (Alexandria, La.), Dec. 22, 1989.

43. Kathy Calongne, "Hunger Strike," *Town Talk* (Alexandria, La.), Dec. 20, 1989.

44. Fred Grimm, "Southern Jails Cashing In on Mariel Inmates," *Miami Herald*, July 16, 1990.

45. "Good Money for Warehousing, and Often Beating, Cubans," *National Catholic Reporter* 27, no. 35 (1991): 12.

46. Lisa Manuel, "The Jail Situation," *Greater Avoyelles Journal*, Dec. 29, 1991.

47. "Alphonse Sez . . . ," *Greater Avoyelles Journal*, Feb. 5, 1989.

48. Belt's most notable legal conflict was with Judge Frank Polozola, who argued that the parish was holding federal prisoners at the expense of state prisoners. See *Williams v. McKeithen*, 939 F.2d 1100 (5th Cir. 1991).

49. "Alphonse Sez . . . ," *Greater Avoyelles Journal*, July 28, 1991.

50. In 1999, after touring several jails, one INS employee wrote to a colleague that he did not believe the immigration service should pursue toll-free calls for detainees. "The telephone system is a big money item to these County Sheriffs. . . . [W]e need to be sensitive to their needs." Quoted in Mark Dow, *American Gulag: Inside U.S. Immigration Prisons* (Berkeley: University of California Press, 2005), 176.

51. U.S. Attorney's Office, "Avoyelles Parish Sheriff William Belt and Others Indicted by Federal Grand Jury," press release, Aug. 8, 2007, https://www.justice.gov/sites/default/files /usao-wdla/legacy/2013/02/27/wdl20070808.pdf.

52. The Belts were not convicted for this offense, despite significant evidence compiled in a five-year investigation by the FBI. News coverage suggested that the Belts' defense team was highly effective in discrediting witnesses: One of the witnesses was described as a "convicted male pedophile," and another was described as a "vengeful, lying" woman. Billy Gunn, "Belt, Wife, Sister, Not Guilty of Federal Charges," *Town Talk* (Alexandria, La.), Nov. 4, 2010.

Sheriffs profiting off of phone contracts continues to be a major issue. A 2019 report by the Prison Policy Initiative found that phone calls from jails can cost more than three times as much as phone calls from state prisons, with sheriffs receiving commissions from telecommunications companies. See Peter Wagner and Alexi Jones, "State of Phone Justice: Local Jails, State Prisons and Private Phone Providers," press release, Prison Policy Initiative, Feb. 2019, https://www .prisonpolicy.org/phones/state_of_phone_justice.html.

53. Cindy Humphreys, "Jailed Cubans Wait for Some Place to Go," *Southern Illinoisan* (Carbondale), March 11, 1990.

54. Pam Swischer, map: "Mariel Detainees in the U.S.," *Miami Herald*, Nov. 25, 1987.

55. Michael Mentzer, "Housing Cubans Helps Pay for Jail Expansion," *The Reporter* (Fond du Lac, Wisc.), Feb. 5, 1987.

56. U.S. Congress, House, Committee on the Judiciary, *Cuban Detainees and the Disturbance at the Talladega Federal Prison: Hearing before the Subcommittee on Intellectual Property and Judicial Administration*, 102nd Cong., 1st sess., 1991, 49.

57. Puerto Rico was facing multimillion-dollar fines for lack of compliance with federal laws regulating prison facilities. In 1993, it began a $5.6 million overhaul of its corrections system. The majority of the prisoners were sent to the rural town of Appleton, Minnesota, where local

officials were struggling to fill the beds of a newly built prison. See Lauren-Brooke Eisen, *Inside Private Prisons: An American Dilemma in the Age of Mass Incarceration* (New York: Columbia University Press, 2017), 83–85.

58. Marion Gremillion, "Sheriff Signs for His 'Super Prison,'" *Greater Avoyelles Journal*, Nov. 12, 1989.

59. *Central Louisiana Bank & Trust Co. v. Avoyelles Parish Police Jury*, 493 So. 2d 1249 (La. Ct. App. 1986).

60. Lease-purchase agreements offered several advantages that made them appealing to communities financing prisons in the 1980s: They did not require a special election, taxpayers did not need to approve new bonds, and they neatly cut around municipal debt limits and restrictions on incurring new debt. See Jan Chaiken and Stephen Mennmeyer, "Lease-Purchase Financing of Prison and Jail Construction" (Washington, D.C.: U.S. Department of Justice, National Institute of Justice, 1987), https://www.ojp.gov/pdffiles1/Digitization/114210NCJRS.pdf.

61. On the relationship between neoliberalism, poverty, and incarceration, see Jordan T. Camp, *Incarcerating the Crisis: Freedom Struggles and the Rise of the Neoliberal State* (Oakland: University of California Press, 2016); on the the RTDS, Inc. proposal, see Thomas W. Tubre, "Letter to the Editor: Prison questions answered," *The Bunkie Record*, Feb. 8, 1990.

62. Eisen, *Inside Private Prisons*, 38.

63. Shull, *Detention Empire*, 206.

64. COM 110.a: To: Arnold Burns, From: Norman Carlson, 19 Dec. 1986 [Electronic Record], Series: Commissioner Files, 1/1/2015–12/31/2019, Records of the U.S. Sentencing Commission, RG 539, NARA2.

65. U.S. Congress, House, Committee on the Judiciary, *Privatization of Corrections: Hearings before the Subcommittee on Courts, Civil Liberties, and the Administration of Justice*, 99th Cong., 1st and 2d sess., 1986, 59.

66. U.S. Congress, House, Committee on the Judiciary, *Privatization of Corrections*, 159.

67. This is a stark contrast to how the companies themselves used penal history. In a 1984 NPR interview, the CEO of for-profit detention company Behavioral Systems Southwest said that "[the] first American prison[s] were private" and that it was time "for private enterprise to again take over the penal system." Shull, *Detention Empire*, 204.

68. Frederic C. Howe assumed the position of commissioner in 1914 and, two years later, chose not to renew Hudgins and Dumas Co.'s contract for food services at Ellis Island. "I wanted the government to do it right, and take the element of profit out of it. . . . [It is] my duty to protect the immigrant who has to run the gauntlet of all kinds of private interests from the time he leaves the steamship until he reaches his destination." Frederic C. Howe, "Denies Scandals at Ellis Island: Commissioner Howe Answers Bennet's Charges of Immorality among Immigrants," *New York Times*, July 20, 1915. Almost immediately, Congressman William S. Bennet, a former attorney for Hudgins and Dumas, launched an all-out attack on Howe. Bennet accused Howe of being "an extremist," "a negligent commissioner," and "a half-baked radical with free love ideas." See Kenneth E. Miller, *From Progressive to New Dealer: Frederic C. Howe and American Liberalism* (University Park: Penn State University Press, 2010), 220.

69. Sunny Schubert and Ron Seely, "Refugees Mean Jobs, Dollars," *Wisconsin State Journal* (Madison), June 1, 1980; Petition to Establish Fort Chaffee as a Permanent Refugee Center, Box 51, Folder "INS—Detention Facilities," SF-RWG.

70. Philip Mattera, Mafruza Khan, and Stephen Nathan, *Corrections Corporation of America: A Critical Look at Its First Twenty Years* (Washington, D.C.: Grassroots Leadership, Institute on Taxation and Economic Policy, 2003), 10. CCA rebranded in 2016 as CoreCivic.

71. Dow, *American Gulag*, 97.

72. Philip Mattera and Mafruza Khan, *Jail Breaks: Economic Development Subsidies Given to Private Prisons* (Washington, D.C.: Institute on Taxation and Economic Policy, 2001), 2.

73. For a more thorough account of CCA's origins, see Shull, *Detention Empire*, 208–10.

74. Norman A. Carlson, Director of BOP, to Arnold I. Burns, Deputy AG, re: Privatization of Corrections, Dec. 19, 1986 [Electronic Record], Series: Commissioner Files, 1/1/2015–12/31/2019, Records of the U.S. Sentencing Commission, RG 539, NARA2.

75. Douglas C. McDonald, "Public Imprisonment by Private Means: The Re-emergence of Private Prisons and Jails in the United States, the United Kingdom, and Australia," *British Journal of Criminology* 34 (1994): 29–48.

76. Charles W. Thomas and Linda S. Calvert Hanson, "The Implications of 42 U.S.C. 1983 for the Privatization of Prisons," *Florida State University Law Review* 16, no. 4 (1989): 933–62.

77. On the history of Section 1983, see Paul Howard Morris, "Impact of Constitutional Liability on the Privatization Movement after *Richardson v. McKnight*," *Vanderbilt Law Review* 52, no. 2 (1999): 489–520.

78. Legal scholars have noted that litigation such as *Medina v. O'Neill* represented a break from the judicial precedents of *Shaughnessy* and *Mezei*, which forbid excluded aliens from challenging the constitutionality of Congress's decision to exclude or detain, offering excludable migrants the ability to challenge the *conditions* of their confinement on due process grounds. Stephen H. Legomsky, "Ten More Years of Plenary Power: Immigration, Congress, and the Courts," *Hastings Constitutional Law Quarterly* 22, no. 4 (1994): 932. See also *Lynch v. Cannatella*, 810 F.2d 1363 (5th Cir. 1987).

79. "Ad hoc" is generally used in the literature on immigration detention to refer to space. Michael Flynn writes that an "ad hoc" facility is one that is "improvised to fulfil a role it is structurally or administratively not intended to." I suggest here that the process of detaining can also be ad hoc, as immigration officials selectively embraced privatization on a one-off basis, with little political or public attention, prior to the advent of privatized immigration detention centers. See Michael Flynn, "Immigration Detention and Proportionality," Global Detention Project Working Paper No. 4, Global Detention Project, 2011, https://www.refworld.org/pdfid/545b38404.pdf.

80. On Danner's, Inc., see Pat Streilein-Kirk, "Captains with Problems Call Danner's," *Port of Houston Magazine*, May 1984, 10.

81. *Medina v. O'Neill*, 589 F. Supp. 1030, 1032 (S.D. Tex. 1984).

82. U.S. Congress, House, Committee on the Judiciary, *Privatization of Corrections*, 117.

83. *Medina v. O'Neill*, 589 F. Supp. 1030, 1042.

84. U.S. Congress, House, Committee on the Judiciary, *Privatization of Corrections*, 102–3.

85. Lily Geismer, *Left Behind: The Democrats' Failed Attempt to Solve Inequality* (New York: PublicAffairs, 2022), 8–9.

86. H.R. 3345—Federal Workforce Restructuring Act of 1994.

87. Congressional Budget Office, "Changes in Federal Civilian Employment," July 1996, https://www.cbo.gov/sites/default/files/104th-congress-1995-1996/reports/fcivempl.pdf.

88. Memorandum for Mack McLarty, re: Privatization of Operations for the New Forrest City, Arkansas, Prison [Electronic Record], Records of the Domestic Policy Council (Clinton Administration), Jose Cerda Files, 1995–1999, William J. Clinton Library, Little Rock.

89. John M. Eason, *Big House on the Prairie: Rise of the Rural Ghetto and Prison Proliferation* (Chicago: University of Chicago Press, 2017), 1.

90. Mayor Danny Ferguson's Letter [Electronic Record], Records of the Domestic Policy Council (Clinton Administration), Jose Cerda Files, 1995–1999, William J. Clinton Library, Little Rock.

91. Kathleen M. Hawk to Dale Bumpers, March 9, 1995 [Electronic Record], Records of the Domestic Policy Council (Clinton Administration), Jose Cerda Files, 1995–1999, William J. Clinton Library, Little Rock.

92. While the federal government had initially intended to privatize four federal facilities scheduled to open in 1996, including Forrest City, it ultimately decided to contract out for only one of the four. National Institute of Justice, "Examination of Privatization in the Federal Bureau of Prisons" (Washington, D.C.: U.S. Department of Justice, Office of Justice Programs, 1999), https://www.ncjrs.gov/pdffiles1/sl000354.pdf.

93. David E. Pozen, "Managing a Correctional Marketplace: Prison Privatization in the United States and the United Kingdom," *Journal of Law and Politics* 19, no. 3 (2003): 259.

94. By 1995, the INS had 1,100 beds in contract facilities, constituting roughly 16 percent of the approximately seven thousand total beds the INS had for detention. U.S. Department of Justice, Immigration and Naturalization Service, "Elizabeth, New Jersey Contract Detention Facility, Operated by ESMOR Inc., Interim Report," 2.

95. John Sullivan and Matthew Purdy, "A Prison Empire: How It Grew," *New York Times,* July 23, 1995.

96. U.S. Department of Justice, Immigration and Naturalization Service, "Elizabeth, New Jersey Contract Detention Facility, Operated by ESMOR Inc., Interim Report," 4.

97. U.S. Department of Justice, Immigration and Naturalization Service, "Elizabeth, New Jersey Contract Detention Facility, Operated by ESMOR Inc., Interim Report," 12.

98. Ashley Dunn, "U.S. Inquiry Finds Detention Center Was Poorly Run," *New York Times,* July 22, 1995.

99. *Jama v. Esmor Correctional Services, Inc.,* 577 F. 3d 169 (3rd Cir. 2009).

100. "The Lessons of Esmor," editorial, *New York Times,* June 21, 1995.

101. "Immigration: York's Ship Comes In," *York Daily Record,* April 12, 1998.

102. The Flores Settlement Agreement, which arose out of the 1997 landmark case that capped detention of minors at twenty days, came out of a private detention center, for example. Plaintiffs Jenny Lisette Flores and Alma Yanira Cruz-Aldama were detained in a Pasadena detention facility operated by Behavioral Systems Southwest, Inc. The case also named CCA, which operated a juvenile migrant detention facility in Laredo, Texas. For a history of the *Flores* case, see Philip G. Schrag, *Baby Jails: The Fight to End the Incarceration of Refugee Children in America* (Berkeley: University of California Press, 2020).

103. Scott Dodd, "Freedom Seekers Find Themselves Wearing Shackles," *York Daily Record,* Dec. 27, 1996.

104. Caryl Clarke, "Detainees' Riot Brings Profit to York," *York Daily Record,* June 28, 1995; Scott Dodd, "Prison Signs Contract with INS," *York Daily Record,* Oct. 11, 1995. While called a

prison, the York County facility did the job of both a jail and a prison, holding both pretrial and sentenced inmates. The county sheriff operated the jail on-site, while the state maintained the portions of the facility for those sentenced to a stay of more than a year.

105. Fauziya Kassindja, *Do They Hear You When You Cry* (New York: Delacorte Press, 1998), 293.

106. Patrick Radden Keefe, "The Snakehead," *New Yorker*, April 16, 2006.

107. On Clinton's changing positions toward refugee refoulement, see David FitzGerald, *Refuge beyond Reach: How Rich Democracies Repel Asylum Seekers* (New York: Oxford University Press, 2019), 71–101.

108. Quoted in Dow, *American Gulag*, 10.

109. "Prison Board Shopping for Inmates to Prevent Lay-Offs," *The Patriot-News* (Harrisburg, Pa.), June 22, 1993.

110. J. P. Kurish, "Prison Plan: Little Risk, Big Payoff?" *York Sunday News*, July 14, 1996.

111. On the Sanctuary movement, see Shull, *Detention Empire*, 104–45; Adam Waters, "Alternative Internationalisms: The Sanctuary Movement and Jim Corbett's Civil Initiative," *Diplomatic History* 46, no. 5 (2022): 984–1009.

112. Caryl Clarke, "INS Disregards Clinton Policy," *York Daily Record*, Feb. 3, 1996.

113. Ying Chan, "Aid for Refugees: Townspeople Push Officials for 'Justice,'" *York Daily News*, Nov. 30, 1993.

114. U.S. Congress, House, Committee on International Relations, *Coercive Population Control in China: Hearings before the Subcommittee on International Operations and Human Rights*, 104th Cong., 1st sess., 1995, 47.

115. The *Golden Venture* cases had varying outcomes: Four years after the ship's arrival, ninety-nine of the passengers had been sent back to China, a third were released or resettled in Latin America, and a small number were granted asylum in the United States. In February 1997, the last fifty-four *Golden Venture* passengers at York County were released by order of President Clinton. See Anna Dubrovsky, "Detainees Released: Six Months Later," *York Daily Record*, Aug. 26, 1997.

116. Wendy E. Solomon, "Immigration: Are We Closing the Door?" *York Sunday News*, Oct. 6, 1996.

117. In the original draft of this press release, the INS described "criminal aliens" as those who had "preyed on the community." U.S. Department of Justice, News Release: INS Removes Record Number of Criminal and Illegal Aliens in Second Quarter, May 13, 1977, VF: Detention and Deportation (INS)—Statistics, USCIS Library.

118. Leslie Gray Streeter, "Friday, Cecilia Jeffrey Was Set Free," *York Sunday News*, April 12, 1998.

119. For additional examples, see Welch, *Detained*, 161–62.

120. Jim Lynch, "Baseball Could Cost County," *York Daily Record*, Jan. 17, 2002.

121. "The [INS] had more armed agents with arrest powers than any other federal agency in mid-1996," reported the *Daily Record*, noting that it now had 12,400 agents, compared with the BOP's 11,300 agents. A budget increase for the INS accompanied the 1996 legislation and officially made the immigration bureaucracy the largest federal law enforcement agency in the United States. President Clinton's 1996 budget called for $171 million to double the capacity of detention facilities, as well as $15 million to build new detention centers. See Barbara Barrett and Anna Dubrovsky, "Laws, Guns, and Money," *York Daily Record*, April 23, 1998; William J. Clinton, *The Budget for Fiscal Year 1996* (Washington, D.C.: Office of Management and Budget, 1996), 77.

122. Solomon, "Immigration."

123. Caryl Clarke, "Warden Looks to Save INS Contract," *York Daily Record*, March 27, 2002.

124. "Feds Make Foolish Decision," editorial, *York Daily Record*, Dec. 24, 2002. Ironically, some of the detainees were moved out of York County and back to a center in Elizabeth, N.J., operated by a private contractor that charged $160 per night.

125. Jim Lynch, "County, INS Hope for Deal," *York Daily Record*, Jan. 15, 2003.

126. Thomas Ginsberg, "Immigration Jail May Close over Contract Dispute," *The Monitor* (McAllen, Tex.), Dec. 27, 2002.

127. "Hooked on Detainee Money," editorial, *York Daily Record*, July 21, 2004.

128. "INS Should Make Deal with County," editorial, *York Dispatch*, Jan. 8, 2003.

129. Robert E. Koulish, *Immigration and American Democracy: Subverting the Rule of Law* (New York: Routledge, 2010), 1.

130. U.S. Department of Justice, Office of the Inspector General, *The September 11 Detainees: A Review of the Treatment of Aliens Held on Immigration Charges in Connection with the Investigation of the September 11 Attacks*, April 2003, 2, https://oig.justice.gov/sites/default/files/legacy/special/0306/full.pdf.

131. U.S. Department of Justice, Office of the Inspector General, *September 11 Detainees*, 75–103.

132. Eleanor Acer and Archana Pyati, *In Liberty's Shadow: US Detention of Asylum Seekers in the Era of Homeland Security* (Washington, D.C.: Human Rights First, 2004), 19.

133. York County settled with ICE for $18.5 million—a sum it funded largely through the reintroduction of immigrant detainees to the county. Eugene Park, "Prison Now a Stopover," *York Daily Record*, June 22, 2008.

134. Wardens at York County threatened incarcerated persons who complained about inadequate medical treatment that if they caused the county to lose its contract, they would be transferred to private detention facilities, which were "a lot worse." Immigrant legal advocates at York County conceded that, while they did not believe asylum seekers should be held in prison, transfers to rural, private facilities would likely be a worse situation. Caryl Clarke, "INS Inmates: Contract Can Go," *York Daily Record*, Dec. 18, 2002.

135. Dan Pens, "Prison Realty/CCA Verges on Bankruptcy," *Prison Legal News*, July 15, 2000; Judith Greene, "Bailing Out Private Jails," *The American Prospect*, Dec. 19, 2001.

136. Naomi Klein, *Shock Doctrine: The Rise of Disaster Capitalism* (New York: Picador, 2008), 371.

137. Pugliese, *State Violence and the Execution of Law*, 24.

138. Volker Janssen, "Private Prisons: Where the Sunbelt Casts Its Global Shadow," in *Caging Borders and Carceral States: Incarcerations, Immigration Detentions, and Resistance*, ed. Robert T. Chase (Chapel Hill: University of North Carolina Press, 2019), 294.

139. County of York, "2015 Budget Narrative," 11–12, https://yorkcountypa.gov/DocumentCenter/View/1055.

140. For another example of contract termination and its financial fallout, see Dow, *American Gulag*, 227–43.

141. Nina Bernstein, "Ill and in Pain, Detainee Dies in U.S. Hands," *New York Times*, Aug. 12, 2008; *Lin Li Qu v. Central Falls Detention Facility Corp.*, 717 F. Supp. 2d 233 (D.R.I. 2010).

142. For examples of Chinese incarceration in St. Albans, see "State of Vermont," *News and Advertiser* (Northfield, Vt.), March 30, 1897; "Champagne Seizure Is Climax of Week's Activities along Border," *St. Albans Daily Messenger*, Aug. 3, 1925.

143. David Rainville, "Sheriff: Vt. Inmates No Loss," *The Recorder* (Franklin County, Vt.), July 20, 2012.

144. Economic and jobs arguments for detention are often vastly overstated, particularly by private prison companies attempting to secure local support. For one example of how a locality reworked its financial statements to make it appear that its private detention facility was producing, rather than losing, revenue for the county, see Karla Molinar Arvizo, "The Detention Drain: How Immigration Detention Hurts New Mexico's Economy" (Washington, D.C.: Institute for Policy Studies, 2019). On debt and the failed economic promise of incarceration, see also Gilmore, *Golden Gulag*.

145. Nina Bernstein, "City of Immigrants Fills Jail Cells with Its Own," *New York Times*, Dec. 27, 2008.

146. "Defendant United States' Memorandum of Law in Support of Motion to Dismiss," *Lin Li Qu v. Central Falls Detention Facility Corporation et al.*, CA-09-CV-0053-S-DLM (2009), 2, https://www.riaclu.org/sites/default/files/field_documents/NgGovMotiontoDismiss.pdf.

147. U.S. Congress, Senate, Committee on the Judiciary, *INS Reform*, 141.

Epilogue: Getting ICE out of Jails

1. Jessica Bulman-Pozen and Heather K. Gerken, "Uncooperative Federalism," *Yale Law Journal* 118, no. 7 (2009): 1256–310.

2. American Immigration Council, "The Cost of Immigration Enforcement and Border Security" (Washington, D.C.: American Immigration Council, 2021), https://www.american immigrationcouncil.org/sites/default/files/research/the_cost_of_immigration_enforcement _and_border_security.pdf; Goodman, *Deportation Machine*, 179–81.

3. Detention Watch Network, "Banking on Detention: Local Lockup Quotas and the Immigrant Dragnet," 2015, 2, https://www.detentionwatchnetwork.org/sites/default/files/reports /DWN%20CCR%20Banking%20on%20Detention%20Report.pdf.

4. For example, "US Border Patrol Tightens Catch-and-Release Policy," *Voice of America News*, Oct. 31, 2009.

5. Congress rejected the Biden administration's proposal to reduce capacity to 25,000 for FY 2023. Aside from being a human rights disaster, this is a phenomenal waste of taxpayer money. See Erica Bryant, "ICE Is Wasting Millions of Dollars on Unnecessary Detention Beds," Vera Institute of Justice, July 20, 2022, https://www.vera.org/news/ice-is-wasting-millions-of-dollars -on-unnecessary-detention-beds.

6. Macías-Rojas, *From Deportation to Prison*, 68.

7. U.S. Government Accountability Office, *Immigration Detention: Actions Needed to Improve Planning, Documentation, and Oversight of Detention Facility Contracts*, GAO-21-149 (Washington, D.C.: U.S. Government Accountability Office, Jan. 2021), 24–29, https://www.gao.gov /assets/gao-21-149.pdf (accessed Jan. 1, 2023). As ICE becomes more desperate for space, it is more likely to offer minimums; laws that increase the number of detention beds and the number of migrants subject to mandatory detention increase the bargaining power of contractees to secure more guarantees.

8. Emily Ryo and Ian Peacock, "The Landscape of Immigrant Detention in the United States" (Washington, D.C.: American Immigration Council, Dec. 2018), 2, https://www

.americanimmigrationcouncil.org/sites/default/files/research/the_landscape_of_immigration_detention_in_the_united_states.pdf.

9. On the least visible of ICE detention sites, see Jacqueline Stevens, "America's Secret ICE Castles," *The Nation*, Jan. 4, 2010.

10. Ryo and Peacock, "Landscape of Immigrant Detention in the United States," 5.

11. U.S. Immigration and Customs Enforcement, "Detention Management: FY 2023 Detention Statistics," 2023, https://www.ice.gov/detain/detention-management.

12. Ryo and Peacock, "Jailing Immigrant Detainees," 67.

13. Frederick Wirt traces the origins of the intergovernmental service agreement to an 1852 Indiana statute authorizing local jails to house fugitives from other jurisdictions for set fees. A national survey of IGSAs in the early 1970s found that 63 percent of reporting municipalities with populations over five thousand participated in an IGSA, with arrangements involving sewage, social services, housing, environmental control, and of course, jails. Frederick M. Wirt, "The Tenacity of Confederacy: Local Service Agreements in the Family of Governments," *Publius* 12, no. 4 (1982): 112–13.

14. Bridget A. Fahey, "Federalism by Contract," *Yale Law Journal* 129, no. 8 (2020): 2326–416. Even in this highly flexible system, ICE has identified ways to further insulate itself. In recent years, ICE has acquired much of its detention space by attaching "riders" to IGSAs between the U.S. Marshals Service and local jails. By adding language to the U.S. Marshals' agreement saying that ICE can also use a jail, the immigration service does not need to create a new agreement with a locality. This is all the more critical as activists interrogate local relationships with ICE. Some counties prefer this approach because it allows them to reap ICE money without the potential backlash associated with a formal agreement with ICE. See Ellyn Jameson, "ICE Detention through U.S. Marshals Agreements," *Georgetown Immigration Law Journal* 35, no. 1 (2020): 310.

15. Ellyn Jameson writes: "But this view of what these agreements are creates an inherent tension. Either an agreement is a procurement contract and should be subject to the regulations that come with that, or it is an intergovernmental agreement in which sovereign authorities cooperate to detain individuals and pay the corresponding fiscal and political costs. The federal government should not be able to have it both ways merely because local governments would not agree otherwise." Jameson, "ICE Detention through U.S. Marshals Agreements," 297.

16. U.S. Department of Homeland Security, Office of Inspector General, "Immigration and Customs Enforcement Did Not Follow Federal Procurement Guidelines When Contracting for Detention Services," OIG-18-53 (Washington, D.C.: U.S. Department of Homeland Security, Feb. 21, 2018), https://www.oig.dhs.gov/sites/default/files/assets/2018-02/OIG-18-53-Feb18.pdf (accessed Jan. 1, 2023).

17. See, for example, Sarah Tory, "How For-Profit Detention Persists in the West," *High Country News*, Sept. 15, 2016. There is a dearth of data on how many jails in the United States are run by private companies. One criminologist calculated that in 2016, 5.4 percent of the jail population was in private facilities—this number has almost certainly increased in the years since. Gerald G. Gaes, "Current Status of Prison Privatization Research on American Prisons and Jails," *Criminology and Public Policy* 18, no. 2 (2019): 271–72.

18. Felipe De La Hoz, "How ICE Is Using Private Contractors to Dodge Local Democracy," *The Intercept*, May 26, 2020.

19. Loyd and Mountz, *Boats, Borders, and Bases*, 117–20.

20. Loyd and Mountz, *Boats, Borders, and Bases*, 177–81.

21. U.S. Government Accountability Office, *Immigration Detention*, 13.

22. U.S. Department of Homeland Security, Homeland Security Advisory Council, *Report of the Subcommittee on Privatized Immigration Detention Facilities* (Washington, D.C.: U.S. Department of Homeland Security, Dec. 1, 2016), 5, https://www.dhs.gov/sites/default/files/publications/DHS%20HSAC%20PIDF%20Final%20Report.pdf (accessed Jan. 1, 2023).

23. Macías-Rojas, *From Deportation to Prison*.

24. Catalina Amuedo-Dorantes and Mary J. Lopez, "Immigration Policy, Immigrant Detention, and the U.S. Jail System," *Criminology and Public Policy* 21, no. 2 (2022): 438.

25. American Immigration Council, "The Removal System of the United States: An Overview" (Washington, D.C.: American Immigration Council, Aug. 2022), https://www.americanimmigrationcouncil.org/sites/default/files/research/removal_system_of_the_united_states_an_overview.pdf.

26. Elliot Spagat, "US Expands Curfews for Asylum-Seeking Families to 13 Cities as an Alternative to Detention," Associated Press, Aug. 4, 2023.

27. There are two models of the 287(g) agreement. Under the jail enforcement model, deputized officers may interrogate suspected noncitizens who have been arrested on state or local charges regarding their immigration status; if they suspect that a migrant may be subject to removal, they issue an immigration detainer. Under the more limited warrant service officer model, local law enforcement officers execute ICE administrative warrants and are permitted to perform the arrest functions of an immigration officer within prisons and jails. However, in this model, the law enforcement officer cannot interrogate an arrested person about immigration status. As of October 2022, ICE had 287(g) jail enforcement model agreements with sixty-four law enforcement agencies in nineteen states. ICE also had 287(g) warrant service officer agreements with seventy-six law enforcement agencies in eleven states. See U.S. Immigration and Customs Enforcement, "Delegation of Immigration Authority Section 287(g) Immigration and Nationality Act," https://www.ice.gov/identify-and-arrest/287g; American Immigration Council, "The 287(g) Program: An Overview" (Washington, D.C.: American Immigration Council, 2021), https://www.americanimmigrationcouncil.org/sites/default/files/research/the_287g_program_an_overview.pdf.

28. Felicia Arriaga, "Relationships between the Public and Crimmigration Entities in North Carolina: A 287(g) Program Focus," *Sociology of Race and Ethnicity* 3, no. 3 (2017): 417–31.

29. Armenta, *Protect, Serve, and Deport*; Debbie Cenziper, Madison Muller, Monique Beals, Rebecca Holland, and Andrew Ba Tran, "Under Trump, ICE Aggressively Recruited Sheriffs as Partners to Question and Detain Undocumented Immigrants," *Washington Post*, Nov. 23, 2021. Amada Armenta's ethnography of 287(g) programs also reveals a more nuanced uncertainty on the part of the law enforcement officers conscripted into immigration law enforcement: As this book has similarly shown, local workers tasked with carrying out this work had a range of understandings about deportation but often legitimized their work through rhetoric that they were simply "helping" the federal government. There is ample room for further historical study on how workers in the United States' evolving deportation regime understood their labor and its political role, as well as on the role of unions for both government and private corrections workers.

30. Despite it formalizing channels for cooperation, statistics on the 287(g) program provide an incomplete picture of federal-local partnership. At the discretion of their head law

enforcement officers, localities have worked with ICE in informal ways that have not required signing memorandums of agreement. See Huyen Pham, "The Inherent Flaws in the Inherent Authority Position: Why Inviting Local Enforcement of Immigration Laws Violates the Constitution," *Florida State University Law Review* 31, no. 4 (2003): 965–1004.

31. Angelika Albaladejo, "Biden Promised to Protect Sanctuary Cities. So Why Is ICE Still Partnering with Local Cops?" *Capital and Main*, April 1, 2022.

32. Zolan Kanno-Youngs, "Biden to Nominate Texas Sheriff to Lead Immigration and Customs Enforcement," *New York Times*, April 27, 2021.

33. U.S. Immigration and Customs Enforcement, "Wake County Sheriff's Office First of 4 Sites in North Carolina to Receive Full Interoperability Technology to Help Identify Criminal Aliens," Nov. 12, 2008, https://www.ice.gov/news/releases/wake-county-sheriffs-office-first-4 -sites-north-carolina-receive-full (accessed March 8, 2020).

34. U.S. Immigration and Customs Enforcement, "Criminal Apprehension Program," https:// www.ice.gov/identify-and-arrest/criminal-apprehension-program (accessed Jan. 24, 2023).

35. Nayna Gupta and Heidi Altman, "Disentangling Local Law Enforcement from Federal Immigration Enforcement," policy brief, National Immigrant Justice Center, Jan. 2021, https:// immigrantjustice.org/sites/default/files/content-type/research-item/documents/2021-01 /Policy-brief_disentanglement_Jan2021_FINAL.pdf.

36. Timantha Goff, Zack Mohamed, Ronald Claude, Moussa Haba, Famyrah Lafortune, Amanda Diaz, and Andrew Quirk, "Uncovering the Truth: Violence and Abuse against Black Migrants in Immigration Detention" (Washington, D.C.: Freedom for Immigrants, Black LGBTQIA+ Migrant Project, Black Alliance for Just Immigration, and UndocuBlack Network, 2022), 11, https://www.freedomforimmigrants.org/report-uncovering-the-truth.

37. Freedom for Immigrants et al., "Uncovering the Truth," 9.

38. Jorge Rivas, "Activists in California Just Proved You Can Push ICE out of Your City," *Splinter*, Feb. 28, 2017.

39. Justin Wm. Moyer, "Transgender Obama Heckler Jennicet Gutiérrez Hailed by Some LGBT Activists," *Washington Post*, June 26, 2015.

40. Jorge Rivas, "Why This Graduating Senior Went on Hunger Strike Three Weeks before Prom," *Splinter*, May 17, 2016.

41. Community Initiatives for Visiting Immigrants in Confinement, Complaint on behalf of thirty-one women in the custody of U.S. Immigration and Customs Enforcement at the Santa Ana City Jail in Santa Ana, California, Jan. 25, 2016, https://static1.squarespace.com/static /5a33042eb078691c386e7bce/t/5a9d9fafc83025905aa47de7/1520279472035/Complaint _SACJ_2016.pdf.

42. Memorandum from Christian Henrichson, Center on Sentencing and Corrections, Subject: Local Jails and U.S. Immigration and Customs Enforcement Detention, Vera Institute of Justice, Aug. 1, 2018, https://www.vera.org/downloads/publications/local-jails-and-ice-detention.pdf (accessed Jan. 1, 2023).

43. Rivas, "Activists in California Just Proved You Can Push ICE out of Your City."

44. Deepa Fernandes, "It's the Last California Jail Used by ICE. And He's the Only Immigrant Detainee Inside It," *San Francisco Chronicle*, Jan. 20, 2022.

45. While most of the legislation limiting IGSAs has come from Democratic-leaning states, it is not as simple as saying that liberal counties do not cooperate and conservative counties do.

Work by political scientist Jillian Jaeger has shown that conservative counties are among those least likely to deport. Instead, it is counties with larger policing budgets that report the highest levels of deportation. Jaeger also makes the critical point that some conservative counties that would ideologically like to work with ICE do not have the resources to do so—this could mean that their jail is too small, but it could also mean that they cannot afford to hold migrants at local expense until ICE can pick them up, as the Secure Communities Program mandates. See Jillian Jaeger, "Securing Communities or Profits? The Effect of Federal-Local Partnerships on Immigration Enforcement," *State Politics and Policy Quarterly* 16, no. 3 (2016): 362–86.

46. Ariel Goodman and "Lautaro," "Why I Led a Hunger Strike against ICE in New Jersey," *The Counter*, Feb. 17, 2021. On the deep, global lineages of hunger striking as a political practice, see Nayan Shah, *Refusal to Eat: A Century of Prison Hunger Strikes* (Oakland: University of California Press, 2022).

47. *CoreCivic, Inc. v. Philip D. Murphy, et al.*, Civil Action No. 23-967 (2023).

48. A federal appeals court similarly gutted California's law banning private prisons and immigration detention centers on the grounds that it violated the supremacy clause, which bars states from passing laws overriding federal statutes. Sophie Nieto-Munoz, "Biden Administration Says Closure of ICE Detention Center in N.J. Would Be 'Catastrophic,'" *New Jersey Monitor*, July 19, 2023; *GEO Group, Inc., v. Newsom*, No. 20-56172 (9th Cir. 2021).

49. "Changes to contracts can impact ICE operations, where ICE may have to depend on its national system of detention bed space to place those detainees in locations farther away," the agency has said, threatening that local activism will only make migrants' lives worse. Giulia McDonnell Nieto del Rio, "There Are No Immigrants Left in New Jersey County Jails. Where Is ICE Sending Them?" *Documented*, Nov. 18, 2021.

50. The Vera Institute reports that people who are represented by lawyers in immigration court are 3.5 times more likely to be granted bond and up to ten times more likely to establish their right to remain in the United States. Nicholas Turner and Erica Bryant, "New York Could Become the First State to Provide the Right to Legal Representation in Immigration Court," Vera Institute of Justice, Nov. 30, 2022, https://www.vera.org/news/new-york-could-become -the-first-state-to-provide-the-right-to-legal-representation-in-immigration-court (accessed Jan. 1, 2023).

51. On the use of surveillance and e-carceration in present-day border regimes, see Camilla Fojas, *Border Optics: Surveillance Cultures on the US-Mexico Frontier* (New York: New York University Press, 2021). The #notechforICE campaign has been critical in directing attention to the ways technology companies have partnered with ICE, as well as in documenting the agency's use of "digital detention" in recent years.

52. Simon Romero, "All over U.S., Local Officials Cancel Deals to Detain Immigrants," *New York Times*, June 28, 2018; Nick Miller, "Sacramento County Cancels Multimillion Dollar Immigrant Detention Contract with ICE," *Capital Public Radio*, June 6, 2018.

53. Santa Ana made a similar decision to replace ICE detainees with U.S. Marshals Service detainees, a decision that incurred comparably little public pushback. Maintaining an IGSA with the USMS means that a future local administration could restart collaboration with ICE with little friction. Jameson, "ICE Detention through U.S. Marshals Agreements," 311.

54. Project South, Georgia Detention Watch, Georgia Latino Alliance for Human Rights, and South Georgia Immigrant Support Network, Complaint on behalf of detained immigrants

at the Irwin County Detention Center and Ms. Dawn Wooten, Sept. 14, 2020, https://
projectsouth.org/wp-content/uploads/2020/09/OIG-ICDC-Complaint-1.pdf.

55. U.S. Senate, Permanent Subcommittee on Investigations, Committee on Homeland Security and Governmental Affairs, *Medical Mistreatment of Women in ICE Detention* (Washington,
D.C.: U.S. Senate, Permanent Subcommittee on Investigations, 2022), 4, https://www.hsgac
.senate.gov/imo/media/doc/2022-11-15%20PSI%20Staff%20Report%20-%20Medical%20
Mistreatment%20of%20Women%20in%20ICE%20Detention.pdf (accessed Jan. 1, 2023).

56. Jacob Kang-Brown and Jack Norton, "More than a Jail: Immigrant Detention and the
Smell of Money," Vera Institute of Justice, July 5, 2018, https://www.vera.org/in-our-backyards
-stories/glades-county-more-than-a-jail.

57. Jameson, "Ice Detention through U.S. Marshals Agreements," 299.

58. U.S. Government Accountability Office, *Immigration Detention*, 17.

59. In December 2019, the National Archives and Records Administration approved an ICE
plan to destroy sensitive records documenting sexual abuse and assault of detained migrants.
Citizens for Responsibility and Ethics in Washington, along with the American Historical Association and the Society for Historians of American Foreign Relations, successfully sued to
prevent the destruction of these records; I, along with historians Kristina Shull, Kristin Hogan-
son, and James Grossman, provided declarations in this case. *Citizens for Responsibility and
Ethics in Washington et al. v. National Archives and Records Administration et al.*, Case No. 20-cv-
00739 (APM) (D.D.C. Mar. 12, 2021).

60. Littman, "Jails, Sheriffs, and Carceral Policymaking," 893–94.

61. Littman, "Jails, Sheriffs, and Carceral Policymaking," 899.

62. Peter L. Markowitz, "Abolish ICE . . . and Then What?" *Yale Law Journal Forum* 129
(2019): 120–48.

63. Min Xian, "A New Immigrant Detention Center Will Open in Former Clearfield County
Prison," *WPSU*, Sept. 30, 2021.

64. Conference on the Detention of Marielito Cubans: Eight Years after the Boatlift, Feb. 25,
1988, Box 2, Folder "Doc. Atlanta 1987–1988," Alberto Muller Papers, Cuban Heritage Collection, University of Miami.

65. Conference on the Detention of Marielito Cubans: Eight Years after the Boatlift, Feb. 25,
1988.

66. Conference on the Detention of Marielito Cubans: Eight Years after the Boatlift, Feb. 25,
1988.

INDEX

Abolish ICE movement, 229
activism: hunger strike, 95–97, 134, 143,
 178–79, 201, 225, 267n48; against ICE, 224,
 225, 229; protests as, 141, 153; resistance
 as, 11–14, 218
ad hoc facility, defined, 300n79
Administrative Procedure Act, 87, 181–83,
 290n45
Ah Tai, 58
alienage laws, 240n22
Alien Criminal Apprehension Program
 (ACAP), 169–70
Alvarado, Sylvia, 129
Amdur, Spencer E., 238n11
American Bar Association, 204
American Civil Liberties Union (ACLU),
 87, 104, 106, 204
American Committee for Protection of
 Foreign Born (ACPFB), 87, 93–94, 97,
 103, 105–6, 267n32
American Federation of Government
 Employees, 204
American President Lines, Ltd., 104–5
American Prison Association, 61, 68
Amnesty International, 131, 194
Angel Island, 90, 101
Anti-Drug Abuse Act of 1986, 170
Antiterrorism and Effective Death Penalty
 Act, 190, 192, 211
appeals system, 63–64
Appleton, Minnesota, 298n57
Arabs, profiling against, 213
Argot, Edward, 80

Arizona State Prison, 72
Ark Toy, 46, 47, 48
Armand, Pierre Marie, 143
Armenta, Amada, 306n29
Arnold, Paulina D., 243n49, 250n108
Asia, war brides from, 7
Asians, religious profiling against, 213
assault, in jails, 82
Asylum Pre-Screening Officer Program,
 293n101
asylum seekers, 120, 139, 208, 293n101.
 See also specific groups
asymmetrical accountability scheme, 295n7
Atlanta Federal Penitentiary, Atlanta,
 Georgia, 54, 71, 72, 76–78, 155, 157, 198,
 199, 296n18
Attica prison rebellion, 180
August, Willeme, 134
Augusta, Georgia, 54
Avoyelles Parish Jail, Louisiana, 198, 199–203

Baca, Herman, 129
Bahamas, 279n111
bail practices, 53, 54–55, 57–58, 254n58,
 254n60
balanced detention resources, 197
Baltimore, Maryland, 25, 71
Baltimore Afro-American (newspaper), 117
Barnes, William, 142
Bates, Sanford, 264n154
Bay County, Florida, 190
Behavioral Systems Southwest, 187
Bell, Griffin, 125

Federal House of Detention, New York
City, 106
federalism, 11–14
federal jails: building of, 84; conditions of,
85; origin of, 260n77; privatization of,
207–8; push for, 68–72; revenue from,
210; in Southwest, United States, 111–16;
trials of, 84–85. *See also specific locations*
Federal Prison Camp, Florence, Arizona, 116
federal prisoners, defined, 244n9
Federal Protective Service, 154
Ferguson, Danny, 208
Fletcher, "Boots," 110
Florence, Arizona, 221
Flores Settlement Agreement, 301n102
Fond du Lac County, Wisconsin, 203
Fong Hoo, 47
Fong Yue Ting, 239n15
Fong Yue Ting v. United States, 19, 98, 239n15
Foong King, 54–55
Ford, Gerald, 275n15
foreign-born radicals, apprehension of, 92–93
Forrest City, Arkansas, 208
Fort Allen, Puerto Rico, 180–81
Fort Chaffee, Arkansas, 151, 152, 154–55, 158,
198–99, 205
Fort Drum, New York, 180
Fort Eglin, Florida, 151, 152
Fort Indiantown Gap, Pennsylvania, 151
Fort McCoy, Wisconsin, 151, 156, 157
Fort Pierce, Florida, 142
Fort Walton Beach, Florida, 153
Frankfurter, Felix, 100
Franklin County Jail, Malone, New York:
Chinese jail at, 28, 32–33; conditions of,
24, 41–48; deaths at, 42–48; description
of, 16, 24; escape from, 43–46; failures of,
74; income from migrant incarceration
in, 17, 25–27; Irish immigrants in, 60;
overcrowding at, 25, 67; photos of, 43;
statistics regarding, 27, 35
Franklin County Jail, St. Albans, Vermont, 216
Franklin County Jail and House of Corrections, Greenfield, Massachusetts, 216

Freeze, Jack, 155–56
Fuente, Alejandro de la, 150

Galveston County Jail, Texas, 81–82, 84
Galveston Daily News (newspaper), 82
García, Deyaneira, 224
Garcia, Ramon, 206
Geary Act, 40–41, 49, 53–54, 239n15, 254n60
Gelman, Clara, 105–6
Georgia, intergovernmental cooperation in,
76. *See also specific locations*
German migrants, 86, 95
Gersten, David, 163
Gin Hop, 103
Giuliani, Rudolph, 184–85
Golden Venture cases, 209–14, 302n115
Grace Commission, 204, 205
Graham, Bob, 145–46, 167, 179
Green, Martin, 163
Guerra-Carillo, Anselmo, 199
Gullage, Richard, 132, 138
Gutiérrez, Jennicet, 224

habeas corpus, 18, 23, 24, 33, 34–35, 36,
53–54, 59, 247n39
Haitian migrants: accommodations for,
280n113; as asylum seekers, 119–20,
130–34; Cuban-Haitian Entrant legal
category regarding, 150–51; deportation
of, 279n111; formalizing detention of,
179–83; at Krome Service Processing
Center, Miami, Florida, 173, 176–79; *Louis
v. Nelson* and, 181, 182, 184; as making
illegal, 134–38; overview of, 130–34;
photo of, 178; policies regarding, 174–75;
on *Saint Sauveur* (sailboat), 119, 173;
statistics regarding, 173, 177
Haitian Program, 135–38
Haitian Refugee Center, 138
Haitian Refugee Center v. Civiletti, 138
Halliburton, 214
Hamilton County Jail, Cincinnati, Ohio, 51
Harrison County Jail, Mississippi, 203
Hart, Hastings H., 68–72